T0323986

Marché Noir

Kenneth Mouré shows how the black market in Vichy France developed not only to serve German exploitation, but also as an essential strategy for survival for commerce and consumers. His analysis explains how and why the black market became so prevalent and powerful in France and remained necessary after Liberation. *Marché Noir* draws on diverse French archives as well as diaries, memoirs and contemporary fiction, to highlight the importance of the black market in everyday life. Vichy's economic controls set the context for adaptations – by commerce facing economic and political constraints, and by consumers needing essential goods. Vichy collaboration in this realm seriously damaged the regime's legitimacy. *Marché Noir* offers new insights into the dynamics of black markets in wartime, and how illicit trade in France served not only to exploit consumer needs and increase German power, but also to aid communities in their strategies for survival.

Kenneth Mouré is Professor of History at the University of Alberta, and taught at the University of California, Santa Barbara. He specializes in twentieth century French history, with particular interest in the policy responses to economic crises. His published works include *Managing the Franc Poincaré* (1991) and *The Gold Standard Illusion* (2002).

Marché Noir

The Economy of Survival in Second World War France

Kenneth Mouré

University of Alberta

CAMBRIDGE
UNIVERSITY PRESS

Shaftesbury Road, Cambridge CB2 8EA, United Kingdom

One Liberty Plaza, 20th Floor, New York, NY 10006, USA

477 Williamstown Road, Port Melbourne, VIC 3207, Australia

314–321, 3rd Floor, Plot 3, Splendor Forum, Jasola District Centre, New Delhi – 110025, India

103 Penang Road, #05–06/07, Visioncrest Commercial, Singapore 238467

Cambridge University Press is part of Cambridge University Press & Assessment, a department of the University of Cambridge.

We share the University's mission to contribute to society through the pursuit of education, learning and research at the highest international levels of excellence.

www.cambridge.org
Information on this title: www.cambridge.org/9781009207690

DOI: 10.1017/9781009207683

First published 2023
First paperback edition 2024

A catalogue record for this publication is available from the British Library

ISBN   978-1-009-20766-9   Hardback
ISBN   978-1-009-20769-0   Paperback

To Sara

Contents

Figures

Tables

Acknowledgments

My curiosity about the exceptional character of the black market in Occupied France was first piqued by Jacques Delarue's *Trafics et crimes sous l'Occupation*. Why did the black market take on such vast proportions in France, and what could be learned from archival records when illicit traffic was organized to have as little visibility as possible and the appearance of legality? In the years since then I have benefited from the resources and interest of many institutions, colleagues and friends in my exploration of archival sources and published work. It is a pleasure to acknowledge their substantial contributions to this work and to thank them for their interest, engagement, expertise and support.

I began serious research for *Marché Noir* with financial support from the German Marshall Fund, Research Fellowship grant no. E5931 V, and as a visiting member of the *Institut d'Histoire du temps présent*. Funds to support research travel while I was a department chair were provided by Deans David Marshall at UC Santa Barbara, and Gurston Dacks and Lesley Cormack at the University of Alberta. Subsequent research, especially for travel to departmental archives in France, was made possible by the Social Sciences and Humanities Research Council of Canada, grant no. IG 435–2013–1219.

In the many archives visited for this research, the help of knowledgeable staff was invaluable in seeking out relevant sources. The Service des archives économiques et financières at Savigny-le-Temple was essential for documenting the state management of economic controls; Laurent Dupuy was enormously helpful in locating records there in the early stages of my research, and Aurélie Aubaddy, for advice in later visits. At the Banque de France, Frédérik Grélard and the archival staff were marvellously efficient in providing documents and answering questions. At the Archives de Paris, Philippe Grand and Brigitte Lainé provided great encouragement and advice. At the Archives de la Préfecture de Police, Commissaire Françoise Gicquel facilitated access to police evidence in various forms. Many archivists assisted in providing access to diverse sources at the Archives nationales, most notably Patricia Gillet,

Sandrine Lacombe and Christine Nougaret. At the Juno Beach Centre in Courseulles-sur-Mer, Marie-Éve Vaillaincourt helpfully arranged interviews with local residents who lived in Normandy during the Occupation.

Library access to published sources was critical. As well as libraries in Paris, most notably the *Bibliothèque de documentation internationale contemporaine* (now *La Contemporaine*), I am grateful to the indefatigable interlibrary loan staff at the UC Santa Barbara Library and at the Rutherford Library at the University of Alberta, and especially to Denis Lacroix at Rutherford Library, for his expertise in resolving online access issues.

I am deeply grateful for the many conversations, suggestions and comments from colleagues and friends that have informed my research and analysis. Fabrice Grenard has been an exceptional source of information and discussions of points of interpretation in puzzling about black market behaviour. Regular conversations about research with Patrick Fridenson, Michel Margairaz and Dominique Veillon have influenced the development of my research and analysis over many years. I would also like to thank the many colleagues in France whose questions and suggestions have encouraged my research: Patrice Baubeau, Bertrand Blancheton, Alain Chatriot, Olivier Feiertag, Noëmie Fossé, Danièle Fraboulet, Pierre-Cyrille Hautcoeur, Hervé Joly, Christophe Lastécouères, Béatrice Touchelay and Philippe Verheyde. Colleagues in North America have contributed in many discussions, conference panels and workshops: Megan Barber, Kyri Claflin, Chad Denton, Sarah Fishman, Mary Furner, Bertram Gordon, Susan Howson, Norman Ingram, Eric Jennings, Fred Logevall, Sandra Ott, Paula Schwartz, Jack Talbott and Lynne Taylor.

Conversations with French people who lived through the Occupation provided fascinating opportunities to hear about their perspectives and points of detail on their lives as children and young adults in the economy of penury. I am very grateful to Jacques Baszanger, Jean-Louis Hautcoeur, Jean-Pierre Hébert, Michel Legallo, Robert Lemanissier, Suzanne Mathieu, Cécile Rol-Tanguy, and Hortense Viatte, for sharing their memories.

I am particularly indebted to the colleagues who read and provided feedback on individual chapters as the book neared completion in the Covid years: Alain Chatriot, Heather Coleman, Patrick Fridenson, Fabrice Grenard, Mary Furner, and Paula Schwartz. For her reading of the entire manuscript and her astute comments, my sincere thanks to Susan Howson. The anonymous readers for Cambridge University Press provided excellent advice, and my thanks to Michael Watson as editor for his longstanding interest in this project. All errors remain my responsibility.

My most important thanks are to my family, for all of life outside the archives, and for their great patience with my research manias. Isabelle Baszanger, I include as family, for our many dinners and extended conversations in Paris and her enduring interest in my research. My brother Bill and sister Erin, for the strong family connections maintained over many years and miles; and my thanks to Erin, as poet and translator, for her ever-helpful advice on translations from French to English. My sons Owen and Christopher provide welcome entertainment and distraction, as much fun as adults as they were when kids. Special thanks to Chris for his valuable feedback on several chapters. My greatest thanks are to Sara Norquay; my companion in life's adventures, the first reader for my written work, ever a source of enthusiasm, wisdom, laughter and love. This book is dedicated to her.

Abbreviations and Terms

ABdF	Archives de la Banque de France, Paris
AD	Archives départementales, followed by name of department
AdP	Archives de Paris – Archives for the Department of the Seine, Paris
AN	Archives nationales, Paris, Pierrefitte
AP	Archives privées, Archives nationales, Paris
APP	Archives de la Préfecture de police, Paris
BA-MA	Bundesarchiv-Militärarchiv, Freiburg im Breisgau
BTP	Batiment et travaux publics – the construction industry
CAC	Centre des archives contemporaines, Fontainebleau
CAH SNCF	Centre d'archives historiques de la SNCF – French national railway archives, Le Mans
CCDR	Commission consultative des dommages et des réparations
CCPI	Comités de confiscation des profits illicites – departmental committees to confiscate illicit profits
CDL	Comités départementaux de libération – deparmental liberation committees
CE	Contrôle économique: short form for the DGCE, which changed its name several times during the period covered
CFLN	Comité français de libération nationale
CHEFF	Comité pour l'histoire économique et financière de la France
CIVC	Comité interprofessionnel des vins de Champagne
CLL	Comités locaux de libération – local liberation committees
CGGIL	Comité de gestion des groupements interprofessionnels laitiers
CSCPI	Conseil supérieur de confiscation des profits illicites – the national review committee for appeals of CCPI decisions
DGCE	Direction générale de contrôle économique

DGCEE	Direction générale du contrôle et des enquêtes économiques
DGEE	Direction générale des études économiques – Bank of France summaries of monthly reports from its branch directors
ETO	European Theater of Operations
GDR	Groupe de recherche, CNRS
IGF	Inspection générale des finances
IHTP	Institut d'histoire du temps présent
INSEE	Institut national de la statistique et des études économiques
JAG	Judge Advocate General (US military)
NARA	National Archives and Records Administration, College Park, MD
OCRPI	Office central de répartition des produits industriels
OPA	Office of Price Administration, US national administration
PTT	Postes, télégraphe et téléphone – French national post office, including telegraph and telephones
PX	Post Exchange stores for US soldiers
RG	Ravitaillement général – the national office for food supply
RG	Record Group, when in NARA file references
SAEF	Service des archives économiques et financières, Savigny-le-Temple
SEITA	Service d'exploitation industrielle des tabacs et allumettes
SHAEF	Supreme Headquarters of the Allied Expeditionary Force
SNCF	Société nationale des chemins de fer – French national railway corporation
SRCRE	Service de coordination des recherches sur la collaboration économique
SHD	Service historique de la Défense, military and police archives, Vincennes
TNA	The National Archives, Kew, UK
ZNO	Zone non-occupée – the unoccupied zone, southern France June 1940 to November 1942
ZO	Zone occupée – the regions occupied by the Germans beginning in June 1940

French terms

Contrôle technique – *Le Service du contrôle technique,* created in December
   1939 to monitor postal communications, expanded in 1940 to listen
   in on telephone conversations as well. Officially under the control of
   the War Department and, from August 1942, under Pierre Laval as
   prime minister.

réfractaires – young men avoiding labour for the Germans in the *Service du
   Travail Obligatoire*

soulte – a premium paid in cash, not recorded on the sales receipt

le système D – making do, using initiative to solve problems

trafiquant – trafficker, black marketeer

transaction – a fine, determined and imposed by control authorities
   including the *Contrôle économique,* especially for black market
   offences

1   The Black Market in Wartime France

On the rue Philippe de Girard in Montmartre the restaurant's front door is closed, as if no longer in business. A young man loiters nearby to direct customers to an entry from the alley. Inside, drinks are ready at the zinc counter and the menu offers exemplary fare for the Occupation years. Rutabagas, leeks and Jerusalem artichokes (*topinambours*) are the staple vegetables. But there are rare meat dishes as well, and pâté, and real coffee, and desserts made with real sugar, and even chocolate, all long unavailable in restaurants abiding by ration restrictions. The restaurant, *Le couvre-feu*, offers period dishes with black-market supplements. The staff are actors costumed to play wartime roles. This is retro café theatre in 1990. The décor and menu give patrons the atmosphere and flavours of the Occupation, without its dangers, or its very real privations.[1]

Black-market activity was pervasive in wartime France, and distributed a growing share of the resources essential for survival. In his last diary entry in December 1942, the Jewish journalist Jacques Biélinky wrote that anyone trying to live on the food from ration tickets alone would starve. 'The black market takes everything, and those who live on their tickets are condemned to starve.'[2] Regional directors of the Bank of France, reporting on economic activity across France, found it impossible in 1942 to calculate the proportion of licit to illicit commerce. The borderline between the two had become too uncertain and the trend clearly favoured growth of the 'parallel economy' outside the law. Official estimates of the volume of black-market traffic and prices understated their real extent. 'From the observation of daily practices that have become normal in commerce and consumption, it is clear that only a slender minority of French people get their provisions and live in conformity with the <u>rules</u>,

---

[1] Suzy Patterson, 'New French Restaurant Re-Creates the Look, Feel and Food of Nazi-Occupied Paris', *Los Angeles Times* 27 May 1990 (reprinted from *The Free Lance-Star*, 13 Apr. 1990).

[2] Jacques Biélinky journal entry for 17 Dec. 1942; quoted by Henry Rousso, 'L'économie: pénurie et modernization', in *La France des années noires*, vol. 1, *De la défaite à Vichy*, ed. by Jean-Pierre Azéma and François Bédarida (Paris: Seuil, 1993), 453.

respecting rations and prices, and those who do so usually lack the resources needed to break this constraint. The vast majority seek supplements outside the normal networks for distribution.'[3] That such daily practices now looked 'normal' to Bank directors shows the importance of the illicit traffic and the changing moral values for everyday consumption. This parallel market continued and increased after Liberation. British visitors in early 1945 remarked on the public character of the black market and the absence of state control: 'without the black market France cannot exist'.[4]

Adapting to wartime shortages required innovation at every level: to find scarce goods, to develop new consumer practices and adjust moral standards in order to secure essentials, as well as to exploit opportunities for profit from the deprivation and desperation of others. The world of consumption was transformed by the prolonged shortages and the urgent need to find essential goods. It fostered a climate of working around the rules, improvising ways of 'getting by' (known as *le système D*), with constant improvisation to evade restrictions and ameliorate shortages. Consumers sought products no longer available in official markets. Shopkeepers tried to restock goods they had sold. Producers needed raw materials, labour and markets. Intermediaries became critically important, seizing opportunities to profit from price movements that under normal circumstances would work in legal markets to encourage the production of needed goods and deliver them to customers. The economist Charles Rist described the changes as a moral and material regression, with 'morally unscrupulous middlemen' now in control.[5] The state, trying to control prices and distribute goods equitably, took an unprecedented role in economic direction, a role for which it was unprepared and ill equipped.

Black markets during the war can be viewed in many ways: as providing essential means for survival, as popular resistance to state tyranny invading daily life, as a system for German exploitation, and as a means for unscrupulous producers and dealers to profit from French misery. The Vichy period fascinates us because the choices made in wartime, in the hazardous circumstances of Occupied France, lay bare fundamental issues of human behaviour and moral values in times of crisis, when

---

[3] Banque de France, Paris, Archives of the Banque de France (ABdF), Direction générale des études économiques (DGEE), 'Résumé des rapports économiques, Zone occupée' (ZO), May 1942, emphasis in original.

[4] The National Archives (UK) (TNA), FO 371/49073, O. Harvey report of 30 Mar. 1945.

[5] Charles Rist, *Season of Infamy: A Diary of War and Occupation, 1939–1945*, trans. by Michele McKay Aynesworth (Bloomington: Indiana University Press, 2016), 364(6 Dec. 1943).

even incidental choices could carry fatal consequences. Individuals made day-to-day decisions based on their immediate circumstances, with limited knowledge of where their choices could lead.

Black-market activity is defined by state laws and enforcement. Price controls and rations to equalize access to limited resources add restrictions; opportunities can then multiply for economic offences and illicit profit. Motives for violating the new laws can range from mothers buying extra milk to feed their children, to factory directors trading finished goods for raw materials to keep their firm running and their workers employed, a Joseph Joinovici selling scrap metal to the Germans for enormous profit, and a Luftwaffe Colonel Veltjens coordinating black-market purchasing by the German military to buy hoarded consumer goods including toys, women's shoes, lingerie and cosmetics.

Marché Noir investigates black-market experience in France during and after the Occupation, with a focus on the logic and pervasiveness of black-market practices and their importance as a response to economic controls. The proliferation of black-market activity engages vital issues in the exercise of state power, the consequences of French collaboration with German authorities, popular resistance to state controls, consumer adaptations to survive the shortages and adversity, and change in expectations for social and economic behaviour. The shortages, controls, and criminal activity persisted after Liberation. *Marché Noir* provides new explanation and analysis of the exceptional character of black-market experience in France. The issues in black-market use engage fundamental questions concerning the effectiveness of state policies, the policing of markets, the economic origins of popular protest, and the difficulties that slowed France's postwar recovery from the economy of penury.

Surviving the Economy of Penury

Everyday life in Occupied France became a struggle to survive shortages. The time and effort needed to locate and purchase essential goods, especially food, made attention to daily needs the principal concern for most civilians. Consumption practices seemed to have retreated to the nineteenth-century. Production fell. Internal borders and the scarcity of vehicles and fuel crippled transport. Industrialists lost access to the raw materials essential to their manufacturing. Farmers desperately needed tools, fertilizer, and transport for their crops. Private exchanges and barter took the place of retail purchase for scarce goods, and trade in second-hand merchandise thrived. Quality was compromised by substitutions, *ersatz* goods and deliberate degradations to extend scarce supplies. With shortages of vehicles and fuel, Parisians relied on bicycles and horse-drawn cabs, the streets strangely quiet.

Consumers adapted to penury, localized economies, and needs-based moral compromise. Mothers ran households without husbands, anxiously seeking food for hungry children. From Nice, the worst-hit urban centre for food shortages, one housewife wrote to a friend in October 1941 that she had queued for three hours to obtain one kilo of chard for her family of five:

It's a true famine, you can no longer find anything. There are terrible scenes of women fainting, crying, children and adults stealing, and as for me, it's a great struggle to keep myself from doing the same. I'm haunted by the idea of stealing when I see food. Two women friends tell me that they've stolen bread. I hope you never experience what we have been living these last two months.[6]

Her letter conveys the shock and desperation of trying to feed her family in the second autumn of the Occupation, with no way of knowing how long such conditions would last or how to adapt should they get worse.

The shortages posed immediate challenges and prompted adaptations at three inter-related levels. First, for consumers, the disappearance of goods essential to everyday life prompted panic buying and hoarding of any goods available, which aggravated the shortages. Constant improvisation was essential to develop methods and means of supply through family, friends or new acquaintances to secure needed goods. Consumer practice changed to provide for essential needs, particularly for those lacking the wealth and time needed to seek supplies outside official markets. Second, for the Vichy regime, fixing prices and controlling the allocation of goods became a paramount concern. The legitimacy of the new French state depended on its ability to protect its citizens and negotiate effectively to resist German demands. Third, in the market itself producers of goods and services, through the growing web of intermediaries needed to connect goods and purchasers, found that scarcity and controls provided both challenges and opportunities. Being able to locate, purchase and transport goods took on far greater importance and value, and the ability to move goods outside state control offered substantial profit.

Food access became the critical realm for everyday black-market use. The condition fundamental for successful food rationing in Britain and the United States was to have sufficient supplies available to guarantee an adequate minimum diet. 'If the assured supply is not forthcoming, all the bother is for nothing.'[7] In France, official rations promised food sufficient

---

[6] AD Alpes-Maritimes, 166W/21; letter of 10 Oct. 1941, quoted in Conseil Général des Alpes-Maritimes, *Les Alpes-Maritimes et les guerres du XXe siècle* (Milan: Silvana Editoriale, 2012), 140.

[7] John Kenneth Galbraith, *A Life in Our Times: Memoirs* (New York: Houghton Mifflin, 1981), 156.

for slow starvation, and too often failed to deliver even that. Consumers had to find food. 'All the bother' in French supply management fostered evasion and hostility to state control. Official markets lost supplies to an alternative economy of barter, bonus payments, and buying from friends, shops, and new intermediaries at prices and in quantities higher than those allowed by state controls.

Black markets are delimited by the state rules for legal market transactions: increased regulation narrows the range for legal commerce and requires means of enforcement. Buying bread fresh from the oven, for example, or an extra loaf, or white bread or croissants for a family breakfast, was no longer allowed as of 1 August 1940.[8] The controls outlawed practices that had been normal, and the restrictions provided both opportunity and incentive for buyers and sellers to replace lost goods and income through illicit activity. The black market attracted sustained public attention. Consumers needed it and were dismayed by its effects. The state's imperative to repress black markets required a major effort to persuade the public. The new regulations needed legitimacy in terms of their perceived outcomes: they had to be seen as effective and fair. To persuade the public that state policies were necessary and effective, the state publicized the abuses and the profits of black marketeers and the punishments in order to deter consumers and would-be *trafiquants* from black-market traffic.

Contemporaries explained black-market activity based on their experiences with shortages and the control administration. Black markets obviously provided goods to those able to pay higher prices, but it wasn't clear whether illicit exchanges were in fact markets ('the black market is less and less a market, and more and more black'), as prices were not determined by open competition.[9] This was true of the prices set by the state in official markets: some saw the black market as the revenge of free market forces, countering state interference.[10]

---

[8] The measures were intended to reduce bread consumption; Dominique Veillon, *Vivre et survivre en France 1939–1947* (Paris: Payot, 1995), 109.

[9] Louis Baudin, *Esquisse de l'économie française sous l'Occupation allemande* (Paris: Éditions politiques, économiques et sociales, 1945), 142.

[10] Contemporary descriptions of the price regime: Max Cluseau, *Taxation, rationnement et science économique: Étude théorique et pratique des prix réglementés et d'une économie distributive* (Paris: Librairie de Medicis, 1943); Jean Dubergé, *Le contrôle des prix en France au regard de la théorie économique* (Paris: Librairie générale de droit et de jurisprudence, 1947); Lucien Laurat, 'Remarques théoriques sur le marché noir', *Revue d'économie contemporaine* (Feb. 1944): 29–32; René Lebrun, *La police des prix: Ses pouvoirs de recherche et de constatation du délit de hausse illicite* (Paris: Dalloz, 1944); and Olivier Moreau-Néret, *Le contrôle des prix en France* (Paris: Sirey, 1941). For the revenge of free market forces, see Olivier Wieviorka, 'Sans esprit de retour? Les libéraux de l'Alliance démocratique et l'expérience vichyste (1940–1944)', *L'Occupation, l'État*

The explanations for the black market immediately after the war emphasized the shortages and state policy. Michel David, writing in 1945, saw the black market as a natural consumer response to shortages which, combined with poor regulation, had encouraged illicit commerce: 'The fisherman, the farmer, the worker, the civil servant, the mother, all of them have trafficked, often innocently, in the black market, in protesting against its demands, but in buying, selling or exchanging everything within their reach.' David noted that the black market had victims as well, and he concluded that it had enriched a handful of profiteers and impoverished the nation.[11] Louis Baudin, surveying French economic experience, devoted a long chapter to explain how shortages and state controls had created a defective system. Spontaneous consumer actions 'corrected' the defect by using barter, new personal connections, and the black market, which was a necessary evil amplified by poor state policies: 'Man is not a saint; when he suffers, he cares little for the rules.'[12]

Jacques Debû-Bridel, in 1947, saw the black market as more sinister. Initially a product of military supply management in 1939, it developed through Vichy collaboration with the German 'suction pump' set up to drain the French economy of resources. Debû-Bridel recognized the need for a patriotic grey market (*marché gris*) to serve French interests, in contrast to the black market supplying Germany with Vichy's help. Having been in the Resistance and served on a departmental committee to confiscate illicit profits, he believed Vichy personnel and administrative practices had been kept in place after Liberation. A corrupt national administration not only tolerated, but also profited from the controls and diversion of goods that sustained the postwar black market: 'The black market, it's the state.'[13] Yves Farge, a Gaullist, *Commissaire de la République* for the Lyon region after Liberation and Minister of Food Supply for most of 1946, also blamed official corruption. The black market had originated as resistance but evolved as a system for corrupt practice protected by officials in government and the judiciary, an 'administrative organization of fraud'. Like Debû-Bridel, he saw black market use as an infection, transmitted throughout the economy and abetted by the state administration.[14]

français et les entreprises, ed. by Olivier Dard, Jean-Claude Daumas and François Marcot (Paris: ADHE, 2000), 241.

[11] Michel David, *Le marché noir* (Paris: SPID, 1945), 141, 144.

[12] Baudin, *Esquisse*, 108–156, quoted at 150.

[13] Jacques Debû-Bridel, *Histoire du marché noir (1939–1947)* (Paris: La jeune parque, 1947), quoted at 206.

[14] Yves Farge, *Le pain de la corruption* (Paris: Éditions du chêne, 1947), quoted at 11.

The officials enforcing state controls told a different story. Jacques Dez worked for the *Contrôle économique* (CE) during the war and completed a dissertation on price controls in 1950. He criticized all previous accounts of the black market as written 'with no concern for objectivity', especially Debû-Bridel, and he faulted their condemnations of the state and the control administration. For Dez, the black market originated in producers withholding goods from official markets to sell for higher profit. Effective price control had been frustrated by tolerance for abuse in government departments other than the ministry of finance (that oversaw the CE).[15] French finance officials recognized the importance of German black-market activity in their evidence gathered for the Nuremberg trials.[16] In 1950, they published an article on 'The German black market in France' in a special issue of the *Cahiers d'histoire de la guerre* on the German exploitation of the French economy. This distilled CE observations of German clandestine purchasing, against which they had been virtually powerless. German black-market operations took place in addition to their requisitions and official purchasing, had been practiced by all German services in France, and relied on the complicity of French *trafiquants* whose 'great familiarity with the national market' assisted in this pillaging of French resources. Implicitly, the *Contrôle économique* bore no responsibility for this black-market activity. The standard *Ausweis* (pass) carried by German transport vehicles stated: 'the truck cannot be checked or even stopped by the French police. Any attempt to do so will be severely punished.'[17]

Another controller, Raymond Leménager, defended the CE in a 768-page manuscript prepared for the *Direction générale des prix et des enquêtes économiques*. He gave a detailed account of the development of controls and their administration, focused on price controls, not the black market. Leménager described the CE challenges in enforcing incoherent legislation, their insufficient staff and resources, and the pervasive and perverse interference by the Germans. The exceptional circumstances of the German Occupation and exploitation made effective price control impossible. The black market thrived as a vital alternative to provide essential goods, but it fulfilled these needs 'in the most iniquitous way, rationing by money ruled'.[18]

---

[15] Jacques Dez, 'Économie de pénurie et contrôle des prix: le contrôle des prix dans l'économie française de 1935 à 1949' (Doctoral thesis, Université de Poitiers, 1950).

[16] Service des archives économiques et financières, Savigny-le-Temple (SAEF) B-0049476 contains Ministry of Finance documentation for this purpose.

[17] ***, 'Le marché noir allemand en France', *Cahiers d'histoire de la guerre* no. 4 (1950), 46–71, quote at 61.

[18] Raymond Leménager, 'Étude sur le contrôle des prix', Jan. 1953, quoted at 724. Copies of his study are available in SAEF, B-0016039 and Archives de Paris, coffre 15.

This was precisely the result that the economic controls were supposed to prevent.

These authors' professional training and experience structured their accounts. They agreed on the importance of German black-market purchasing and interference in French control enforcement. They differed on the degree to which bad policy, state incompetence, and corruption had aggravated the shortages, inequities, and price inflation. They noted the incoherence of state policy, lopsided enforcement and the popular alienation from policies and police that failed to control prices and provide equitable access to scarce goods. The state had focused too narrowly on catching and punishing the small fry, while major profiteers went free, with the state sometimes complicit in their illicit traffic. The social and cultural dimensions of black-market activity, essential as context, went unremarked; as did the black-market growth to serve communities of interest when the state failed to manage supplies, and when state controls and controllers lost legitimacy.

The two most influential works about the black market in Paris appeared in the 1950s: Jean Dutourd's novel *Au bon beurre* (1952), depicting the black-market profiteering by a dairy shop owner and his wife, and Claude Autant-Lara's film *La traversée de Paris* (1956), following two porters' misadventures crossing Paris at night, lugging suitcases of freshly butchered black-market pork. Both works were products of resentment and frustration.[19] Meanwhile, survey histories gave, at best, passing attention to black markets, acknowledging that the activity was widespread and engaged almost everyone, with wide variation depending on a person's wealth and location. Black markets benefited the farmers and the rich, earned extraordinary profits, and demonstrated ineffectual surveillance and corruption in the state regulation of markets.[20] Economic historians, by contrast, gave black markets little attention.[21]

Jacques Delarue's *Trafics et crimes sous l'Occupation* (1968) marked a notable exception. Delarue drew from his experience in the *Police judiciaire* to shed light on dark aspects of the Occupation – French complicity in German black-market activity, the destruction of the Vieux Port in Marseille in 1943, and the murderous path of the SS division Das Reich in June 1944. His account of the black market revealed the thorough integration of French *trafiquants* in the German exploitation of French

---

[19] See Kenneth Mouré, 'Black Market Fictions: *Au bon beurre, La traversée de Paris*, and the Black Market in France', *French Politics, Culture and Society* 32(1) (2014): 47–67.

[20] Most notable, for breadth of coverage, see Henri Amouroux, *La vie des Français sous l'Occupation* (Paris: Librairie Arthème Fayard, 1961); he titled his chapter on the black market 'Le crémier-roi', in reference to *Au bon beurre*.

[21] Alan S. Milward, *The New Order and the French Economy* (Oxford: Clarendon Press, 1970); Alfred Sauvy, *La vie économique des Français de 1939 à 1945* (Paris: Flammarion, 1978).

resources. Delarue stated that black-market experience was the most per-sistent dimension of Occupation experience and memory in France. Of all the key words of the Occupation, 'the term "black market" is without doubt the one that has remained engraved in most memories'. He focused not on the everyday, small-scale black market with which most people engaged, but on its underbelly, *les dessous du marché noir* that worked with French organ-ized crime (the 'milieu') and operated with German approval.[22]

Since the 1980s the reorientation of Vichy research has given greater attention to the social and cultural dimensions of Occupation experience, often in regional studies, and has drawn on newly available archival evidence to deepen our understanding of the context for and the local adaptations to the Occupation. Coping with shortages, particularly in food supply, was vital. Local economies, their provisioning and their adaptations to use black markets, demonstrated the normalization of illicit transactions. In agriculturally rich regions like Normandy and Brittany, black marketeers sought out farmers and competed for their produce. In the cities and in regions of monoculture in southern France, efforts to import food supplements fostered new strategies to meet con-sumer needs. Research organized by the *Institut d'histoire du temps présent* detailed the experience of shortages at the regional and departmental levels, differentiating the departments according to food supply – abun-dance to feed other regions, penury, and those with a rough balance able to feed their residents.[23] English-language historians gave new attention to black markets as a means for survival in regional studies; most notably Lynne Taylor's work on experience in the Nord and Pas-de-Calais.[24]

---

[22] Jacques Delarue, *Trafics et crimes sous l'Occupation*, revised ed. (Paris: Fayard, 1993; original ed. 1968), quote at 17. Grégory Auda explores the *milieu* in detail in *Les belles années du 'milieu' 1940–1944: Le grand banditisme dans la machine répressive allemande en France* (Paris: Éditions Michalon, 2002).

[23] Dominique Veillon and Jean-Marie Flonneau, eds., 'Le temps des restrictions en France (1939–1949)', *Les Cahiers de l'IHTP*, 32–33 (1996); they classify departments by food availability as 'nourriciers', 'affamés' and 'en situation intermédiaire'.

[24] Lynne Taylor, *Between Resistance and Collaboration: Popular Protests in Northern France, 1940–45* (New York: St. Martin's Press, 2000), and ibid., 'The Black Market in Occupied Northern France, 1940–4', *Contemporary European History*, 6(2) (1997): 153–176. Significant English language studies with black-market attention include John F. Sweets, *Choices in Vichy France: The French under Nazi Occupation* (Oxford: Oxford University Press); Robert Zaretsky, *Nîmes at War: Religion, Politics and Public Opinion in the Gard, 1938–1944* (University Park: Pennsylvania State University Press, 1995); Megan Koreman, *The Expectation of Justice: France 1944–1946* (Durham, NC: Duke University Press, 1999); Robert Gildea, *Marianne in Chains: In Search of the German Occupation 1940–45* (London: Macmillan, 2002); and more recently Shannon L. Fogg, *The Politics of Everyday Life in Vichy France: Foreigners, Undesirables, and Strangers* (Cambridge: Cambridge University Press, 2009) and Sandra Ott, *Living with the Enemy: German Occupation, Collaboration and Justice in the Western Pyrenees, 1940–1948* (Cambridge: Cambridge University Press, 2017).

French local studies provided valuable details on consumers' and manu-facturers' reliance on illicit trade.[25]

The first national study of the black market in France based on archival research, Paul Sanders' *Histoire du marché noir, 1940–1946* (2001), showed the wealth of information now available in diverse state archives: the ministry of finance (and the *Contrôle économique*), justice, and the Gendarmerie, and the German military archives.[26] Sanders distinguished between the black market for essentials, especially food, in which almost everyone in France took part, and a professional black market ('marché noir du métier') that supplied the Germans and French industry. He stressed the importance of German purchasing and critiqued the linkage of black-market activity with Resistance.[27]

Fabrice Grenard's *La France du marché noir* (2008) provided a more comprehensive chronology and analysis, with thorough archival research to analyse the legislation defining black-market activity, the logic and strategies employed by *trafiquants*, the public perceptions and participa-tion in black-market activity, and the enforcement challenges faced by state agencies, especially the *Contrôle économique*.[28] Like Sanders, Grenard distinguishes between differing motivations and logic for black-market use, developing a more complex analysis: a black market linked to subsistence (consumers and agriculture); a black market of adaptation to economic constraints (industry and commerce); a black market for profit and speculation (intermediaries); and a black market of solidarity on the part of all those not recognized or favoured by the Vichy regime (Jews, *réfractaires* avoiding the labour draft, and clandestine mem-bers of the Resistance).[29] Grenard has also contributed detailed black-market studies to the series of conferences organized by the CNRS research group GDR 2539 on the theme 'French business during the Occupation'. This group, under Hervé Joly's direction, encouraged new

---

[25] The most valuable for black-market work include studies of agriculturally rich Normandy: Michel Boivin, *Les Manchois dans la tourmente de la Seconde Guerre mondiale, 1939–1945*, 6 vols. (Marigny: Eurocibles, 2004) and Yves Lecouturier, *Le marché noir en Normandie 1939–1945* (Rennes: Éditions Ouest-France, 2010).

[26] Paul Sanders, *Histoire du marché noir 1940–1946* (Paris: Perrin, 2001).

[27] Sanders, *Histoire du marché noir*, 262, 292–307.

[28] Fabrice Grenard, *La France du marché noir (1940–1949)* (Paris: Payot, 2008); Grenard has also contributed significant black-market studies to the colloquia organized by the GDR 2539 discussed below. He summarizes his key findings for English readers in '"The Black Market Is a Crime Against Community": The Failure of the Vichy Government to Bring About an Egalitarian System of Distribution and the Growth of the Black Market in France During the German Occupation (1940–1944)', in Tatjana Tönsmeyer et al. (eds.), *Coping with Hunger and Shortage under German Occupation in World War II* (Cham, Switzerland: Palgrave Macmillan, 2018), 83–97.

[29] Grenard, *La France du marché noir*, 283–286.

research on business histories during the Occupation, including the experience of workers, consumers, specific firms and industrial sectors, and presented research findings in a series of conferences from 2002 to 2009.[30]

In this same period, new research on black markets elsewhere in Europe during the Second World War has improved our knowledge of the pervasiveness of black markets and their importance in consumer and producer adaptations to shortages. Black markets developed as a means of exploitation by the German administrative regimes in Occupied Europe, and as a means of resistance and survival by oppressed populations. Even in Britain, with no German occupation but facing serious material shortages, and in Germany itself, exploiting wealth from the countries it had conquered and imposing harsh penalties on domestic black-market activity, black markets produced economic, social and cultural changes. Shortages impacted everyone. Black markets were a direct response to shortages and the economic controls devised to manage their impact.[31]

The Black Market

Illicit activity, often unrecorded or disguised, became a critical part of everyday life. Shannon Fogg, studying how the rural population in the Limousin region dealt with the material shortages that dominated their lives, found that behaviour changed throughout the community in a 'banalization and normalization of illegality'.[32] This had far wider influence than the 'outlaw culture' in the Resistance described by Roderick Kedward; it spread throughout French consumer practices without regard for politics.[33] This normalization of illegality, an essential

---

[30] The topic had been the subject of an earlier conference organized by the IHTP in 1986, with publication of some of the contributions in A. Beltran, R. Frank and H. Rousso, eds., *La vie des entreprises sous l'Occupation* (Paris: Éditions Belin, 1994). Complete information on GDR 2539 activities and publications can be found on their website: http://gdr2539.ish-lyon.cnrs.fr/. It lists their twelve published volumes of conference papers.

[31] The European context is discussed briefly in Chapter 10. For Britain, see Ina Zweiniger-Bargielowska, *Austerity in Britain: Rationing, Controls, and Consumption 1939–1955* (Oxford: Oxford University Press, 2001) and Mark Roodhouse, *Black Market Britain, 1939–1955* (Oxford: Oxford University Press, 2013). For Germany, see Gustavo Corni and H. Gies, *Brot-Butter-Kanonen: Die Ernährungswirtschaft in Deutschland unter der Diktatur Hitlers* (Berlin: Akademie Verlag, 1997), and Malte Zierenberg, *Berlin's Black Market, 1939–1950* (Houndsmill: Palgrave Macmillan, 2015).

[32] Fogg, *The Politics of Everyday Life*, 17.

[33] Roderick Kedward, 'The Maquis and the Culture of the Outlaw (With Particular Reference to the Cévennes)', in *Vichy France and the Resistance: Culture and Ideology*, ed. by Roderick Kedward and Roger Austin (London: Croom Helm, 1985), 232–251,

element in the development of strategies to cope with shortages, is central to *Marché Noir* and my analysis of the purposes black markets served and the reasons for their power, prevalence and persistence.

My approach in *Marché Noir* is organized by sectors of economic activity, to provide clear analysis of the logic for and the impact of black-market activity in each kind of activity. The sectoral differences in needs and in demand for goods influenced the availability and the necessity for black-market goods. Local communities and the resources available within them became intensely important for how individuals adapted behaviour during the Occupation and demanded retribution after Liberation.[34] Strategies for survival are a recurrent theme. As Tatjana Tönsmeyer notes, in a volume on food shortages under German occupation, attention to 'coping strategies' is essential to understand wartime experience.[35]

Marché Noir addresses key issues in the economic and social adaptation to wartime shortages, the development and use (and abuse) of state policy, and conflicts between state authority and the interests of producers, shopkeepers and consumers. The first and most obvious issue is the need to evaluate the role of *state policy and its impact on market activity*. All states used price controls and rationing to contain inflationary pressures, to allocate materials according to priorities for the war effort, and to distribute scarce goods more equitably among consumers who would otherwise bid against each other. Otherwise, the wealthy would maintain or increase their prewar consumption at the expense of those lower on the income scale. France offers a complicated case in which the controls were extensive, convoluted, and increasingly contravened and ineffective. The presence of a 'national' government in Vichy meant that French officials implemented this regulatory regime. The growth and the importance of black-market activity in France demonstrated the failure of Vichy's

and H. R. Kedward, *In Search of the Maquis: Rural Resistance in Southern France 1942–1944* (Oxford: Clarendon Press, 1993), 56–57, 95–100.

[34] Martin Conway emphasizes the importance local experience in his analysis of postwar retribution in Belgium; the point is valid for much of Occupied Europe. Martin Conway, 'Justice in Postwar Belgium: Popular Passions and Political Realities', in *The Politics of Retribution in Europe: World War II and Its Aftermath*, ed. by István Deák, Jan T. Gross and Tony Judt (Princeton, NJ: Princeton University Press, 2000), 133–156.

[35] Tatjana Tönsmeyer, 'Supply Situations: National Socialist Policies of Exploitation and Economies of Shortage in Occupied Societies During World War II', in *Coping with Hunger and Shortage under German Occupation in World War II*, ed. by Tatjana Tönsmeyer, Peter Haslinger and Agnes Laba (Cham, Switzerland: Palgrave Macmillan, 2018), 3–4, observing that historians have focused more on German exploit-ation than on civilian responses. One important study explicitly addressing the survival strategies for women in France is Hanna Diamond, *Women and the Second World War in France 1939–1948: Choices and Constraints* (Harlow: Pearson Education Ltd., 1999).

control regime and the loss of legitimacy for controls, controllers and the state itself. The handbook prepared for Allied troops who would land in France put this bluntly: 'The unsuccessful campaign to suppress the black market affords the most extreme example of the inefficiency, the division and overlapping of responsibility and the proliferation of governmental agencies which are so characteristic of the Vichy régime.'[36] Chapter 3 provides a critical evaluation of the operations of the main enforcement agency, the *Contrôle économique*.

When controls work well, minimal enforcement should be needed. Market players engaged in buying and selling will support controls they see as fair, useful and legitimate. W. B. Reddaway wrote of wartime rationing in Britain that success and the avoidance of a black market depended upon designing a system 'relatively easy to enforce, and which will, indeed, to a large extent "enforce itself"'.[37] The French control system did not enforce itself: it became a target for protest and sometimes violent aggression by its intended beneficiaries. The degree to which market players support regulation and regulate their own conduct is critical to maintaining order in a liberal society. The more controls are seen as pernicious, the greater the policing power needed to enforce them. Resistance to state authority can take many forms, and the black market offers an opportunity to study and reflect on the state's ability to manage economic conduct by observing French experience 'at the grass-roots level, among those whose fight was located in the fine meshes of the web of power'.[38] Food protests and consumer resistance are covered in Chapter 6; attacks on controllers in Chapter 8.

The importance of regulating behaviour and adapting institutions to govern economic conduct is essential to understanding black-market use as social and economic behaviour. The shock of defeat and occupation in 1940 reversed the long-term evolution of state controls towards greater market freedom. With the ensuing shortages of material goods, the state introduced not only new rules, but new policing agencies to enforce rules and contain market disorder. The changes in conduct and the alienation of support for controls show how rapidly the initial public support for effective regulation was disappointed. Managing shortages of essential

---

[36] SAEF 5A-0000183, *France, Basic Handbook, Part III (revised edition): France Since June 1940* (Jan. 1944), 73.

[37] W. B. Reddaway, 'Rationing', *Lessons of the British War Economy*, ed. by D. N. Chester (Cambridge: Cambridge University Press, 1951, reprinted Greenwood Press, 1972), 192.

[38] Michel Foucault, 'Truth and Power', in Paul Rabinow, ed., *Michel Foucault: Beyond Structuralism and Hermeneutics* (New York: Pantheon Books, 1982), 59; Foucault's concept of 'governmentality', the conduct of conduct and its self-regulation, is important for evaluating the market responses to government controls.

goods had been a longstanding function of state authority; in times of famine, the eighteenth-century state had served as 'baker of last resort'.[39] How the French state failed in this role during the Occupation and the immediate postwar years provides grounds for reflection on the power of the state and the limits on its power to regulate markets.

The second issue is *the dynamic for black-market growth*. Chapters 4, 5 and 6 look at the practical problems and the incentives for black-market development in agriculture, industry and commerce, and consumer strategies for survival. The scale of black-market activity in France was not a product of greed alone. Rational economic choices underlay decisions about what goods to produce, where and how to distribute them, and who would have access to purchase them. The massive demand, the enormous purchasing power available in France – especially in German hands – and the needs of diverse consumers created an array of market incentives that worked outside the official markets with its prices and rations fixed by the state. The demand and the potential for profit incentivized entrepreneurial problem-solving that migrated substantially from official to clandestine markets.

Consumer vulnerabilities and resistance, and strategies for provisioning and survival, are a third key issue. The politics of everyday life in conditions of adversity include consumer willingness (or not) to tolerate controls and their alternative strategies for provisioning. Consumer tactics of consumption under adverse conditions have a political content that can challenge the structures of power in government, markets and the production and delivery of goods.[40] The exchanges negotiated outside state rules, to the mutual benefit of buyer and seller, constituted a recovery of some consumer agency in a system of constraint. The study of everyday life under coercive regimes has become increasingly important in understanding how power is exerted and resisted in the social and economic realms, especially in times of stress and under authoritarian regimes. Historical study of popular adaptations to survive shortages has discounted the degree to which states exert 'totalitarian' power under Nazism, Fascism and Stalinism, and recognized the agency of ordinary citizens and their ability to exploit gaps in the regimes of control and use regime rhetoric to counter the power of the state apparatus.[41] Ordinary

---

[39] Steven Laurence Kaplan, *The Bakers of Paris and the Bread Question, 1700–1775* (Durham, NC: Duke University Press, 1996), 12 and 492 (playing on the classic phrase for the importance of central banks in financial crises as the lender or banker of last resort).

[40] Michel de Certeau, *The Practice of Everyday Life*, trans. by Steven Randall (Berkeley: University of California Press, 1984).

[41] Alf Lüdtke, ed., *The History of Everyday Life: Reconstructing Historical Experiences and Ways of Life*, trans. by William Templer (Princeton, NJ: Princeton University Press, 1995), and Paul Steege, Andrew Stuart Bergerson, Maureen Healy and Pamela E. Swett,

consumers and their routines of daily life in extraordinary circumstances allow us to see the rigidities in state power and the flexibility of popular resistance by non-political agents whose ideals and values are expressed in actions rather than words. Even those most willing to believe in Vichy's proclaimed values of 'work, family and fatherland' adopted survival strategies that weakened support for the regime and undermined the values Vichy claimed it would restore.

One revealing dimension of Vichy's failures, discussed in Chapters 7 and 8, was the result of its effort to establish a 'moral order' in France. The everyday realities of shortages and the normalization of illegality made many observers, particularly state officials, fear a national decline in moral standards. Wartime prefects and post-Liberation *Commissaires de la République* warned of a 'profound moral crisis', demonstrated by the increased theft, the active black market, and the preference of youth for the easy profits of crime over honest hard work.

The fourth issue is that of *social fracture in time of economic stress*. Economic controls were supposed to share the sacrifices imposed by economic contraction and German exploitation to equalize the burden. Marshal Philippe Pétain explained food rationing in October 1940 as a 'cruel necessity', imposed by the defeat, in the face of which 'we want to assure the equality of all in making sacrifices. Each must take their part in the common hardships, without allowing some to be saved by their wealth and impose greater misery on the others.'[42] But an equal sharing of misery was impossible. On the vital matter of food rations, consumers were organized in categories by their needs according to age, work and

'The History of Everyday Life: A Second Chapter', *Journal of Modern History*, 80(2) (2008): 358–378. For influential studies everyday life, during the First World War in Germany, see Belinda J. Davis, *Home Fires Burning: Food, Politics, and Everyday Life in World War I Berlin* (Chapel Hill: University of North Carolina Press, 2000); for Austria, see Maureen Healy, *Vienna and the Fall of the Habsburg Empire: Total War and Everyday Life in World War I* (Cambridge: Cambridge University Press, 2004). For Russia during the war and Revolution, see Mary McAulay, *Bread and Justice: State and Society in Petrograd, 1917–1922* (Oxford: Oxford University Press, 1991). Later experience in the Soviet Union is examined in Sheila Fitzpatrick, *Everyday Stalinism. Ordinary Life in Extraordinary Times: Soviet Russia in the 1930s* (Oxford: Oxford University Press, 1999), and Julie Hessler, *A Social History of Soviet Trade: Trade Policy, Retail Practices, and Consumption, 1917–1953* (Princeton, NJ: Princeton University Press, 2004). For Fascist Italy, see Luisa Passerini, *Fascism in Popular Memory: The Cultural Experience of the Turin Working Class*, trans. by Robert Lumley and Jude Bloomfield (Cambridge: Cambridge University Press, 1999); Kate Ferris, *Everyday Life in Fascist Venice, 1929–1940* (Houndsmill and New York: Palgrave Macmillan, 2012), and Philip Morgan, 'The Years of Consent? Popular Attitudes and Forms of Resistance to Fascism in Italy 1925–40', in *Opposing Fascism: Community, Authority and Resistance in Europe*, ed. by Tim Kirk and Anthony McElligott (Cambridge: Cambridge University Press, 1999), 163–179.

[42] Philippe Pétain, *Discours aux Français, 17 juin 1940 – 20 août 1944*, ed. Jean-Claude Barbas (Paris: Albin Michel, 1989), 84.

gender (with extra food for pregnant and nursing mothers and babies), which assumed equal needs within each category as a matter of convenience. (The rationing system is explained in Chapter 2.) Needs within categories were not identical, and the categories and registrations became opportunities for fraud. Beyond the problem of categories, access to goods varied not just by income (whether one could afford the black market), but also by proximity to goods, which varied by region, occupation, social status and personal connections. The *Contrôle économique* claimed that price controls were essential in order 'that relations between French people not be ruled by the law of the jungle, and to save the weak from being sacrificed for the benefit of the strong'.[43] Inept controls transferred output and consumption to black markets, where 'the law of the jungle' increased the power of the wealthy.

The two most notable fractures in access to goods were between the rich who could afford black-market prices and the middle and working classes who could only rarely do so, and between urban residents needing food and rural populations. In both rural and urban experience, there were also profound differences between productive polycultural regions and those heavily committed to a single-product monoculture. Police and prefects reported frequently on the gap between the rich and the rest, a division into 'two distinct clans' one of which could provision itself normally in using the black market, the other – the middle and working classes – lacking essential goods.[44] Rather than equality, state rationing established a control system that was inconsistent (varying in degrees of control) and corrupt, increasing popular belief in unequal treatment. Prefects in departments with strong agricultural sectors complained of peasant greed: 'Unfortunately, the knowledge of privations on the part of those in cities, notably the factory workers, leaves the peasant indifferent. A selfish materialism continues to rage in the countryside.'[45] Such differences fuelled deep animosities and social divisions during the Occupation, and demands for retribution when Liberation released local residents from the constraints of state control.[46] In the postwar economic purge, covered in Chapter 9, many black-market profiteers

---

[43] Fourmon, 'Nécessité d'une politique des prix', *Contrôle économique*, 1 (Nov. 1943): 10.

[44] Archives de la Préfecture de Police (APP), Paris, 220W 4, 'Situation à Paris', 16 June 1941. A housewife in Amboise likewise complained in 1941 that 'there are two categories of consumers, the rich who eat and those who queue for an hour only to be told that there is nothing left'. Quoted in Gildea, *Marianne in Chains*, 114.

[45] AN AJ/41/373 (Indre-et-Loire), prefect monthly report, 31 May 1942.

[46] See Megan Koreman, *The Expectation of Justice: France 1944–1946* (Durham, NC: Duke University Press, 1999), and Marc Bergère, *Une société en épuration: Épuration vécue et perçue en Maine-et-Loire. De la Libération au début des années 50* (Rennes: Presses universitaires de Rennes, 2004).

seemed, to the citizens they had exploited, to escape punishment. The breadth of the black market and its 'essential' nature for survival made postwar justice appear flawed: black-market practices continued, some newly re-legalized, and the state opted in 1947 for fiscal measures to tax rather than punish the actors and activities needed for reconstruction.

To thrive as it did in France, the black market needed to escape disruption and suppression by the state: it sought invisibility. The *Contrôle économique* observed in 1945: 'Its essential characteristic is to be very hard to pin down, it leaves no accounts and can only be proven in starting from very slight evidence.'[47] The archival documentation for black-market activity comes mainly from state efforts at repression. Particularly important in France are the records of the *Contrôle économique*, supplemented by judicial and police records, prefect reports, and the contemporary press. Some writers showed astute observation and penetrating analysis of black-market operations and the difficulties they posed for suppression. The language in their reports reveals rising frustrations in combatting the spreading and effective social resistance to officials and economic controls.

The nature of this evidence and its bias, in recording the suppression of illicit activity, leaves many elements of that activity obscured, but it allows for analysis of the origins and the dynamics of black market growth as an essential part of the survival strategies of those adapting to economies of constraint (producers, consumers, and those engaged in the commerce connecting them): constraint by the shortages of goods, by tighter limits on licit commerce, and by controls to contain prices and distribute scarce goods. Patrick Modiano's father survived the war as a black marketeer. In his search for details, Modiano characterized many of his father's associates as 'phantoms': 'They are very shady travellers who pass through train stations without my ever knowing their destination, supposing that they have one.'[48]

Representations of economic life in fiction, based on observations of life under the Occupation, often complement the archival evidence. As imaginative reconstructions, they do not carry the official status granted to prefects' reports and *Contrôle économique* analyses (which vary widely in quality, originality of analysis, and degree of departure from formulaic response to meet official reporting requirements). But the fictions display the biases, the rancour and the hopes of French citizens adapting their behaviour to the economy of penury. This is particularly interesting after

---

[47] Direction du contrôle et des enquêtes économique (DCEE), *Rapport sur l'activité de la DCEE au cours de l'année 1945* (1946), 37.
[48] Patrick Modiano, *Un pedigree* (Paris: Gallimard, 2005), 24.

the war, when accounts of war experience were written knowing the outcomes of wartime changes. Writers try to render past experience comprehensible (events as they happen are not) and write to serve current needs, to legitimize or critique the present, and to give direction for future action. In France, reconciling wartime collaboration and submission to the Germans with the Allied victory and Liberation produced a 'Gaullist resistancialist myth', with de Gaulle serving as inspiration for a broad national will to resist. Twenty-five years later (Henry Rousso's 'broken mirror' phase of the Vichy syndrome, 1971–1974) this resistancialist mirror was shattered by new research challenging the extent of resistance and the logic and impulse behind French collaboration.[49] Robert O. Paxton's *Vichy France: Old Guard and New Order* (1972) was the key paradigm-changing book, setting a new agenda for research to understand the importance of collaborationist initiatives in France, and opening the way for a new generation of research on collaboration and compromise.[50] As elsewhere in Europe, stories constructed a 'usable past' to serve present concerns; to recover and move on from the tragic experiences in war.[51]

For France, until the 1990s, that usable past gave little attention to the black market, which owed so much to the conditions of penury and exploitation imposed by the Germans and was linked in its worst cases to collaboration and brutal exploitation. The breadth of illicit exchange and improvisation was less visible; its very breadth made it less spectacular. But the details and logic reveal a black-market experience that was more complex, more controversial, and more important than had been recognized, as an essential element in economic survival.

[49] Henry Rousso, *The Vichy Syndrome: History and Memory in France since 1944*, trans. by Arthur Goldhammer (Cambridge, MA: Harvard University Press, 1991); Pierre Laborie, *Le chagrin et le venin: La France sous l'Occupation, mémoire et idées reçues* (Paris: Bayard, 2011).

[50] Robert O. Paxton, *Vichy France: Old Guard and New Order 1940–1944* (New York: Knopf, 1972). On Paxton's impact, see essays in Sarah Fishman et al., *France at War: Vichy and the Historians* (New York: Berg, 2000), and Moshik Temkin, '"Avec un certain malaise": The Paxton Trauma in France, 1973–74', *Journal of Contemporary History*, 38 (2) (2003): 291–306.

[51] Robert G. Moeller, *War Stories: The Search for a Usable Past in the Federal Republic of Germany* (Berkeley: University of California Press, 2001), and Richard Ned Lebow, Wulf Kansteiner and Claudio Fogu, eds., *The Politics of Memory in Postwar Europe* (Durham, NC: Duke University Press, 2006).

2   L'économie de misère

Defeat and military occupation had a devastating impact on French economic output and civilian consumption. Black market development in France responded to the shortages and the hastily conceived state efforts to manage them. The shortages touched everyone. For rich and poor, the strictly rationed food, the empty shelves and lengthy queues, made the war years a struggle for survival in *l'économie de misère*. This chapter establishes the context for black-market growth in France in reviewing the economic impact of defeat and Occupation policies. It explains the severity of the contraction in the supply of goods, the state logic for controls on prices and markets, the unreliability of wartime statistics, and the organization of the system for rationing food (where black markets had their most pervasive influence).

The public face of penury and the rapid growth of the illicit economy pose a problem of assessment for how severely the shortages affected the economy overall, as well as particular sectors and individuals. The effects were inequitable and depended on access to alternative markets. At one extreme, people with no extra income, assistance, or access to alternative food sources went hungry; indeed, some starved. Such was the fate of 45,000 inmates who died in mental asylums in the period 1940–1942.[1] At the other extreme, those with wealth, freedom from control, and black-market access could feast lavishly.[2] If the shortages were obvious, the causes were not. From the shock of defeat in June 1940, visible changes such as the loss of imports from Atlantic trade, the end of imports from North Africa in November 1942, and industry's need for imported raw materials were readily evident. For many, the shortages in food, clothing

---

[1] The state increased inmate rations in December 1942 in belated response to the death toll. See Isabelle von Bueltzingsloewen, *L'Hécatombe des fous: La famine dans les hôpitaux psychiatriques français sous l'Occupation* (Paris: Flammarion, 2007), and for broader analyses of internee vulnerability, Isabelle von Bueltzingsloewen ed., *'Morts d'inanition': Famine et exclusions en France sous l'Occupation* (Rennes: Presses universitaires de Rennes, 2005).

[2] Black-market restaurants provide classic examples; see Kenneth Mouré, 'La capitale de la faim: Black Market Restaurants in Paris, 1940–1944', *French Historical Studies*, 38(2) (2015): 312–314, 320–323.

and household consumer goods seemed to be the result of German requisitions and plunder. 'Most of the population is deceiving itself on the scale of German takings', Alfred Sauvy observed in March 1942. 'They seriously overestimate the amount of food taken, going so far as to think that this is the difference between prewar consumption (or before June 1940) and the current rations.' This common belief implied that when the Germans were gone, consumption would return quickly to its prewar level.[3] Sauvy, as an economist and statistician, knew that German demands on the French economy were just one factor, taking needed goods from output that had fallen significantly. The damage to output would require an extended period of recovery after liberation.

The reasons for scarcity, the lines of causation, and the adaptations to distribute goods outside legal markets created a complex web of problems. At every step the design of new rules to regulate distribution, seeking to bring order and equity to the economy of penury, created opportunities for evasion, illicit supply and illegal activity. Alternative markets proliferated in rapid response to the shortages, the new regulations, unsatisfied demand, and opportunities for profit. The statistical record exaggerates the decline in goods, counting those sold in official markets. Black markets and the parallel economy thrived, accentuating the decline in recorded output and moderating the impact on actual consumption.

Economic Contraction

In defeat, France lost not just political independence and status, but access to international markets and the power to decide national economic and financial policies in the interests of French producers and consumers. Through collaboration, Vichy hoped to gain some autonomy and to reorder the French economy for recovery and growth in a Europe controlled by Germany. German administrators allowed neither independence nor policies to serve French interests. German policies, although neither consistent nor carefully planned for sustained exploitation, successfully extracted resources from France as the wealthiest of its occupied territories. The French contribution to the German war economy was greater than that of any other single occupied country.[4] Through

---

[3] Institut de Conjoncture, 'Situation économique au début du mois de mars 1942', 56–57. These reports compiled by Alfred Sauvy, known as the *Bulletins rouge brique*, are available in the library of the Institut d'histoire du temps présent, Paris.

[4] Alan S. Milward, *War, Economy and Society 1939–1945* (Berkeley: University of California Press, 1977), 135–149; Peter Liberman, *Does Conquest Pay? The Exploitation of Occupied Industrial Societies* (Princeton, NJ: Princeton University Press, 1996), 36–68; and

a combination of high 'occupation costs' intended to support on-going military operations outside of France, and coercive purchasing and transfer policies, the German authorities 'secured a massive and, perhaps, unparalleled transfer of resources from France'. The occupation costs paid by France were more than 36 per cent of French economic output (GDP) in 1941 and 1942, and 55.5 per cent in 1943.[5] This figure is for the payments made into German accounts, covered mainly by Bank of France advances to the state.

The transfer of real wealth employed a variety of methods. The occupation payments show the funds transferred officially to the Germans for direct purchases. This purchasing power had limited ways to find goods in a world of fixed prices in official markets, German requisitions, lost imports and reduced production.[6] The payments in francs increased the currency in circulation from 101.7 billion francs in 1938 to 569.1 billion in 1944.[7] This six-fold increase in paper currency increased the means to purchase with significantly fewer goods available. Inflation was inevitable. Fixed prices in official markets diverted currency and goods to black markets, where the prices responded to the increased purchasing power and material scarcity.

The speed of the defeat in June 1940 caught French and German authorities by surprise. The French had not planned for defeat, nor the Germans for such sudden victory. German policy developed in three overlapping phases. In summer 1940 they focused on immediate plunder, taking resources to defeat Britain and win the war in the West. A design for longer-term exploitation developed in autumn 1940 and in 1941 as it became clear that victory in the West was not imminent. The invasion of the Soviet Union and the failure to win a decisive victory in the East

Hein Klemann and Sergei Kudryashov, *Occupied Economies: An Economic History of Nazi-Occupied Europe, 1939–1945* (London: Berg, 2012), 99.

[5] Filippo Occhino, Kim Oosterlinck and Eugene N. White, 'How Much Can a Victor Force the Vanquished to Pay? France under the Nazi Boot', *Journal of Economic History*, 68(1) (2008): 1–45, quote at 2, figures from Table 1, 7. On German logic for setting the payments at far above actual occupation costs, see Marcel Boldorf and Jonas Schermer, 'France's Occupation Costs and the War in the East: The Contribution to the German War Economy, 1940–4', *Journal of Contemporary History*, 47(2) (2012): 294–300.

[6] Occhino, Oosterlinck and White, 'France under the Nazi Boot', 9; Michel Margairaz, 'La Banque de France et l'Occupation', in *Banque, Banque de France et Seconde Guerre mondiale*, ed. by Michel Margairaz (Paris: Albin Michel, 2002), 37–47. Margairaz calculates the total wealth taken by Germany at 850 billion francs (47).

[7] See INSEE, *Mouvement économique en France de 1938 à 1948* (Paris: Imprimerie nationale, 1950), 338 for contemporary accounting. Later recalculation of the currency in circulation determined an increase from 93.43 billion francs in December 1938 to 574.90 in December 1944; Jean-Pierre Patat and Michel Lutfalla, *Histoire monétaire de la France au XXe siècle* (Paris: Economica, 1986), 258–261. M2 (paper and metallic currency plus demand deposits) increased from 255.4 billion in 1939 to 847 billion in 1944; ibid., 105.

altered planning again in 1942. Germany needed to increase the contributions from occupied territories, with less concern for long-term sustainability as the war on the Eastern Front became one of attrition. The three phases of German policy – plunder, planned exploitation, and then maximum extortion – overlapped.[8] Policy developed through the interaction of central directives with considerable opportunity for improvisation, adaptation and disagreement among military authorities and civilian agencies vying for power, influence and resources. In the competitive climate fostered by the opportunities to loot a richer economy, German military needs, interagency rivalries, differences of opinion between administrators in Paris and Berlin, and individual initiatives produced no coherent plan for exploitation. Those who could exploited their opportunities, abusing power and privilege to advance their own interests.

The Bank of France repeatedly used the term *asphyxie* – suffocation – to describe the economy. In November 1941: 'Anemia, paralysis, suffocation, etc. . . . all these terms, borrowed from medical vocabulary, are at the same time expressive and insufficient' to capture the total, interrelated complex of problems that they found unprecedented.[9] Industrial production fell: from 1938 in the last full year of peace (and a year of low output), it had fallen by 35 per cent in 1941, 46 per cent in 1943, and 59 per cent in 1944. The Germans gave priority to the industries that served their needs. More than 50 per cent of French iron and steel went to German use, 90 per cent of the armoured cars and lorries manufactured in 1942 and 1943, and nearly 100 per cent of the output for cement, aircraft, and aircraft motors.[10] Agricultural output declined in almost every category, on average from 20 to 40 per cent (varying by crop), while land under cultivation fell slightly. For some crops, output per hectare fell considerably. Real gross domestic product fell by 50 per cent from 1938 to 1944.[11] By 1943, French consumption had

---

[8] See the essays by Arne Ratdke-Delacor, Hans Umbreit and Paul Sanders in *L'Occupation, L'État français et les entreprises*, ed. by Olivier Dard, Jean-Claude Daumas and François Marcot (Paris: ADHE, 2000), 11–52; Ratdke-Delacor, 'Produire pour le Reich: Les commandes allemandes à l'industrie française (1940–1944)', *Vingtième Siècle*, 70 (2001): 99–115; and Boldorf and Scherner, 'France's Occupation Costs'.

[9] ABdF 1069201226 24, DGEE, 'Résumé des rapports économiques', ZO, Nov. 1941. Grenard et al. term the situation in summer and autumn 1940 the worst economic crisis in France in the twentieth century; Fabrice Grenard, Florent Le Bot and Cédric Perrin, *Histoire économique de Vichy: L'État, les hommes, les entreprises* (Paris: Perrin, 2017), 54.

[10] Milward, *The New Order and the French Economy*, 132–133, with studies of output in key industrial sectors, 181–253.

[11] Michel Cépède, *Agriculture et alimentation en France durant la IIe Guerre mondiale* (Paris: Éditions M.-Th. Génin, 1961), 311; Sauvy, *La vie économique*, 239; real GDP calculated from Angus Maddison, *The World Economy: Historical Statistics* (Paris: OECD, 2003), 50.

fallen 60 per cent from its level in 1938.[12] German policies damaged the productive power of the French economy and crippled the distribution of goods.

The French economy suffered repeated shocks. The intense battle for France in May–June 1940 had damaged industrial and transportation infrastructure and equipment, homes, and productive farmland. In addition to repairing the war damage, three significant factors posed economic challenges to the new state, its producers and citizens. These make clear the reasons for the economy of penury in Occupied France and the enduring problems slowing recovery after Liberation. The first was the isolation of the French economy, severing ties that had integrated France in a global economy of trade and finance. Although a rich agricultural economy, France imported 20 per cent of its food supply prewar,[13] particularly edible fats, cereals, wine, and tropical goods such as tea, coffee and rice. In addition, it depended on imported fertilizers (94 per cent of phosphate needs) and energy. More than half of France's electricity came from hydroelectric power, but northern France relied heavily on coal-generated power. Domestic coal provided only 70 per cent of national needs; France had imported more coal than any other country before the war.[14] It relied on petroleum imports for all but 8 per cent of its consumption. Energy supplies fell to 50 per cent of prewar coal consumption and less than 5 per cent for petroleum during the Occupation.[15]

French industry depended on international trade for many raw materials. France imported 99 per cent of its mineral oils, nearly 100 per cent of its copper, lead and zinc, 100 per cent of its rubber, and most of its raw textile fabrics – 100 per cent of cotton and jute, 92 per cent for wool, 88 per cent for silk.[16] Commerce with French territories across the Mediterranean eased some shortages in 1941 and 1942, until the Allied landings in North Africa closed that option in November 1942, ending badly needed imports of vegetable oils, fruits, wheat and wine. The loss of

---

[12] R. Froment and P. Gavanier, 'Le revenu national français', *Revue d'économie politique*, 57 (1947): 929.
[13] Barral, 'Agriculture and Food Supply in France', 91.
[14] Milward, *The New Order and the French Economy*, 38.
[15] AN F/37/120; Commission Consultative des Dommages et des Réparations, 'Prélèvements allemands de matières premières: Charbon', and 'Prélèvements allemands de matières premières: Produits pétroliers'.
[16] Sauvy estimates assessing the impact of the closing of German Atlantic trade in Service d'observation et conjoncture économique, '*Situation économique* no. 1 (vers le 15 Aout 1940)', 6; he concluded the lack of raw materials was the principal obstacle to economic recovery.

vegetable oils from colonies meant a 40 per cent decline in national supply and required a reduction in fat rations by one-third.[17]

German demands were the second factor damaging output, separable into the demands for financial resources and for material and labour. Occupation costs provided the main mechanism for exploitation. These were announced on 8 August, setting payments at 20 million RM per day. This did not include the cost of quartering troops, to be paid directly by the French government, and gave no account of how the amount had been set or what relation it bore to actual costs for the army of occupation (as distinct from the armed forces in France for other purposes). The payments were reduced temporarily to 15 million RM per day from May 1941 to December 1942; then raised to 25 million RM per day from December 1942 to July 1944. The payments were required in French francs, at an exchange rate of 20 francs to the RM. This over-valued the RM by more than 50 per cent: thus France paid 400 million francs per day initially, and 500 million per day in 1943 and 1944, deposited at the Bank of France in advance every ten days.[18] This gave Germany sufficient purchasing power in August 1940, General Huntziger declared, to pay for an army of 18 million men; enough that 'the Germans will be able to buy the whole of France'.[19]

The Occupation costs imposed 'a massive and perhaps unparalleled transfer of resources', a major contribution to the German war economy: 479 billion francs, greater than one year's prewar GDP in France.[20] These funds helped supply Germany's war effort against Britain and the Soviet Union, and restored and resupplied the troops temporarily in France for rehabilitation, on rotation from the Eastern Front.[21] France also served as a place for German private gain, draining consumer goods by official and private purchasing, drawing on legal and black markets. This included official purchasing of raw materials and supplies, troops engaging in direct purchase, and deliberate use of the black market to buy hoarded and illicit goods.[22]

---

[17] AN AJ/41/2142, Bonnafous to Michel, 24 Nov. 1942, and figures cited in 'Entretien du 24 novembre 1942 au Majestic'.

[18] Milward, *The New Order and the French Economy*, 55; Pierre Arnoult, 'Comment, pour acheter notre économie, les allemands prirent nos finances (1940–1944)', *Cahiers d'histoire de la guerre*, 4 (1950): 5–8.

[19] Milward, *The New Order and the French Economy*, 61; Arnoult, 'Comment, pour acheter notre économie', 6; AN AJ/41/107, Huntziger conversation with Hemmen, 21 Aug. 1940.

[20] Occhino, Oosterlinck and White, 'France under the Nazi Boot', 2, 8.

[21] Boldorf and Scherner, 'France's Occupation Costs', 303, 315.

[22] On the share of black-market purchasing in German spending, see Christof Buchheim, 'Die Besetzten Länder im Dienste der Deutschen Kriegswirtschaft während des Zweiten Weltkriegs: Ein Bericht der Forschungsstell für Wehrwirtschaft', *Vierteljahrshefte für Zeitgeschichte*, 34(1) (1986): 129–131.

In their first weeks in France German soldiers used *Reichskreditkassenschein* (RKK), an occupation currency issued from trucks following the troops. Although their issue was suspended in France in October 1940, RKK remained convertible until December 1943, and were brought to France and spent in large quantities by troops on rotation from the Eastern Front.[23] In trade relations with France, Germany benefited from clearing arrangements negotiated in November 1940 to disconnect the German payment for imports in Reichsmarks from the payments made to exporters in France, in francs.[24] In theory, clearing arrangements facilitate a balanced exchange. In practice, these were designed to allow Germany to run a large trade deficit without paying for imported goods.[25] Lastly, outright looting and theft accounted for an estimated 154 billion francs in material gain for the Germans.[26]

German labour demands exacted a further toll. France mobilized 4.2 million men in 1939–1940. More than 1.8 million soldiers were taken prisoner in May and June 1940. In December 1942, 1.1 million French prisoners remained in Germany, many of them assigned to work Kommandos (on farms, in industry and mines) rather than remaining in camps.[27] Germany needed skilled workers to sustain its war effort. By 1942 the labour shortage was 'the overwhelming preoccupation of the German war economy'.[28] France, with its industrialized economy held hostage, offered good prospects for labour recruitment and coercion. French workers were encouraged to volunteer for work in Germany with the promise of higher wages, more and better food, and employment security. The fixed wages and low rations imposed in France made work in Germany look attractive for some, but volunteers were quickly

[23] Milward, *The New Order and the French Economy*, 54–56; Boldorf and Scherner, 'France's Occupation Costs', 309–311; Kenneth Mouré, 'Spearhead Currency: Monetary Sovereignty and the Liberation of France', *International History Review*, 42(2) (2020): 280.

[24] Jonas Scherner, 'The Institutional Architecture of Financing German Exploitation: Principles, Conflicts, and Results', in *Paying for Hitler's War: The Consequences of Nazi Hegemony for Europe*, ed. by Jonas Scherner and Eugene N. White (Cambridge: Cambridge University Press, 2016), 49; Klemann and Kudryashov, *Occupied Economies*, 207–215.

[25] The German clearing account deficit climbed from 55 million RM at the end of 1940 to over 8.5 billion RM in 1944.

[26] Milward, *The New Order and the French Economy*, 81; Adam Tooze, *The Wages of Destruction: The Making and Breaking of the Nazi Economy* (London: Allen Lane, 2006), 385.

[27] Yves Durand, *La vie quotidienne des prisonniers de guerre dans les Stalags, les Oflags et les Kommandos 1939–1945* (Paris: Hachette, 1987), 11, 296; Richard Vinen, *The Unfree French: Life under the Occupation* (New Haven, CT: Yale University Press, 2006), 190–191.

[28] Tooze, *Wages of Destruction*, 513ff; by late 1944 there were nearly 8 million foreign workers in Germany, more than 20 per cent of the labour force and one third of the workers in armaments (517).

disabused by their experience there.[29] Volunteers to work in Germany numbered 48,567 in September 1941, and perhaps 75,000 in autumn 1942.[30] Fritz Sauckel, the Nazi plenipotentiary for labour mobilization, sought to recruit skilled workers in Western Europe, but in 1942 resorted to coercion. In France, the *relève* in June 1942 promised to release POWs in return for skilled workers who volunteered to work in Germany, and this turned to compulsion with a law to requisition workers in September 1942, and then to conscription with the *Service du travail obligatoire* (STO) in February 1943. Labour conscription brought a total of nearly 650,000 French men and women to work in Germany in 1943–1944.[31]

The third factor challenging French economic management was the capacity to feed its population. The loss of labour affected both agriculture and industry. Of the 1.8 million French POWs, about 500,000 were agricultural workers, 13 per cent of the prewar male labour force. A POW census of 25 May 1941 showed 350,000 agricultural and forestry workers, 31 per cent of the prisoners at that time.[32] Transport difficulties and the fragmentation of French territory, with passage obstructed between zones, complicated the organization of food supply. The main division between Occupied and Unoccupied France gave the Germans direct access to a high percentage of French industry and mines, manufactured goods, and grain and dairy output in agriculture. The northern departments of the Nord and Pas-de-Calais, placed under the German military administration in Brussels, suffered severe food crises as German troops there bought up the local supplies desperately needed by civilians.[33]

---

[29] On volunteers and their work experience, see essays by Fabrice Virgili and Mark Spoerer in *Travailler dans les entreprises sous l'Occupation*, ed. by Christian Chevandier and Jean-Claude Daumas (Besançon: Presses universitaires de Franche-Comté, 2007), 359–391, and the account of French experience as prisoners, volunteers and conscript labour in Vinen, *The Unfree French*. For working conditions in Germany for French volunteers and POWs, Ulrich Herbert, *Hitler's Foreign Workers: Enforced Labor in Germany under the Third Reich*, trans. by William Templer (Cambridge: Cambridge University Press, 1997), 195–197, 273–278, 292–295. For French conscript labour, see Patrice Arnaud, *Les STO: Histoire des Français requis en Allemagne nazie 1942–1945* (Paris: CNRS Éditions, 2010).

[30] Henry Rousso estimates there were never more than 70,000 volunteers by mid-1942, in 'L'économie: pénurie et modernization', 470. Arnaud estimates there were about 75,000 in autumn 1942, with another 20,000 to 30,000 added from then to the end of the war, and nearly 600,000 conscripts; Arnaud, *Les STO*, 23. French statistics after the war counted 765,952 French workers as deported to work in Germany. J. Vergeot, 'Dommages, repartitions, reconstruction', *Revue d'économie politique*, 57 (1947): 949.

[31] Yves le Maner and Henry Rousso, 'La domination allemande', in A. Beltran, R. Frank and H. Rousso, eds., *La vie des entreprises sous l'Occupation* (Paris: Belin, 1994), 26–29.

[32] Cépède, *Agriculture et alimentation*, 209–210. When Vichy tried to repatriate agricultural workers, 683,000 prisoners claimed to be eligible, hoping this would get them home.

[33] Taylor, *Between Resistance and Collaboration*, 30–37, Étienne Dejonghe and Yves Le Maner, *Le Nord-Pas-de-Calais dans la main allemande* (Lille: La Voix du Nord, 2006), 75–76, 124–128.

Feeding France's urban population, its workers, its mothers and children, posed a major challenge for the Vichy government. Their adoption of food rationing, explained below, came in September 1940 at German insistence, and imposed starvation level rations dictated by the Germans.

To recapitulate, three factors shaped French economic experience after June 1940. The severing of most international ties threw the hexagon back on its internal resources, imposing economic contraction. The German victory and occupation damaged output and took significant quantities of French raw materials, food, financial resources, stocks of goods, new production and labour. The very life of the nation was at risk in the contraction and disruption of its food supplies.

Under the impact of defeat the French economy contracted, with high unemployment, internal fragmentation, and great uncertainty as to when and under what terms recovery would be possible. Industrial production in August 1940 was estimated at one quarter to one third of normal, and the threat of German appropriation of material resources made negotiation and the restoration of a French 'presence' a matter of urgency.[34] The grain harvest was imperiled, the ownership and output of industry in doubt, imports jeopardized, and the availability of essential food supplies and transport uncertain. French GDP would decline steadily, despite German efforts to sustain production in the sectors they needed for their war effort. Real GDP in 1940 fell 11.5 per cent from its level in 1938; in 1941 it was down 30 per cent, in 1943 down 40 per cent[35] (Figure 2.1).

Alfred Sauvy calculated an industrial output index for the Occupation years based on second quarter output in 1939 as 100.[36] This index fell to 54 per cent in 1941, 45 per cent in 1943, and 33 per cent in 1944.[37] The sectors with the smallest contraction were those of use to the Germans and less reliant on raw material imports. Gas and electricity remained strong until 1944, particularly hydroelectric power. Construction, cement, metallurgy and vehicle construction (military), as priorities, produced at only half their prewar levels in 1942–1943.[38] These were industries the Germans sought to exploit. Table 2.1 provides an index for the contraction of output of indicative products (1938=100). Output in

---

[34] Michel Margairaz, État, finances et économie: Histoire d'une conversion (1932–1952) (Paris: CHEFF, 1991), 503–506.
[35] Maddison, The World Economy, 50.
[36] INSEE, Le mouvement économique en France (1938–1948), 9–10.
[37] Sauvy, La vie économique, 155.
[38] Sauvy, La vie économique, 155–156; the surveys of industrial production in S. Béracha, 'La production industrielle', Revue d'économie politique, 57 (1947): 1247–1273, and INSEE, Le mouvement économique en France (1938–1948) focus on the recovery after Liberation with few statistics on wartime production.

Figure 2.1 France: Real GDP 1938–1950 (1938=100)
Calculated from Angus Maddison, *The World Economy: Historical Statistics* (Paris: OECD, 2003), 50.

1938, already 25 per cent below its interwar peak in 1929–1930, serves as a base year as the last calendar year of peace.[39] The wartime contraction is evident in declining output and declining per capita food consumption. German exactions took industrial and consumer goods from a shrinking economy and food supplies from a damaged agricultural sector.

The German administration froze prices and wages on 20 June 1940 in their first economic measure, to maximize their purchasing power in France. French authorities already believed price controls to be essential. They fixed French prices on 9 September 1939 and started to develop a more robust price control administration with the power to punish price infractions and determine whether increases were justified. With the defeat in June, a shattered economy, and the need to pay exorbitant Occupation costs, prices were of great concern for authorities in the Bank

[39] Alfred Sauvy gives index figures for industrial production; the average for 1938 (1929=100) was 76. Sauvy, *Histoire économique de la France entre les deux guerres* vol. 3 (Paris: Economica, 1984), 316, 323, 327.

Table 2.1 *French Economy 1940–1945 (1938=100)*

	1940	1941	1942	1943	1944	1945	Sources
Real GDP	88.4	69.9	62.7	59.5	50.3	54.5	Maddison, 50
Industrial Production		65	59	54	41	42*	Sauvy, 239
Retail prices Paris	129	150	175	224	285	393	ME, 278
Steel		69.3	72.2	82.4	49.8	26.6	ME, 227
Aluminium		146.7	100	102.2	57.8	82.2	Sauvy, 239
Cement		82.1	57.8	72.3	35.5	42.6	ME, 232
Military trucks		116	90.9	47.2	25.2	82.1	ME, 230
Civilian vehicles		5.7	1.5	0.01	0.09	0.9	ME, 230
Cotton		28	10	6	3*		F 37 120
Wool		21	27	17	14*		F 37 120
Shoes*		81.5	71.0	57.4	35.7		F 37 120
(leather soles)		(50)	(31)	(25)	(19)		
Consumption per person							
Wheat	54.8	62.7	55.2	64.7	66	50.2	ME, 200
Potatoes	61	43.4	43.4	41.7	47.2	37.6	ME, 200
Meat	60.9	48.7	45.5	37.9	39.1	51.4	ME, 200
Milk	78	72.2	66.4	67.2	57.7	63.9	ME, 200
Sugar	44.2	46.2	51.2	52.5	43.3	52	ME, 200
Coffee	75.7	20.5	14.2	4.7	1.8	26.6	ME, 200

* Shoe statistics are the indexed output for all shoes and, in brackets, the shoes with leather soles. Industrial production in 1945 is the figure for May 1945; numbers for cotton and wool in 1944 are for January to May.

Sources: Maddison, *The World Economy*, 50; Sauvy, *La vie économique*, 239; INSEE, *Mouvement économique en France (1938–1948)*, 200, 227, 230, 232; and F 37 120, Commission consultative des dommages et des réparations, *Prélèvements allemands de matières premières*. Monographie M.P. 15, *Textiles* (Paris: Imprimerie nationale, 1947) and Monographie M.P. 16, *Cuirs et pelleteries* (Paris: Imprimerie nationale, 1948).

of France and the Ministry of Finance, to preserve the franc against the threat of massive inflation.[40]

Vichy Statistics

The statistical record gives an impression of precision at odds with the reliability of the metrics for economic activity. The state's need for data

[40] Margairaz, *L'État, les finances et l'économie*, 542–547.

prompted an unprecedented effort to document economic activity, including the creation of a new *Service national des statistiques* in 1941 (in 1946 it merged with the economic studies section of the Ministry of National Economy to become INSEE, the *Institut national de la statistique et des études économiques*).[41] Vichy administrators needed to report stocks and output to the German Occupation authorities and negotiate the level of German requisitions. They tried to control prices, restore domestic production, and manage the shortages of raw materials and essential consumer goods. In a world of sudden scarcity, particularly for essentials in daily life, the state made a huge effort to identify where goods were and who should get them.

Industrialists, retailers and farmers all complained of the new paperwork this imposed. Demands on farmers for reports on land under cultivation, livestock and crop yields resulted in a law in October 1941 which limited the number of declarations they could be required to file to two per year, one in spring and one in autumn.[42] The increased effort to gather information yielded data of low quality. For producers in agriculture, individual declarations replaced estimates made at the commune level. Their reported output would be subject to requisitions, taxation, and sale at official prices. In industry and commerce, off-record transactions provided lucrative business opportunities. For the state, since the Germans would take all they could from French resources, under-reporting would reduce German demands. Almost everyone had an interest in under-reporting, omitting or disguising output. It was fiscally prudent for individuals and firms, and it could be seen as a 'patriotic duty' by individuals and even by state officials.[43] The entire reporting system

---

[41] Wartime developments are explained by participants in François Fourquet, *Les comptes de la puissance: histoire de la comptabilité nationale et du plan* (Paris: Encres, 1980), 34–41.

[42] Pierre Fromont, 'La production agricole', *Revue d'économie politique*, 57 (1947): 1202, states that farmers had been required to go to local mayors' offices 22 times for declarations to that point in 1941. The *Contrôle économique* estimated that 50 per cent of the wheat production in the Côtes-du-Nord was undeclared and sold to buyers other than the state; Louis Bahurel, 'Les fraudes en matière de blé dans le département des Côtes-du-Nord', *Contrôle économique* no. 3 (May 1944): 181–194. For Vichy initiatives to improve accounting and accountability in industry, see Béatrice Touchelay, *L'État et l'entreprise: Une histoire de la normalisation comptable et fiscale à la française* (Rennes: Presses universitaires de Rennes, 2011), 173–222.

[43] Both the national statistical service (INSEE) and the *Revue d'économie politique* survey report on agriculture during the war characterized under-reporting as a patriotic duty. INSEE, *Mouvement économique en France (1938–1948)*, 57; Fromont, 'La production agricole', 1203. Similar comments in Cépède, *Agriculture et alimentation*, 145, 163, 287, 311; and Pierre Barral, 'Agriculture and Food Supply in France during the Second World War', in *Agriculture and Food Supply in the Second World War*, eds. Bernd Martin and Alan S. Milward (Ostfildern: Scripta Mercaturae Verlag, 1985), 90. The Germans recognized that French statistics were systematically falsified and unreliable: BA Freiburg, RW 19/ 3361, 'Lage der französischen Industrie und Bedingungen ihres Wiederaufbaues und Einordnung in die europäische Wirtschaft', 22 Dec. 1941. Jean Fourastié and Henri

thus produced misleading results. One illustrative example, from the critical realm of food supply, was the *Office national interprofessionnel de céréales* lamenting in 1942 that it was impossible to know how much grain would be harvested: 'We know that unfortunately all the declarations are wrong. Everyone declares a false figure in order to favour their own interests.'[44]

In addition to the need for caution regarding the quantities reported, the decline in the quality of many goods aggravated shortages and made the quantities less comparable. This decline in quality is not visible in the quantitative record. Sellers compromised quality to stretch supplies. Foods were affected: shortages of food and transport meant that perishable supplies were often sold in poor condition, damaged in transit or storage, and forced consumers to choose between buying poor quality or nothing at all.

The changes in quality for bread, regulated as a staple of French diet, show adulteration as official policy. The sale of white bread and pastries was forbidden, and bread could be sold only after it had been out of the oven for twenty-four hours, beginning 1 August 1940. The rate of utilization (*taux de blutage*) for grain milled into flour was increased. The average rate for milling wheat prewar was 74 per cent (white bread is made from flour using about 70 per cent of the grain); the rate was increased to 80 per cent in June 1940, to 90 per cent in January 1942, and to 98 per cent in April 1942, rendering the bread almost impossible to digest. One doctor described the concoction as a 'sticky, heavy dough, impossible to cook and to digest'.[45] Nutrition experts advised that pushing the rate above 90 per cent added no food value and increased digestive problems and illness. German authorities insisted, returning the rate to 97 per cent after a brief reduction (to 90 per cent) in late 1943.[46] Bakers

Moutet lauded the importance and accuracy of statistical evidence in their analysis of France's place in the world economy in 1945. Revealingly, their statistics for France relied on prewar years, leaving the wartime years in several tables blank. In their comparative analysis of productive capacity, they noted that a statistical comparison was impossible: 'because the usable statistics, while abundant in other countries, are in France non-existent or random'. Jean Fourastié and Henri Montet, *L'économie française dans le monde* (Paris: Presses universitaires de France, 1945), quote from 73.

[44] Meeting of the ONIC comité de gestion, 21 May 1942, quoted in Alain Chatriot, 'L'ONIC ou la régulation étatique et professionnelle d'un marché politiquement sensible (1940–1953)', in *Histoire des modernisations agricoles au XXe siècle*, ed. by Margot Lyautey, Léna Humbert and Christophe Bonneuil (Rennes: Presses universitaires de Rennes, 2021), 143.

[45] Quoted in Steven L. Kaplan, *Le pain maudit: Retour sur la France des années oubliées 1945–1958* (Paris: Arthème Fayard, 2008), 163.

[46] Dates for rate changes are given in the report on cereals in AN F/37/120; Commission Consultative des Dommages et des Réparations (CCDR), *Céréales panifiables*, 45. Utilization rates and the harmful effects of rates above 80 per cent are discussed in AN

were permitted to add up to 5 per cent flour from beans, barley, corn, or rice.[47] Other additives in unknown quantity, from potato to buckwheat to sawdust, yielded a black bread that saved on wheat flour at the expense of digestibility. The black market offered better bread, white bread and pastry.

Flour, milk, butter and coffee were easily and frequently adulterated. Clothing was scarce, sometimes available only if old clothes were exchanged along with the coupons needed to obtain new items. (Easier for the affluent than the poor, when consumers had to hand in two used articles to purchase one new.) Leather and rubber were in very short supply, reducing the availability of footwear essential for work and travel. Shoes were made with wooden soles (scored to make them flexible), and with uppers from experimental materials ranging from straw and paper to felt and fish skin. Owners lucky enough to have leather-soled shoes added metal plates or nails to the soles to reduce wear on the leather.[48] Such changes in quality remain invisible in the quantitative record, but seriously aggravated the decline in supply.

Official prices, the essential measure for the success of state policy, show the state insistence on price stability rather than the realities of market exchange. Bank of France managers noted repeatedly that rising prices were not recorded well in official price indices. The manager in Roubaix observed in February 1942 that the widespread practice of under-the-table payments (*soultes*) increased the real prices paid. 'There's no longer any correlation between the official accounts and business as it is actually transacted.'[49] In March the Bank explained, 'in all branches of the economy we see an extreme <u>disorder in</u> prices, which makes it impossible now to calculate any valid index or to determine what used to be called the <u>level of the cost</u> of living'.[50] As practices for charging extra evolved and as the parallel economies for barter and black market

---

AG/3(2)/352, 'Notre pain quotidien', undated but in a period of 98 per cent utilization. Kaplan reviews 'the black legend' of poor-quality bread during the war in *Le pain maudit*, 162–163; he has slightly different utilization rates for the war period, 144. The regulations were more easily enforced in cities than in rural areas, where official rates could be ignored.

[47] Veillon, *Vivre et survivre*, 118.

[48] Dominique Veillon, *La mode sous l'Occupation* (Paris: Payot & Rivages, 2014), 83–96.

[49] ABdF 1069201226 25, DGEE, 'Résumé des rapports économiques', ZO, Feb. 1942; Fabrice Grenard, 'La soulte, une pratique généralisée pour contourner le blocage des prix', in *Les entreprises de biens de consommation sous l'Occupation*, ed. by Sabine Effosse, Marc de Ferrière le Vayer and Hervé Joly (Tours: Presses universitaires François-Rabelais de Tours, 2010), 29–43.

[50] ABdF 1069201226 25, DGEE, 'Résumé des rapports économiques', ZO, Mar. 1942. Underlined in the original.

transactions distributed an increasing share of goods, the official indices showing moderate price increases become less and less accurate.

Louis Baudin characterized French economic direction during the Occupation as a 'Vaudeville économique', leading off his list of problems with 'the impossibility of establishing meaningful statistics'.[51] Nonetheless, the statistics furnish an essential perspective on the trends in output, prices, shortages, and the impact of German exploitation. They are indicative rather than exact. They show the nature of the problems faced and the logic for the adaptations and policy initiatives needed to manage a situation of serious shortages with potential for economic disaster.

Rationing

Marshal Philippe Pétain explained in October 1940 that the rationing of raw materials for industry and food for consumers was 'a painful necessity' after defeat. France needed to be rebuilt from a heap of ruins to create a new order. The liberal economy failed in the 1930s. Two principles would guide construction of the new economic order: the economy must be organized and it must be controlled. Sound money with stable prices and wages would allow the recovery and growth of production. This required two systems of control: the first over international trade to serve national purposes, the second a 'vigilant control of consumption and prices, in order to maintain the purchasing power of the currency, to prevent excessive expenditure, and to provide greater justice in the distribution of goods'.[52] The ambitions were lofty and the agenda clear. Control prices to prevent inflation, and ration goods to ensure equitable distribution. But how could that be achieved?

Rationing took place at two levels: in apportioning supplies for producers and in limiting the purchase of goods by consumers. Vichy developed new bureaucracy to allocate raw materials and parts needed by producers. Industry-wide *Comités d'organisation* were established to direct the allocation of raw materials between firms in each industry, and the legislation was slapped together in mid-August 1940. The *Comités* set a layer of French allocation offices between the German authorities and French industry and prevented the re-organization of French industry by the Germans. The Germans then insisted on a centralized direction to coordinate the allocations to the *Comités d'organisation*. The *Office central de répartition des produits industriels* (OCRPI – Central Office for the

---

[51] Baudin, *Esquisse de l'économie française*, 150.
[52] Pétain, *Discours aux Français*, 84 (9 Oct. 1940) and 88–93 (10 Oct. 1940).

Distribution of Industrial Products) was created to this end in September. The Germans held substantial power over appointments to the committees and their allocation policies.[53] The system gave predominant influence to large firms and to industrial leaders with Vichy sympathies. It consolidated Vichy control and accepted German domination. Firms lacking sufficient weight or political connections, and producing goods not in demand by the Germans, had to look elsewhere for their productive inputs.

The most immediate and widely felt impact was in rationing food supplies. The exodus from invading troops in May and June 1940, the Wehrmacht seizure of warehoused supplies, disruption of the harvest, shortages of transport and the complex fragmentation of French national territory by German internal frontiers all combined to create immediate shortages and fears for future supply. This triggered consumer reflexes to buy and hoard, and departmental authorities blocked exports from their regions. The improvised local measures to allocate food needed consistency and centralized coordination. Vichy introduced measures to restrict sugar, pasta, wine and oils at the end of July. A comprehensive system was designed in August, under German pressure, and came into force on 23 September. The Germans set ration levels by a 'unilateral and irrevocable' decision, to punish French consumers with quantities equivalent to those suffered by Germans during their 'turnip winter' during the First World War.[54]

Evading restrictions to obtain sufficient food that official rations did not provide was by far the most widespread motivation for black-market activities. Consumers were allocated rations according to their ration category, which was determined by their age and, for adults, their labour (see Table 2.2). The initial adult bread ration allowed 350 grams per day, reduced to 275 in April 1941. Adult meat rations began at 360 grams per week, were cut to 250 grams in April 1941 and to 180 grams in January 1942. In many regions this dropped to 90 grams. And the official rations were not always available.[55]

---

[53] Grenard et al., *Histoire économique de Vichy*, 62–65; Richard F. Kuisel, *Capitalism and the State in Modern France: Renovation and Economic Management in the Twentieth Century* (Cambridge: Cambridge University Press, 1981), 132–144; and Hervé Joly, ed., *Les Comités d'organisation et l'économie dirigée de Vichy* (Caen: Centre de recherche d'histoire quantitative, 2004).

[54] For German pressure and the initial ration levels, see Kenneth Mouré, 'Food Rationing and the Black Market in France (1940–1944)', *French History*, 24(2) (2010): 265–268; the quote is from AN F/60/1546, Général de Corps d'Armée to M. le Maréchal de France, 'Plan de rationnement alimentaire', 8 Sept. 1940.

[55] Cépède, *Agriculture et alimentation*, 149–152, and his comparison of ration allocations and actual consumption, 381–399; Eric Alary with Bénédicte Vergez-Chaignon and Gilles Gauvin, *Les Français au quotidien 1939–1949* (Paris: Perrin, 2006), 209–219.

Table 2.2 *Ration Categories in Occupied France*

Ration Categories	Number (in Jan. 1942)	Ration calories (3rd quarter 1942)	Normal daily needs
E Under 3 years	1,684,000	1350	900
J1 3–6 years	1,784,000	1400	1400
J2 6–12 years	4,244,000	1300	1800–2400
J3* 13–21 years	5,184,000	1400	3000–3300
A 22–70 years	10,292,000	1150	2200–2800
T 21–70 engaged in heavy labour	7,481,000	1500	3200–5400
C 21 years and older, agricultural labour	6,866,000	Varied by region	
V 70 and older (excludes those in C)	1,820,000	1100	2000–2400

* J3 category added in June 1941; initially the A category included ages 13 to 70, as did T and C; pregnant women were included in J3 to increase their rations.
Sources: Cépède, *Agriculture et alimentation*, 150, 367, 390; Alary et al., *Les Français au quotidien*, 212.

Consumers faced a wearying, convoluted process to obtain their rations. Municipal offices issued ration documents; consumers registered and then queued to receive their ration books and coupons. Buyers used coupons to purchase monthly and quarterly rations (sugar, coffee); for daily and weekly essentials like bread, cheese, meat and fats, they had to exchange coupons for tickets each month. The coupons valid for exchange, which could vary in timing and quantity according to the local stocks available, were announced in the local press. The tickets were an entitlement to purchase the rationed food. Consumers had to keep their tickets in order, exchange coupons for tickets when the goods were available (*déblocage*), use the correct tickets, and queue at the shops where they had registered, hoping their ration entitlement would be available when they reached the counter.[56] The increased complexities in responsibility for food acquisition fell heavily on women as an addition

[56] Alary et al., *Les Français au quotidien*, 210–211, and Dominique Veillon, *Paris allemand: Entre refus et soumission* (Paris: Tallandier, 2021), 321–322 n4, and 328 n1.

to their housekeeping work. The extra time and attention required made this particularly difficult for consumers who were elderly, single, and/or working long hours.

Shopkeepers replenished goods based on the tickets they submitted as proof of stock sold to customers – if replacements were available. This created many frustrations: in the paperwork involved with handling ration documents; in not having reliable access to resupply (which encouraged hoarding and black-market purchase and sales); and in encouraging fraud in handling the coupons and tickets in their exchanges with customers and in submitting them to suppliers. The difference for shopkeepers between 'normal' prewar markets with sufficient supply and the Occupation markets were scarcity, increased regulation and paperwork, and vastly reduced predictability.

The system of controls required new state agencies to implement and enforce an unprecedented state intervention in markets. Effective control would depend on the quality of information gathered (not good, as we have seen), the qualities of the new administrative agents and agencies, and the development of policies and practice to win public confidence and compliance. The German invasion and the civilian flight in May–June 1940 brought defeat, disorder and economic dislocation. The Vichy regime claimed it would restore economic order and build a place for France in a German-dominated Europe. This would, in turn, bring greater stability and better prospects for growth than the Republican regime of the 1930s. The worst, they assumed in summer 1940, would soon be over.

3   Curing the Thermometer: Price Controls and the Black Market

The shock of defeat and the need to restore order in a distraught and damaged nation set the context for the abandonment of republican government and support for Philippe Pétain to lead an undefined *État français*. Economic controls seemed more necessary than ever in order to share sacrifice and keep economic conditions from getting worse. Price controls and rationing would be essential, as would the development of administrative capacity to design and enforce controls.

The office for price control became the state agency most responsible for enforcement of controls in its 1942 recreation as the *Direction générale du contrôle économique*. The *Contrôle économique* earned a reputation for incompetence, corruption, and abuse of power. The reputation, not well-deserved, increased resistance to state controls. One controller, Raymond Leménager, wrote a detailed history of the CE to rehabilitate work he believed had been 'misunderstood, unjustly slandered, and sometimes odiously attacked'.[1] Another, Jacques Dez, wrote in 1950: 'there are few administrations that have amassed against them so much discredit'.[2] How the CE earned this reputation is linked to its strategy for enforcement during the Occupation and its persistence after Liberation.

Henri Culmann, who worked for the ministries of commerce and industrial production during the Occupation, later characterized the price controls as 'curing the thermometer': focused on the measure of prices, rather than the conditions that created inflationary pressure.[3] Facing serious shortages, the state fixation on price control and rationing would neither increase output nor bring more goods to market. The controls were a regime of constraint to manage penury: to live with the shortages rather than to combat them.

---

[1] Quote from SAEF B-0016041, 'Essai sur le Contrôle Economique'. SAEF files B-0016038 to B-0016042 have documents for his study; a complete version of his unpublished manuscript (1953) is in B-0016039.

[2] Dez, 'Économie de pénurie', i.

[3] Henri Culmann, *À Paris sous Vichy: Témoignage et souvenirs* (Paris: Les Éditions la Bruyère, 1985), 52.

The control legislation set boundaries to separate licit from illicit commerce, and in doing so, delimited black market activities. As new legislation took effect, prefects commenting on illicit commerce set the term 'marché noir' in quotation marks and used terms like 'commerce noir'. The prefect for the Department of the Seine, describing the food supply to Paris in September 1940, observed 'The development of crooked commerce (*commerce marron*), which always finds ways to have vehicles and fuel, and which buys at any price with the certainty to resell at a profit.'[4] As illicit traffic increased, 'the most important problem at this time' according to a cartoon in *L'Œuvre* in October 1940, the quotation marks disappeared. *Marché noir* became the familiar term for the growing 'parallel' economy.[5] The new rules to combat this traffic, punish offenders and deter potential *trafiquants*, required energy and imagination for new agencies and methods to police transactions and make the controls effective.

The Germans prohibited price increases in June 1940. They required that the French ration food in September, and repeatedly criticized French policing of markets and prices as inadequate. Their insistence on price controls, which facilitated their purchasing, aligned with the objectives of the French administration. French measures to ration food and raw materials and fix prices, planned in the spring of 1940 and delayed by the invasion, established a more robust administration in the fall of 1940. Culmann's observation that control efforts treated symptoms rather than their causes was not evident in the turmoil of defeat and the uncertainty for France's economic future. The control measures developed to meet immediate problems, reacting to problems rather than anticipating them, and scrambling for solutions with little time or decision-making autonomy. Although positive in their intent to contain inflation and share sacrifice, the controls' consequences proved to be pervasive, complex, and frequently perverse. Black markets developed to escape the system of controls.

This chapter reviews control efforts during the Occupation, focusing on the *Contrôle économique* and its enforcement strategies. The control efforts did restrain official prices and increase compliance with new regulations, but the controls were reactive in nature and subject to significant German interference. The popular dislike of controls and controllers developed as products of administrative choices and practices, particularly the focus on prices in retail markets and the conviction that harsh punishments would bring compliance with regulations that promised

[4] AN AJ/41/390 (Seine), prefect report, 13 Sept. 1940.
[5] Grenard, *La France du marché noir*, 18.

equity but delivered deprivation. They provide a striking example of the difficulty of imposing regulations that alienate the producers and consumers they claim to serve.

Controls and the Black Market

All belligerents in the Second World War used controls to allocate resources to war purposes. Price controls and rationing replaced the market determination of prices and allocation of goods through its normal 'rationing by price' to limit inflation and focus on war production. The French government decreed a price freeze on 9 September 1939 to protect consumers and preserve the franc and avoid repeating the First World War experiences of inflation and currency depreciation. The 1939 measure required exceptions and exemptions: for agricultural prices to be set by the Ministry of Agriculture, for wholesale prices for raw materials, and to allow price increases when supply costs rose. The Vichy regime established a new fixed price regime (by a law of 21 October 1940) and comprehensive rationing measures under German pressure.[6] In markets crippled by shortages, the unsatisfied consumer demand for rationed goods shifted to complementary and replacement goods, requiring the extension of controls to cover them as well. Buyers looked to illicit transactions. The legislation and the efforts to enforce controls and punish offenders developed in response to market activity. Allan H. Meltzer notes as his 'second law' of regulation: 'Regulations are static. Markets are dynamic.'[7] New regulations, in reducing the range for licit transactions, create opportunities for evasion and contravention. The dynamic growth of black-market activity in France provides a significant example of entrepreneurial innovation to

---

[6] The price legislation is summarized in Philippe-Jean Hesse and Olivier Ménard, 'Contrôle des prix et rationnement: l'action du gouvernement de Vichy en matière de régulation de l'offre et de la demande', in *Le droit sous Vichy*, ed. by Bernard Durand, Jean-Pierre Le Crom and Alessandro Somma (Frankfurt am Main: Vittorio Klostermann, 2006), 165–208; and briefly in Michel Margairaz, 'L'État et les restrictions en France dans les années 1940' and Jean-Marie Flonneau, 'Législation et organization économiques au temps des restrictions (1938–1949)' both in *Les cahiers de l'IHTP*, 32–33 (1996): 25–41, 43–58. On early price controls, Olivier Moreau-Néret, *Le contrôle des prix en France* (Paris: Librairie du Recueil Sirey, 1941), 1–3, 10–13, and Louis Franck, *French Price Control from Blum to Pétain* (Washington, DC: Brookings Institution, 1942).

[7] Allan H. Meltzer, *Why Capitalism?* (Oxford: Oxford University Press, 2012), 9. Meltzer's first law is 'Lawyers and bureaucrats regulate. Markets circumvent regulation.' He thus separates personal responsibility for the regulations from the abstract action of 'markets', as if some natural law moves markets rather than the decisions of human actors. I would rephrase his first law to give market players, not the market, agency: 'Lawyers and bureaucrats regulate. Buyers and sellers circumvent regulation.'

exploit new opportunities, and the power of demand to foster new supply and distribution.[8]

The sudden shortages and early controls following the defeat in 1940 sparked a rapid growth of illicit activity. The state struggled to understand the nature and the extent of illicit commerce in order to suppress it. Contemporaries distinguished between the varying forms of illicit trade: a *marché gris* for infractions outside the law but tolerated by the state as necessary to meet family needs; a *marché brun* for the sales to German authorities, over which French authorities had little power; a *marché rose* for transactions among friends; even a *marché blanc* for the sale of milk without ration tickets.[9] The array of colours captured the diversity of activities, distinguishing variations in their nature and economic gravity. These different transactions often overlapped and intertwined. I will usually refer to all these activities as black market, using the language of the state and enforcement officials for the violation of economic controls. The intermediate categories were not applied with consistency or precision.

The kinds of black-market activity are best differentiated by following the goods, who bought them, and the motivations for the traffic. Not all illicit trade was for profit: the increase in barter and the resale of used goods indicate how people found ways to acquire goods for everyday needs by evading rather than violating legislative prohibitions. The greatest potential profit lay in selling to the Germans, who used black market purchasing systematically to obtain merchandise, especially hoarded goods.[10] Luftwaffe Colonel Josef Veltjens, appointed to coordinate German black-market purchases in Occupied countries in 1942, spent over 1.1 billion Reichsmarks from May to November in four countries.[11] In France, occupation payments provided abundant funds for the

---

[8] Although authorities rarely acknowledged the direct connection between restrictions and black-market growth, Admiral Darlan did so in June 1941, stating that the spread of the black market was 'the direct consequence of the considerable increase in restrictive legislation and quotas in economic affairs'. AN F/7/14900, Darlan and Achard to all prefects and sub-prefects, 4 June 1941.

[9] Yves Lecouturier, *Le marché noir en Normandie 1939–1945* (Rennes: Éditions Ouest-France, 2010), 5.

[10] Sanders, *Histoire du marché noir*; and 'Economic Draining: German Black Market Operations in France, 1940–1944', *Global Crime* 9 (1) (2009): 136–168. Götz Aly documents widespread black market purchasing by German troops in *Hitler's Beneficiaries: Plunder, Racial War, and the Nazi Welfare State* trans. by Jefferson Chase (New York: Holt Paperback, 2008). German black-market use across Europe appears in many essays in Tönsmeyer et al., *Coping with Hunger and Shortage under German Occupation*.

[11] SAEF B-0049476, Veltjens, 'Rapport fondé sur l'expérience du Délégué pour les Missions spéciales', 15 Jan. 1943. The other countries were Belgium, the Netherlands and Serbia.

purchases. German authorities bought goods with little concern for price; they had the purchasing 'power' to prevail over French laws (which they berated French authorities for failing to enforce). Joseph Joinovici and Michel Szkolnikoff, infamous billionaire *trafiquants*, made their fortunes in selling French goods to the Germans (Chapter 5). More typical were the many businesses that worked for the Germans because German contracts did not need to respect French official prices, and could provide access to raw materials, transport, higher profits, and protection from French controllers.

Illicit commerce among French buyers and sellers was far more common, more varied in its forms, and the main target for French controllers. Trade in industry and commerce often violated price and ration controls. Sellers used billing and payment deceptions to disguise transactions, with premiums paid under the table. Some kept more than one set of books to record official prices for state monitoring, and accounting practices used various forms to conceal or obscure the real prices paid. Deceit in sales and accounts was one dimension that challenged enforcement; another was the transport of goods. Suppliers and consumers developed ways to evade, obstruct or stretch the rules for possession and transport of goods. This included shipping forbidden goods in 'family parcels' (*colis familiaux*); setting aside scarce products for favoured customers who would pay a premium; buying direct from farmers and selling for profit to urban residents and restaurants; and fraud in the use of ration cards and tickets that included theft, counterfeiting and trafficking in ration documents. Illicit slaughter of livestock was common in rural areas, as was milling or sifting flour for white bread and pastry. The difference between actions for profit or to serve family and community was not always clear. Traffickers disguised their for-profit trade as family support.

The scale of illicit activity defies precise counting. The most accurate figures, used by the CE to demonstrate its effectiveness, are those for the offences caught and punished by control administrations. To what extent these are the tip of the iceberg cannot be known; state officials assumed they caught only a fraction of the illicit transactions, and public opinion believed that the *gros trafiquants* escaped punishment, often thanks to state protection. Table 3.1 shows the numbers of cases filed by control agencies in France from 1940 to 1947. (The years are determined by the sharp decline in enforcement after June 1947 and the CE annual reports issued only for the years 1943 to 1947.) The cases reported and the kinds of activity they display tell us more about control effort than about the extent of black-market activity. The case numbers include warnings and many small fines for minor infractions.

Table 3.1 *Black Market Infractions 1940–1947*

	1940	1941	1942	1943	1944	1945	1946	1947
# case reports centralized at CE	27,528	214,016	199,485	379,405	285,786	302,313	234,650	191,891
% filed by CE	33%	46%	49%	45%	46%	39%	33%	31%
% filed by Gendarmerie			33.2%	35%	30%	34%	34%	36%
% filed by police			12.9%	12%	19%	21%	24%	25%
Nature of offence								
Infractions by producers	1.2%			19%	16%	15%	14%	11%
by wholesalers	12.4%			4%	4%	4%	6%	7%
by retailers	76.7%			42%	43%	41%	52%	64%
by individuals				35%	37%	40%	28%	18%
Punishment by CE								
Number of cases	11,784	166,029	153,527	278,771	264,250	242,050	174,255	
Warnings	2,625	33,324	27,117	33,249	35,776	36,900	34,050	
						(14%)	(22%)	(41%)
Transactions	9,159	132,705	126,410	196,010	142,730	119,700	70,180	
				(58%)	(46%)	(42%)	(35%)	(17%)
Fines and confiscations				(15%)	(28%)	(37%)	(34%)	(34%)
Businesses closed	511	1,763	1,588	4,339	2,508	3,300	3,021	6,180
Imprisonments				2,274	1,405	2,425	49	0
Funds to Treasury from CE fines and confiscations (millions frs)				1,215	1,575	2,073	3,055	2,757

Sources: Grenard, 'Le cadre legislatif', 191–194; DGCE/DGCEE annual reports, 1943–1947.

Two elements in this breakdown merit emphasis. First, the import-ance of the *Contrôle économique*: they reported 45 to 49 per cent of the cases in the period 1941–1944. Second, the focus on retail commerce: in every year with statistics available, the largest category for infractions is retailers, closely followed by individuals. Combined, they constitute 80 per cent of the cases from 1943 to 1947.[12] The 1.84 million cases from 1940 to 1947 provide a large sample to analyse the dimensions, the practices and the logics for black market transactions, and to understand the often misdirected efforts at enforcement. The state records for the system of policy and enforcement are essential to understand how this system provoked disappointment, resentment, and then anger and outright opposition, alienating the public it was meant to serve.

Price Police

The *Contrôle économique* began life as the *Service de contrôle des prix* in 1936, created by the Popular Front to prevent 'unjustified' price increases for essential goods. It would become the main state agency to enforce marketplace controls.[13] The devaluation of the franc in 1936, the price freeze after a second devaluation in 1937, and legislation to prepare for war in July 1938 and September 1939 prompted the development of department-level committees to monitor prices, with no patrolling of markets or real power to punish unjustified increases. Vichy gave teeth to the *Service de contrôle des prix* and promised a regime of stable prices with its law of 21 October 1940 to codify price legislation and increase the fines for violations, a tacit admission that previous legislation had been

---

[12] Statistics in Fabrice Grenard, 'Le cadre législatif et institutionnel de la lutte contre le marché noir dans la France des années 1940–1946' (Mémoire pour le DEA, Institut des études politiques, 2000), 191–194, and Grenard, *La France du marché noir*, 313.
[13] Leménager provides a chronology of the changing names in his 'Étude sur le contrôle des prix', 124–132:

Date of name change	Title for service
20 May 1940	Service de contrôle des prix
31 December 1941	Service générale de contrôle économique
6 June 1942	Direction générale du contrôle économique
8 February 1944	Direction générale du contrôle des prix
23 November 1944	Direction générale du contrôle économique
29 April 1946	Direction générale du contrôle et des enquêtes économique
27 December 1948	Direction générale des prix et du contrôle économique
January 1952	Direction générale des prix et des enquêtes économique

ineffective.[14] The new controls appeared as products of Vichy collaboration with German occupation forces, but they were consistent with earlier French efforts to control prices and distribution. Controls would share sacrifice and assure 'the same rights to everyone regardless of their wealth', Pétain explained, and preserve the value of the franc. Camille Marchand, the prefect of police, declared that controls would maintain calm in markets: 'public order depends on the level of prices'.[15]

Jean de Sailly (1906–2001), appointed to direct the *Contrôle des prix* in November 1940, had been an *inspecteur des finances* since 1931. He disliked the Popular Front, which he thought too interventionist, preferring the 'liberal' policies of Paul Reynaud. De Sailly took the post to help restore order and to protect France against German depredations. 'In a regime of penury, the strongest profit most from disorganization', he later explained, 'and because of that, maintaining some control in the economy was, in a system of penury, the lesser evil'.[16] Under his direction the *Contrôle des prix* would expand its remit to include rationing and transport violations, and then take on the vital role of coordinating enforcement to suppress the black market as the *Direction générale du contrôle économique* in June 1942.

The new controls required policing power to ensure they were followed in market transactions. This generated enforcement agencies with little coordination and conflicting zones of competence. The *Brigade financière* of the Paris police, responsible for investigating financial fraud, had its scope extended to include supervision of economic controls. So did the Gendarmerie, to enforce controls in rural markets and on the roads used for transport. The Ministry of Agriculture established an office of food administration (*Service du ravitaillement général*) in October 1939, with *Brigades mobiles* to oversee collection, transport and distribution. The Ministry of the Interior created a *Police économique* in November 1940 to investigate criminal economic activity including the black market.[17]

---

[14] Hesse and Ménard, 'Contrôle des prix et rationnement', 171–172; this law was preceded by laws of 20 May 1940 granting powers to enforce price legislation, and a decree of 17 Sept. 1940 giving these powers to the *Service de contrôle des prix*. Fabrice Grenard provides a concise history of the *Contrôle économique* in 'L'administration du contrôle économique en France, 1940–1950', *Revue d'Histoire Moderne et Contemporaine*, 57(2) (2010): 132–158.

[15] Pétain comments from speeches on 13 Aug. 1940 and 10 Oct. 1940, *Discours aux Français*, 73, 84; Marchand from AN 72AJ/1853, report on the meeting of the *Comité départemental de surveillance des prix* for the département of the Seine, 31 Mar. 1941.

[16] CHEFF Archives orales, interview of Jean de Sailly by Agathe Georges-Picot, 21 and 29 June 1989.

[17] AN F/7/14900, Bouthillier and Perouton to all prefects, Circulaire no. 206, 26 Nov. 1940, for the *Police économique*; Moreau-Néret reviewed the range of state administrations given responsibility for prices and the early development of the Contrôle des prix, in *Le contrôle des prix*, 261–273.

This fragmented authority needed coordination, de Sailly argued, with competent staff sharing information on offenders and the offences under investigation under one administration and guided by one set of rules. Repression of the black market would be its central task. The growth of the black market was 'the most visible manifestation of a generalized economic disorder'.[18] The *Service de contrôle des prix*, renamed the *Service général de contrôle économique* in January 1942, was renamed again to oversee enforcement as the *Direction générale du contrôle économique* (DGCE) in June. De Sailly emphasized his administration's competence to lead the effort, including their ability to distinguish between serious black-market offences needing exemplary punishment and minor infractions by families desperately in need of food. The *Police économique* and the Gendarmerie would work with the CE. The notoriously corrupt *Brigades mobiles* from the food supply administration would be 'integrated' into the CE with a purge of its agents and improved training.[19]

The CE direction of enforcement was short-lived. The Milice, the national police force established in January 1943 to combat the Resistance, claimed suppression of the black market as part of its duties. Its contribution in this regard was negligible, but in January 1944, Milice chief Joseph Darnand took charge in a consolidation of French police as the *Secrétaire général au maintien de l'ordre*. This put Darnand in control of all police forces. A decree in February transferred the CE's policing powers to a *Direction de police économique*. De Sailly and the DCGE did not want to be under Darnand's control. The CE returned to price supervision, as the *Direction générale du contrôle des prix*, remaining under the ministry of finance.[20]

The development of the *Contrôle des prix* from monitoring prices by committee to active surveillance of prices in 1940, and then to responsibility for all market activity, required the rapid assembly of competent staff, supplies and organization for effective action. Price controllers

[18] SAEF 1A-0000402, Jean de Sailly, 'Note au sujet du Contrôle Économique', 14 May 1942; also 'Projet de circulaire au sujet de la coordination des Services Économiques', 15 May 1942.
[19] SAEF B-0049888, de Sailly, Notes de service no. 131, 6 July 1942, and no. 162, 21 Sept. 1942; Grenard, *La France du marché noir*, 139–140. De Sailly wanted a serious 'purge' to determine the agents' 'moral and professional aptitude'.
[20] On the police reforms, see Jean-Marc Berlière, *Police des temps noirs: France 1939–1945* (Paris: Perrin, 2018), 607–611; on the changes to the *Contrôle économique*, SAEF B-0049888, Laval to regional and department prefects, 'Réorganisation du Contrôle Économique. Application de la loi du 8 Février 1944', 28 Feb. 1944. On de Sailly's hostility to Darnand and the Milice, DGCE, *Rapport sur l'activité de la DGCE au cours de l'année 1944*, 8; and Leménager, 'Étude sur le contrôle des prix', 626–630.

needed knowledge of state law and administration and of the industries, commerce, and accounting practices to be monitored. The first controllers in 1939, often retired civil servants, had been designated as auxiliaries and served without pay.[21] The decree of 20 May 1940 authorized the creation of a central administration and enabled department services to hire controllers. A decree of 17 September established the new price control agency as a temporary service. Price control mobilized retired civil servants and borrowed staff from financial services, especially the customs administration (about one third), tax administrations (*Contributions indirectes* and *Contributions directes*), and the post office.[22] Many were moved by administrative transfers;[23] some of those transferred were among the least capable in their original positions. New agents were hired on temporary contracts of three to six months. The staff complement climbed from 1,900 in late 1940 to a maximum of 7,117 in 1943. Numbers then fell: to fewer than 7,000 in 1944 and 1945, then more rapidly to 4,530 in January 1948, and 3,526 in 1950.[24] In September 1951 the CE argued it needed a force of 1,523 agents.[25]

Price controllers needed to know the ever-changing price and ration legislation, and they were given basic instruction in economics, accounting and law.[26] The CE established a *Centre d'études* in 1942 to improve agent training in law, finance, accounting and economics. They added advanced courses in 1943 for specialists to conduct investigations in particular branches of industry.[27] But they could train only a few agents

[21] Moreau-Néret, *Le contrôle des prix*, 263–264.

[22] Moreau-Néret, *Le contrôle des prix*, 264–270. In the Charente-Inférieure, retired civil servants worked as volunteers to enforce price legislation in the fall of 1940. AN F/1a/ 3676, Inspection générale des services administratifs, 'Rapport à Monsieur le Ministre, Secrétaire d'État à l'Intérieur', 19 Oct. 1940. The report's author was sceptical that the auxiliaries had the knowledge to review commercial accounts and determine illicit price increases; he records the difficulty of agent competence in initial hiring.

[23] See DGCE, *Rapport sur l'activité de la DGCE au cours de l'année 1944*, 10–11, and the overview in Michel-Pierre Chélini, *Inflation, État et opinion en France de 1944 à 1952* (Paris: CHEFF, 1998), 235–236. Former controller Jacques Dez comments on the problem of transfers 'to get rid of (the word is not too strong) all the agents judged undesirable' in 'Économie de pénurie', 123. The CE had to assure borrowed personnel that working for the CE would not hurt their careers in their home administrations; SAEF B-0049888, note de service no. 87, 29 Mar. 1942, 'Détachement au Service Général de Contrôle économique'.

[24] Chélini, *Inflation, État et opinion*, 235 Table 75, and reports in SAEF, 5A-0000018; figure for 1940 personnel from Grenard, 'Le cadre législatif', 41. The most complete list of CE personnel is in an undated Leménager note in SAEF B-0016038.

[25] SAEF B-0057639, J. Bernad, J. Guichard, R. Leménager, A. Morin and P. Rachou, 'Rapport sur l'organisation et le fonctionnement du Service', 28 Sept. 1951.

[26] SAEF B-0016039, Leménager, 'Étude sur le contrôle des prix', 176–180.

[27] SAEF B-0049888, Note de Service no. 72, 27 Feb. 1942; DCEE, *Rapport sur l'activité de la DCEE au cours de l'année 1945*, 18–20; Hervé Dumez and Alain Jeunemaitre, *Diriger l'économie: L'État et les prix en France (1936–1986)* (Paris: L'Harmattan, 1989), 151.

at a time, and the CE *Notes de service* indicate that practical experience counted heavily in how well controllers actually performed in the field.[28] Compared with the staff transferred from financial services, new agents hired on temporary contracts needed more training and were less capable of detailed investigations. They were often assigned to the easier tasks, monitoring food rationing and retail prices. They needed little training to verify if pretzels were sold at the correct price and weight, or whether shops followed regulations for signage, sales receipts and ration tickets.

Their primary focus was retail sales. Agents, assigned initially to supervise prices in their own communities, had fewer opportunities to catch infractions and enforce price compliance if they were known to shopkeepers. When shopkeepers knew that controllers were present, they charged legal prices and suspended illicit sales.[29] Controllers filed fewer case reports in regions where they served for extended periods, particularly in rural areas.[30] Agents were sent therefore to communities where they would not be readily identified. There they needed lodgings; this delayed transfers and incurred expense for agents staying in hotels.[31]

The control administration struggled with supply shortages. They needed offices for central and departmental administrators, office supplies, and means of transport to patrol markets and pursue illicit traffic. Office space was hard to find, as were furniture and supplies.[32] The service introduced measures to economize on paper use, reducing the size of pages for reports, using both sides of each page, avoiding the use of envelopes, and sending official notices in bulk.[33] But transport posed the most serious difficulties; it was crucial to interdict black market traffic, which frequently relied on trucks and black-market fuel. The surveillance of markets outside major urban centres and the pursuit of suspects required mobility. At the end of 1943 the CE had the use of 373 automobiles for all of France, 242 of them owned by the agents. Fuel allocations in 1942 allowed as little as 10 litres per

---

[28] Dez reports that from 1943 to 1947 the Centre d'études trained 650 specialists, the largest numbers to work in industry (especially construction and textiles) and in food processing and distribution (especially dairy); 'Économie de pénurie', 130. The need for practical experience and the importance of specialist training are evident in SAEF B-0049888, Notes de service, no. 335, 30 July 1943 and no. 419, 5 Feb. 1944.

[29] Baudin, *Esquisse de l'économie française*, 154; he notes that when a controller was in the neighbourhood, 'the delighted clients benefit from official prices'.

[30] Dez, 'Économie de pénurie', 111: 'In rural sectors, the Contrôle des prix agents quickly knew too many people and became too well known. Their actions ended in being completely useless, their functions a sinecure.'

[31] SAEF B-0049888, Note de service no. 446, 29 Mar. 1944.

[32] SAEF B-0049888, Note de service no. 130, 2 July 1942.

[33] SAEF B-0049888, Notes de service nos. 141, 24 July 1942; 298, 4 June 1943; and 374, 26 Oct. 1943.

vehicle per month.[34] The CE arranged for agents to purchase bicycles at a reduced price, especially for rural areas where bicycles were essential.[35] In December 1943, CE agents had 2,183 bicycles in use, all but six privately owned.[36] Many controllers relied on public transit. They were allocated cards for train travel at reduced fares, but the number of cards was insufficient and did not give them priority to obtain seats on the over-filled trains.[37] Travel between departments required advance approval, as did the transport of bicycles, which incurred extra cost.[38] The CE thus lacked the mobility essential for rapid action against black-market traffic, especially in rural areas.[39]

The *Direction générale du contrôle économique*

The administrative reconfiguration in 1942 put the DGCE in a position to coordinate enforcement and improve public opinion and compliance, as well as to advise on control legislation and policy. De Sailly argued in May 1942 that his *Contrôle des prix* staff were best suited to take charge of enforcement because of their ability to exercise informed judgement on the severity of the offences they dealt with. His argument showed concern for growing black-market activity and the increasing animosity and resistance to price controls and food shortages. Fabrice Grenard's account of the CE recognizes that their efforts restrained the rise of official prices during the Occupation, but terms their record 'a complete failure' between 1942 and 1946. The judgement is well deserved in terms of the CE battle with the black market and its alienation of public support.[40] Retail price inflation (official prices in Paris) was held under 20 per cent per year from 1940 through 1942, surged to 38 per cent in 1943, and would reach 60 per cent annually from 1946 through 1948 (Table 3.2).

The CE administrators blamed their failures on the bad policies set by the state, which they tried to administer with insufficient personnel. They

---

[34] Leménager, 'Étude sur le contrôle des prix', 182–183; Dez, 'Économie de pénurie', 154–156; SAEF B-0049888, Note de service no. 49, 3 Jan. 1942.

[35] SAEF B-0049888, Note de service no. 141, 19 Nov. 1941; agents would purchase the bicycles and receive an indemnity for their use that would eventually reimburse the cost.

[36] Leménager, 'Étude sur le contrôle des prix', 182; Dez, 'Économie de pénurie', 155.

[37] SAEF B-0049512, 'Brigade Centrale de Contrôle Économique Année 1942'.

[38] SAEF B-0049888, Note de service no. 303, 8 June 1943. An agreement in August allowed them to use coupons for their bicycles without paying out of pocket. SAEF B-0049514, 'Note pour Monsieur le Chef du 3ème Bureau', 26 Aug. 1943.

[39] Even adequate footwear for agents was in short supply; the Customs service offered extra work shoes and fabric for uniforms, restricting the offer to members of their staff, to meet 'immediate and urgent' needs. SAEF B-0049888, Note de service no. 225, 27 Jan. 1943.

[40] Grenard, 'L'administration du contrôle économique', 156, and 'The Black Market Is a Crime Against Community', 91–92.

Table 3.2 *Retail Prices in France, 1938–1950 (1938=100, Annual Averages, Paris)*

Year	Retail price index	Annual % change
1938	100	
1939	108	8%
1940	129	19%
1941	150	16%
1942	175	17%
1943	244	39%
1944	285	17%
1945	393	38%
1946	645	64%
1947	1030	60%
1948	1632	58%
1949	1676	3%
1950	1864	11%

Source: INSEE, *Annuaire statistique de la France 1966, résumé rétrospectif* (Paris: Ministère de l'économie et des finances, 1966), 286.

claimed their staff complement was 'notoriously insufficient for the task to be accomplished', citing Belgium as a better example (where black-market activity was more extensive, indicating that the number of controllers was not the key to effective enforcement).[41] De Sailly lamented in 1943: 'I notice more and more that the Service, despite all our efforts, is overwhelmed because of lack of personnel, the inadequacy and slowness of sanctions, and above all because the regulations it is charged to apply are in many sectors faulty; it [the Service] finds itself confronting infractions that are generalized and almost inevitable.'[42]

One Paris daily, *Le Petit Parisien*, ran a six-part series on the CE in December 1943, titled 'The difficult mission of the Contrôle économique'. In contrast to frequent criticism in the press, this series

[41] DGCE, *Rapport sur l'activité de la DGCE au cours de l'année 1943*, 5. In 1943 Belgium's price control administration had between 7,000 and 8,000 staff; with controllers in the department of agriculture and food supply, the number of controllers was about 20,000. But the black market was far more active and widespread, and essential to civilian food supply. Jean Colard, *L'alimentation de la Belgique sous l'Occupation Allemande 1940–1944* (Louvain: Nouvelles publications universitaires, 1945), 30 (for the number of controllers).

[42] SAEF 1A-0000402, de Sailly to Minister of the National Economy and Finances, 14 Apr. 1943; cover note for a report arguing that he had insufficient staff, 'Note au sujet de la position des Services français de contrôle en ce qui concerne le marché noir', Apr. 1943.

Figure 3.1 Direction générale du contrôle économique; *Le Petit Parisien*, 3 Dec. 1943. Bibliothèque nationale de France.

lauded CE efforts to control prices and counter black-market traffic (Figure 3.1). It highlighted 'the importance and the difficulties of repression, as well as the competence, devotion, and probity of its agents', and echoed the CE complaints of insufficient staff to battle 'a black market that is better organized each day'.[43]

Typical press coverage gave attention to economic hardship, the black market (arrests, condemnations, confiscations), and cases of misconduct by *fonctionnaires*. Abuses were regrettably frequent (see Chapter 7): the press reported food supply officials selling to the black market, municipal employees trafficking in ration documents, and thefts by staff working in food collection, transport and distribution, all of whom had opportunities to traffic in the goods and documents they

---

[43] *Le Petit Parisien*, 2–9 Dec. 1943; SAEF B-0049516, Contrôle économique, Département de la Seine, 'Rapport mensuel du mois de décembre 1943'.

handled.[44] The price controllers did not handle goods, except those they confiscated; their main opportunities for abuse lay in accepting bribes to overlook or profit from the offences they uncovered.[45]

The belief that effective control depended on policing markets, exemplary punishment and enforcement power was essential to CE practice. They claimed they would do better with more staff, but while the force of policing could be increased, tighter enforcement of bad policy would not reduce public hostility, nor improve ineffective controls. In its first annual report (for 1943) the CE stated that it faced an atmosphere of public 'incomprehension' and 'hostility'.[46] In the evaluation that follows, CE policies and enforcement strategy are reviewed to explain the increasing public opposition to controls and controllers.

Public hostility was the product of insufficient rations and inequitable distribution, to which market conflict with controllers added first irritation and then disillusion with the state control measures. Controllers were agents of state interference. They held unusual power to investigate and punish infractions. Their written statements were considered proof of an offender's guilt. Price controllers could issue warnings for minor and first-time offences, send serious cases to the courts for prosecution, or confiscate goods and impose an immediate penalty known as a *transaction*. If the offender agreed and the controller's supervisor approved, the *transaction* was then to be paid within fifteen days.[47] This was intended to encourage prompt payment from the income gained by illicit sales. It avoided delay in bringing cases to trial and swamping the courts with petty cases, where magistrates treated many offenders with leniency.[48] Controllers served as policeman and judge. For the CE, a *transaction* was not considered a fine, but rather a 'contract' in which the state renounced legal action in exchange for payment by the offender.[49] Their statistics separated cases according to how they were concluded: with *transactions*, fines and

---

[44] On food supply scandals, see Fabrice Grenard, *Les scandales du ravitaillement: Détournements, corruption, affaires étouffées en France, de l'Occupation à la guerre froide* (Paris: Payot, 2012).

[45] Dez, 'Économie de pénurie', 219, 'This Administration having no goods to distribute, could traffic only in its repressive powers.'

[46] DGCE, *Rapport sur l'activité de la DGCE au cours de l'année 1943*, 34–36.

[47] Moreau-Neret, *Le contrôle des prix*, 298–304. Transactions, fines and confiscations imposed by the CE were used in about two-thirds of the cases they dealt with each year.

[48] A. Heilbronner, 'Le ravitaillement', *Revue d'économie politique* 57 (1947): 1659. The complaint of court leniency was common in CE reports; but as Dez noted, many cases sent to the courts were not serious offences, but rather cases with weak evidence and resistance from the delinquent. Dez thought the courts were sympathetic to the defendants as victims of legislation imposed by the Germans. Dez, 'Économie de pénurie', 174–175.

[49] DGCE, *Rapport sur l'activité de la DGCE au cours de l'année 1944*, 32.

confiscations, legal proceedings, or warnings. In 1943, 58 per cent resulted in *transactions*, 15 per cent with fines and confiscations, and only 9.5 per cent in prosecutions.[50]

The CE had the power to close businesses that were in violation of economic laws for periods from one to three months. This punished clients and employees as well as owners. To protect the employees, owners still had to pay their full salary while closed. Customers had to find other providers, especially if they had registered to obtain rationed goods.[51] The CE advised closures of three to six months so that consumers would find new providers and the closed business would provide 'continuous publicity' of the government's determination to punish 'economic fraudsters'.[52] Department prefects could detain traffickers for periods of up to six months by 'administrative internment' and were encouraged to use interments and to forbid those guilty of serious or repeated infractions from continuing in business. Rapid action would counter public belief that black marketeers profited enormously from public misery.[53] But the shortages continued.

Policing retail markets gave the CE visibility for its price control effort and reportable results. The administration used the number of cases filed and the fines imposed as its metrics to demonstrate effective action and argue for more resources. They asked for additional staff in April 1943 based on these metrics for 1942, stating 'The results we have obtained prove in any case the active role of the Service', claiming credit for half of the cases filed, four fifths of the *transactions* levied, and most of the 'big cases'.[54] German authorities judged them by these metrics. René Bousquet, as head of the police under Vichy, told CE directors in July 1943 that it was essential that their director 'can present an impressive picture of infractions caught and ... sanctions imposed. He must be

[50] DGCE, *Rapport sur l'activité de la DGCE au cours de l'année 1944*, 33–35.

[51] Moreau-Néret, *Le contrôle des prix*, 305–306, and controllers' reports including, in 1941: 'Among the punishments considered, one of the most efficacious was the temporary suspension of business. Unfortunately, with current difficulties in food supply and the system of customers registering with their suppliers, temporary closure of a business was not practical. Customers would suffer from such a measure, much more than would shopkeepers, and they would be the first to protest against it.' SAEF 4A-0000003, A. Lebelle, 'Note sur l'insuffisance de la répression en matière de contrôle des prix', 26 July 1941.

[52] SAEF B-0049896, Circulaire no. 18, 10 June 1943.

[53] SAEF B-0049896, Circulaire no. 18, 10 June 1943; B-0049888, Note de service no. 385, 20 Nov. 1943.

[54] SAEF 1A-0000402, 'Note au sujet de la position des Services français de contrôle en ce qui concerne la lutte contre le marché noir', Apr. 1943. In the figures cited for 1942 they claimed a total of 200,000 *procès-verbaux*, but a paragraph later state that only 11,800 were 'truly black-market cases'.

able to show that when the *Contrôle économique* is given the means, it will produce results.'[55]

This emphasis on case numbers and penalties had two perverse consequences. First, the metrics served as misleading proxies for CE effectiveness. The number of citations demonstrated CE effort, not whether they were gaining or losing ground against the growing black market. Second, it promoted practices that fostered public irritation. Even with the increased efforts in training and research to pursue black-market cases at the production level in 1942, retail transactions remained the main target. These tasks required less training and the number of infractions seemed to demonstrate significant results: more than 1.1 million infractions caught during the Occupation years. The vast majority were petty infractions: charging higher prices, failure to have price tickets on all goods or to issue proper sales receipts, failure to post menus and prices both indoors and out in restaurants, lack of receipts for goods being resold.[56] In Bordeaux, for example, the CE reports filed in 1944 include a plethora of fines for infractions by street pedlars, who sold small quantities of goods at higher prices and did not ticket their merchandise. One pedlar was fined at least six times for selling fruit and vegetables from June to August 1944.[57] The number of *procès-verbaux* climbed impressively. The impact on the black market was negligible.

This focus on marketplace infractions had critics in state administration. Henry Cado, delegated prefect in the Aisne, a typical rural department, observed of the list of infractions reported to him in early 1942: 'Most of these cases are people caught transporting a kilo of butter or a kilo of wheat, and a few cases of clandestine slaughter of one or two hogs. Meanwhile, tons of rationed goods are disappearing from the official market.'[58] The Paris police noted public discontent with the black market, the scarcity of goods and the cost of living. By 1942, Parisians 'complained bitterly' about the state controllers charged with suppressing the black market, who 'go after the little people and let the true *trafiquants* slip through'.[59] Pierre Mendès France, describing the life he observed in rural France as he waited for passage to London after escaping a Vichy prison in 1941, saw recourse to black market goods as 'a palliative,

---

[55] AN 3W/90, 'Conférence des directeurs régionaux tenue à la DGCE les 6 et 7 juillet 1943 sous la présidence de Monsieur de Sailly', 12 July 1943; Grenard, *La France du marché noir*, 199.

[56] The Archives de Paris 1W series has some 900 cartons of *Contrôle économique* reports for the Occupation period; my sampling of cartons suggests that most infractions recorded were minor.

[57] AD Gironde, 62W/9 and 62W/10: the seller, V. Aggabi, had at least two previous convictions in 1942.

[58] AN AJ/41/363 (Aisne), prefect monthly report, 3 Feb. 1942.

[59] APP 220W 10, 'La situation à Paris', 10 Aug. 1942.

inglorious but very useful to supplement miserable rations'. He shared the common view that the CE targeted the small fry and minor infractions: 'But they never pursue the *grands trafiquants* who destroy the organization of the country's food supply and provision the real black market.'[60] The pursuit of easy targets discredited controllers and was mocked in the press, as in a cartoon in *L'Œuvre* in 1942, depicting a tearful schoolboy arrested at school for possession of his snack of bread and jam (Figure 3.2).

The CE administration recognized that punishing ubiquitous minor infractions turned the public against them without solving the shortages or the diversion of goods. German and French administrators advocated

La lutte contre le marché noir

(Dessin de Ploq.)

— J'ai arrêté cet individu devant la porte de l'école. Il était porteur d'un petit panier qui recelait une tartine de confiture.

Figure 3.2 'La lutte contre le marché noir', *L'Œuvre*, 3 Jan. 1942. This image has undergone some editing in order to improve its legibility. Bibliothèque nationale de France.

---

[60] Pierre Mendès-France, *Liberté, liberté chérie* … (New York: Didier, 1943), 455, 457; similar comments recorded in Grenard, *La France du marché noir*, 127–132, and Veillon, *Vivre et survivre*, 184.

'exemplary' punishments, believing that rapid and severe repression would deter breaches of the rules, particularly by retailers (in Table 3.1 a main target for their attention). Immediate action against price offences would have a salutary effect through the speed and the local knowledge of the penalties.[61] The implicit logic assumed freedom of choice for sellers and consumers. It ignored the impact of shortages in official markets, food most of all, that required individuals to extend their purchasing networks outside the law. The impact was recognized officially in allowing substantial shipment of food in 'family parcels' in 1940 and 1941,[62] and in legislation on hoarded goods that distinguished between stocks for family needs and profiteering (8 February 1941).[63] In mid-March 1942, new legislation increased the penalties for deliberate, clandestine black-market activity to provide 'exemplary punishment', with prison terms up to ten years and fines up to 10 million francs. It also stated official tolerance for infractions committed 'uniquely for personal or family needs'.[64] De Sailly claimed the CE staff's financial and legal training enabled them to distinguish between profiteering that merited exemplary punishment and the widespread minor infractions to acquire essential goods that needed empathy and toleration.[65] Bousquet articulated this distinction in a note to regional prefects:

We need to bring an end to the annoying interventions and clearly excessive fines to which consumers have too often been subject, when they are simply trying to assure normal food supply for their family. All measures that, without serving the general interest, would be of a nature to irritate public opinion, which is already troubled by food supply difficulties in large cities, must be rigorously proscribed.[66]

This recognized that many marketplace infractions, if technically 'black market', were necessary adaptations to grave supply deficiencies, and as such should not be punished. But controllers still targeted retail markets

---

[61] German expert Dr. Kleberg stated in a speech in June 1941: 'Exemplary punishments are indispensable, especially for serious infractions. This repression is the essential foundation for relative stability of prices, the basis for sound social policy.' AN 72AJ/1853, *Les nouveaux temps*, 20 June 1941. For French administrators' belief in prompt, exemplary punishment, see SAEF 4A-0000003, 'Note sur l'insuffisance de la répression en matière de contrôle des prix', 26 July 1941, and Moreau-Néret, *Le contrôle des prix*, 284, 302.

[62] Family parcels receive detailed attention in Chapters 4 and 6.

[63] Moreau-Néret, *Le contrôle des prix*, 289–291.

[64] This shift in Vichy regulation of transactions and definition of black-market activity is described in Grenard, *La France du marché noir*, 123–137. The law specified goods that could be confiscated, including all means of transport belonging to the delinquent.

[65] SAEF 1A-0000402, 'Note au sujet du Contrôle économique', 14 May 1942.

[66] AN 3W/90, Bousquet to regional prefects in the occupied and unoccupied zones, 2 July 1942.

and transport, where they could obtain rapid and numerically impressive results.

Agent practices generated further hostility. Their administrative power to punish offences immediately facilitated their focus on numbers. The CE not only argued its effectiveness by the number of case reports filed, but also obtained a share of the fines imposed and goods confiscated; agents could benefit from the penalties they imposed. Control personnel in the field were not well paid. The lowest rank of agents, according to February 1942 salary scales, earned barely 10,000 francs per year; *inspecteurs principaux* earned 37,000 to 42,000; directors at the department and regional level could earn up to 60,000 francs per year. Salary supplements calibrated to their base salary could add from 4,200 to 12,000 francs per year.[67] Agents were reimbursed for a limited range of their expenses if their investigation resulted in a case being filed.[68]

Article 74 of the pricing decree of 21 October 1940 established a *fonds commun*, to receive one tenth of the funds recovered from price control fines, transactions and confiscations, and to be divided between CE agents and other services engaged in price control.[69] In principle, reward would be calibrated according to the agents' time in the field, rank and the results obtained by their work.[70] This gave financial incentive to maximize the number of cases filed, confiscations, and the fines or (until October 1941) *transactions* imposed. Part of the service's concern with reward for its agents was to guard against their taking bribes. Georges Fourment, writing in the CE's house journal, observed that working for the CE required 'an honesty beyond question', as *trafiquants* would not hesitate to bribe control officials, with sums far greater than their civil servant salaries.[71] State officials taking bribes were subject to

---

[67] SAEF B-0049888, Note de service no. 123, 23 June 1942, reproduces the salary scales and supplements approved in October 1941.

[68] Dez, 'Économie de pénurie', 155.

[69] SAEF B-0056460; in October 1941 the CE eliminated the 10 per cent levy on transactions, leaving it in place on fines and confiscations. The fund was terminated in February 1945.

[70] SAEF B-0049888, Note de service no. 1, 26 June 1941, provided initial explanation of the point allocation system to reward agents in the field. The second Note de service on 7 July 1941 detailed payment of informers from this fund. Subsequent notes, Note de service no. 23, 6 Oct. 1941, explained how allocations should take place from the *fonds commun* for activity in the first half of 1941, and was revised in no. 43, 10 Dec. 1941, for reward in the second half of 1941. Although the point allocation and reward calibration should have provided the greatest reward to cases involving large-scale networks and black-market activity before goods reached final markets, the number of personnel with the training and opportunity for exposing such serious operations were few compared to those monitoring retail market transactions.

[71] Georges Fourment, 'L'évolution du marché noir et sa répression', *Contrôle économique*, 3 (May 1944): 234–235.

administrative internment, along with the *trafiquants* who tried to bribe them.[72] De Sailly emphasized, explaining his need for more staff in September 1944, that as well as technical expertise CE agents needed to be of the highest moral calibre: 'that one can imagine the temptation for an agent, in uncovering an important black market operation that left no evidence, who was offered a sum greater than several years of his salary to close his eyes for a few moments'.[73] The CE service notes to its staff and the suspicions voiced in the press and letters of denunciation all indicated there was need to counter temptations. Leménager claimed that CE agents resisted taking bribes.[74] But he, and CE directors de Sailly and Burnod, acknowledged that the problem compromised their agents and cast all CE activity in a bad light.[75]

In September 1944, summarizing his need for more staff, de Sailly blamed the temporary and auxiliary agents for abuses during the Occupation: 'Unstable, poorly paid, insufficiently trained, they are not as well prepared to resist the numerous temptations confronting them, despite the sanctions for those who succumb. They are responsible, almost entirely, for the poor reputation of the *Contrôle économique* in certain milieux.' Because they had less training and aptitude, the auxiliaries were mainly deployed to monitor retail sales and food supplies.[76] In these markets they had maximum contact with retailers and consumers and were the public face of the CE.

The CE relied on two other methods to uncover black market activity, both of which illustrate the difficulties in detecting illicit trade. Agents provoked black market sales in posing as buyers, and they paid informers for tip-offs. In December 1940 an illiterate, unemployed worker bought a chicken from a farmer for his own consumption. A CE agent persuaded him, against his initial inclination, to sell it to a purported German buyer (another CE controller) who would pay significantly more. The *Tribunal correctionnel de la Seine* dismissed this 'black market' case in May 1941 as morally reprehensible procedure. The CE warned agents thereafter against the use of entrapment.[77] But the CE considered such purchasing

---

[72] SAEF B-0049896, Circulaire no. 18, 10 June 1943.

[73] SAEF B-0057659, 'Note pour le Ministre', 19 Sept. 1944.

[74] Leménager, 'Étude sur le contrôle des prix', 534–535.

[75] In December 1946 there were seventy-three CE agents under suspension for serious (unspecified) offences. SAEF B-0049893; Burnod, 'Note pour Messieurs les directeurs', no. 08 2147, 2 Dec. 1946. Leménager notes controllers were remarkably honest given that they were 'poorly paid, poorly fed, poorly dressed and sometimes poorly housed'; Leménager, 'Étude sur le contrôle des prix', 503.

[76] SAEF B-0057659, 'Note pour le Ministre', 19 Sept. 1944.

[77] SAEF B-0049888, Note de service no. 12, 27 Aug. 1941 warns CE agents against the practice. Grenard has a similar example from Lille in 1941, *La France du marché noir*, 130.

essential and tried to tread a fine line between the danger that courts would dismiss a *délit provoqué* and the need to prove a suspect's willingness to transact sales at illegal prices and quantities, which rarely yielded written evidence.[78]

Trafiquants outsmarted some agents. Large-scale operators investigated their clients and developed contacts to identify CE personnel. They preferred dealing with buyers they knew. If they suspected a buyer was a CE inspector, they could drop the deal, or arrange to obtain a large down payment without delivering any goods. One CE agent set up a black-market purchase of 10 tonnes of sugar in Paris in December 1942. He paid 100,000 francs of state funds and 5,000 francs of his own as a deposit, only to have the seller disappear with the cash.[79] In 1943 an agent in Lille paid 400,000 francs for a purchase arranged by men characterized as 'crooks' rather than 'ordinary *trafiquants*'. The CE reported that the agent 'demonstrated, in the circumstances, a naivete truly surprising for an agent familiar with the risks of the job'.[80]

The CE relied on informers for serious black market traffic, stating they were 'indispensable' to identify operations by *trafiquants* working 'in a very closed milieu'.[81] A decree in February 1941 set parameters for the use and payment of informers: they could be paid up to one third of the penalties imposed on individuals caught (fines, transactions, and goods confiscated) to a nominal ceiling of 12,000 francs (which could be exceeded in cases of high value). The best informers, the CE advised, were honest shopkeepers hurt by black market traffic, who offered information without expecting remuneration. But the service had to use informers acting from personal interest, including 'professional informers clever at obtaining secrets that they will immediately sell'. Payment was essential to obtain such information.[82] In 1942 and 1943 the CE increased its scale of payments and improved its procedures to protect informers.[83]

---

[78] Jean Mazard, 'La provocation en matière d'infraction aux lois économiques', *Contrôle économique*, 2 (Feb. 1944): 110–118, and criticism of the practice in Fernand-Charles Jeantet, *Le code des prix et les principes fondementaux du droit pénal classique* (Paris: Domat-Montchrestien, 1943), 84–87. From the DGCE annual report for 1944: 'The fraud is essentially fugitive, so it is often indispensable, to expose it, that agents present themselves as buyers.' DGCE, *Rapport sur l'activité de la DGCE en 1944*, 26.

[79] SAEF B-0049514, agent report of 8 Dec. 1942 and CE note of 20 Jan. 1943.

[80] SAEF B-0049514; notes of 6 Nov. and 4 Dec. 1943. Because of the agent's good record, he was not dismissed, but he was excluded from the distribution of *fonds commun* for the second half of 1943.

[81] SAEF B-0009860, DCEE, *Rapport sur l'activité de la DCEE au cours de l'année 1945*, 37.

[82] SAEF B-0049888, Note de service no. 2, 7 July 1941.

[83] They decided to record informers' services by coded numbers rather than by name. SAEF B-0049888, Notes de service nos. 24, 29 Sept. 1941; 34, 3 Nov. 1941; 113,

Denunciations offered a third, far less reliable source of information. As in Nazi Germany, the Soviet Union and Fascist Italy, Vichy France encouraged citizens to inform on each other. The scarcity of goods promoted denunciations for material gain.[84] Millions of letters were written to German and French authorities during the Occupation. The most frequent denounced food supply irregularities and black-market trade.[85] In 1943 'La Rose des Vents' on Radio-Paris condemned black-market activity and moral decline in France, and called on listeners for denunciations to restore French morality. They forwarded letters to the police, who sent them on to the CE.[86] Most proved groundless. Of seventy-one investigations, five had uncovered black-market activity several months later. Controllers and police found that denunciations were 'most often the expression of personal vengeance or rancour', leading to 'isolated investigations requiring a deployment of means and an expenditure of effort disproportionate to the final result'.[87] Shannon L. Fogg, in her analysis of letters in the Limousin region, makes a point valid for national experience: 'Rather than building a stronger community through the purge of harmful elements such as black marketeers, hoarders, and cultural outsiders, denunciations encouraged lying, dissimulation, and self-interested actions.'[88]

The price controls did restrain inflation during the Occupation. The CE agents, liked or more often not, were present in markets to enforce price discipline and did so with visible success (see Table 3.2). The *Centre*

23 May 1942; 166, 26 Sept. 1942; 203, 29 Dec. 1942; 338, 2 Aug. 1943; 374, 26 Oct. 1943; and 475, 8 May 1944. The *Police économique* and the *Ravitaillement général* paid informers; their systems were regularized according to CE rules in 1942. The CE criticized the RG practice of immediate payment of 10 per cent and more of the products seized, which informers promptly resold on the black market. SAEF 4A-0000003, Inspector General of Finances Poisson to Minister of Finance, no. 309/1942, 8 Sept. 1942.

[84] Robert Gellately and Sheila Fitzpatrick, eds., *Accusatory Practices: Denunciation in Modern European History 1789–1989* (Chicago: University of Chicago Press, 1997); and Robert Gellately, *The Gestapo and German Society* (Oxford: Clarendon Press, 1990). For earlier work on denunciations in France, see André Halimi, *La délation sous l'Occupation* (Paris: Alain Moreau, 1983); he claims (7) there were 3 to 5 million letters of denunciation written during the Occupation. For current work, see Laurent Joly, ed., *La délation dans la France des années noires* (Paris: Perrin, 2012).

[85] Laurent Joly, 'Introduction', *La délation dans la France des années noires*, 45; and Shannon L. Fogg, 'Denunciations, Community Outsiders, and Material Shortages in Vichy France', *Proceedings of the Western Society for French History* 31, (2003): 271–289.

[86] SAEF B-0049515, 'Rose des Vents' correspondence.

[87] SAEF B-0009860, DGCEE, *Rapport sur l'activité de la DGCEE au cours de l'année 1946*, 38. Fabrice Grenard analyses the unreliability of black-market denunciations in 'La dénonciation dans la répression du marché noir', in *La délation dans la France des années noires*, 139–161. Robert Gildea judges that such letters were principally a means to settle personal accounts; *Marianne in Chains*, 116, 76–78.

[88] Fogg, 'Denunciations', 274–275.

d'études improved expertise for the investigation of the production and distribution of black-market goods, which the CE belatedly realized was critical to supply for the marketplace transactions downstream. The DGCE developed a coordinated filing system to identify sources and track black-market goods to their point of production and to trace networks of distribution.[89] Of the 1.1 million case reports filed, 96,717 were sent for judgement in the courts; 607,014 resulted in *transactions* and 2.1 billion francs paid in penalty.[90] The figures reflect the ubiquitous and small-scale nature of black-market traffic. Although the majority of cases were for minor infractions, more significant results were obtained when trained agents investigated producers and supply networks. The CE reported the significant arrests, confiscations and convictions in the press, as well as monthly values of black-market goods confiscated, to demonstrate effective repression and discourage potential *trafiquants*.

German Demands

German interference disrupted French efforts to make controls effective. The occupying forces made extensive black-market purchases, protected their suppliers from prosecution by French authorities, and rebuked the French for not prosecuting black-market traffic with sufficient vigour. Their interference challenged the policing of markets on two levels. First, it protected a powerful sector from state control. German violations had to be referred to the German military authorities, and evidence was difficult to obtain when French officials had no authority to stop, search or detain the Germans engaged in black-market traffic. German army units used military vehicles and passes to carry black-market merchandise. Military demand for resources exploited the black market, particularly for metals, clothing, food and alcohol. Leather from hides provides an illustrative example. In 1943, de Sailly notified the *Sicherheitsdienst* in Paris of the large volume of hides delivered to German purchasing offices from the illicit slaughter of livestock, carried in trucks with German military passes. In the previous three months his services had recorded 147 tonnes of hides, from ten departments, purchased in this way, usually for *Dienststelle No. 20.803* at

---

[89] SAEF B-0049714 has notes developing the filing system beginning in Nov. 1941. A draft note explaining the system stated: 'If, in effect, the services of the CE must bring all their powers to bear on combatting the black market, they cannot disregard that one of the most effective means to destroy clandestine traffic is precisely in better organization and control of production and distribution', 18 Feb. 1942.

[90] Grenard, *La France du marché noir*, Annexe 1, 313, from results reported in SAEF B-0009860.

the Saint-Ouen docks outside Paris.[91] This traffic gave German protection and funding to French *trafiquants* involved in illicit slaughter and the transport of the hides, meat and other foods.

Second, French *trafiquants* took advantage of German power and immunity, using German vehicles for transport, appealing for protection when caught by French authorities, and claiming German connections to escape imprisonment and the confiscation of their goods. The Germans demanded the release of dealers working for them, the return of goods, and the handing over of French judicial dossiers for economic offences to German authorities. They rarely punished French *trafiquants*, and many files simply disappeared.[92]

In one case, described as 'typical marché noir', Maurice C. of Croissy-sur-Seine bought butter and meat in Normandy and sold it to the German military in Caen. He sold goods the Germans did not want to French customers at black-market prices. Interrogated in February 1943, he refused to answer questions, stating: 'You won't be able to do anything, the German authorities will order you to close this case.' He had 50 kg of butter and 30 kg of veal from business the previous day; sales to French customers that day had earned 27,000 francs. The Germans demanded his case file and halted the French prosecution. The public prosecutor for the *Cour d'appel de Paris* complained, 'Such practices tend to render illusory the repressive measures decreed by the government. In creating shocking inequalities between delinquents, according to whether or not the Occupation authorities take an interest in their fate', they damaged control efforts and discouraged judicial prosecution.[93]

The German interference gave reason, sometimes highly visible, for popular belief that French controls were ineffective, served German interests, and targeted individuals without high-level protection. French controllers were officially permitted to stop French vehicles with German passes beginning in summer 1943, and then to stop German vehicles as well, but official permission did not mean they dared do so in practice.[94] In January 1944, when the CE retreated to price control to separate their functions from Darnand's economic police, it instructed agents to give less information to the Germans and to stop confiscating the goods they

---

[91] SAEF 1A-0000402, de Sailly to commander of the *Sicherheitsdienst* in Paris, undated, citing cases from late 1942 and early 1943.

[92] AN AJ/41/335 and AJ/41/336 contain correspondence regarding files taken by the Germans.

[93] AN AJ/41/335, Attorney General Cavarroc to the Keeper of the Seals, 6 Apr. 1943, and Attorney General at Versailles to Attorney General for the Paris Court of Appeal, 31 Mar. 1943.

[94] SAEF B-0049888, Note de service no. 296, 31 May 1943; Leménager, 'Étude sur le contrôle des prix', 598–599.

sought – fuel, lubricants, gold, tyres, and hides. For cases where the Germans blocked the prosecution of French *trafiquants*, controllers were asked to keep copies of their records in secure locations, for use in future prosecution.[95]

The German interference altered policy and enforcement at three levels evident in the next chapters. First, German policy demands gave the French authorities little leeway to correct flawed policies or to launch initiatives to foster economic recovery. Second, German requisitions, purchasing, and financial extortion exacerbated the shortages and price inflation. The French economy lost a significant part of its declining domestic output to German consumption. Third, German black-market purchasing encouraged and developed illicit activity, protecting black market producers and *trafiquants*, and seriously compromising French authority and morale.

Leménager concluded that German Occupation made French price control impossible. Disobeying economic controls became patriotic, a national duty.[96] The CE was slow to reach this conclusion, after having alienated public support for controls and achieved only limited success in restraining black-market growth. The Allied invasion and liberation from German control was expected to bring rapid improvement in material conditions. The transition from Vichy to a provisional government under de Gaulle in the summer of 1944 marked a phase of retreat and reorientation for the *Contrôle économique*. The renewal of enforcement after Liberation would encounter greater resistance and have weaker results.

Control Efforts Pause

The Normandy invasion returned France to a state of war. It disrupted transport and supply in north-western France, damaged homes, factories, and transport infrastructure, and created new challenges in enforcing controls amidst the disorder produced by military conflict.[97] Food supplies to Paris had been dwindling. For three weeks in March 1944 there were no meat rations available, and two thirds of Paris bakeries had to close for lack of wood to fire their ovens. Workers had their hours reduced because of power

---

[95] SAEF B-0016041, from the memoir of a controller in Limoges sent to Leménager; and Leménager, 'Étude sur le contrôle des prix', 593–595.

[96] Leménager, 'Étude sur le contrôle des prix', 721, 729.

[97] The physical damage began earlier from Allied bombing of transport infrastructure; the situation was described as 'one of the most serious the French administration has had to deal with' by the regional prefect for Normandy: AD Seine-Maritime 40W/114, monthly report for April, 9 May 1944.

shortages.[98] In May, shortages of fresh vegetables and the decline in family parcels increased fears that Paris would face starvation when the Allies invaded.

The diverse agriculture in Normandy supplied much of northern France, especially the cities. The post office and the SNCF suspended the shipment of family parcels from nineteen northern and western departments on 6 June, and from a further seventeen later in June.[99] Official supplies of fresh fruit and vegetables and dairy goods, milk especially, plummeted.[100] Parisians took the metro to buy food grown in suburban gardens; in July, garden owners refused to sell to them, keeping their produce for black-market buyers.[101] They cycled to regions where they could still buy vegetables, meat and dairy goods. In Gournay-en-Bray, east of Rouen, hundreds of cyclists came each week to buy food, especially butter – an estimated 15 tonnes per week. Two on a tandem bicycle carried 80 kgs of butter.[102] The Germans proposed forbidding cyclists to cross department boundaries, and local officials recommended tighter control on road traffic and the confiscation of butter in excess of 2 or 3 kg per person. The 'scandalous' prices for butter suggested that most went to the rich and to black-market restaurants.[103] German troops trafficked in butter, selling it to civilians as they retreated East.[104]

Residents feared Paris would starve. Annie Vallotton commented in her diary, 'Life is becoming really crazy and the black market is flourishing as never before.'[105] The police reported widespread fears of famine and growing anger in the lengthening queues for food, where customers often waited in vain. Customers complained that shopkeepers reserved food for black-market customers; shopkeepers blamed wholesalers for the high prices.[106] Teacher Berthe Auroy wrote on 14 July that nine out of ten food

[98] APP 220W 15, 'Situation à Paris', 3 Apr. 1944. Workers on reduced hours were paid 75 per cent of their normal salary.
[99] AN F/90/21623, 'Suppression du service des paquets', undated.
[100] APP 220W 15, 'Situation à Paris', 12 June 1944.
[101] APP 220W 16, 'Situation à Paris', 10 July 1944.
[102] AN F/7/14895, Comité central des groupements interprofessionnels laitiers, Regional Director of Service to the Intendant de Police, prefecture of the Seine-Inférieure, 17 July 1944; Intendant for maintenance of order in the Rouen region to the Director of Security for the Zone nord, 17 July 1944.
[103] AN F/7/14895, Comité central des groupements interprofessionnels laitiers, Regional Director of Service to the Intendant de Police, prefecture of the Seine-Inférieure, 17 July 1944; Feldkommandant Dr Kuhr to the prefect of the Seine-Inférieure, 18 July 1944.
[104] Pierre Audiat, Paris pendant la guerre (Juin 1940 – Août 1944) (Paris: Hachette, 1946), 267.
[105] Gritou and Annie Vallotton, C'était au jour le jour: Carnets (1939–1944) (Paris: Payot et Rivages, 1995), 289; Charles Braibant, La guerre à Paris (8 Nov. – 27 Août 1944) (Paris: Corrêa, 1945), 491, 498 (26 June 1944).
[106] APP 220W 15, 'Situation à Paris', 26 June 1944.

stores had closed, and the tenth was nearly empty: Paris was starving.[107] The prefect of the Seine summarized the situation at the end of June:

The black market establishes itself with increased insolence and, to satisfy immediate needs, even the poorer households are forced to spend their last resources on food, paying higher and higher prices. It is a great scandal, and if energetic measures are not taken to remedy the situation, the consequences could be very serious. The population will not understand how public authorities could be powerless against the excesses of clandestine commerce.[108]

Jean de Sailly reported that spring fruits and vegetables were selling at two to five times their legal prices in Paris markets, and that his agents could no longer enforce price controls. They suspended control activity in Belleville despite police protection. The public was determined to get food, 'indifferent to the surpassing of legal prices', and hostile to control efforts.[109] Mayors in communities close to Paris asked to raise prices for local produce. In working-class districts, discontent ran high; many parents limited themselves to one meal a day to feed their children.[110] De Sailly observed that the equitable distribution of food required a minimum of goods. 'It is impossible to impose discipline in the food market when official rations do not permit one to live.'[111]

Controllers faced growing opposition and had reduced mobility as fuel allocations stopped. They were 'totally paralyzed' de Sailly reported, with no gasoline for their cars or the *vélomoteurs*. 'All movement by our agents in rural areas has become impossible, and all surveillance or repression of the black market has thus come to a halt.'[112] The CE advised controllers to dismantle cars and *vélomoteurs*, and to hide their parts to prevent their being taken by the retreating Germans.[113] A plan to suspend price controls in the event of a supply crisis was not activated; de Sailly insisted the controls remained essential.[114] But the CE could not deal with the increasing shortages, black-market traffic, and consumer hostility in the disruptive period of Liberation.

[107] Berthe Auroy, *Jours de guerre: Ma vie sous l'Occupation* (Paris: Bayard, 2008), 312.
[108] AN AJ/41/390 (Seine), prefect monthly report, 5 July 1944.
[109] SAEF B-0057659, 'Note au sujet du contrôle du marché des fruits et légumes dans le département de la Seine', 20 June 1944.
[110] SAEF B-0057659, de Sailly notes to the Secretary of State for Food Supply, 24 and 27 June 1944; APP 220W 15, 'Situation à Paris', 26 June 1944.
[111] SAEF B-0057659, 'Note sure les prix du marché noir dans la Région parisienne entre le 1er Mai et le 25 Juin 1944', 29 June 1944.
[112] SAEF B-0057659, de Sailly to Ministerial Counselor Bauch, 27 June 1944.
[113] SAEF B-0049888, Note de service no. 497, 26 July 1944.
[114] SAEF B-0057659, de Sailly, 'Note pour le ministre', 1 July 1944.

Conclusions

The most striking aspect of the control efforts to August 1944 is the gulf between CE determination to enforce marketplace restrictions and their inability to contain black-market growth. The CE claimed success based on case numbers, insisting it could do even better with more resources. It blamed its difficulties on poor state policy and German interference. Both factors complicated its work. But the CE enforcement strategies supported the state's logic for controls and generated hostility, non-compliance, and loss of the popular support needed to curb black-market growth. Henri Culmann's critique that the CE focused on 'curing the thermometer', stepping back from counting violations to consider the emphasis on marketplace price controls as misdirected, has merit. The policing of markets increased consumer frustration with the control system and discouraged producers from bringing goods to market.

Black-market activity after the defeat in 1940 spread in response to shortages, uncertainty, and a growing need to break consumption rules. The state agencies for control enforcement had few resources and no overall strategy other than to punish price infractions where they found them, which for the CE was mainly in retail markets. The consolidation of enforcement in the *Direction générale du contrôle économique* improved organizational coherence but kept the focus on policing restrictions. The laws and CE advice to controllers evolved to allow exceptions for people who were simply trying to feed their families, but black-market traffic adapted to exploit the opportunities this provided. Commerce, especially for goods with dispersed production (notably food from farms), moved increasingly to the black market. The control administration adapted slowly to changing behaviour, hobbled by German interference that fostered black-market activity, disrupted enforcement, and castigated French efforts as weak and ineffective.

Effective price control and rationing depend on the state obtaining compliance with the new regulations. The state's influence on economic behaviour is exercised through power relations that can rely on threat, on surveillance, and on persuasion.[115] Market surveillance and the threat of 'exemplary punishment' proved insufficient. Persuasion in Occupied France, with regard to the legitimacy of economic controls, faced three challenges. First, the imposition of strict controls under German Occupation linked the shortages, 'miserable rations' and the transfer of goods from official to parallel markets, to the presence of the Germans *and* the willing collaboration of the Vichy regime. It was easy to blame the Germans for the early problems in 1940, but responsibility was quickly reassigned to the Vichy administration. Vichy personnel

---

[115] Michel Foucault, 'The Subject and Power', *Critical Inquiry*, 8(4) (1982): 791–793.

faced guilt by association and by collaboration in their responsibility for measures that deprived French consumers.

Second, the need for state intervention to manage shortages and organize limited resources to rebuild the French economy was clear in the turmoil of defeat in 1940. Police reported a public desire for price controls and the suppression of black-market traffic. But as we shall see in the next three chapters, the willingness to respect rules and comply with constraints suffered rapid decline by failing to deliver the promised results. The system failed to provide essential goods to consumers, corrupted the state administration, and tilted obviously in favour of the Germans, the wealthy and the dishonest. Producers, their goods and needy consumers all obtained better results in black-market trade. As de Sailly observed, belatedly, in June 1944, it was impossible to impose discipline when following official policies did not allow people to survive.

The third challenge to legitimacy lay in the logic for enforcement. Respect for economic rules relies significantly on individuals' perceptions of the fairness of the system and whether it works to the benefit of their immediate community of family and friends. This was critical for matters of immediate survival – food, shelter and clothing. The focus on enforcement in retail markets had its broadest impact on ordinary, urban, working- and middle-class consumers for whom official rations were insufficient. Compliance with the law declined as consumers saw the resources from which they were entitled to draw their share shrinking, to the benefit of those working outside the rules: the Germans, the wealthy, government officials, customers in black-market restaurants, and the friends and neighbours who developed connections and sources outside official markets.[116]

As the public lost confidence in the system, they blamed French administrators and controllers for the operation of a system that exploited their vulnerability. They revived practices for exchange by negotiation to locate goods and agree on price. These market practices were no longer legal. Vichy claimed it would restore 'moral order', but the policies of fixed prices and rationing established a regime that outlawed basic market negotiations of price. Official markets adjusted quantities instead: supplies and new production went increasingly to the black market. How state policy worked, how producer and consumer strategies for survival evolved, and how the black market thrived, are subjects explored in the next three chapters which cover developments in agriculture, industry and commerce, and consumer behaviour.

---

[116] Public interest in strict policing of the black market is reported in APP 220W 1 and 2, 'Situation à Paris' reports for 23 Sept., 21 Oct. and 11, 18 and 25 Nov. 1940; Maurice Prax in *Le Petit Parisien*, 14 Mar. 1941; and Grenard, *La France du marché noir*, 17–18, 53–58.

4 *La terre, elle, ne ment pas*: Agriculture and the Black Market

'La terre, elle, ne ment pas', Philippe Pétain proclaimed in June 1940. 'Elle demeure votre *recours*. Elle est la patrie elle-même.' A field lying fallow is a part of France that dies. Reseeded in crop, it is a part of France reborn.[1] His phrase 'The earth, it does not lie' would be repeated on posters, in books, in speeches, to emphasize the deep rural roots of 'true France': based in the land, the culture and the values of rural life, the economy of family farms, and thus intimately binding the Vichy trinity of *travail, famille, patrie* (work, family, fatherland).[2] Working the land embodied core values to which France would return after decades of distraction and degeneration under the Third Republic. Vichy would promote a culture of hard work and honesty, a restoration of local traditions, and the return to origins would bring a national rebirth rooted in the land that did not lie.

The land did not lie, but those who worked it quickly learned that Vichy rhetoric was not matched by policies to promote their interests. The immediate need for increased output – to replace imports and meet German demands – should have made agricultural yield a top priority. Vichy propaganda celebrated *le paysan* and the rich fruits of French agriculture, as well as the moral and ethical values gained in working the land.[3] But Vichy's economic controls encouraged a culture of evasion, illicit transactions and deliberate lies. This was particularly true in agriculture. Illicit traffic in food became the most widespread domain of black-market activity, touching all consumers and changing how farmers worked the land and sold its fruits. Agricultural diversity made France nearly self-sufficient when it functioned as a national economy. The

---

[1] Pétain, *Discours aux Français*, 66.
[2] On 'true France' see Herman Lebovics *True France: The Wars over Cultural Identity, 1900–1945* (Ithaca, NY: Cornell University Press, 1992); and for its place in Vichy ideology, Gérard Noiriel, *Les origines républicaines de Vichy* (Paris: Hachette, 1999), 48–50, 96–98, 212–213.
[3] Christian Faure, *Le projet culturel de Vichy: Folklore et révolution nationale, 1940–1944* (Lyon: Presses universitaires de Lyon, 1989).

fracture into occupation zones and the disruption of transport narrowed economic horizons. Interests contracted to operate on a local and regional basis. National policies had inconsistent and inequitable local effects, making them look inept, if not perverse. This fostered local communities of interest, local and regional solutions to immediate problems, and community resistance to national policies.

Vichy coupled praise for the peasant character with a simplistic belief that the elements of that character, as imagined by the state, would flourish when given public recognition. But peasant character was rooted in the soil they worked, in the demands of intense physical labour and the inability to control the weather or market prices. Their responsibilities extended outwards from the primary importance of caring for their family, livestock and land, and then to friends and local community. Their vulnerability to influences beyond their control imposed a need for sharp market practices to seize the potential benefits from unpredictable harvests and unyielding markets. Their traditions and the embedded nature of market practices would bring rapid disillusion with Vichy policies and adaptation to maintain their primary interests in the new order of shortages, market disruption and invasive state controls.

This chapter begins with a summary of Vichy agricultural policies as the context to understand farmers' responses to the shortages they faced, and the impact of German demands and state policies. It then explores how farmers developed 'alternative markets' for their produce, and how tensions caused by the inequities in food access made the rural-urban divide a fault line fracturing national cohesion.

Vichy Agricultural Policy

Agricultural policy had to cope with multiple crises: manpower losses (soldiers and prisoners of war), shortages of critical supplies, and German demands for agricultural goods and interference in French policy. Feeding the French population dominated the list of challenges. His government's first task, Pétain declared, was to procure sufficient food for all, rationed 'so that everyone, poor and rich, have their fair share of the resources of the nation'.[4] The urgent need to increase supply met immediate and ever-increasing difficulties. Vichy's aspirations to launch a 'retour à la terre' (return to the land) that would bring agricultural labour back from cities and industrial employment to agricultural work

---

[4] Pétain, *Discours aux Français*, 73 (13 Aug. 1940). In four years, Vichy had five ministers of agriculture and eight directors of food supply. Cépède, *Agriculture et alimentation*, 67.

on the farm proved unrealistic.[5] The programme attracted few adherents, even when rural life offered better access to food. Vichy slowed, but could not reverse, the migration from rural to urban employment, and its rhetoric proclaiming support for agriculture and farmers rapidly lost credibility. Vichy policies developed as crisis management, trying to feed French citizens and satisfy German demands as productive capacity declined and farmers became increasingly hostile.[6]

The *Corporation paysanne* is emblematic of Vichy aspirations and failure. Created by decree on 2 December 1940, it was to be a foundational element in restructuring the French economy along corporatist lines. It would represent the interests of all peasants and agricultural organizations.[7] The hollowness of Vichy policy was clear in the Corporation's failure to represent farmers' interests. It served as a vehicle to press for compliance with state policies: fixed prices and obligations to deliver to the state. The state demanded information on crops and livestock and imposed quotas for delivery to state collection. Minister of Agriculture Max Bonnefous claimed in 1943 that the state wanted *Corporation paysanne* officials to be 'neither collectors nor gendarmes'. But the Corporation's main role by then was to press compliance with state controls. When he took control as minister in December 1942, Bonnefous told the Germans that the Corporation had been 'an organization of peasant demagoguery that embarrassed the government. It must be made into an organization that aids the government.' Farmers saw the Corporation as an arm of the despised food supply administration.[8] Even in regions where the Corporation took over cooperatives protecting peasant interests, such as the corporatist *Office central* of Landernau in Brittany, it met hostility and growing resistance.[9]

---

[5] This had been a longstanding hope; Jules Méline published a book of that title in 1905.

[6] Pierre Barral, *Les agrariens de Méline à Pisani* (Paris: A. Colin, 1968), 258 and 265; on Vichy agricultural policy, Cépède, *Agriculture et alimentation*, 60–68, and Pierre Barral and Isabel Boussard, 'La politique agrarienne', in *Le gouvernement de Vichy 1940–1942: Institutions et politiques* (Paris: Armand Colin, 1972), 211–233.

[7] Hervé Budes de Guébriant, 'La corporation paysanne', in *Le gouvernement de Vichy*, 241–244, and Alain Chatriot, 'Syndicalismes et corporatisme agricole en France', in *Le corporatisme dans l'aire francophone au XXe siècle*, ed. by Olivier Dard (Berne: Peter Lang, 2011), 29–48.

[8] Isabel Boussard, *Vichy et la Corporation paysanne* (Paris: Presses de la fondation nationale des sciences politique, 1980). Suspicions that the Corporation's function was to report on farm assets, crops and livestock for state purposes show up in reports to prefects; AD Pyrénées-Atlantique 1031W/8, Corporation nationale paysanne, Département des Landes to Prefect, 3 Mar. 1943. Gildea finds similar conflict in the Loire region, where peasants took control of the regional Corporation and resisted state demands; Gildea, *Marianne in Chains*, 130–131. Bonnefous quoted in Cépède, *Agriculture et alimentation*, 92 n. 1.

[9] On the *Office central des œuvres mutuelles agricole du Finistère*, see Suzanne Berger, *Peasants against Politics: Rural Organization in Brittany 1911–1967* (Cambridge, MA: Harvard University Press, 1972); on resistance to the *Corporation paysanne*, 134–139.

German interests dominated Vichy policy, which sought to meet German demands that worsened the material shortages in French agriculture. The German demands for agricultural goods, negotiated on an annual basis, took a significant part of the falling French output, and were a matter for acute resentment, taking disproportionate quantities of some essential materials. They took 80 per cent of French supplies of straw and hay needed to feed livestock, making it impossible for many farmers to maintain their herds in winter. Compelled to slaughter animals they could not feed, farmers often did so themselves to ensure that the meat went to people they knew.[10] German livestock requisitions took mature animals, leaving herds weaker in age and weight (the impact thus greater than the decline in head of livestock).[11] Horsepower was essential to German military needs. They took the best workhorses, paying no attention to farmers' needs.[12] The Resistance newspaper *Libération* commented in February 1942: 'The Germans require that Vichy provide 55,000 horses. Too bad if French agriculture dies a bit more. Collaboration.'[13] German military units purchased meat, dairy goods and cereals direct from farms, as did German agencies and individual soldiers. This steady drain on supplies was beyond the control of French authorities.[14]

The most immediate shortage was labour. France mobilized 1.3 million men from agriculture in 1939–1940; defeat and the large number of French taken prisoner reduced manpower for the harvest in 1940. Farmers in uniform had been given leave to help with seeding before the German attack, and the Germans authorized the temporary release of 926,000 French soldiers from POW camps to help with the harvest in twenty-eight departments.[15] The grain harvest in 1940 was only half that of the record harvest in 1938. Vichy claimed that agriculture had lost 20 per cent of its prewar work force. And labour continued to move from farms to industry, to work for the Organisation Todt building German defences in France, and to work in Germany as volunteers and as labour conscripts.[16]

---

[10] AD Ille-et-Vilaine 43W/3, prefect monthly report from the Finistère, 1 Apr. 1942.

[11] AN F/23/481 is one of many sources where this is reported; in this case, a 1943 report from Ille-et-Vilaine.

[12] AD Ille-et-Vilaine 43W/3, prefect monthly report from the Finistère, 1 June 1942.

[13] Cited in Eric Alary, *L'histoire des paysans français* (Paris: Perrin, 2016), 205.

[14] AN F/23/470, Galmiche, 'Inspection effectuée dans le Département d'Eure-et-Loire', 26 Sept. 1940; AN F/23/500, 'Rapport de l'Inspecteur général Jeantreau (Inspection des 3 et 4/12/1940), Département de la Mayenne', 10 Dec. 1940; AN AJ/41/366 (Calvados), prefect monthly reports from Nov. 1940 through June 1941.

[15] AN F/60/1547, Boissière to Eckelmann, 26 July 1940.

[16] AN F/23/405, 'Note lue par le ministre, M. Bonnafous, devant M. Backe, Ministre de l'Agriculture et du Ravitaillement du Reich', 1 Mar. 1943; Cépède, *Agriculture et alimentation*, 209–210.

The material shortages had a cumulative impact. Motor vehicles and fuel were in ever-shorter supply for farm equipment and transport; German requisitions reduced the number of draught horses by 20 per cent. Farm tools, equipment and work clothing were often obtainable only through barter or the black market. Twine for harvest, usually made from sisal imported from Mexico, had to be manufactured in France from less durable material. The military demand for chemicals in arms production reduced the availability of pesticides, herbicides and fertilizer, causing an immediate drop in output and a cumulative decline in soil quality.[17] The shortages affected farmers' opinions of the state. Vichy rhetoric on the importance of agriculture rang hollow when policies failed to meet farmers' needs.

The state needed data and personnel to manage the scarce resources and output. Data previously compiled at the commune level now had to be reported by individual declarations. The proliferation of require-ments and paperwork exasperated the farmers, who recognized that the less they reported to the state, the more easily they could avoid state requisitions and payment at official prices.[18] As the prefect for the Basses-Pyrénées was told, regarding the peasant response to new requirements: 'Many of them do not understand why they do not have freedom to dispose of their crops, since they consider these to be their own property.'[19] The new reporting requirements and the enforcement of requisitions were bitterly resented.[20] Pierre Limagne noted Vichy's desire to control everything: 'Vichy wanted to take charge of everything, legislate, publish ukases, and impose on the peasants (who detest the paperwork and interference above all else) a thousand formalities.'[21] The Bank of France director in Caen observed that, as the machinery of administration increased, 'the first result is an inflation of circulars and declarations of all sorts'.[22] Frustrated farmers under-reported their livestock, dairy and poultry numbers, their land under cultivation and their crop yields. They under-delivered on their assigned quotas for dairy, meat and cereal crops.

[17] Cépède, *Agriculture et alimentation*, 207–252.
[18] Fromont, 'La production agricole', 1202.
[19] AD Pyrénées-Atlantiques 1031W/3, Sub-prefect in Oloron report to the prefect, 29 Aug. 1941.
[20] The hostility is evident in Gérard Boutet's recounting of the Occupation years in *Ils étaient de leur village* ... vol. 3, *Ils ont vécu l'Occupation* (Paris: Jean-Cyrille Godefroy, 1990), 130–134.
[21] Pierre Limagne, *Témoignage sur la situation actuelle en France par un dirigeant français d'Action Catholique* (Montréal: Éditions de l'arbre, 1941), 99.
[22] ABdF 1069199311 7, 'Note pour la direction des études économiques', 4 Feb. 1941.

Agricultural Practice

In this world of new demands and constraints, producers assessed their likely profit or loss in deciding crops and livestock, markets and buyers, and they avoided official markets when fixed prices required selling at a loss or below expectations of reasonable profit. They adapted output, consumption and sales to meet the needs and the interests of their families, their farms, and their communities, as well as their potential profit.

Farmers had little power over market prices, and none whatsoever over the prices fixed by the state. But their numbers and geographic distribution did give them great potential to avoid state control. Farmers' decisions on what to grow and bring to market, and where and to whom to sell their goods, took advantage of the rapid growth of alternative markets. The state needed their cooperation to make its policies effective. Massive enforcement would be needed to compel every farm to abide by unwelcome rules. Three areas of state policy met with wide resistance.

The most immediate realm of interference was the restrictions on farm consumption. The ration category for *cultivateurs* allowed them higher rations of bread and meat. But trying to reduce farm consumption of the goods they produced, especially during seasons of heavy labour, and for dietary staples like bread and wine, showed that the state neither understood nor respected the norms and needs in agricultural work. Restrictions on bread, dairy goods and meat depended on farmers' willingness to comply. Prefects, sympathetic to the farmers, advised that allowing normal consumption and relaxing ration requirements would increase farm deliveries to official markets. Otherwise, produce would be withheld for family use and for sale on the black market.[23] Prefects urged allowing farmers to decide their own consumption of the goods they produced. 'Every producer seeks first to meet the needs of his family and his farm.'[24] In a perceptive report on peasant psychology in January 1943, the Ministry of Agriculture recognized that 'the peasant does not accept being short of the goods he produces'.[25] Peasants were

---

[23] AN AJ/41/368 (Charente-Maritime), prefect monthly reports of 25 Nov. 1941 and 25 Jan. 1942. In the second report the prefect argued that 'the peasant doesn't believe or agree that he should be rationed in the same way as those who live in cities, when he is the one who produces the wheat, wine, vegetables and supplies the cattle'. Policy to reassure farmers could make a huge difference to supply nationally, in ending 'the deception or the fraud by each cultivator, multiplied by the large number of almost all the farmers in France'. Bank of France directors made similar comments in their reports on the occupied zone in January and June 1941; ABdF 1069201226 23.

[24] AD Ille-et-Vilaine, 43W/3, prefect monthly report from the Finistère, Mar. 1942.

[25] AN F/10/4962; 'La psychologie paysanne devant les problèmes de la production et du ravitaillement', 20 Jan. 1943, underlined in original.

hostile not only to state efforts to dictate consumption of their own goods, but also to controls on what they could feed their animals. The restrictions on cereals and dairy products forbade feeding grain (especially wheat) to poultry or livestock, and dairy by-products to hogs. In a period of scarce feed, low prices set by the state for dairy products and cereals, and the high black-market value for dairy, poultry and meats, farmers ignored these rules.

The second area of resistance, and by far the most important, was to state price-fixing. Low state prices provided the single greatest motivation for withholding goods from official markets. The price freeze in September 1939 and the more rigorous measures in 1940 affected decisions on what goods to produce, and where and how to sell them. In the first weeks of the Occupation, Paris lost food supplies to nearby markets offering higher prices.[26] As price coordination developed, setting higher prices to draw goods to Paris, this encouraged a 'black commerce' from producing regions in Normandy and Brittany. The prefect of Ille-et-Vilaine lamented in November 1940 that pricing policy benefited neither the producer nor the consumer: 'The only ones to profit from this situation, harmful to the whole population, are the clandestine *trafiquants* and some wholesalers.'[27] The Bank of France director in Angoulême noted in 1942 that *Ravitaillement général* price policies seemed oblivious to 'peasant psychology'. With low official prices, farmers sought 'clandestine sales' as legitimate compensation for their 'official sales'.[28] The initial price measures in September 1939 had recognized that agricultural prices differed from other goods (their seasonal and regional variation in availability), and had changed the purpose of price regulation. Price policies in the 1930s had guaranteed producers an adequate return (especially for wheat) in an era of low prices, and tried to sustain or increase output.[29] Vichy's measures were to curb inflation and served German needs.

Alienation from official markets sparked the development of new avenues for sales. If fixed official prices did not cover costs, farmers could switch to produce other goods and seek alternative markets. This was critical in the choices for production and marketing of meat. But even when costs could be recovered at the fixed prices, alternative markets offered higher returns. Low prices increased farm consumption and sales to buyers willing to pay more. Profit was not the sole concern: helping family and friends, avoiding the state and requisitions, and ensuring that scarce supplies went to French consumers rather than the Germans all

[26] Archives de Paris, Perotin/1012/57/1 3, reports of 8 Aug. and 13 Sept. 1940.
[27] AN AJ/41/373 (Ille-et-Vilaine), prefect to minister of the interior, 20 Nov. 1940.
[28] ABdF 1069201226 25, DGEE, 'Résumé des rapports économiques', ZO, Jan. 1942.
[29] Moreau-Néret, *Le contrôle des prix*, 53–56.

played a part. Some farmers sold to Germans under compulsion, many for substantial profit. The price regime was the critical factor reducing the food delivered to official markets and encouraging alternative sales. A report to the prefect of the Seine-et-Oise stated this bluntly in September 1941: 'Goods disappear from the regulated market.'[30]

The third factor prompting opposition was the state's inability to assure provision of essential supplies and services, especially transport for perishable foods like milk, eggs and meat. Essential goods – from fodder for draught animals and livestock, to machinery and tools, fertilizer, work clothing, and household goods – rose in price, if they could be found at all. Farmers sought connections to obtain goods they needed through exchanges with family and friends, barter, and the black market.[31] Individual initiatives, the Bank of France reported, increasingly sought 'direct transactions, irregular or clandestine, which are gathered under a term as extensive as it is imprecise, of "marché noir"'. Barter predominated: 'useful goods exchanged for other useful goods, most often without reference to money or to price'. Cash gave way to material exchange, 'or, as the farmers say, for "things", vastly preferable to any fiduciary representation'.[32] Black-market *trafiquants* traded goods to obtain farm produce and obscure the details of quantities, prices and profits. They traded bicycles for butter in the Morbihan.[33] The Gendarmerie observed of barter: 'It is practiced at all levels, from the producer exchanging farm produce with the artisan who repairs his equipment, to the consumers who barters this or that good for the food they want.'[34] Some farmers would sell only to buyers who offered goods they needed.[35] The prefect in Ille-et-Vilaine concluded: 'The practice of exchange (often on a small

[30] AD Yvelines, 1W/8, 'Rapport mensuel sur la situation économique agricole du département', Sept. 1941. The author noted that the quality of *Ravitaillement général* staff made closer supervision on the farms impractical: 'I remain convinced that controls at the farm will not work, the quality of the controllers guarantees their incompetence.'

[31] INSEE, *Enquêtes diverses sur les prix et les consommations de 1942 à 1944* (Paris: Imprimerie nationale, 1947), 33, and prefect monthly reports in 1941 and early 1942. A synthesis from the occupied zone put it this way: 'the infractions by farmers take on more and more the form of barter, exchanging rationed foods for industrial goods'. AD Seine-Maritime 40W 115, Ministry of the Interior, 'Synthèse des Rapports des Préfets de la Zone occupée', Feb. 1942.

[32] ABdF 1069201226 25, DGEE, 'Résumé des rapports économiques', ZO, Jan. 1942.

[33] AD Ille-et-Vilaine 43W/6, prefect monthly report for Morbihan, 31 May 1943; butter became a currency of exchange in bartering; the prefect blamed this for the decline in butter supply after the war; AD Ille-et-Vilaine 43W/138.

[34] AN AJ/41/24, 'Synthèse des rapports mensuels des Commandants des Légions de Gendarmerie de la Zone Libre (Avril 1942)'.

[35] AN AJ/41/24, 'Synthèse des rapports mensuels des Commandants des Légions de Gendarmerie de la Zone Libre', July and Sept. 1942.

scale, constituting what one could call "family exchange") is becoming established as custom.'[36]

Farmers engaged in three levels of sale and exchange, displaying the gradation of values in the economic and social relations for marketing farm produce.[37] The first level is the exchanges negotiated to meet family and farm needs that could no longer be satisfied in the marketplace. Clothing for work and for children, basic farming tools and materials, repairs to farm hardware, and planting needs could often be met locally by trading favours and goods. Equipment and repairs could be paid for with food. Artisans and tradesmen in towns knew local farmers and exchanged services for goods.[38]

A second level of exchange and sale was to help family and friends, those nearby and those who had moved to cities. At the local level, discreet sales to friends or gifts to family shared farm output with residents in local towns and provided extra income. This was particularly important for the illicit slaughter of livestock. Over greater distances, families transferred goods in various way: visits on weekends and in summer, sending children to stay on holidays with rural relatives where they would be better fed, and sending family parcels (colis familiaux) by post or by rail. Within families, such exchange need not involve monetary payment, but it could easily develop from family assistance to commercialized exchange. The colis familiaux were not restricted to immediate family, but they distinguished between the parcels sent to meet family needs and those with food intended for resale as black-market goods or to supply restaurants.[39]

The third level of exchange, selling goods for profit, in clear violation of price and ration laws, was the most important in volume and in value and diverted a large quantity of goods from official circuits. It usually involved selling to individuals who came to farms looking to supplement the limited food available in towns and cities. This included direct sales to Germans, to black market dealers, and the shipment of food by truck or by parcel to buyers in cities. Alfred Sauvy noted in July 1942 the strong

---

[36] AN AJ/41/373 (Ille-et-Vilaine), delegate prefect monthly report, 31 Mar. 1943. Bank of France directors noted this as well in 1943; ABdF 1069201226 26, DGEE, 'Résumé des rapports économiques', Zone Sud, Jan.–Feb. 1943.

[37] Robert Gildea distinguishes concentric circles in black market dealings, the prices rising as the distance from the farmer to the final buyer increased. Gildea, *Marianne in Chains*, 115–117.

[38] Robert Lemanissier's uncle was a cobbler in Normandy who made and mended goods for farmers and bought food from them. Interview, 7 Nov. 2014. René Limouzin took violin lessons in exchange for a pound of butter or a dozen eggs; *Le temps des J3: Une adolescence paysanne pendant la guerre de 1939–1945* (Paris: Éditions les monédières, 1983), 94–96.

[39] On family parcels, further details in Chapter 6.

inverse correlation between the increasing number of 'family parcels' arriving in Paris and the steep decline in butter collected in Normandy for official markets.[40] Butter, dairy goods, eggs and meat were the main foods in this black-market traffic. Prefect reports from rich agricultural departments, particularly in the north and west of France supplying Paris, indicate the importance of this illicit trade.

The evolution of the reports by the prefect of the Mayenne demonstrates the gradual recognition of black-market traffic through direct sales. In March 1941, he reported purchases by 'persons not from the department who visit farms and purchase poultry, butter and eggs at any price, and send them to their families or carry them on their return trip (Région Parisienne)'. He did not yet see this as black-market activity.[41] By the end of the summer, he saw 'traffic called "marché noir"'. In December 1941 he noted that farmers raised geese for sale to individual purchasers, Germans and Parisians, rather than bringing them to market, and he described one case as 'black market on a massive scale'.[42] In April 1942 he called for closer surveillance of family parcels, which served as cover for clandestine traffic and supplied 'a true black market'. A few weeks later, he increased surveillance in train stations, where parcel traffic clearly exceeded the bounds of 'family' provisioning.[43] In September he stated that the peasants, not normally involved in the black market, now made direct sales at black-market prices: 'There is a new state of affairs, very unfortunate, against which we need to react energetically.' This included sending 'so-called family' parcels destined for restaurants in Paris.[44] The director of price controls in Mayenne had noted earlier, 'The mentality of the peasant in our region is such that, whatever the price, he always tries to charge more.'[45]

As regulations increased, the price controls prompted recurrent observations that low prices reduced the goods brought to market. As one observer told the prefect in Pau, 'The effect of fixed prices, contrary to the intended purpose, is to withdraw goods from public access and reserve them for people with the time and the means to buy at home.'[46]

---

[40] Institut de conjoncture, 'Situation économique au début du mois de Juillet 1942', Rapport no. 11; statistics repeated in Sauvy, *La vie économique*, 134.

[41] AN AJ/41/378 (Mayenne), prefect monthly report for March 1941, 5 Apr. 1941.

[42] AN AJ/41/378, prefect monthly reports for October and November, 30 Oct. 1941 and 2 Dec. 1941; the geese sold for 800 to 1000 frs.

[43] AN AJ/41/378, prefect monthly reports for March and April, 3 Apr. 1942 and 31 Apr. 1942 [sic].

[44] AN AJ/41/378, prefect monthly report for July–August, 1 Sept. 1942. In subsequent reports he noted the increasing traffic to Paris and declining official collection; monthly reports of 4 Jan. and 3 Mar. 1943.

[45] SAEF B-0049656, 'Note pour la 4ème Division', 16 Sept. 1941.

[46] AD Pyrénées-Atlantiques, 1031W/200, André Servat to prefect, 14 Jan. 1941.

Alternative Markets

Low official prices were the main factor diverting food supplies to alternative markets. Where the food went and at what price was more complicated. Potential profit figured in farmers' choices for production and sales, but in company with concerns for family and farm, for solidarity (or not) among neighbours who identified their community interests as distinct from those of the distant state, for extended family elsewhere in France, and for relations with local authorities and their tolerance or rigour in disciplining extralegal activity.

Farm consumption increased. Ephraim Grenadou, a farmer in the Loire Valley, claimed that he ate 50 per cent more and gained weight during the war; mortality rates in regions of high agricultural diversity and productivity declined.[47] Perceptive critics, including prefects, suggested that farmers would deliver more to markets if France followed German practice, allowing them to eat what they wanted from their own produce. One German official, comparing French and German food policy, commented 'You can't really ration peasant consumption; he lives amid his produce and it is very easy to hide or deceive.'[48]

In addition to looking after their immediate family, farmers were aware of the shortages in cities. Many had relations in cities, to whom they gave goods on visits and sent packages by mail.[49] The memoirs and journals written by city residents often mention their visits to rural relatives and the packages that provided an essential supplement to the insufficient rations. They rarely mention payment; this was not considered black-market traffic and any payment was by mutual accord. Traffic to supply family extended easily to friends, and to friends of friends, and then to strangers in exchange for payment. Colette's *Lettres aux petites fermières* record her correspondence with two admirers in Brittany who sent food from their farm, including eggs and chickens, more than she and her husband could eat. Colette sent payment in gratitude rather than as fixed charges for

[47] Ephraïm Grenadou, *Grenadou, paysan français* (Paris: Éditions du Seuil, 1966), 173. Mortality rates from Cépède, *Agriculture et alimentation*, 403–407; he cites increases in the Bouches-du-Rhône (57 per cent), Rhône (29 per cent), Seine and Seine-et-Oise (24 and 23 per cent) for high mortality rates, and the Indre, Mayenne and Orne for declines of 10–11 per cent. Grenadou's farm was in the agriculturally rich Eure-et-Loir near Chartres, southwest of Paris.

[48] AN F/60/591, 'Observations relatives à la réunion du CEI du 1er Octobre 1941', 4 Oct. 1941; AN F/60/1010, Lieutenant-Colonel Vialet to the deputy premier, 14 Oct. 1941; quote reported by Vialet.

[49] Grenadou admitted to some black-market activity, including sharing meat with neighbours; Grenadou, *Grenadou, paysan français*, 172–174; also Célia Bertin, *Femmes sous l'Occupation* (Paris: Stock, 1993), 226–228.

parcel contents.[50] City residents placed ads in rural newspapers seeking farmers who would send regular food packages.[51]

Prefect reports from Brittany record the surge in family parcels sent from this region and Normandy. In the Morbihan, the prefect estimated in May 1941 that the volume of parcels to cities carried 10 tonnes of food each day, 300 tonnes per month.[52] The prefect of the Côtes-du-Nord estimated a similar volume in April 1942, 6,700 parcels per day, or 300 tonnes per month.[53] The prefect in Maine-et-Loire lamented that postal transport in his department was 'swamped' (*débordé*) by parcel shipments.[54] The prefect in Ille-et-Vilaine noted that nearly 100,000 visitors came to his department in the summer of 1941 and bought up butter, poultry and pork at any price.[55] The *Contrôle des prix* determined that one farmer near Villechien (La Manche) had shipped 449 parcels from several local train stations between November 1940 and October 1941, weighing more than 16 tonnes, to more than 100 clients, mainly in Paris.[56] Prefects complained of outsiders buying food and negotiating 'parcel contracts' for the winter.[57]

Black-market traffic adapted to utilize the family practices allowed by state officials, particularly the use of family parcels. Monitoring packages sent by post seemed an obvious method for control, but interrogating the senders and recipients yielded poor results. The persons interviewed had 'complete liberty to furnish a range of plausible explanations without any verification being possible'.[58] CE investigations often found that intermediaries sent packages to multiple destinations, using several post offices in one region to hide the volume of goods. Restaurants received packages sent by farmers, family members, and clients of the restaurant.[59] Substantial traffic, particularly to restaurants, was often transported by truck or carried by travellers on trains. One farm in Troisgots (La Manche) supplied a *valisard* (someone carrying food in suitcases)

---

[50] Colette, *Lettres aux petites fermières*, ed. by Marie-Thérèse Colléaux-Chaurang (Paris: Le Castor Astral, 1992).

[51] Veillon, *Vivre et survivre*, 174; Veillon cites the 31 Aug. 1941 issue of *Rustica* with twenty such ads.

[52] AN AJ/41/381 (Morbihan), prefect monthly report, 3 May 1941.

[53] AD Ille-et-Vilaine, 43W/3, prefect monthly report, 1 Apr. 1942.

[54] AN AJ/41/376 (Maine-et-Loire), prefect monthly report, 2 Nov. 1941.

[55] AN AJ/41/373 (Ille-et-Vilaine), prefect monthly report, 1 Sept. 1941.

[56] Michel Boivin, *La vie quotidienne des Manchois sous l'Occupation 1940–1944* (Marigny: Éditions Eurocibles, 2014), 148–149; details on the 16,295 kg recorded in n. 495.

[57] AN AJ/41/389 (Sarthe), prefect monthly report, 4 Sept. 1942.

[58] SAEF B-0049511, M. Robert, 'Envois par la poste des denrées rationnées', 12 Dec. 1942.

[59] SAEF B-0049510 and B-0049511 have evidence on parcel traffic in 1942 and 1943.

caught at the station in Saint-Lô, en route to Paris, with nearly 200 kg of meat and dairy products in five cases and two suitcases.[60] As well as direct sales to the Germans and the traffic to urban consumers, farmers contributed to local consumption by their sales to friends, and exchanges of goods with retailers. Farmers developed local strategies to evade controls. To obtain white flour, they brought more grain to millers than was marked on their transport papers and paid the extra grain to the miller for the white flour (forbidden by law but widely violated). Such an exchange could only be detected by weighing the grain in transit to ensure that it matched the weight on the transport documents. The number of farms, small mills and remote locations made controlling such private exchanges virtually impossible.[61] These exchanges maintained local traditions: tightening Vichy controls increased the recourse to fraud.[62] Local adaptations included deals with gendarmes and local authorities, who needed food for their families and preferred to see local resources consumed in their community. Gendarmes in towns near Dijon warned farmers of imminent control measures, and in return were 'well-treated regarding price'.[63]

Alternative markets for the two most significant black-market foods – butter and meat – show the range of inventive power, the variety of methods, and the social context for black-market supply. Butter, eggs and cheese (*beurre, oeufs et fromage*) were the classic black-market products; the products and those who sold them were referred to as 'les B.O.F.'[64] The black market for meat was one of the most difficult to police because of the combined effects of low rations, German demand, and the opportunity for almost any farm to raise and sell some livestock and poultry. Cities, including Paris, had weeks in which no meat rations were available, while black market restaurants remained well supplied.

Most of the nation's butter (85 per cent) was produced in the Occupied zone. Butter had high value for its fat content and the flavour it added in cooking. Output and official collection plummeted in 1941–1942. The

---

[60] Boivin, *La vie quotidienne des Manchois*, 147–148. The contents included beef, a leg of mutton, 33 kg smoked ham, 24 kg fresh ham, 30 kg fresh pork, 34 kg salted pork, one turkey, 3 chickens, paté, sausage, 47 camemberts, butter, lard, white beans, liver, cream, and 2 bottles of Calvados.

[61] AD Ille-et-Vilaine 43W/4, regional prefect report for Bretagne, 8 Aug. 1942.

[62] AN AJ/41/376 (Manche), prefect monthly report, 1 Sept. 1943.

[63] Henri Drouot. *Notes d'un Dijonnais pendant l'Occupation allemande, 1940–1944* (Dijon: Éditions universitaires de Dijon, 1998), 43 (7 Apr. 1942) and 697 (30 Aug. 1943); Grenadou, *Grenadou, paysan français*, 173, 178; Jean Orieux, *Souvenirs de campagnes* (Paris: Flammarion, 1978), 330–331.

[64] Louis Calaferte portrays common views in conversation, including repeated references to 'The bofs are getting richer', in *C'est la guerre*, trans. by Austryn Wainhouse (Evanston, IL: The Marlboro Press/Northwestern University Press, 1999), 124, 138, 141.

dairy herd declined; some milk cows were slaughtered to meet German requisitions for meat, some because farmers had insufficient fodder. Yield per cow fell by about 30 per cent. The Germans took only 2 per cent of the milk collected by the state, but from 12 per cent to more than 30 per cent of the butter. Exact amounts are unknown because they made large direct purchases.[65] German requisitions sometimes required more butter than had been collected by French authorities, leaving nothing for consumers even in areas of strong production, as happened in the Morbihan and Côtes-du-Nord in the spring of 1942.[66] In Caen the butter ration allowed residents only 100 grams per month in April 1942. As one controller observed, the scarcity justified and encouraged black-market purchasing. Cutting rations in producing regions increased black market sales.[67] The *Service nationale des statistiques* tried to determine the 'real' price for butter in the years 1942 to 1944. They found that state collection took nearly half of total output, while black and grey markets together took more than 30 per cent.[68]

Selling to the Germans was direct and profitable. One couple in the Calvados was caught with 68.5 kg of butter bought from neighbours for resale to the Germans.[69] A farmer in the Pas-de-Calais sold the Germans butter and meat at higher prices than if he delivered to the French food administration. After the war he was subject to a confiscation of 800,000 francs for illicit profits and fined a further 2.4 million francs as there was no evidence the sales had been coerced. He appealed the decision; after

[65] AN F/37/120, CCDR, *Produits laitiers* (Paris: Imprimerie nationale, 1947). The statistics in this report are based on reporting years starting in the spring each year (1 May), with the Germans taking per cent of the butter collected in 1940–1941, 11 per cent the next year, 16 per cent in 1942–1943, 26 per cent in 1943–1944, and 33.6 per cent from May through August in 1944. Compared to the prewar average, consumers had only 40 to 52 per cent in the years 1940 to 1943.

[66] AD Ille-et-Vilaine 43W/3, prefect monthly reports of 1 Apr. 1942 (Côtes-du-Nord) and 31 May 1942 (Morbihan).

[67] SAEF 4A-0000003, X. des Franc, 'Note sur les restrictions dans les villes de province', 17 Apr. 1942.

[68] INSEE, *Enquêtes diverses*, 35–40; their percentages for 1943 include German consumption in the official collection, which skews results in that year, increasing the percentage going to the *Ravitaillement général* at the expense of the other categories. Their 'real price' was a weighted average of official, grey and black-market prices, determined according to departmental surveys of the proportion of production going to different markets.

[69] AD Seine-Maritime 40W/126; the couple had been doing this for several months, paying from 70 to 140 frs per kg for butter they resold at an unspecified price. They were subject to administrative internment for four months. In a similar case, punished after the war, a farmer in Calvados bought from neighbouring farms and sold to the Germans and to the French black market. He had 750,000 frs confiscated as illicit profit and was fined an additional 1.5 million. SAEF 30D-0000267, case no. 8437R.

review, his fine was increased to 3 million francs.[70] Workers in the Organization Todt benefited from having vehicles, fuel and permits, to purchase butter, meat, milk and eggs for their own consumption and to sell in Paris.[71]

Milk deliveries plunged, in part because farmers chose to make more butter. Milk collection was unreliable, with uncollected milk turning sour, especially in hot weather. Butter, easier to conserve and transport, had greater black-market value. After meeting the needs of immediate family, beneficiaries included friends and distant family, often traded for goods, in mutually beneficial exchange to evade price regulation.[72]

Although postal regulations did not allow shipping perishable foods, the post was the most accessible means to send food and it became a major conduit for traffic in butter. Postal employees did not enforce the rules, 'in a broad spirit of social understanding'.[73] Mailing butter was expressly forbidden in October 1941, with little effect. In 1943 the volume of parcel traffic from Brittany and Normandy had increased from prewar levels by five to ten times. The regional prefect for Brittany estimated in June 1942 that postal traffic was 35,000 packages daily from his region (four departments). Parcels from the Mayenne reached a record daily average of 8,586 in 1943.[74] Intermediaries shipped food from multiple stations, gave false names and addresses, and falsified their lists of parcel contents. One supplier mailed butter from the Côtes-du-Nord to Paris restaurants in packages labelled 'leeks';[75] a farmer in the Alpes-Maritimes routinely sent butter and cheese in parcels, listing only the vegetables as content.[76] The CE and the Gendarmerie reported constant adaptations to conceal forbidden goods, sending food to family, friends and community at or below official prices.[77]

State collection enabled food supply administrators to engage in their own black-market commerce. Some officials collecting dairy products

[70] SAEF 30D-0000057, case no. 1905R; his case was reviewed and the fine increased by the *Conseil supérieur de confiscation des profits illicites*.
[71] AD Ille-et-Vilaine 43W/4, prefect monthly report for Morbihan, 31 July 1942.
[72] AD Seine-Maritime 40W/114, prefect monthly report, August 1943; INSEE, *Enquêtes diverses*, 16, 19; city residents traded bicycle tyres, lengths of cloth and Belgian tobacco.
[73] M. Paul, 'Histoire des PTT pendant la deuxième guerre mondiale (1939–1945)', unpublished manuscript, Ministère des PTT (1967), 285; copy in the Bibliothèque historique des postes et télécommunications, Paris.
[74] AD Ille-et-Vilaine 43W/3, regional prefect report of 3 June 1942; Paul, 'Histoire des PTT', 285–287.
[75] SAEF 30D-0000115, case no. 6262.
[76] AD Alpes-Maritimes 159W/46, case 1195-R.
[77] Boutet, *Ils ont vécu*, 138–139 and 154. The *Service des statistiques nationales* distinguished between the *marché noir* and the *marché amical* for friends and family; the line between the two was not clear.

kept a share for black-market sale or their own consumption, officially reporting only part of the goods they collected, and paying farmers extra for the milk and butter they sold on the black market. The prefect of the Côtes-du-Nord asked police to check the cars of state collection officials to verify that they reported all the butter collected, and to punish officials who engaged in this widespread practice.[78] Dairy collection was administered by the *Comité de gestion des groupements interprofessionnels laitiers* (CGGIL). Industry representatives serving on the committees could take advantage of their position to protect producer interests.[79] Two CGGIL officials supplied the German embassy in Paris with two tonnes of butter per month and gave dairy goods to the French police, probably in exchange for protection from prosecution. The Germans stopped the *Police économique* inquiry into this case, but the investigation reopened after Liberation.[80] In the Mayenne, three collection officials were suspended for falsifying receipts and selling butter on the black market in the summer of 1942.[81] One wholesaler in the Somme supplied butter to the Germans and to the directors of French services (*Ravitaillement général*, *Contrôle économique* and the prefect) to avoid prosecution. Such cases were regarded as common practice.[82] The illicit traffic in butter thus engaged producers, friends, black market intermediaries and state officials.

The illicit slaughter and distribution of black-market meat likewise touched all levels in commerce and administration. Illicit slaughter became the offence most frequently punished by administrative internment in producing regions. Meat infractions were widespread in restaurants, and meat products were the greatest in number (31.2 per cent) and value (43 per cent) of black-market goods seized in 1944.[83] The traffic developed in response to declining meat output and increased regulation. The Germans took about 14 per cent of the reduced meat output in 1941, 20 per cent in 1942 and 33 per cent in 1943. French consumers thus obtained a fraction of their 1938

---

[78] AD Ille-et-Vilaine 43W/4, prefect of the Côtes-du-Nord monthly report for July 1942. 8 Aug. 1942. Prefects made similar reports from Morbihan, Ille-et-Vilaine (AD Ille-et-Vilaine 43W/3 and 43W/4) and Mayenne (AN AJ/41/378, report of 1 Sept. 1942).

[79] AN F/23/405, 'Étude sur la collecte des produits laitiers', 19 Jan. 1943.

[80] SAEF B-0049479, from a list of arrests requested by the Minister of Food Supply, 4 Oct. 1944.

[81] AN AJ/41/378 (Mayenne), prefect monthly report, 1 Sept. 1942.

[82] AN F/23/408, 'Affaire Lemaire', Note (M. Julienne) for Inspector General Jeannin, 21 Feb. 1944.

[83] SAEF B-0009860, DGCE, *Rapport sur l'activité de la DGCE au cours de l'année 1944*, Table 3. Butter accounted for 16.7 per cent of the cases and 7.7 per cent of the value of confiscations.

consumption levels through official rations: 35 per cent in 1941, 32 per cent in 1942, 24 per cent in 1943.[84]

State regulations for livestock set standards for sanitary slaughter and the distribution of meat to wholesale and retail outlets, making illicit slaughter a concern for reasons of health as well as control of distribution. The state created *commissions de reception* in June 1941 for the legal purchase of livestock. State purchasing groups competed to hire industry professionals for livestock purchase. Privileged buyers (including restaurants) were allowed supplies in advance of retail shops.[85] The suppliers, restaurants, shopkeepers and consumers all looked to alternative markets. The best quality meat, and by 1943 probably the greatest quantity, went to the black market. One official estimated that in some regions, black markets obtained twice as much as the official supply. And the best animals went to the black market: *trafiquants* supplied farmers with underweight cattle to meet their official requisitions.[86]

The illicit slaughter served three distinct markets. The most profitable was selling directly to the Germans. In addition to deliveries negotiated with the French state, German military units set up their own supply systems to provision military canteens and the restaurants they patronized. They had massive purchasing power, trucks, fuel, transit passes to carry animals and butchered meat, and virtual immunity from French control. When French police stopped such vehicles, German authorities intervened to recover the meat and liberate their French *trafiquants*. The intensity of traffic varied by region and season as German deployments changed. Departments on the Atlantic coast with substantial livestock often had the heaviest concentrations of troops, and *Organisation Todt* workers constructing the Atlantic Wall in 1943 and 1944.

Trafiquants supplying the Germans used their expertise and connections to develop broader black-market commerce. Michel S., a livestock buyer at the La Villette slaughterhouses in Paris before the war, became a purchaser for the town of Bourges and for the French army. In 1940 the German army employed him to purchase meat and coordinate with the French food supply administration. His license allowed him to travel anywhere, day or night, to supervise meat purchases. In 1941 he claimed to supervise 110 employees and transact business worth 40 million francs

---

[84] Calculated from statistics in AN F/37/120, CCDR, *Viande*.

[85] Sylvain Leteux, 'Débats et tâtonnements dans l'organisation du marché de la viande en France (1931–1953)', in *Organiser les marchés agricoles: Le temps des fondateurs. Des années 1930 aux années 1950*, ed. by Alain Chatriot, Edgar Leblanc and Édouard Lynch (Paris: Armand Colin, 2012), 136–138; and 'Le commerce de la viande à Paris: qui tire profit de la situation?' in *Les entreprises de biens de consommation*, 81–98.

[86] AN F/60/1010, Formery to Laval, 27 July 1943.

per week.[87] Like many administrations, the *Ravitaillement général* had staff working with the Germans to gain access to food and privileges. They delivered large quantities of food to the Germans with the knowledge of French authorities and left little evidence for postwar prosecution.[88]

Farmers in regions of troop concentration could be subject to serious pressure to sell to nearby units, with the threat of theft and violence if they did not comply. But some welcomed and sought this commerce: it was profitable and seemed secure, given the German command of resources and policing authority. The committees investigating illicit profits after Liberation imposed heavy fines to punish voluntary sales. One farmer in the Calvados was fined 1.5 million francs for illicit slaughter and selling to the Germans, twice the amount of his estimated profits.[89] Another in the Pas-de-Calais, already mentioned, had his fine increased from 2.4 to 3 million francs on appeal, justified by new evidence that he had sold to the Germans voluntarily.[90]

The second market, selling to French consumers, could involve substantial networks to collect, transport and distribute black-market meat. One group engaging in large-scale supply to Paris had ten members, buying in the region of Neufchatel (Seine-Inférieure). On 22 January 1943, the Gendarmerie found large metal cases being shipped to Paris that contained 967 kg of meat, 567 cheeses and 7 kg of butter. The group, working with the complicity of SNCF employees, had engaged in illicit slaughter to sell meat in Paris since September or October 1942. They slaughtered the livestock on the farms and shipped from local stations to the Pont-Cardinet station in Paris. They used Pont-Cardinet as the last stop before the Gare Saint-Lazare, which had tighter control. They often employed a German army truck and driver for the transport to stations, and shipped the meat as 'accompanied baggage', which did not require detailing the contents. Marcelle D., responsible for much of the organization, was the wife of an SNCF employee who registered some of the shipments; she was having an affair with Charley H., who took charge of the meat and sold it when it reached Paris.[91] The group included two farmers, a farm worker, a butcher's helper, a shopkeeper, and three unemployed men who had organized the ring. Such networks supplied meat to clients in Paris, including butchers'

[87] SAEF B-0049509, Inspector 702, 'Rapport', 16 Apr. 1945, and 'Demande de permis de circulation', 23 Oct. 1941.

[88] SAEF B-0049509, 'Note sur la collaboration économique en matière de la viande', undated, ca. 1945.

[89] SAEF 30D-0000267, case 6833R; the fine was reduced to 750,000 frs on appeal

[90] SAEF 30D-0000057, case 1905R.

[91] AD Seine-Maritime 40W/125, prosecutor in Neufchâtel-en-Bray to Attorney General, Appeals Court, Rouen, 12 May 1943.

shops and restaurants. Hippolyte Gancel described a similar network near Saint-Lô, selling meat and butter from local farms to the Germans and to customers in Paris, shipping goods by train with the complicity of a local stationmaster, a tax official, a policeman, and the German authorities in Saint-Lô.[92]

The third level, and the most widespread, was illicit slaughter for local consumption. This traffic tended to be small-scale, serving local communities, and charging prices that provided farmers a better return without earning significant profit. In January 1942, Gendarmerie reports from the unoccupied zone on the rising number of cases of illicit slaughter found that 'these are animals slaughtered for families, destined to feed a restricted circle of people living close by'. Difficulty in obtaining feed for livestock and official prices that did not cover costs encouraged this clandestine slaughter.[93] Subsequent reports noted rising case numbers, mainly to meet family and community needs: 'in most cases it is the slaughter of a calf, a hog, or a sheep that the peasant shares with his friends or neighbours, at a price above the official price and without requiring tickets'.[94]

Suppression of illicit slaughter was virtually impossible. There were too many farms, often isolated, and the enforcement agencies had few staff, fewer vehicles, and derisory fuel allowances to patrol large departments.[95] Farmers adapted to follow the letter of the law. Allowed to keep two hogs for family consumption, 'The cultivator declares two hogs; he kills one clandestinely, buys another, and thus still has two.'[96] Mayors were required to report the slaughter of livestock. 'But they don't know anything', Henri Drouot commented: 'since the war, the hogs no longer squeal when their throats are cut . . .'[97]

[92] This memoir is a melodramatic fiction based on Gancel's experience as a schoolteacher in Normandy. Hippolyte Gancel, *Crime et Résistance en Normandie* (Rennes: Éditions Ouest-France, 2008), 56–61.

[93] AN AJ/41/24, 'Synthèse des rapports mensuels des Commandants des Légions de Gendarmerie de la Zone Libre (Janvier 1942)'.

[94] AN AJ/41/24, 'Synthèse des rapports mensuels des Commandants des Légions de Gendarmerie de la Zone Libre (Février 1942)' and 'Synthèse des Rapports Mensuels des Commandants des Légions de Gendarmerie de la Zone Libre (Mai 1942)' (quoted).

[95] In March 1942, the fuel allocation for the *Inspection général du ravitaillement* in the Eure-et -Loire was 20 litres. AN F/23/408, 'Synthèse des rapports d'inspection effectuées au cours de la période du 15 mars au 15 avril', 16 Apr. 1942.

[96] AN AJ/41/24, 'Synthèse des rapports mensuels des Commandants des Légions de Gendarmerie de la Zone Libre (Janvier 1942)'. The rules changed in October 1941; initially farmers could keep one hog for family consumption and could have a second only after delivering one hog to the RG. On impact of this change, see AN AJ/41/393, prefect to Minister of the Interior, 3 Dec. 1941.

[97] Drouot, *Notes d'un dijonnais*, 121 (2 Mar. 1941); René Limouzin describes the illicit slaughter of pigs as 'la fête du cochon' in *Le temps des J3*, 82–83.

Local authorities often sympathized with community efforts to improve food access, keeping local goods in their region, pushing for higher prices, and turning a blind eye to illicit slaughter for local consumption. The mayor of Lignières-Sonneville (Charente) refused, in October and November 1941, to provide the *Ravitaillement général* with cattle for slaughter because the prices paid were unsustainable for the farmers.[98] Local mayors supported his resistance to department-level pressure, threatening to refuse to deliver cattle to the state administration.[99] The low prices diverted livestock to serve local needs, with the complicity of mayors, local butchers, and sometimes the Gendarmerie. The state needed the hides from illicit slaughter, and its mild fines made it look like the black market for meat was tolerated.[100]

The meat producing regions in the Occupied zone developed illicit slaughter on a larger scale. The prefect for the Manche attributed the trend in August 1941 to the reduced meat rations in rural areas. In response, farmers slaughtered calves and sheep for family consumption, a net loss to state collection.[101] The prefect of the Seine-Inférieure explained illicit slaughter as a daily occurrence, practiced by everyone, the butcher, the farmer with pastureland, and factory workers. Most of the product went to the black market in Le Havre or Paris, but 'it should be noted that some of this meat is sold at accessible prices to local workers and that the butchers are satisfied with making only a small profit'.[102]

Farmers devised methods to conceal livestock and slaughter. They kept cattle in isolated fields and reported the cattle they sold to black market networks as stolen.[103] They used changing seasonal pasture to explain the movement of livestock between departments for black-market delivery. In the Mayenne, stock bought by state purchasing commissions was often reclassified for shipment out of department, particularly through the canton of Landivy, which gave access to three neighbouring departments.[104] Prefects stated that the number of farms made it impossible to survey them all for illicit slaughter. 'The battle against illicit slaughter continues non-stop and yields some results, but it shouldn't

[98] AD Charente 1W/70, sub-prefect in Cognac to the prefect, 28 Nov. 1941.

[99] AD Charente 1W/70, sub-prefect in Cognac to the prefect, 19 Nov. 1941.

[100] AN F/23/415, 'Note pour M. le Ministre d'État à l'agriculture et au ravitaillement', 25 Oct. 1943.

[101] AN AJ/41/376 (Manche), prefect monthly report of 31 Aug. 1941.

[102] AD Seine-Maritime 40W/114, 'Synthèse des rapports des préfets de la région de Rouen du mois d'avril 1943'.

[103] AN AJ/41/390 (Seine), prefect monthly report for March-April, 30 Apr. 1943.

[104] AN F/23/500, 'Rapport de l'Inspecteur du ravitaillement Clayeux sur le bétail dans la Mayenne', 21 Feb. 1944. He detailed the types of fraudulent paperwork used to ship cattle by rail and by truck.

be hidden that the services of the *Contrôle économique* or the Gendarmerie will never have enough manpower to fight this practice, which is that much more harmful in generally working in conjunction with the black market.'[105]

The price factor was fundamental to the incentives for illicit slaughter. When official prices did not cover the cost to feed livestock to mature weight, the animals were slaughtered for local consumption and black-market sale. This was especially true for hogs. Pork was seldom available in official markets: high German demand and low official prices diverted it to alternative markets.[106] In some regions, butchers bought direct from the farm, paying higher prices for meat they sold at the legal price.[107] Butchers in Ille-et-Vilaine sold meat from illicit slaughter at prices 'about normal'. This corrected the mispricing of livestock to benefit local consumers. Butchers went to the farms, 'to do their work on site and the meat, soon butchered, is distributed to neighbours without leaving a trace'.[108] In 1944, the *Contrôle économique* advised against imposing heavy fines on butchers selling meat from illicit slaughter in Lyon, as this would transfer the slaughter from butchers' shops to farms. The CE conceded the reality of consumer needs and the effect of low official prices: 'one can't in fact pursue impossible goals, and oblige the population to give up meat almost entirely as a result of the failings of the collection agencies, when the meat is there, on the spot'.[109]

Poultry and rabbits were subject to price controls without ration restrictions. People raised them on farms and in homes in the city for their own consumption. Poultry numbers declined for lack of feed, whereas rabbits increased.[110] The Gendarmerie in the ZNO explained why eggs, chickens and rabbits were *unfindable* in legal markets in 1942: they were sold directly from the farm, for family consumption and the black market.[111] One gendarme traveling by bus to Marseille saw passengers at the customs entry to the city declare a total of sixty dozen eggs; one

---

[105] AN AJ/41/392 (Deux-Sèvres), prefect report for March-April, 5 May 1943.

[106] The Bank of France commented on the disparity: 200 francs per kg paid for piglets live, and 25 francs per kg as the on the hoof legal price for hogs: 'One can see how in these conditions, no fattened animals would be brought to market.' ABdF 1069201226 27, DGEE, 'Résumé des rapports économiques', May 1944.

[107] AD Seine-Maritime 40W/114, regional prefect in Rouen, monthly report, Sept. 1943.

[108] AD Ille-et-Vilaine 43W/8, prefect report for February–March 1944.

[109] SAEF B-0057659, de Sailly to Regional Prefect Bonnefoy, 1 Apr. 1944. The *Service national des statistiques* estimated that farmers, black and grey markets took 35 to 50 per cent of the livestock. INSEE, *Enquêtes diverses*, 54, 56.

[110] INSEE, *Enquêtes diverses*, 53; and 'Le mystère des lapins', in Jules Véran, *En faisant la queue: ou les spectacles du jour* (Paris: Librairie Aristide Quillet, 1942), 19–24.

[111] AN AJ /41/377 (Marne), prefect monthly report, 30 June 1942.

passenger had forty rabbits and fifty partridges.[112] Jean Orieux described the train station in Limoges during the Occupation as 'a true barnyard', as noisy as a town marketplace with the raucous squawking of roosters, hens, ducks, geese and turkeys. The noise and the smell made the traffic obvious, but there were no birds in sight. Controllers apparently were deaf, blind, and had no sense of smell (and they were concerned about their own food access).[113]

The wine industry's experience was structured more significantly by German purchasing. Unlike carbohydrates, fats and protein, wine is not a dietary essential. But many in France considered it a necessity with significant health benefits. It would fight bacteria, improve one's physical constitution and raise morale. Experience in the First World War had established 'le pinard des poilus' (the wine ration for the soldier) as essential for the troops.[114] Philippe Pétain praised wine as 'the beneficial stimulant for morale as well as physical force' that helped bring victory in 1918. Advocates deemed state measures to reduce wine consumption in early 1940 (including three 'days without' in cafés and bars) to be a danger that would increase fraud, crime and alcoholism.[115]

Defeat brought two major threats to French wine consumption. First, the regional nature of production relied on transport for national distribution. The chaos of defeat, followed by German division of the country, subjected the national market to German control over means of transport. Second, massive German purchasing caused immediate shortages and favoured sales to German buyers. The Germans established purchasing offices in major production centres, led by men from the German wine industry who often had long collaborative relationships with producers and expert knowledge of French wines. In Christophe Lucand's analysis, French producers were far more interested in profit than in resisting German demands. The Germans bought wine, champagne and hard liquor with eager assistance from French negotiators, while price controls and rations for French consumers fostered widespread and highly remunerative black markets.

---

[112] AN AJ/41/24, 'Synthèse des rapports mensuels des Commandants des Légions de Gendarmerie de la Zone Libre (Septembre 1942)'; similar comments occur in each month after April. Reports on poultry and eggs 'rare and almost unfindable in markets' from the Calvados (AJ/41/366, report of 1 Jan. 1941); the Gironde (AJ/41/372, 23 July 1941); Marne (AJ/41/377; 31 Oct. 1942); as well as in the Mayenne and the Vendée.

[113] Orieux, *Souvenirs*, 330–332.

[114] Christophe Lucand, *Le pinard des Poilus: Une histoire du vin durant la Grande Guerre (1914–1918)* (Dijon: Éditions universitaires de Dijon, 2015).

[115] Christophe Lucand, *Le vin et la guerre: Comment les nazis ont fait main basse sur le vignoble français* (Paris: Armand Colin, 2017), 40–55; quote at 43 from Pétain's preface to Gaston Derys, *Mon docteur le vin* (1935).

German thirst for champagne provides the most spectacular case of German exploitation. France produced 30 million bottles per year in the 1930s. In the four years from mid-1940 to mid-1944, the Germans took 86.3 million bottles: 64.3 million in direct purchase, nearly 20 million in 'hidden' purchases, and 2.5 million in pillaging French resources in 1940.[116] French producers organized the *Comité interprofessionnel des vins de Champagne* (CIVC) to negotiate official prices and coordinate the provision of essential materials, including sugar. The massive sales to all branches of the German military at negotiated prices earned large profits. The additional 'hidden' sales to individual German purchasers, black-market restaurants and cabarets, and exports to favoured foreign markets (Belgium in particular) charged 'exorbitant' prices and often sold low-grade champagne as top quality.[117]

A French analysis in 1945 commented, regarding the official account books for the major champagne firms: 'the accounts ... are in good health, in very good health, in fact in some cases in plethoric health'. The attitude of producers, the author remarked, had been 'more than kind', and the CIVC had not exercised even the slightest slowing down of collaboration with the enemy.[118] German buyers took the bulk of French output in official purchases, facilitated black market distribution with Wehrmacht trucks carrying illicit traffic, and increased the demand in black-market restaurants and canteens serving Germans and their collaborators. The military also bought large volumes of cognac and Armagnac; Armagnac production increased tenfold from 1938 to 1943. The Wehrmacht tried to increase its purchases by 200 per cent in 1943, stating that cognac was 'vital' for their troops in Russia.[119]

The wine trade received close attention from German specialists like Heinz Boemers, who was in charge of wine purchasing in the Bordeaux region and led the organization to coordinate wine purchasing throughout France (the *Hauptvereinigung der deutschen Weinbauwirtschaft*). The combination of deliveries negotiated with French authorities, direct purchasing by the armed forces and police, and French black-market demand generated sharp competition. Wine output fell by roughly 40 per cent in the 1942–1943 and 1943–1944 seasons, and imports from North Africa (12 million hectolitres per year) ended in

---

[116] AN F/37/120, CCDR, *Vins et spiritueux*, 45.
[117] Lucand, *Le vin et la guerre*, 252–255, 265.
[118] SAEF B-0049509, Direction générale des études et recherches, Reims, 'Le vin de Champagne sous l'occupation', 28 Feb. 1945.
[119] Lucand, *Le vin et la guerre*, 267–277; vital for troops claimed by Dr Reinhart in discussing alcohol deliveries for 1943–1944 in AN F/1a/3855, conversation in the Hôtel Majestic, 10 Sept. 1943.

November 1942. The wine available for French consumption from the 1942–1943 harvest was just 46 per cent of the prewar average, and 52 per cent the following year.[120] The impact on consumption was greatest in non-producing departments. But even in the Gironde, famous for Bordeaux wines, the prefect complained of shortage in 1941. He blamed massive German purchasing and reduced supplies from the Midi and Algeria.[121] Consumption in the Seine region (Paris), which averaged 9.8 million hectolitres per year prewar, fell to 3 million in the last three years of the Occupation.

In all, the Germans took an estimated total of 10.2 million hectolitres of wine from 1940 to 1944, according to the postwar commission investigating damage to the French economy.[122] This calculation underestimates the volume of illicit purchasing; the total appropriation could have been as much as 50 per cent higher.[123] Consumption by producers increased during the Occupation,[124] and vintners held back large quantities for barter and direct sales. They also routinely understated their output, in part to 'deceive the Germans', but more significantly to increase their revenue and profit.[125]

Fraudulent practices were more common in the wine industry than in other commercialized agriculture for two reasons. First, after a crisis decade of overproduction and low prices in the 1930s, the power and pervasiveness of German purchasing yielded astonishing profits to those willing to collaborate. Wine producers were better organized, and their representatives worked more closely with the Germans than did other branches of French agriculture. This included the supply to restaurants, hotels, casinos and residences taken for German use, and usually supplied

---

[120] AN F/37/120, CCDR, *Vins et spiritueux*, 37; slightly higher figures are given in the agriculture report for the Occupation years in *Revue d'économie politique*; Froment, 'La production agricole', 1218, 1232.

[121] AN AJ/41/372 (Gironde), prefect monthly report, 26 June 1941. The Bordeaux region produced higher quality wines and imported wines from the Midi and Algeria for 'current consumption'.

[122] AN F/37/120, CCDR, *Vins et spiritueux*, 37, 39.

[123] Christophe Lucand reviews the figures and estimates the total German take to have been 15 to 17 million hectolitres; Lucand, *Le vin et la guerre*, 383–386.

[124] Froment, 'La production agricole', 1232.

[125] AN F/23/441, Rapport de renseignement no. 21, 8 Apr. 1946, reporting on fraud in the wine industry. The Chamber of Commerce in Beaune estimated in December 1943 that almost all producer declarations understated their wine output, often by 50 per cent or more; Lucand, *Le vin et la guerre*, 228. The Bank of France thought vintners in the Bordeaux region declared only 50 per cent of their 1943 harvest; Sébastien Durand, 'Consommer les vins dans la France en guerre: étude croisée des deux conflits mondiaux', paper presented at the Society for French Historical Studies annual meeting, 2018, Pittsburgh, PA.

by direct purchasing. This traffic took advantage of German purchasing privileges and transport to sell to French purchasers.

Second, the regional shortages and inequities in access were aggravated by the rationing regime, which distinguished between ordinary wines (*vins de consommation courantes* – VCC) and quality wines (*vins d'appellation contrôlées* – VAC). The VAC had greater price freedom, allowing a steeper rise in prices and, as a consequence, an increased volume of sales through increased output *and* a surge in the sale of VCC wines as VAC, especially in restaurants. The prefect of the Gironde asked the ministers of finance and agriculture to fix VAC prices in 1941, reporting they had quadrupled between late March and late May.[126] In February 1943, the state required that one litre of the adult ration of four litres per month (far below average consumption) must be VAC. The higher cost put the fourth litre beyond reach of many working-class consumers.[127] The new restrictions increased the demand for black-market wine and the fraud in retailing.

Differences in regional access to wine meant that non-producing departments could go for months with wine rations unavailable or reduced to one litre. Restaurants had higher priority in the supply system than households, and they often charged high prices for alcohol to recoup the cost of black-market food. The restaurants serving Germans, collaborators and the wealthy relied on black market supplies; they recovered costs by charging extra for aperitifs, wine and digestifs. The Paris police estimated in late 1941 that restaurants received only 40 per cent of their prewar wine supply; the black-market supply flowed to restaurants for the rich.[128]

In comparison with the family and community functions of black-market activity for butter and meat, the wine trade engaged a larger-scale traffic, concentrated profits in the hands of renowned vintners, and had greater German influence, to create a flourishing black market that served the wealthy and the privileged.

Social Fracture

The urban working and middle classes struggled to survive on starvation rations and often believed the farmers to be eating well – too well – and growing rich on black-market profits. Black-market food was rarely

[126] AN AJ/41/372 (Gironde), prefect monthly report, 26 June 1941.
[127] Complaints recorded by the Paris police, APP 220W 11, 'Situation à Paris', 8 and 22 Mar. 1943, and by the Gendarmerie, AN AJ/41/395, 'Synthèse relative à l'état moral et matériel de la population dans les territoires de la zone occupée au cours du mois d'Avril 1943'. The Gendarmerie thought the measure one of the most unpopular yet, requiring many families to give up wine consumption to keep within their budgets.
[128] APP BA 1806, note of 6 Jan. 1942, citing a PCF tract, 'Vers la ruine des petits débitants de vins et restaurateurs'.

affordable for those with restricted incomes. The anger over profiteering, evident in reports by prefects and the state *Contrôle technique,* swept farm practices into one rubric of self-interest and greed. Prefects believed that the *paysans* acted in selfish interest with no larger view of national purpose: 'In the countryside, the spirit of lucre frequently dominates the actions of our *paysans,* who only see in the present situation a source of great profits, easily realizable.'[129] The prefect in Rennes observed: 'A selfish materialism continues to rage in the countryside ... the *paysan* remains withdrawn into himself, moved only by the lure of gain. He only delivers his products to state requisitions in protesting and trying to cheat ... '[130] Such reports continued in 1943: 'Selfishness persists on the part of the *paysan,* always greedy for gain, and often heedless of the major reforms to the structure of the state carried out by the National Revolution.'[131]

This animosity played out in two registers in the last months of the Occupation and the Liberation. First, the anger had its source in the food shortages, the obvious inequities of access, and the belief that farmers preferred to sell to the black market rather than deliver for legal distribution. The *Contrôle technique,* eavesdropping on telephone conversations and intercepting mail, created a new rubric in 1943 for comments displaying 'Resentment towards the peasants'.[132] They frequently noted the 'Growing hostility towards the *paysans,* who abuse the situation, who have everything yet complain all the same, who take pride in practicing the black market ... '[133] The chief of police in Rouen noted in August 1944, regarding the black market's impact on the cost of living and the profits to farmers and shopkeepers, the deep division and hatred between the well-to-do and those exploited in the war: 'The population that has suffered expects justice to be done and that the newly enriched be forced to cough up their gains.'[134]

Hatred fostered violence, the second register for this social fracture, especially in early 1944. Farmers believed to have profited from selling to the Germans and the black market were attacked, forced to pay 'fines', and robbed of any cash, jewellery, alcohol and food they had on hand. In some cases, aggressors declared they were in the Resistance. Others claimed to be German police. Commenting on the rising tide of violence,

---

[129] AN AJ/41/373 (Indre-et-Loire), prefect monthly report, 3 Jan. 1942.
[130] AN AJ/41/373 (Ille-et-Vilaine), prefect monthly report, 31 May 1942.
[131] AN AJ/41/372 (Gironde), prefect monthly report, 2 June 1943.
[132] AN F/7/14930, *Contrôle technique* monthly reports.
[133] AN F/7/14929, note of 29 Apr. 1943.
[134] AD Manche 1370W/134, Secretary General for the police in for the Rouen region, 12 Aug. 1944. 'La population qui a souffert attend que justice soit faite et qu'on fasse rendre gorge aux enrichis de fraîche date.'

one report noted 'The victims are reputed to have sold to the black market, particularly to the Occupation troops.'[135] The farmers who reported thefts claimed amounts stolen that rose in some cases to hundreds of thousands of francs. The irregularity of the attacks makes identifying assailants, their purpose, what they took and why, a matter of conjecture. Some attackers were indeed *résistants*; some were angry neighbours; some were 'faux maquis' seizing on the opportunity for violence and profit.[136]

The fracture is obvious. But the line of fracture was neither as clear nor as clean as the quotes above suggest. Prefect and police reports reflected their frustration in observing the growing anger. Alongside this anger, many city residents benefited from family parcels and direct purchases that made a greater difference in their consumption than their black-market use.[137] The countryside provided vital supplies in bypassing official markets. For the farmers, the findings from investigations to confiscate illicit profits show a mixed record. These cases often began from CE reports of infractions, including cases halted by German intervention and cases based on public notoriety.[138] When the confiscation appeals committee reviewed cases, it looked closely at evidence for the products sold, the prices, and the efforts to avoid law enforcement. In some cases, they annulled the initial confiscations when farmers convinced them that they had sold their produce to friends and local workers, serving community needs, often at or below the prices set by the state.[139] In cases with clear black-market activity, especially those who actively sought German clients, higher fines were imposed, and increased when appeals misrepresented the illicit sales.[140]

According to postwar confiscation estimates, the profits from illicit traffic in farm goods could be in the millions of francs, and merit fines at triple the level of the profits. But these figures were estimates and dealt with the largest-scale cases. The belief that peasants grew rich exaggerated the amount of profits and their distribution. Certainly, a minority made significant profits, especially in selling to the Germans and the large-scale black-market traffic that escaped controllers. The money

---

[135] AN F/60/1527, report from the Calvados, 8 Apr. 1944.
[136] Fabrice Grenard, *Maquis noir et faux maquis 1943–1947* (Paris: Vendémiaire, 2011), 47–59.
[137] Sauvy's 1943 calculations as to where consumers found food in addition to their rations are reproduced as a pie chart showing the proportions of calories obtained in J.-L. Leleu, F. Passera, J. Wuellien and M. Daeffler, eds., *La France pendant la Seconde guerre mondiale: Atlas historique* (Paris: Fayard, 2010), 145.
[138] The confiscation process for illicit profits is explained in Chapter 9.
[139] SAEF 30D-0000386, case 16674, selling butter and meat to friends, Pas-de-Calais.
[140] SAEF 30D-0000267, case 1313, from Vienne, and case 6833, Calvados.

they gained was often hoarded because there were few goods, especially the machinery and tools needed for farm work. Inflation diminished the value of their hoarded currency. Historians who have assessed rural wealth accumulation find it to have been modest, and agriculture desperately needed new investment after the war.[141] The bitter resentments of the Occupation and Liberation periods were a product of the shortages, the obvious inequities in access and the injustice in who suffered, and the frustrations with ineffective state policies.

Conclusions

Vichy's aspirations to restore French agriculture as the foundation for national renewal failed. French farmers faced the multiple problems of prices fixed by the state, interference in their decisions for production and consumption, and shortages of the materials and transport essential to their work. Output fell and farmers opted increasingly for alternative markets rather than deliver to the state. An analysis by the Ministry of Agriculture in 1943 stated bluntly that for producers, 'the official food supply seems to them a swindle'. That farmers preferred to sell direct to French consumers was 'a current of opinion that must be taken into account, and against which it is impossible to fight'.[142]

Low fixed prices were the main factor driving sales to alternative markets, but three other factors influenced farmers' decisions about output and marketing, and encouraged misreporting and redirecting output in opposition to state policy. The first was the increase in state requirements to report production, which they found intrusive, annoying and contrary to their interests. A report to London in December 1943 noted: 'More and more, the farmer uses the force of inertia, making no declaration, making no delivery, waiting for them to come and take the merchandise from him ... The Saône et Loire, notably, is in a state of general, open rebellion.'[143] Pierre Barral later concluded, 'If the statistics are abundant, because they multiplied the questionnaires, they are certainly false: those reporting, and then the state authorities, minimized their results in order to reduce state impositions and deliveries to the occupier.'[144] Second, restrictions on farm consumption and the use of

[141] Cépède, *Agriculture et alimentation*, 448–453; Annie Moulin, *Les paysans dans la société française: de la Révolution à nos jours* (Paris: Seuil, 1998), 200; Alary, *L'histoire des paysans français*, 291; Grenard, *La France du marché noir*, 287.

[142] AN F/10/4962, 'La psychologie paysanne', 20 Jan. 1943.

[143] AN F/1a/3772, ZAC/4/25100, 'La production du blé en Saône et Loire (1943)', 6 Dec. 1943.

[144] Barral, *Les agrariens*, 266.

feed for livestock and poultry were impossible to enforce without the farmers' cooperation. When the rules were an affront to their autonomy and dignity, they resisted; the interests of their family and farm came ahead of respect for state rules.[145] Third, the state failed to assure the availability of materials and equipment essential to farm work, including draught animals and household goods ranging from work clothes, boots and gloves, to tools, bedding and linens.

Prefects reporting the spread of direct sales from farms, even when critical of a rural 'greed for lucre', depicted the *paysans* as acting rationally in response to the demand for food, and recognized that a significant share of their illicit traffic to avoid state controls supplied family, local communities and French citizens rather than the Germans. Vichy's project for national regeneration did not sustain the farm, family and local interests that were essential to generate a feeling of shared national solidarity. In their experience, the Vichy controls served German needs, and were imposed and enforced by an administration they experienced as inefficient, interfering and unpatriotic.

---

[145] AD Ille-et-Vilaine, 43W/3, prefect monthly report for the Finistère, Mar. 1942.

5   Market Forces: Industry and Commerce

The geographic diffusion of agricultural activity and the fact that everyone needed to eat made the black market for food the most widespread and difficult to suppress. But the highest profits lay in industry and commerce. The infamous 'black-market billionaires' made their fortunes in trafficking rather than producing goods. From the defeat in June 1940, French industry faced major challenges to resume production and avert business failure. Their most direct and reliable access to raw materials, energy, labour and transport was in working for the Germans. As well as privileged access, this provided opportunities for higher profits, black-market purchase of scarce and hoarded goods, and protection from French controllers. For many producers, economic collaboration and the black market became essential to survival, and the two intertwined.

The Bank of France summarized the situation for commerce in the Unoccupied Zone in mid-1941 as one of paralysis. Manufacturers, wholesalers and retailers scrambled to obtain supplies. Apart from the firms working for the Germans, and thus obtaining raw materials, manufacturers were unable to produce for clients because of material shortages and fixed prices. In commerce, 'The sellers wanting to obtain supplies now have only one means to do so: recourse to the "black market".[1] The Bank stated in November 1941: 'The existence of black markets is today prevalent across France; in every city, every town, in every cluster grouping only a few inhabitants, practices that could or must be categorized under this name are rampant . . . A leading role is played by producers and sellers and, in fact, by anyone who holds or can procure "real values".[2]

Compared to working for or selling to the Germans, the markets for French consumers were doubly inferior. They had lower priority and purchasing power, and they were subject to price and ration controls that the Germans routinely flouted. The flow of goods and effort to

---

[1] ABdF 1069201226 24; DGEE, 'Résumés des rapports économiques', ZNO; on raw materials for those working for the Germans in June–July 1941; on paralysis and resort to black market, Oct.–Nov. 1941.

[2] ABdF 1069201226 24, DGEE, 'Résumés des rapports économiques', ZO, Nov. 1941.

serve the Germans and to meet French black-market demand altered standards for behaviour. As illicit transactions became normal practice, greater effort was needed to disguise or hide purchases, quantities and prices. Intermediaries became key players, bringing supply to meet demand. Charles Rist captured the changes in December 1943 in commenting on France's 'material and moral regression' and the reign of 'morally unscrupulous middlemen'.[3]

The most infamous profiteers were the black-market billionaires, Joseph Joinovici and Michel Szkolnikoff. Their spectacular gains made them national symbols of a corrupt and violent economic underworld, serving the Germans, protected from the French police, and gathering intelligence for the Abwehr and the 'French Gestapo' of the rue Lauriston. Their profiles fit the Vichy stereotype of black-market profiteers as un-French: both were immigrants from Eastern Europe, with shady interwar careers, and both were Jews exploiting hardship and depriving French citizens of needed goods.[4]

Their cases merit attention in observing the extremes that illustrate fundamental aspects of the black market for manufactured goods and raw materials, and the difficulties in documenting illicit commerce. German spending in Occupied France totalled 862.5 billion francs; black market purchases were at least 126.7 billion francs (15 per cent), perhaps as high as 200 billion.[5] The Germans relied on French intermediaries to locate and purchase raw materials and finished goods, many having been hoarded as the Occupation started, or produced later for the black market. French intermediaries could tap into local knowledge, make business connections, and allay sellers' concerns about dealing with the Germans. The German purchasing agencies and individual buyers developed an extensive, competitive and anarchic system of purchasing that officials tried to bring under control in 1943, when their spending had run down their occupation funds at the Bank of France.[6]

Vichy propaganda about the black market being foreign and ethnically distinct was a propaganda fiction. The French were early, active and

---

[3] Rist, *Season of Infamy*, 364 (6 Dec. 1943); Rist's phrase was 'intermédiaires sans scrupules'.

[4] Vichy propaganda initially emphasized that foreigners and Jews were responsible for the black market; Grenard, *La France du marché noir*, 65–71.

[5] Sanders, 'Economic Draining', 141, and *Histoire du marché noir*, 170–171.

[6] ***, 'Le marché noir allemand en France', *Cahiers d'histoire de la guerre*, 4 (1950): 63–64; Sanders, *Histoire du marché noir*, 263–272. The German black market is also covered in SAEF B-0049476, DGCE, 'Caractère officiel du marché noir allemand'; 'Le marché noir allemand en France', 26 Oct. 1945; 'Note de la Direction général du contrôle économique concernant les méthodes allemandes employées pendant l'occupation pour détruire l'économie française'; and Lieutenant-Colonel Veltjens, 'Marché noir allemand en France', 15 Jan. 1943.

essential players. The German system to manage penury and exploit French resources was neither well planned nor efficient. The proliferation of new rules, and the impunity with which they could be broken, encouraged improvisation to secure goods, privileges and profit. This chapter considers supply side behaviour: the producers needing materials to manufacture goods, the retailers improvising to replenish stock, and the dealers who connected products and buyers, Rist's 'unscrupulous middlemen'.

Industry in Occupied France

Occupation hit industry much harder than agriculture. The loss of manpower and access to raw materials, energy and transport produced a steep decline in output. Industrial output privileged the materials and finished goods desired by the Germans. Alfred Sauvy's general index for industrial production (1938=100) falls to 65 in 1941, 59 in 1942, 54 in 1943 and 41 in 1944.[7] The general index hides major differences between the sectors working for the Germans, where output did not fall as far, and the sectors of no interest to them. The Germans took a growing share of falling output as the economy was restructured to serve their needs and to restrict the production dependent on foreign trade. French estimates in 1944 of the percentages of activity undertaken for the Germans, although imprecise, show the areas of concentration for German interests (Table 5.1).

Bank of France directors in the Occupied Zone estimated that the Germans were taking 80 per cent of French industrial output in October 1941, indicating their alarm at the extent and efficiency of German exploitation.[8] But working for the Germans gave access to the raw materials and transport needed to produce and move the goods they wanted. 'The French industrialist knew', one official stated, 'that if he worked for Germany he would have orders, receive full payment quickly, and have priority in supplies'.[9] Collaboration allowed businesses to continue producing. The Germans offered business and profit as 'the best

---

[7] Sauvy, *La vie économique*, 239. The postwar review of the French economy in the *Revue d'économie politique* and the INSEE statistical summary for the years 1938 to 1948 do not give industrial production figures for the years 1940 to 1946, but the INSEE volume does provide 'imperfect' index figures for May each year with 1930 = 100: May 1941 = 72; May 1942 = 61; May 1943 = 55; May 1944 = 44. INSEE, *Mouvement économique en France de 1938 à 1948*, 64.

[8] ABdF 1069201226 24, DGEE, 'Résumés des rapports économiques', ZO, Oct. 1941.

[9] André Fanton d'Andon, cited in Richard F. Kuisel, *Capitalism and the State in Modern France: Renovation and Economic Management in the Twentieth Century* (Cambridge: Cambridge University Press, 1981), 141.

Table 5.1 *French Industrial Production for Germany in 1944 that it is in per cent*

Industry	Share of output to Germany
Aeronautics	100
Automobiles and cycles	90
Lime and cement	90
Steel	90
BTP (construction)	85
Naval construction	80
Fuel	80
Iron	70
Electronics	65
Leather and pelts	55
Textiles and clothing	30

Source: Institut de conjoncture, 'Coût pour la France de l'occupation allemande: Bilan approximatif et provisoire au 30 juin 1944' (August 1944). Sauvy was the main author; he gives similar figures, in some cases with lower percentages, in *La vie économique*, 150–163. Rousso provides OCRPI figures that differ slightly, and which he notes overstate output for the Germans in order to obtain more fuel and raw materials, and do not include figures for firms working as subcontractors. Rousso, 'L'économie: pénurie et modernisation', 472.

clients of the moment'.[10] Immediately after defeat, many companies rushed to negotiate deals in order to maintain their output and employment. Collaboration also offered potential for a place in the new European economy serving German masters.[11]

Rather than allocating by price competition in the market, French authorities allocated goods through regulation. They froze prices and gave producers a degree of self-regulation through new sectoral *Comités d'organisation* and a national office for raw materials distribution, the *Office central de répartition des produits industriels* (OCRPI).[12] These committees

[10] Renaud de Rochebrune and Jean-Claude Hazera, *Les patrons sous l'Occupation*, revised ed. (Paris: Odile Jacob, 2013), 297.

[11] Annie Lacroix-Riz stresses the French initiative in seeking these contracts in *Industriels et banquiers sous l'Occupation: La collaboration économique avec le Reich de Vichy* (Paris: Armand Colin, 1999); see also Philippe Burrin, *France under the Germans: Collaboration and Compromise*, trans. by Janet Lloyd (New York: New Press, 1996), 250–261, and Margairaz, *L'État, les finances et l'économie* vol. 1, 591–629.

[12] Kuisel, *Capitalism and the State*, 132–144; Margairaz, *L'État, les finances et l'économie* vol. 1, 511–518 and 570–583; Hervé Joly, ed., *Les comités d'organisation et l'économie dirigée du régime de Vichy* (Caen: Centre de recherche d'histoire quantitative, 2004); and

depended on French state support and German approval. They inserted a layer of French administration between German demands and French industry, in a structure serving German interests.[13] The *Comités d'organisation* allocated goods in the interests of the producers who dominated the committees and the OCRPI. This disadvantaged smaller producers and artisans, who often had to rely on black-market suppliers if they were to work at all.[14] As in agriculture, the state need for information imposed demands for detailed reporting that alienated business owners and generated unreliable data.[15] Robert Catherine explained in 1943 that the authoritarian allocation of essential goods fostered illicit commerce: 'the black market is a fatal corollary of the distribution'. In industry, unlike the 'parallel market' in agriculture that supplied family and friends, raw materials and finished goods *all* went to the black market, either direct from producers or through abuses in the allocation system.[16]

Without access to raw materials through German contracts, firms often bought on the black market to survive, and these purchases required black-market sales to recoup costs.[17] Initially, many manufacturers hoarded supplies to protect against German looting and requisitions. In import-dependent sectors like textiles, hoarded reserves were quickly exhausted. The *Contrôle économique* lamented in 1941 that suppressing illicit activity was difficult because German officials protected their own black-market commerce.[18] In Paris alone, interventions by the infamous Bureau Otto to protect suppliers numbered more than 3000 from 1940 to 1944.[19]

Black-market practices spread, whether or not firms worked for the Germans. The most common practice, under the table payments (*soultes*)

Jean-Guy Mérigot, *Essai sur les comités d'organisation professionnelle* (Paris: Librairie générale de droit et de jurisprudence, 1943).

[13] Arne Radtke-Delacor, 'Die "Gelenkte Wirtschaft" in Frankreich: Versuch einer vergleichenden Untersuchung der technokratischen Strukturen der NS-Besatzungsmacht und des Vichy-Regimes (1940–1944)', in *Figurationen des Staates in Deutschland und Frankreich 1870–1945*, ed. Alain Chatriot and Dieter Gosewinkel (Munich: R. Oldenbourg Verlag, 2006), 251. How this complex, layered system worked for automobile production is explained in Talbot Imlay and Martin Horn, *The Politics of Industrial Collaboration during World War II: Ford France, Vichy and Nazi Germany* (Cambridge: Cambridge University Press, 2014).

[14] Cédric Perrin, 'Les artisans la consommation en période de pénuries', in *Les entreprises de biens de consommation*, 54, 58.

[15] Kuisel, *Capitalism and the State*, 139.

[16] Robert Catherine, 'Répartition et marché noir', *Collection droit social*, XVI (June 1943), 32.

[17] Grenard, *La France du marché noir*, 118–122.

[18] Leménager, 'Étude sur le contrôle des prix', 583–586, 589–594.

[19] SAEF B-0049476, 'Caractère officiel du marché noir allemande', undated; and Rochebrune and Hazera, *Les patrons sous l'Occupation*, 198.

not recorded on receipts, became normal procedure.[20] Accounting practices disguised illicit commerce to evade state control. Former controller Jacques Dez explained the variety of practices used to disguise illicit commerce. The accounts could simply record legal prices rather than the prices paid, or bill for a quantity or quality of goods to increase the seller's gain (overstating the quantity or the quality of the merchandise delivered). They could be imprecise as to details in order to use the same bill for multiple transactions, or they could use a code to disguise the actual price. Receipts could be issued by fictional businesses to make verification impossible.[21] Prices could include excessive costs for packaging. And of course, the simplest method was to issue no receipt at all.[22] Grappling with the problem of accounting fraud in late 1941, Jean de Sailly called for greater effort by the *Contrôle économique* inspectors, as the use of *soultes* and falsified accounts was spreading and would render control impossible, compromising tax collection and leading to the ruin of 'honest businessmen'.[23]

Many firms kept more than one set of books. One Belgian and Dutch company serving the Germans in France claimed its account books had been destroyed by flooding in the Netherlands. Investigators determined in 1946 that the firm had kept two sets of books, an 'A series' for legal transactions and a 'B series' for the illegal (*opérations occultes*).[24] Some firms destroyed records to obstruct prosecution. More often, receipts gave insufficient information to identify firms and prices. An investigation in the Seine-et-Oise in August 1944 found that many records for commerce with the Germans consisted of typed bills, unsigned, 'issued by suppliers with simple names found throughout France, like: DUPONT, DUBOIS, DURAND, DUVAL, MARTIN, MATHIEU, suggests this is something other than a coincidence of surnames'.[25] Honest bookkeeping was rare. The Boucherie Marbeuf, which supplied meat to Paris hotels

---

[20] Grenard, 'La soulte', 29–43.

[21] The *Contrôle économique* found the spread of this practice frustrating but could find no better solution than to ask that controllers submit the names and addresses of such firms so that they could compile a list of non-existent sellers; they noted that services had been set up to supply such false identities. SAEF B-0049888, Note de service no. 120, 19 June 1942.

[22] Dez, 'Économie de pénurie', 150–151.

[23] AD Ille-et-Vilaine 118W/72, director of the *Contrôle des prix* to department heads of service, note commune no. 137 (probably Oct. 1941).

[24] AdP Perotin 3314/71/1/8 56, dossier 1307, 'Rapport d'ensemble', 28 Feb. 1946. Pierre-Antoine Dassaux notes the manipulation of statistics and keeping a secret set of books by the pasta firm Rivoire et Carret in 'Entre espoirs et déceptions: l'industrie des pâtes alimentaires', in Effosse, et al., *Les entreprises de biens de consommation*, 134–137.

[25] SAEF 4A-0000002, Administration of Indirect Taxes, 2ème Direction de Seine-et-Oise, 'Contrôle du chiffre d'affaires de Juvisy', 4 Aug. 1944.

requisitioned by the Germans, was commended after the war for its honest accounting, 'a proof, quite rare during the war, of the sincerity and honesty of their bookkeeping'.[26]

How the accounting fraud worked in practice is evident in specific examples. In the hosiery industry, which sold a large part of its output to the Germans, *soultes* and the use of counterfeit textile ration tickets became standard practice. An investigation in 1942 gathered evidence from retail infractions in Paris to lay charges against twenty *bonnetiers* (makers of stockings and knitted goods) in the Troyes region, who charged premiums from 60 to 700 francs per dozen pairs of silk and rayon stockings. More than 50 per cent of the textile points banked by the Paris retailers were counterfeit. One survey of twenty-four credit agencies storing textile points found that in one week, 74 per cent of the points were counterfeit.[27] The Établissements Marange, a clothing store in Castres (Tarn) developed a system for using official prices on their bills to clients, with *soultes* required for purchases. The cash payments that did not figure on the official receipt were pinned to slips recording the transaction details and destroyed at the end of each day. The supplementary charges were recorded in code using the key CHIEN MORDU, with each letter representing a number from 1 to 0 (thus a 150 franc *soulte* would be recorded as CNU). Controllers checking the store on in July 1941 found slips recording the extra payments with cash attached in a desk drawer. They calculated that supplementary payments from 1 March to 15 July totalled 1.2 million francs, averaging 36.2 per cent above licit prices, plus another one million francs from sales without receipts.[28]

Bicycles became an essential means of transport – for individuals, for state officials, for transit in Paris including by *vélo-taxi*, and even for Occupation forces. Bicycles were subject to rising prices, frequent theft, and an active trade in parts needed for maintenance. Powered by human energy rather than petrochemical, they were in great demand with opportunity to radically increase their output. Alfred Sauvy thought output could easily quadruple and employ 100,000 workers.[29] Annual production prewar had been about one million bicycles.[30] But production fell by

[26] AdP Perotin 3314/71/1/8 16, dossier 342, Robert Firmin to Pieters, undated.

[27] SAEF B-0049512, 'Brigade centrale de Contrôle économique année 1942'.

[28] AN F/12/10511 for documents detailing this case. The state seized clothing and fabric worth 2,350,000 francs and charged the firm with price and accounting infractions.

[29] Service d'observation et conjoncture économique, 'Situation économique no. 1 (vers le 15 Août 1940)'.

[30] Service d'observation et conjoncture économique, 'Situation économique no. 1 (vers le 15 Août 1940)'; postwar statistics stated annual production was 450,000 constructed by bike companies, another 650,000 put together by wholesalers. AN/F/37 119, CCDR, *Automobiles et cycles* (Paris: Imprimerie nationale, 1948).

half in 1941, and it shrank to 200,000 in 1943 and just 100,000 in 1944.[31] The manufacture of parts was concentrated in the region of Saint-Étienne; the parts were shipped to urban retailers for assembly. Producers complained through the *Chambre syndicale des cycles* that their *Comité d'organisation* (for cars and cycles), created in October 1940, distributed only a fraction of the raw materials that the industry had used prewar. They found the *Comité* allocations process incoherent and asked for an explanation of how producers could obtain the metal they needed.[32]

Constraints on bicycle production included not only the limited access to raw materials, but also progressive restrictions on the use of brass, aluminium and copper alloys, and the scarcity of rubber (for tyres) and leather (for saddles). Manufacturers continued production initially by drawing on their stocks of materials, completing orders months after they were placed. They sold bicycles without tyres or saddles because they had no rubber or leather.[33] Smaller firms that assembled bicycles could not respect the prices set for 'standard' models because they no longer had consistent parts and prices from their suppliers.[34] By the autumn of 1943, the industry was in extreme crisis. New bikes for French customers were usually bartered rather than sold.[35] German demands threatened to take most of the French output.[36] Tyres were in extremely short supply, rationed at the department level to ensure they went only to persons with 'an absolute need' and no alternative transport.[37] Consumers riding bicycles to search for extra food bought tyres on the black market at 1,100 to 1,300 francs each in September 1943.[38]

---

[31] SAEF 5A-0000061, Cusin, 'Cycles et motorcycles'.

[32] AN F/12/10831, letter from vice-president of the union to the *Comité d'organisation* for autos and bicycles, 30 June 1941.

[33] ABdF 1069199311 20, Bank of France director in Saint-Étienne monthly report of 2 Apr. 1941.

[34] ABdF 1069199311 20, Saint-Étienne monthly reports, 2 Jan., 2 May and 4 Aug. 1941.

[35] ABdF 1069199311 20, Saint-Étienne monthly reports, 7 June, 3 Aug., 1 Sept. and 1 Oct. 1943.

[36] They demanded 35,000 new bicycles per month in 1943 (more than 75 per cent of French production) and 300,000 new bicycles in 1944; the numbers were negotiated down, German direct orders amounting to 11 per cent of output in 1943 and 31.6 per cent in 1944. AN F/37/119, CCDR, *Automobiles et cycles*.

[37] AD Manche 2Z/308, prefect notices to mayors and sub-prefects concerning bicycle tyre distribution, 1 Sept. and 23 Oct. 1941, 21 Mar. 1942.

[38] Using a bicycle to bring food from the countryside was the theme of a 1943 song, 'On Two Wheels'. The final chorus proclaimed, 'Avec deux pneus, et deux sacoches/On oublie tout sous le ciel bleu/Vers la campagne la plus proche/Gaiement on roule et ça va mieux/Un p'tit cousin nous remplit les poches/Et l'on revient, l'estomac moins creux/Avec deux pneus, et deux sacoches/On s'ravitaille, on est heureux!' [On two wheels with two panniers/We leave our cares behind/Bike to the nearest countryside/Gaily we go to find/A little cousin to fill our pouches/Then home we go, less empty/On two wheels with

State officials in rural areas relied on bicycles for their official duties. For mayors, police, controllers, postmen and food supply officials, bicycles became the essential means of transport. In the Seine-et-Oise, police were allocated one tyre per bicycle per year for state-owned bicycles. Of poor quality, one official tyre might last two to three months.[39] Municipal employees obtained tyre purchase coupons if their bicycle was essential to their work and if their need, based on the wear on their tyres, was rated 'indispensable'.[40]

The black market for bicycle parts flourished, with manufacturers buying materials and selling parts on terms that reflected the scarcity and strong demand.[41] The number of small producers with specialized products and the focus on manufacturing parts facilitated illicit trade and resistance to German demands for 'concentration'. Manufacturers bartered to obtain parts; one in 1941 shipped food parcels to his suppliers.[42] The shortage of parts meant bicycles were no longer constructed according to the model specifications for which the CO had set prices. The Bank of France reported a thriving black market, especially in spare parts; 'the bicycle has become a medium of exchange'.[43] Even priests, needing bicycles to serve rural parishes, paid a premium. The curé in Dampniat ordered a man's bicycle, official price 1640 francs. He received a woman's bicycle 'cadre 55 type B' for 2120 francs. It was delivered by the firm owner, who refused to give him a receipt or allow him to try the bike, telling him he was lucky to have it, as it was worth 6500 francs on the black market.[44]

The shoe industry suffered acute crisis. Military demand for leather made raw hides a black-market commodity in high demand; clandestine slaughter supplied black-market meat and hides. France had manufactured 69 million pairs of shoes in 1938. This fell to 35.4 million in 1942, and 18.7 million in 1944, with a large percentage produced under contract for the Germans. Less than half were made with leather in 1942 and 1943.[45] Célia Bertin commented that leather for shoes was not

two panniers/Content, with food aplenty!] With thanks to Erin for this translation. Copy in AN/AB/ XIX/ 4114.

[39] AD Yvelines 1W/10, Chief Inspector, Head of Regional Public Security, to the prefect of the Seine-et-Oise, 6 Nov. 1943; AD Manche 1370W/134, Police de Granville report of 15 Nov. 1943; Gendarmerie nationale, Seine-et-Oise, 'Synthèse' for Sept. 1943.

[40] AD Manche 2Z/308, prefect of la Manche to mayors and sub-prefects, 23 Oct. 1941.

[41] AN F/12/10831, Ott (Chief Engineer for the District of Lyon) to Lehideux (director of the Comité d'organisation for automobiles and cycles), 4 June 1941.

[42] AN BB/18/3388, case 7361 A41.

[43] ABdF 1069199311 20, director in Saint-Étienne, monthly report, 4 Aug. 1941.

[44] SAEF B-0049524, Curé Sauceras to M. le Directeur, 24 Aug. 1943. He added a postscript that the owner's father, as the two drove away, must have commented 'What a fool, that curé'.

[45] SAEF B-0057658, 'Étude sur la structure économique au point de vue du jeu de la concurrence: Industries du cuir', 30 Sept. 1948. The Revue d'économie politique's postwar

'unfindable' but 'the object of a costly black market'.[46] Shoe rationing began in January 1941 and the system put in place, like that for clothing, fostered extensive abuse. Rationing based on need required accurate knowledge of what consumers owned, and how urgently their shoes and clothing needed replacement. Retailers developed means to evade or defy the rationing rules. One report, trying to fix the rationing system in 1945, argued that basing the system on firm inventories in 1941 had rendered control more difficult from the outset. The author titled the section on the controls to ration shoes and clothing 'The control is impossible.'[47]

Manufacturers had trouble obtaining leather, nails, glue, needles and thread. Bank of France directors reported on the difficulties in 1940, and consumer frustration when they queued at town halls to prove their urgent need for permits to acquire shoes, then found no shoes in stores. Plans negotiated with the Germans for textile and leather goods in 1941 included a commitment to deliver 3.4 million pairs of ladies and children's shoes to the Germans.[48] German authorities seized stocks of raw material and soldiers bought up retail supplies. Chaussures Pillot, which had struggled to survive in the Depression, thrived during the Occupation, selling 75 per cent of its boots to the Germans by official figures, and probably more through black-market sales.[49] By 1942, depleted French supplies allowed an adult in a city just one new pair of shoes every four years. Children aged one to three were allowed three pairs each year; the low-quality materials meant the shoes lasted two to four months.[50] Wooden-soled *galoches* were an affliction for boys, as the soles often broke in rough play.[51] The clack of the wooden-soled 'chaussure nationale' on pavement became a signature sound of street life in

summary of the war years gave no annual figures for most industrial output in the war years, but for shoes gave figures for the pairs produced in 1938 and in 1944; rubber-soled shoes fell from 43,650,000 pairs to 6 million; leather-soled shoes from 20 million to 3,350,000. S. Béracha, 'La production industrielle', *Revue d'économie politique* 57 (1947): 1272.

[46] Bertin, *Femmes sous l'Occupation*, 85.

[47] AN F/1a/3248, prefect of the Loire, 'Rationnement des articles textiles et des chaussures', 18 Jan. 1945.

[48] The Plan Kehrl for textiles and Plan Grunberg for leather goods allocated a large proportion of French inventory and new production to Germany; Margairaz, *L'État, les finances et l'économie*, 609–613.

[49] Sanders, *Histoire du marché noir*, 178, 208–212; based on the Affaire Aubaut dossier in AdP, 1320W/85.

[50] AN F/12/10189, 'Étude sur la distribution des produits chaussants', sent by J. E. J. Fenestrier to M. Rouquier, directeur du commerce intérieur, 23 June 1943. The shoe allocation in the Pas-de-Calais allowed adults one pair of shoes every eighteen months, and 6,000 children were unable to attend school in late 1941 because they had no shoes. AN AJ/41/386 (Pas-de-Calais), prefect monthly reports of 4 Nov. 1941 and 3 Dec. 1941.

[51] Interview with Jean-Louis Hautcoeur, Paris, 22 May 2015.

Occupied Paris. Maurice Chevalier captured the moment with his refrain, 'I love the tap-tap of wooden soles.'[52]

The competition to obtain leather pitted consumer needs against German military demand. Leather for gloves was allocated, by 1943, exclusively for German purchase.[53] German purchasing offices bought vast quantities of hides from illicitly slaughtered cattle and hogs on the black market, often at ten times the official price. Hides shipped to Germany from the docks at Saint-Ouen outside Paris averaged 1,200 tonnes per month. German authorities protected the traffic, releasing arrested traffickers and taking the hides seized by French police.[54] French shoe manufacturers used any artificial and substitute materials they could find; wooden soles, most notably, to replace leather and rubber, and a variety of experimental materials that included artificial fabrics, waxed paper, felt, straw, fish skin, and a wood fibre mixed with 'xanthégénate' – a substance of which no one knew the composition.[55]

The importance of the black market for a firm to maintain output, increase profits and serve German demand is well-documented in a postwar illicit profits investigation of a surprising field for war production: cosmetics. The firm involved had been caught and fined for black-market sales and falsified accounts in 1943. They reported losses in 1942, 1943 and 1945. In the illicit profits investigation in 1947, the production manager estimated that four-fifths of the company's wartime output had been off the book for black-market sale, with considerable profit.[56] The owner admitted that when raw materials could only be obtained on the black market, he had authorized sales on the 'lateral market' to cover the cost of black-market materials.[57] The production manager said he had been instructed to buy raw materials 'in any way possible, even the

---

[52] Michel, *Paris allemand*, 230; lyrics 'J'aime le tap-tap des semelles en bois' from 'La symphonie des semelles en bois', sung by Chevalier in 1943.

[53] Florent Le Bot, 'Confisquer les profits illicites?' in Bergère, ed., *L'épuration économique en France* (Rennes: Presses universitaires de Rennes, 2008), 290. The postwar commission to assess damages found that leather available to French consumers during the Occupation averaged 19 per cent of prewar needs. The market in France had been reduced by 582,000 tonnes in lost imports and 225,000 tonnes taken by the Germans. AN F/37/120, CCDR, *Cuirs et pelleteries* (Paris: Imprimerie nationale, 1948), 45.

[54] AN BB/35/80, Régis Ribes to Jacques Barnaud, 5 Sept. 1942; SAEF 1A-0000402, de Sailly to Befehlshaber the commander of the security police (Sicherheitspolizei), undated, reporting 157 tonnes of hides from the Gironde, Mayenne, and Maine-et-Loire in illicit traffic protected by the Germans in 1942 and early 1943.

[55] Veillon, *La mode sous l'Occupation*, 83–96. For xanthégénate as an unknown substance, Henri Michel, *Paris allemand* (Paris: Albin Michel, 1981), 230.

[56] AdP Perotin 3314/71/1/8 44; report by M. Chevallier, inspector for Indirect Taxes, 19 Nov. 1944. The documentation for this case is unusually rich because the production manager had a falling-out with the owner and left the firm.

[57] AdP Perotin/3314/71/1/8 44; 'Exposé', undated (stamped with date the 22 Nov. 1954).

black market' and to sell output on the black market without issuing receipts.[58] German purchasing, especially after the ban on wearing lipstick in Germany ended in 1942, took an increasing share of the black market sales. Two German buyers (Brandt and Hamel) bought 2,210,000 tubes of lipstick from early 1943 to August 1944, with workers doing night shifts to produce one million tubes for Brandt in June 1944.[59] The initial CCPI decision in July 1948 confiscated 250 million francs in illicit profits and fined the owner 375 million francs.[60]

The incoherence in German black-market policy is unintentionally evident in the reports by Lieutenant-Colonel Josef Veltjens, who tried to bring coherence and efficiency to German purchasing. In May 1942 Hermann Göring appointed Veltjens, a First World War flying ace and friend, to end the 'anarchy' of German purchasing in France, Belgium, the Netherlands and Serbia.[61] Veltjens argued that by centralizing purchasing, he could exhaust black-market supplies for the Reich's military needs on the best financial terms, and end the competition between German purchasers and the corruption in military and civilian administrations. He would organize black-market purchasing and prohibit the independent purchases by 'all civilians, companies, also German authorities, units of the German Wehrmacht or other organizations' who were using the black market.[62]

In January 1943, Veltjens reported on his success. He claimed that German troops had been powerless to stop the spread of black markets in occupied territory, which predated their arrival. But he attributed the growth of black-market activity to purchasing by German military units buying black-market goods they could not obtain in Germany. This purchasing reached such proportions that military authorities could not control its growth or abstain from bidding against each other. Veltjens established offices in each occupied country to coordinate purchasing and prices. He reported the total spending on black market goods from July through November 1942 (RM 1,107,792,818.64, of which RM 929,100,000, 84 per cent, in France), and included an evaluation of the *Weihnachtsaktion* (Christmas Action) in 1942, which purchased RM 244 million of gifts in France to send to Germany – including cosmetics and toys. Ultimately, Veltjens advised that Germany should continue

---

[58] AdP Perotin/3314/71/1/8 57, dossier 1344, report dated 31 Mar. 1949.

[59] AdP Perotin/3314/71/1/8 44; 'Exposé', undated.

[60] The confiscation and fine were reduced in 1954 to 195,289,214 francs, based on recalculation of the firm's illicit sales.

[61] Sanders, *Histoire du marché noir*, 234–252.

[62] BA-MA Freiburg RW 19 2397, Veltjens, 'Bevollmächtigte für Sonderaufgaben am Beauftragten für den Vierjahresplan', 21 May 1942.

black-market purchase of hoarded stocks until they were exhausted. He concluded that ending the black market required harsher control and punishment by national authorities (justice, police, and economic controllers). He did not explain how the French could do this when the Germans protected their own black-market traffic from enforcement by French police.[63]

German authorities did curtail black-market use in 1943. Hermann Göring announced on 2 April 1943 that purchasing agencies would be closed and that 'All black purchases ... must cease, effective immediately.'[64] Official agencies like the Bureau Otto closed, but unofficial purchasing continued on a substantial scale.[65] The German black-market use had multiple repercussions. It reduced supplies available to French consumers, raised prices, fostered networks of French *trafiquants*, encouraged illicit production and transport, compromised French policing efforts, and delegitimized French controls. The change in German policy and the closer collaboration it required with French officials to suppress the black market further discredited French controllers.[66] Black-market practice could not be ended by decree.

Company Canteens

Workplace canteens became an important source for food to boost the productivity of undernourished employees and to retain workers offered better wages and food access in German-run factories. During the economic slump after defeat in 1940, the state encouraged the creation of factory canteens to feed not only workers, but the unemployed and workers' families as well. The need increased as the enduring nature of shortages became clearer in 1941.[67] As well as encouraging their creation, the state set strict accounting standards for supplies and ration tickets to ensure that canteens ran on a non-profit basis and sold no food outside the canteens.[68] As the food situation deteriorated, prefects warned of

[63] SAEF B-0049476, Veltjens, 'Rapport fondé sur l'expérience du délégué pour les missions spéciales', 15 Jan. 1943.
[64] AN 3W/90, Document 760, interview of Jean Michel Boreux on 30 Jan. 1948; and AN F/37/4, 'Entretien du 2 avril 1943 à l'Hôtel Majestic'.
[65] Milward, *The New Order*, 140–146; Grenard, *La France du marché noir*, 188–193; Sanders, *Histoire du marché noir*, 263–272.
[66] Mouré, 'La capitale de la faim', 329–333, for the control effort using 'German methods'; Grenard, *La France du marché noir*, 194–203, for the modest results of collaboration.
[67] CAC 39AS/391, A. Parodi for the Secretary of State for Industrial Production and Labour, 16 Aug. 1940, and R. Belin, Secretary of State for Labour, 31 Dec. 1941.
[68] See Grenard, *La France du marché noir*, 113–115, and 'La question du ravitaillement', in Chevandier and Daumas, *Travailler dans les entreprises*, 398–402. The new regulations are detailed in notes from René Belin (Secrétaire d'Etat au Travail) to prefects, labour

increasing need for the canteens. The process to create new canteens was simplified, and canteens and the number of workers they served increased. The prefect of the Rhône anticipated in 1942 that the number of workers eating in factory canteens in Lyon, Saint-Étienne and Grenoble would triple from October to December.[69]

Firms developed innovative purchasing methods to feed their workers. The *Ravitaillement général* was responsible for supply, but with serious food shortages, the canteens were encouraged to buy their own vegetables and to grow gardens to feed workers. In northern departments under German administration, firms bought black-market food to distribute to workers at a loss or as salary supplements.[70] The number of workers served in canteens in the Nord doubled from May to November 1942.[71] In February 1943, the Ministry of Agriculture reported that 500,000 workers obtained meals in French factories and another 300,000 in German arms factories.[72] Workers wanted the canteens to be managed honestly and at cost (no profit to the firm); they were needed to deal with the impossibility, otherwise, of getting enough food.[73]

The authority given to canteens for the purchase and transport of food opened significant opportunities to develop black-market traffic. In July 1941, one administrator saw factory cooperatives and canteens as 'ideal terrain for the black market'.[74] The December 1941 state explanation for canteen privileges specified that the foods purchased 'must be used exclusively for the preparation of meals and must never be distributed or sold as goods to be taken away'.[75] Such admonitions were of little concern to those managing the food supplies.

Firms with vehicles and permits could purchase food direct from farms, opening opportunities for abuse of the privileges at every level. The Bank of France canteen, which had served 700 staff lunches daily before the war, served more than 2,000 daily in 1943. In July 1943, a Bank truck with an authorization to transport used bank notes back to Paris was stopped at a roadblock and found to be carrying ten tons of sugar and

inspectors, directors of food supply, etc., 31 Dec. 1941, Secretary of State for Food Supply to prefects and food supply directors, 29 Dec. 1941, copies in CAC 39AS/391.
[69] AD Rhône 182W/3, prefect to the regional prefect, undated, likely Oct. 1942; he forecast the number of workers needing meals would rise from 40,000 to 129,000.
[70] AN AJ/41/342, 'La mentalité dans la "zone interdite"', 22 Aug. 1941.
[71] AN AJ/41/384 (Nord), prefect monthly reports, 3 June and 5 Dec. 1942.
[72] AN F/37/4, Reinhardt notice on the authorization of new canteens sent by the Minister of Agriculture to Casanoue, 18 Feb. 1943.
[73] APP 220W 11, 'Situation à Paris', 11 Jan. 1943, reproducing a report by the Comité d'études économiques et syndicales, 'La création des cantines-coopératives professionnelles ou interprofessionnelles'.
[74] Grenard, *La France du marché noir*, 114.
[75] CAC 39AS/391, Belin letter of 31 Dec. 1941.

864 litres of eau-de-vie. The transport papers had been signed by the director of the staff buffet. The press suggested that the Bank regularly made such purchases, to be resold in Paris for huge profit. One newspaper claimed the Bank was 'one of the most important black-market organizations in France'.[76] Police in Argenteuil (just outside Paris) reported that canteens in metal industry factories, established to show management concern for their workers' welfare, served as cover for black-market activity for the owners' profit.[77] The SNCF and PTT canteens fed thousands of workers. Their abuses provoked multiple citations for infractions that included the purchase of illicitly slaughtered meat, the transport of foods without authorization, and possession of illicit stocks of meat.[78]

The canteen for workers at the firm Pétroles Jupiter in Rouen provides an example of how efforts to feed workers could evolve into larger-scale traffic. They created the canteen in early 1942 to feed 200 workers. The employee assigned to buy vegetables locally to supplement their official supply (through the *Groupement de restaurateurs* in Rouen) made arrangements with a butcher in Etreville (Eure) to buy 100 kg of meat each week. In the summer of 1942 he went a step further, setting up a clandestine abattoir on company property, and began purchasing animals locally, bought butchering tools and hired a butcher. Meat in excess of the canteen needs was sold in a shop in the nearby town of Petit-Couronne.[79]

In January 1943, food supply and Sûreté officials raided the abattoir and found two calves being butchered and 75 kg of meat. The Sûreté charged seven men including the administrative director of Pétroles Jupiter, two butchers and two farmers. The butcher in Petit-Couronne was also arrested for selling meat from the illicit slaughter. The prefect interned the men and recommended terms of six months to one year. Although he admitted that the canteen buyer was not really a 'black market *trafiquant*', he believed a lesson was needed for business leaders using illicit means to feed their workers, 'without concern for the repercussions of their actions on food supply for the general population'.[80]

[76] ABdF 1060200101 71 for Bank of France documentation of the Affaire Hubert, and press reports in SAEF B-0049602; quote from *Aujourd'hui*, 5 July 1943.

[77] AD Yvelines 1W/10, Intendance de la Police de Seine-et-Oise et Seine-et-Marne, 9 Aug. 1943: 'The canteens and cooperatives serve too often to hide black market activity for the profit of the bosses and their immediate circle', and 'Enquête dans les usines métallurgiques', 6 Aug. 1943.

[78] SAEF B-0057660, L. Cruse, 'Note pour Monsieur le Directeur du Cabinet', 23 Jan. 1945, and a list of SNCF infractions in L. Cruse, 'Note au Ministre: Transports irréguliers de denrées ou produits contingents effectués pour le compte de la S.N.C.F.', 26 May 1945.

[79] AD Seine-Maritime 40W/130, 'Affaire Boudin' documents, Jan. and Feb. 1943.

[80] AD Seine-Maritime 40W/130, delegate prefect to the regional prefect, 1 Feb. 1943.

The firm's administrative director claimed he was unaware of the abattoir and the sales of meat (the Sûreté stated meat was sent to the Jupiter head office in Paris). The mayor and citizens of Petit-Couronne protested the internment of their town butcher and the closing of his shop; a citizens' petition claimed that 'everyone' knew about the sales, including RG officials.[81] Food supply officials charged that the Sûreté inspectors helped themselves to the confiscated meat, and the CE objected that their investigation had been obstructed by 'external interventions'. The case was reviewed in Paris by a *Commission interministérielle* that ordered the release of all the men involved.[82]

The Pétroles Jupiter case, unusual for its scale of black-market sales, was typical in its effort to meet local needs and its support from local residents. Civil engineer Victor Guillermin worked for the Société anonyme des Hauts-Fourneaux de la Chiers in Longwy (Moselle, near the Franco-Belgian border). Of food distribution in the factory canteen, he observed that the management ate much better than the workers, and that the men who organized the distribution of ration cards took extra cards for their families. In early 1944 the company was selling a significant part of its output off the books and using the profits in part to buy food for the canteen.[83] Guillermin referred to the Belgians in charge of the food rationing as 'the kings of the black market' and commented: 'Dealing directly or indirectly with the handling of food supplies has *many* advantages.'[84]

In addition to providing food in canteens, employers paid workers in kind, with raw materials or finished goods. In-kind payments supplemented wages that could not be raised when the cost of living climbed. Goods in high demand could be exchanged for things workers needed, food in particular, and also encouraged the barter economy that overlapped with 'honest' black-market activity seeking essentials for everyday life. The Dunlop factory in Montluçon paid workers in part with bicycle tyres.[85] The Michelin plants near Clermont-Ferrand established gardens to help feed workers, paid workers partly with tyres, which they could exchange for food and scarce goods, and traded tyres and inner tubes with

---

[81] Cédric Perrin cites a case of similar community protest in a village near Tours, when a butcher was arrested for illicit slaughter. They argued this was not black market as he sold to the needy in the community at prices below their official level. Cédric Perrin, 'Les artisans de la consommation', 52.

[82] AD Seine-Maritime 40W/130; P. Dubuisson, 'Note pour Monsieur le Préfet régional sur l'affaire d'abattage clandestin de Petit-Couronne', 17 Apr. 1943, and regional prefect to the delegate prefect, 19 Apr. 1943.

[83] IHTP ARC 091, Guillermin agendas, 3 Sept. 1942; 23 to 26 Oct. 1942; 3 Apr. 1944.

[84] IHTP ARC 091, Guillermin agendas, 29 July 1944, emphasis in original.

[85] Grenard, 'La question du ravitaillement', 397.

other firms in a vast barter system that accumulated a massive hoard of food supplies, discovered by food supply officials in 1945.[86] The state tobacco monopoly decided in 1942 to allocate monthly cigarette quotas to all its workers to reduce theft, regardless of whether they smoked or not, and including women who were not eligible for tobacco rations (women received 6 packets per month; men received 10).[87] The decision reflected the value of cigarettes for barter, providing all employees with this supplement. Most of these payments, as well as employee thefts (which increased in worksites producing tradeable goods), remain largely invisible. Artisans producing goods in smaller workshops used barter and payment in kind for their black-market traffic, particularly those preparing foods.[88] Paying workers in tradeable goods also helped to compensate them for the freeze on wages, and gave private sector workers an advantage over civil servants in their common quest to obtain essential goods.[89]

Retail Commerce

In the summer of 1940 French consumers hastened to buy goods they feared would disappear, and German soldiers snapped up food, clothing and consumer goods that were scarce in Germany. Initial German policy was one of plunder: seize military resources to defeat Britain and win the war in the West, requisition stocks, and encourage soldiers to purchase consumer goods for themselves and their families.[90] French officials remarked on the German greed for goods. Their shopping sprees were encouraged by the shortages in Germany, the opportunity to ship goods home for free, their spending allowances, and an exchange rate that overvalued the German mark. Even the German soldiers were surprised. Martin Meier, a twenty-two-year-old from Berlin, sent his wife thirteen packages (to keep within the weight limit for parcels without charge), telling her on 4 July that 'All the stores are already empty. You can't imagine all the stuff the German soldiers are buying.'[91] Their purchasing benefited from the exaggerated occupation cost payments, initially

---

[86] Grenard, 'La question du ravitaillement', 405; André Gueslin, ed., *Les hommes du pneu: Les ouvriers Michelin à Clermont-Ferrand de 1940 à 1980* (Paris: Éditions de l'atelier/Les éditions ouvrières, 1999), 294, 297–298.

[87] SAEF B-0061904, *Comité technique* meeting of 24 Mar. 1942.

[88] Perrin, 'Les artisans de la consommation', 49–51.

[89] ABdF 1069201226 26, DGEE, 'Résumés des rapports économiques', ZO, Mar. 1943.

[90] Boldorf and and Scherner, 'France's Occupation Costs', 314. They estimate that nearly half the German material gains in 1940 were via 'war loot' (plunder).

[91] Aurélie Luneau, Jeanne Guérout and Stefan Martens, eds., *Comme un Allemand en France : Lettres inédites sous l'Occupation 1940–1944* (Paris : L'Iconoclaste, 2016), 50–53, and letters from Heinz Rahe, 58–59, Ernst Guicking, 82 and Gottfried S., 94–95.

400 million francs per day.[92] The Germans did not have to queue for service and shopkeepers welcomed their zeal to purchase almost any goods, at any price.

But replenishing empty shelves proved difficult. Parisian department stores sought goods in the Unoccupied Zone. The Paris police reported in September 1940 that commerce found it impossible to resupply; stocks were rapidly exhausted and many articles were no longer available.[93] When news spread in early 1941 that clothing would be rationed on a points system, consumers rushed to buy all the clothing they could find.[94] The shortages of fuel limited available transport to bring new stock, and power shortages in 1941 required moving goods from store interiors to be near windows to save on electricity, and the early closing of stores in December 1941.[95] In September 1941, Bank of France directors reported that resupply was all but impossible without recourse to illicit traffic, especially for clothing and shoes: 'only the houses that restock using the black market and sell merchandise fraudulently, without tickets, can maintain a regular flow of sales as winter approaches. The others will soon have to cease business.'[96]

Commerce adapted to the new circumstances, including serving German needs, and obtained stock from Jewish-owned stores 'aryanized' by the Vichy administration.[97] Bankruptcies and liquidations fell sharply.[98] Remarkably, with fewer goods available, the numbers of stores increased. Opening a business gave new shop owners an opportunity to purchase goods wholesale, and to keep them for personal use, including to barter for food. For goods sold to customers, they needed to make higher profit. Bank of France directors commented on the paradox that stores with fewer

---

[92] Pierre Arnoult, 'Comment, pour acheter notre économie, les Allemands prirent nos finances (1940–1944)', *Cahiers d'histoire de la guerre*, 4 (1950): 1–28.

[93] APP 220W 1, 'Situation à Paris du 10 au 16 septembre' (1940). Noted as well by Bank of France directors; ABdF, 1069201226 22, DGEE, 'Résumés des rapports économiques', ZO, Aug.–Oct. 1940.

[94] APP 220W 3, 'Situation à Paris' reports for 3 and 31 Mar. 1941; APP 220W 4, 'Situation à Paris' report for 5 May 1941, noting that Au Bon Marché had laid off 500 staff and expected to lay off a further 400. On the implementation of clothes rationing, see Veillon, *La mode sous l'Occupation*, 107–110.

[95] APP 220W 6, 'Situation à Paris', 8 Dec. 1941.

[96] ABdF, 1069201226 24, DGEE 'Résumés des rapports économiques', ZO, Sept. 1941.

[97] On aryanizations, see Philippe Verheyde, *Les mauvais comptes de Vichy: L'aryanisation des entreprises juives* (Paris: Perrin, 1999); Jean-Marc Dreyfus, *Pillages sur ordonnances: Aryanisation et restitution des banques en France 1940–1953* (Paris: Fayard, 2003); Florent Le Bot, *La fabrique réactionnaire: Antisémitisme, spoliations et corporatisme dans le cuir (1930–1950)* (Paris: Presses de la FNSP, 2007); and the summary in Grenard et al., *Histoire économique de Vichy*, 239–263.

[98] INSEE, *Mouvement économique en France de 1938 à 1948*, Table 39, 249. For bankruptcies, the monthly average had been 508 in 1929 and 402 in 1938. This fell to 77 in 1940 and 1942, and to 44, 46 and 40 in the years 1943, 1944 and 1945.

goods and shorter hours seemed to earn substantial profits. 'If the black market is a domain apart – and ever growing – the frontiers separating it from the regular market are not clearly defined .... Regular commerce declines from day to day, while occult transactions continually increase under the pressure of urgent needs and assisted by the insufficiency of the penalties for its use.'[99] Enterprising owners diversified their product lines to profit from unsatisfied demand. One enterprising grocer in Surgères (Charente-Maritime), arrested in April 1942, faced charges covering a full range of black-market offences: illegal extension of commerce, illegal increase in prices, illicit stocks of merchandise, payment of *soultes*, and the violation of rationing and receipt requirements. The goods confiscated from his shop were valued at 7 to 8 million francs, included fabric and clothing worth more than 4 million francs, vast quantities of alcohol, and diverse foods including 3,800 cans of asparagus and 1,200 cans of pâté.[100]

In both zones, clandestine commerce drew heavily on farm produce and commercial stocks, with 'scandalous fortunes' earned in the exchange of goods even when official prices were recorded on paper. Textiles in the Troyes region provide a representative example. The Bank of France reported in July 1941 that manufacturers no longer had to worry about attracting customer orders with rebates or discounts, or reduce the price on damaged goods, or worry about product variety and packaging. Everything sold.[101] The Bank also noted the 'singular degradation of commercial practices' as black-market activity and barter increased. 'All the markets are distorted, stocks are declining, and more important are being hidden, and individual ingenuity is such that authorities find they are powerless to stop this trend, which is causing so much harm to the country.' There was no way to measure the volume of commerce in legal and illegal markets, and there was no question that the latter were gaining ground.[102] A postwar report on illicit profits in textiles found black-market practice at all levels of production, from owners selling with *soultes* and fraudulent billing, to workers, foremen, and accountants: 'Everyone takes part: associates, directors, multiple middlemen, carriers, retailers, down to the firm's caretaker (one deposited one million francs in the currency exchange).'[103]

'The ingenuity of individuals' is the key phrase. This ingenuity means on the one hand that generalizations do not capture the variety and pervasiveness of shopkeeper adaptations, within and outside the rules set by the state. On

[99] ABdF, 1069201226 26, DGEE, 'Résumés des rapports économiques', ZO, Jan. 1943.
[100] AN AJ/41/368 (Charente-Maritime), prefect monthly report, 25 Apr. 1942.
[101] ABdF, 1069201226 24, DGEE, 'Résumés des rapports économiques', ZO, July 1941; ZNO, June-July 1941.
[102] ABdF, 1069201226 24, DGEE, 'Résumés des rapports économiques', ZO, Aug. 1941.
[103] SAEF 30D-0000004, 'Note sur le comité de confiscation de l'Aube', 12 July 1946.

the other hand, the creative energy fostered innovations. The new practices to resolve shortages and evade regulation were seldom recorded by the shop-keepers and are only partially revealed in the state efforts to suppress black market activity. For rationed goods, shopkeepers had to keep account of ration tickets and, for many scarce goods, sell only to registered customers. The infractions caught and punished by controllers were most often small in scale, and punished shopkeepers more often than farmers, manufacturers or consumers.[104] The most common offences, as illustrated by the grocer above, concerned prices, quantities and failures in paperwork. Control enforcement punished either the price and quantity infractions or the failure to follow requirements for transactions records (leaving no evidence).

When caught with stock for which they had no receipts, shopkeepers often claimed that they did not know the person from whom they had bought goods and had no receipt. They evaded restrictions by bartering goods without the use of cash or ration tickets, which further complicated the difficulties for controllers seeking evidence. The Gendarmerie com-mented in 1943, 'The inventive genius of crooked sellers renews itself incessantly to throw off the police services.'[105] Controllers caught per-haps one offence in ten, and imposed penalties often less than the profits gained from illicit commerce. The Gendarmerie declared that the frequent use of 'transactions' as penalties had 'failed irremediably'. One *trafiquant* shrugged off his fine with the comment, 'After all, what is a transaction? . . . it's all part of the profits and losses.'[106]

Serving customer demand and escaping state control created a dynamic for innovation that focused on the critical stage of moving goods between producers and customers. Many infractions did not draw significant profit but provided the remuneration necessary to produce and deliver goods to alternative markets. These markets drew goods of higher quality and delivered them to friends, family and French consumers. Increasingly, parallel markets were justified on patriotic grounds. For residents in the Nord and the Pas-de-Calais, under military administra-tion from Brussels, the Occupation recalled local experience in the First World War. Industrial collaboration was required, but some manufactur-ers tried from the outset to deliver as little as possible to the Germans: 'The black market is elevated to the rank of a patriotic institution'.[107]

[104] Grenard, *La France du marché noir*, 313.
[105] AN AJ/41/395, 'Synthèse relative à l'état moral et matériel de la population dans les territoires de la zone occupée au cours du mois de Mai 1943'.
[106] AN AJ/41/395, 'Synthèse relative à l'état moral et matériel de la population dans les territoires de la zone occupée', reports for April and July 1943.
[107] AN AJ/41/342, 'La mentalité dans la "Zone Interdite"', 22 Aug. 1941, emphasis in original.

By 1943 such sentiments had spread across France, fashioning the black market as a way to keep goods out of German hands. It could justify exchanges within families, direct sales from farms, and serve as an excuse for profit from scarcity and for the wealthy to enjoy black market luxuries. François Maspero's rich uncle in *Le sourire du chat* polishes off his meals with the self-satisfied claim, 'Another one the Boches won't get.' Escaping the queues, the hunger and the insecurity of daily life that were the lot for most French citizens, Maspero's uncle claims, was a form of patriotism: 'Getting food on the black market, in all good faith, that is his resistance.'[108] Black marketeers rejected Vichy regulations and authority that disadvantaged producers, retailers and consumers. For Gertrude Stein and Alice B. Toklas, living during the Occupation in the department of the Ain, between Lyon and the Swiss border, 'the blessed black market' supplemented their inadequate rations. Local shopkeepers who sold black-market goods 'said it was their patriotic duty to sell what the Germans forbade. In which case was it not mine to purchase what they offered?'[109]

Black-market meals in restaurants illustrate the challenges for state control and the variety of ruses to evade controllers. The state set rules for the quantities of food served and prices for restaurant meals in 1940, and in May 1941 established restaurant categories from A to D with specific price ranges and meal composition.[110] Restaurant owners had to conform to regulations governing prices, rations, days without, and to collect ration tickets, post daily menus, keep record of their menus for two weeks, provide accurate written receipts to customers, and keep receipts for their purchases. The new requirements needed close surveillance; the number of restaurants made this difficult. The contraction of food supplies reaching Paris in late 1940 and the demand from customers wanting adequate meals made illicit commerce inevitable. The Paris police admitted in November 1940 that the decline in meat delivery to Paris required restaurants either to reduce their menus drastically or to resort to the black market.[111] Control operations, reported weekly by Paris police, found widespread infractions. Customers wanted food that

---

[108] François Maspero, *Le sourire du chat* (Paris: Éditions du Seuil, 1984), 137.

[109] Alice B. Toklas, *The Alice B. Toklas Cookbook* (New York: Harper and Brothers, 1954), 205, 212.

[110] The lowest category D restaurants could charge up to 18 francs for a meal, category A from 35 to 50 francs. A fifth 'exceptional' category, charging up to 75 francs, was added in July 1941, and six Paris restaurants serving the Germans were exempt from all rules, 'hors catégorie', from Nov. 1941 to June 1942. Special status and exemptions continued for many restaurants serving the Germans. Mouré, 'La capitale de la faim', 317.

[111] AN AJ/41/2147, Col. de Mazerat, 'Situation des restaurants à Paris', 8 Nov. 1940.

owners could obtain only on the black market, and willingly paid extra to cover the cost. If rationing measures were strictly observed, most Paris restaurants would have to close.[112]

The German authorities complained that restaurants provided a wealth of black-market foods, with 200 restaurants in Paris where one could eat as much as one wished.[113] When the Germans closed their *hors catégorie* restaurants (which had no restrictions on quantities or prices) in June 1942, they insisted on combined Franco-German control efforts, attempting to check all restaurants in targeted neighbourhoods. These made little progress and compromised French authority, demonstrating their collaboration in enforcement against restaurants that served French diners. But the German troops and Occupation authorities still wanted to enjoy the best of Parisian haute cuisine without control interference.[114] They bought and transported supplies, and protected the restaurants they patronized from French control. For restaurant owners, controls crippled their ability to meet 'normal' customer demand and increased their need for black-market goods. Official supplies were insufficient. One category A restaurant owner explained that the official supplies he received to serve 100 dinners daily in 1943 sufficed to feed only one third of his clients at legal ration levels.[115]

The most common infractions illustrate the extent of demand over the levels set by controlled prices and rations: overcharging (*hausse illicite*), serving larger portions than allowed and food not listed on the menu, fraudulent billing (to hide black-market costs), serving meat on days and at times not permitted, and the possession of food stocks with no bill of sale. These demonstrate the restaurant efforts to offer clients 'normal' meals in the economy of penury and restrictions, exceeding ration allowances and charging extra to cover the costs.[116] Owners found creative means to improve their menus with extralegal supplies. In agriculturally rich regions, restaurants drew on local resources, buying direct from farms and exploiting family connections to rural producers. In larger cities, restaurants relied on intermediaries. Category A and B restaurants, with higher prices, could better afford and arrange sources of supply. Category C and D restaurants had fewer options, and many

[112] SAEF B-0049757, note dated 1941 on control operations in the Paris region beginning 31 Mar. 1941; APP BA 1808, note of 29 Nov. 1941.
[113] AN F/37/4, 'Entretien du 2 avril 1943 à l'Hôtel Majestic'.
[114] Mouré, 'La capitale de la faim', 329–332.
[115] SAEF B-0049756, exposé by M. René Laffont, 1943; Mouré, 'La capitale de la faim', 318.
[116] SAEF B-0049757, note dated 1941 on control operations in the Paris region, observing that restaurants offered food 'necessary to their commerce' and charged extra to cover costs rather than for profit.

closed in the evenings for lack of food.[117] Renowned restaurants with German patrons and protection had fewer problems with supply. Fabienne Jamet, owner of the renowned brothel the One Two Two (at 122 rue de Provence) had German permits for vehicles, fuel and the transport of food and alcohol. Captain Radecke of the Bureau Otto, a regular patron, had been 'only too happy' to provide them.[118] But most restaurants sought French suppliers. Owners with a vehicle and fuel bought direct from farms; more often they received packages sent by post or rail and dealt directly with farmers or through *trafiquants* to tap rural connections. The massive increase in family parcels to cities included food supplies to restaurants.[119]

Restaurant staff invented creative ways to serve, to charge for higher costs, and to guard against state controllers. Official menus conformed to regulations, with extras on a separate bill that was destroyed after payment. In restaurants not assured of protection from controllers, they offered extras only to known customers. Commercial travellers with opportunities to buy food helped supply black-market items. Restaurants dodged price controls by charging extra for alcohol (not included in set meal prices). When Liliane Schroeder dined with her mother in a category A restaurant in 1941, they ordered extra *haricots blancs*, and were charged for liqueurs they had not consumed. 'The liqueurs, that is the beans', their waiter explained.[120]

Common restaurant infractions included billing practices to disguise the prices charged, serving tactics such as alternate menus, serving foods not on the menu, and serving meat or sausage concealed under vegetables or pasta.[121] When controllers arrived at a restaurant, staff blocked their entry to give customers time to hide food they had been served, and entry to the kitchen so staff could move black market supplies off the premises. Local owners warned each other of control operations when the German authorities insisted on large-scale operations in 1942 to check all restaurants in one neighbourhood. The plans for such operations emphasized

---

[117] SAEF B-0049516, 'Rapport mensuel sur l'activité du Service départemental du Contrôle économique de la Seine pendant le mois de décembre 1943'.

[118] Fabienne Jamet, *One Two Two* (Paris: O. Orban, 1975), 125.

[119] AN F/1cIII/1168; rapport mensuel juillet-août 1942, 1 Sept. 1942; SAEF B-0049529, Director of the Contrôle économique in Vienne to the Director of the DGCE, 16 Aug. 1943.

[120] Liliane Schroeder, *Journal d'Occupation: Paris, 1940–1944. Chronique au jour le jour d'une époque oubliée* (Paris: François-Xavier de Guibert, 2000), 94.

[121] AN AJ/40/784, de Sailly to CE regional and departmental directors, Annexe IV, 2 July 1942. Charles Braibant observed meat served under potatoes on a 'jour sans', *La guerre à Paris*, 266–267 (30 Aug. 1943).

surprise, even for the controllers, to prevent them tipping off the restaurants.[122] The proliferation of black-market practices, allowing wealthy clients to eat copious meals while most consumers waited in interminable queues for scanty rations, was a visible affront to Vichy claims of equal sacrifice, and a visible failure of state enforcement. Pierre Laval noted, in calling for greater control efforts in 1943, that the restaurant offences were 'among those that contribute the most to demoralize public opinion and keep the public from bending to an economic discipline that is indispensable'.[123]

Laval's 'indispensable economic discipline' required docile tolerance of the shortages, mismanagement and inequities that discredited the Vichy administration and increased consumer recourse to the black market. In the case of restaurants, German interference had great visibility. Their claims that black-market restaurants thrived and that French control efforts were incompetent ignored the role of German demand, the restaurant need for black-market supplies, and the obstruction of French control efforts when they interfered with German personnel. Hermann Göring complained in August 1942 that *the French* ate far too well in their luxury restaurants; 'The excellent cuisine chez Maxim's must be reserved for us.'[124] The restaurants and night clubs patronized by German personnel were often exempt from French controls, either by order, as were the six restaurants classed as *hors catégorie* in 1941, or by their ability to frustrate control efforts.[125] When controllers attempted to impose fines, confiscations, or to close such restaurants, the owners called in German authorities to quash the disciplinary actions. When the maximum legal meal price in a class E restaurant was set at 75 francs, black-market restaurants like L'Aigle or Alexis charged 700 and 1,000 francs per person, with German protection from French controllers.[126]

The CE instructed its agents to keep a record of these cases, and restaurants protected by the Germans were targeted for punishment immediately after Liberation in 1944. Many were closed for periods

[122] Mouré, 'La capitale de la faim', 319–320, 329–331.

[123] AD Seine-Maritime 40W/125, head of the government to the prefect of police and regional and department prefects, DGCE Lettre commune no. 18, 'Contrôle des restaurants', 31 May 1943.

[124] 'Göring et la "collaboration": Un beau document', *Cahiers d'histoire de la guerre*, 4 (1950): 79.

[125] Bertram Gordon notes there were sixty restaurants in Paris under German military supervision to serve troops in late 1942; Bertram M. Gordon, *War Tourism: Second World War France from Defeat and Occupation to the Creation of Heritage* (Ithaca, NY: Cornell University Press, 2018), 129.

[126] SAEF B-0049508, report by Rougerie and Genicq, 22 Apr. 1942; de Sailly to prefect of police, 23 Sept. 1943.

ranging from three months to two years.[127] They had often been supplied by German army personnel or by French *trafiquants* using German
trucks. On several occasions, French controllers stopped Wehrmacht
trucks carrying large quantities of meat bound for Paris restaurants.
They could not confiscate the meat or punish the French *trafiquants*.
An investigation in the Nantes region in September 1943 found that
twenty-five out of seventy French truck drivers employed by the
Wehrmacht were gathering food locally to sell on the black market in
Paris. The drivers also mailed food parcels from several post offices to
keep a low profile for their illicit commerce.[128] German military units
purchased meat from illicit slaughter, and French police had no authority to stop their trucks. After repeated complaint, the CE obtained this
authority in May 1943, but only if there was no German soldier in the
vehicle.[129]

Luxury restaurants in Paris also served the rich and powerful among
the French collaborators and administrative elites. A restaurant control by the CE in October 1942 found most of the clients at Maxim's,
Lapérousse and La Tour d'Argent to be French. At La Tour d'Argent,
the menu followed rationing rules, they collected tickets, and charged
high prices for alcohol. At Maxim's, under German management (by
Berlin restaurateur Otto Horcher),[130] customers rarely consulted the
menu. They ordered as they wished, without regard for quantities or
price, ordering mutton, steak and poultry, followed by cheeses, desserts and liqueurs (on a day without alcohol), and finishing with real
coffee served with real sugar. The report described the customers as
'people who seem to belong to the world of business born of the
circumstances of the present time'.[131] Below the elite restaurants,
those in categories A and B served a more diverse French clientele,
with food and liquor from the black market and extra charges to cover
costs. German protection and Vichy collaboration made possible
a hierarchy of privileged consumption in restaurants that gave visible
and provocative proof of Vichy's inability to deliver equality of
sacrifice.

---

[127] SAEF B-0049477 and B-0057659 contain correspondence for the closing of these
restaurants.
[128] Christophe Belser, *La Collaboration en Loire-Inférieure 1940–1944*, vol. 1, *Les années
noires* (La Crèche: Geste éditions, 2005), 281.
[129] Mouré, 'La capitale de la faim', 326–327; SAEF B-0049888, Note de service no. 296,
31 May 1943.
[130] On Horcher's restaurant empire, see Giles MacDonogh, 'Otto Horcher, Caterer to the
Third Reich', *Gastronomica* 7(1) (2007): 31–38.
[131] SAEF B-0049508, report by inspector Savarit, 30 Oct. 1942; copy in APP BA 1808.

Middlemen

The most notorious Occupation *trafiquants*, the 'black-market billion-aires' Josef Joinovici and Mendel (Michel) Szkolnikoff, offer extreme cases demonstrating the strategic position of middlemen. Joinovici, in particular, attracted interest then and now for his close connections with German authorities and the French Gestapo of the rue Lauriston, his support for the Resistance that gave him police protection when Paris was liberated in August 1944, and for the arrests, betrayals and murders in his wake. The violence and melodrama have prompted press attention, admiring biographies, and recently an award-winning 6-volume *bande dessinée* that borrows film techniques and inspiration for its title from spaghetti western director Sergio Leone. *Il était une fois en France* announces on its back cover: 'Orphan. Immigrant. Scrap metal dealer. Billionaire. Collabo. Resistor. Criminal for some, hero for others ... Joseph Joanovici was all that and more. This is his story.'[132]

Both Joinovici and Szkolnikoff were born in Eastern Europe, Szkolnikoff in Szarkowszczyzna, Russia (now Belarus) in 1895, Joinovici in Kichinev (Bessarabia, now Moldovia) in 1902. Both were Jews and arrived as immigrants in interwar France. Joinovici came in 1925 and established himself as a scrap metal dealer, taking over the family business of one of his first employers. He was proprietor of the Société de triage et de récupération from 1932, and established Joinovici Frères with his brother Mordhar (Marcel) in 1936. By 1939 his firm was one of the largest scrap dealers in France, with reported earnings from his two firms in excess of 6 million francs and a reputation for dealing in stolen goods.[133] Szkolnikoff arrived in 1933, having travelled from Danzig to the Netherlands to avoid Nazi persecution, and then to Belgium and Paris. He came from a family of textile merchants, had lived in several East European cities before Danzig, and engaged in both textiles and banking with several bankruptcies and prosecutions for fraud in Brussels and Paris. He escaped expulsion from France in 1937 only because he was 'without country', living in France on a Nansen passport for refugees. He remained in France under surveillance by a police inspector, Louis Trayaud, whom he would hire as a manager in 1940. His company Textima profited from war demand for cloth in 1939–1940.

<hr>

[132] Fabien Nury and Sylvain Vallée, *Il était une fois en France*, 6 vols. (Grenoble: Éditions Glénat, 2007–2012). For analysis of this series as a new phase in 'the Vichy syndrome', commercializing interest in Vichy experience, see Chris Reyns-Chikuma, 'Mémoire et histoire dans un roman graphique en six volumes: double jeu, infotainment, obsession française?' *Modern and Contemporary France*, 22(2) (2014): 207–229.

[133] Henry Sergg, *Joinovici: L'empire souterrain du chiffonnier milliardaire* (Paris: Le Carrousel-FN, 1986), 18–19; Auda, *Les belles années du 'milieu'*, 74–75.

Defeat in June 1940 brought dangers and opportunity. German purchasing often sought the sales expertise and connections of German entrepreneurs familiar with French industries.[134] French intermediaries provided connections and screened the fact that the ultimate purchasers were German. The Germans provided protection, authorizations for purchase and transport, funding, and generous profit. Intermediaries benefited from German authority and their disregard for normal accounting procedures in black-market purchasing (which would normally record prices, quantities, and where and how much profit was made). German authorizations enabled them to engage in purchasing throughout France and disregard economic controls and controllers.[135]

Joinovici bought scrap metal for the Bureau Otto beginning in 1942. Established in Paris under engineer Hermann (Otto) Brandl in July 1940 as a branch of German military intelligence (the Abwehr), the Bureau Otto became the most extensive and wide-ranging German purchasing office, in addition to its intelligence gathering, secret police and anti-Resistance activities. It treated French dealers on a first-name basis: 'they dealt only with "Pierre", "Paul" or "Jacques" and required samples of their wares and anonymity', paying in cash, 100 to 150 million francs daily. The principal cashier, Jean Georges, recalled having paid out 322 million francs in one afternoon in December 1942.[136] Joinovici started working with the Germans in 1940 (with Wifo – *Wirtschaftliche Forschungsgesellschaft* – the Economic Research Company, created in 1935 to build fuel storage depots),[137] who requisitioned his metal stocks. His contacts and knowledge of the French scrap metals market allowed the Germans to tap resources throughout France. A Joinovici employee wrote to the Ministry of Industrial Production in January 1942, 'When the Germans arrived in France, they found in our company a business with perfect organization and thorough familiarity with the recovery of non-ferrous metals.' In November 1941, Joinovici met Dr Fuchs of the Abwehr, and a few weeks later began purchasing for the Bureau Otto. His main contact, Captain Wilhelm Radecke, described Joinovici's aid to the German war effort as 'extremely useful, indispensable even, for the economic plan'.[138]

---

[134] This is particularly well documented for the wine industry; Lucand, *Le vin et la guerre*.

[135] See Fabrice Grenard, 'Contourner les règlementations liées aux pénuries et à la fragmentation du marché: le marché noir en ZNO et les circuits d'échanges clandestins inter-zones', in *L'économie de la zone non-occupée 1940–1942*, ed. by Hervé Joly (Paris: Comité des travaux historiques et scientifiques, 2007), 119–138.

[136] Rochebrune and Hazera, *Les patrons sous l'Occupation*, 193–202, 248 (quote); SAEF B-0049476, DCGE, 'Caractère officiel du marché noir allemand', undated.

[137] André Goldschmidt, *L'Affaire Joinovici: collaborateur, résistant ... et bouc émissaire* (Toulouse: Éditions Privat, 2002), 26–28.

[138] Quoted in Rochebrune and Hazera, *Les patrons sous l'Occupation*, 214.

Beyond purchasing metals for the Germans, Joinovici was involved in the physical elimination of rivals, and he supplied equipment and uniforms for the North African Brigade established in January 1944 by Henri Lafont, ostensibly to combat the Resistance in the Limousin and Dordogne regions, but the Brigade mainly worked to intimidate and terrorize civilians.[139] As an Eastern European Jew, Joinovici is a surprising collaborator. To conform to anti-Semitic legislation, he dissolved one firm and aryanized Joinovici Frères, where he and his brother kept roles as 'technical consultants'. Both Joinovicis were arrested in September 1941 – probably for fraud although he later claimed it was for sabotage of the German war effort – and were released several months later.[140] The Joinovicis were vulnerable to persecution as Jews by the Germans and by Vichy authorities, which his German handlers exploited to require his services.[141] Joinovici's collaboration could thus be seen as a strategy for survival, but his close connections with Henri Lafont, leader of the infamous Gestapo of the rue Lauriston, his black-market traffic, and his actions against the Resistance and betrayal of partners show a darker agenda than simple adaptation to survive. His part in the violence, greed, lavish living and national disloyalty in this milieu are not just products of compulsion. As one biographer described the scenario, 'Front-wheel drive and police behind ... an epic of gangsterism the cinema has used for the best films and for the duds.'[142]

The dark side included his betrayal of friends and a Resistance network, his close connections with German intelligence officers, with the French Gestapo of the rue Lauriston, the murder of competitors, the provision of supplies for the North African Brigade, and the murders of five monks in a seminary hiding Resistance arms and a twenty-year-old *résistant*, Robert Scaffa, in July 1944. Conscious choices rather than coercion lie behind these actions. Joinovici's efforts to save friends from the Germans, to support the police resistance group *Honneur de la Police*, and his betrayal of Bonny and Lafont in August 1944, can also be seen as an opportune change in strategy as the certainty of German defeat became clear. In postwar testimony Joinovici emphasized his support for the Resistance, but the role accords poorly with his exploitation of connections to German authorities and the French Gestapo while the Germans were in control.

---

[139] Berlière, *Polices des temps noirs*, 157–162.
[140] Stephen H. Kargère, 'L'affaire Joinovici: Truth, Politics, and Justice, 1940-1949' (PhD dissertation, Brandeis University, 1999), 20–24, 47–51; Jeffrey Mehlman, 'The Joinovici Affair: The Stavisky of the Fourth Republic', *French Politics, Culture and Society*, 32(1) (2014): 103; and Auda, *Les belles années du 'milieu'*, 123–125.
[141] Kargère, 'L'affaire Joinovici', 67–73, and Auda, *Les belles années du 'milieu'*, 126–127.
[142] Alphonse Boudard, *L'étrange Monsieur Joseph* (Paris: Robert Laffont, 1998), 162.

So long as he provided goods needed by the Germans, Joinovici profited from their need for intermediaries to exploit and intimidate French owners of goods they wanted. His recognition in 1944 as a *résistant* complicated the efforts to bring him to justice. In liberated France, investigators could locate witnesses for his resistance activities far more easily than for his relations with the Germans. Many witnesses of criminal collaboration with the Nazis had been killed, retreated with the Germans, or gone to ground to avoid arrest.[143] Joinovici claimed that he had not furnished metals for the German war effort: he had worked at the Saint-Ouen docks as a *réceptionnaire*, a receiving clerk, and that French metal firms delivered to the Germans of their own accord. 'I never delivered a gram of merchandise to the occupation authorities; I was a simple réceptionnaire, not a supplier.'[144] But his income, lifestyle and close connections to the Bureau Otto and the Lafont gang were hardly those of a clerk. Tried for intelligence with the enemy in 1949, Joinovici was convicted of economic collaboration, sentenced to five years in prison and a fine of 600,000 francs, and confiscation of personal goods to the value of 50 million francs.

In contrast to Joinovici, Michel Szkolnikoff can serve as a prototype for the *trafiquant 'pur'*, focused on purchasing, without the connections to gangsters and German intelligence that complicate the Joinovici record.[145] After the fall of France, Szkolnikoff bought surplus textiles at write-off prices. These he sold to the *Kriegsmarine* in November 1940 and became a key purchaser for their textile needs, aryanizing his company to conform to Vichy's anti-Jewish legislation. With the *Kriegsmarine* as his principal client, Szkolnikoff told his staff in December that they no longer needed to keep accounts: 'we're completely covered by the Germans'.[146] When the *Contrôle économique* tried to enforce controls in 1941, Textima blocked their efforts. The CE worked from bank statements to reconstruct Textima's commerce with the Germans after Liberation. In 1941, Textima refused to provide documents and obstructed the control investigation, which noted the intentional disappearance of cheques and invoices, and 'the absence of accounts and major concealment of the turnover and profit'. Szkolnikoff invested his black-market earnings through real estate holding companies registered in Monaco, to buy up hotels in Monte Carlo, Nice, Marseilles and Paris.[147]

---

[143] APP PJ 50, summary of the evidence gathered against Joinovici dating from Feb. 1946.

[144] AN F/7/15336, 'Procès Joinovici, 11ème séance', 20 July 1949.

[145] Delarue, *Trafics et crimes*, 61 and Rochebrune and Hazera, *Les patrons sous l'Occupation*, 229.

[146] Delarue, *Trafics et crimes*, 62–65 and Pierre Abramovici, *Szkolnikoff: Le plus grand trafiquant de l'Occupation* (Paris: Nouveau monde, 2014), 39–42.

[147] SAEF B-0033931, 'Affaire Szkolnikoff', undated, and 'Liste des immeubles et fonds de commerce appartenant au groupe Szkolnikoff', 11 Dec. 1944.

When price controllers took action against his firm in 1941, Szkolnikoff called in German officials to reclaim the textiles seized by controllers and halt their proceedings against him. French officials did record the rapid growth of his receipts from the *Kriegsmarine*: more than 8 million francs in January 1941, 19 million in February, and more than 59 millions from 1 to 24 March.[148] From September 1940 to its closing down in lieu of aryanization in December 1941, Textima's sales totalled more than 158 million francs.[149] Szkolnikoff went on to make an estimated 2 to 4 billion francs, purchasing real estate in Paris and on the Côte d'Azur on a scale that demonstrated his vast new wealth. He began transferring his profits to Spain before the end of the war and died in June 1945 when French DST agents kidnapped him to bring him back to France for trial.

Joinovici and Szkolnikoff demonstrate key aspects of black-market business and the importance of intermediaries. First, the Germans were the largest-volume buyers, enabling and protecting traffic that served their needs. Their support displayed the internal rivalries and lack of coordination characteristic of the 'polycratic' Nazi regime with competing centres of authority. Intermediaries played a vital role connecting buyers with available goods, particularly in moving outside official markets. German agencies employed them to locate and purchase French resources. Second, French authorities were subordinate, subservient, and their legitimacy was damaged by German exploitation and protection of black-market traffic. Vichy's authority was publicly defied, most visibly in the thriving black-market restaurants. Third, the purchasing based on personal connections encouraged abuse and made the prosecution of infractions far more difficult. As Commissaire Petit of the *Police judiciaire* observed in 1946, Joinovici's profits were unknown: 'given the absence of any accounts, any purchase receipts, and any records of payment, all the operations of these *trafiquants* took place strictly on conditions forbidden by the regulations, but in full accord with the Occupation authorities'. Their profits were anyone's guess.[150]

Conclusions

The lack of evidence for most low-level black-market traffic makes the scale of activity a matter of guesswork; as it was for controllers at the time, and for the postwar efforts to confiscate illicit profits. The cases of Joinovici and Szkolnikoff dramatize the fundamentals that structured black-market activity in industry and commerce. The shortages and

---

[148] Delarue, *Trafics et crimes*, 65.   [149] Abramovici, *Szkolnikoff*, 53.
[150] Petit report to the *Direction générale du contrôle économique*, 25 Jan. 1946, cited in Goldschmidt, *L'affaire Joinovici*, 41.

economic controls privileged those with access to goods and transport, and with influence to escape controls. Intermediaries who could deliver goods to consumers outside market controls profited from that ability. German purchasing augmented and legitimated black-market use, and it disrupted and discredited French control efforts. The *Contrôle économique* conceded in 1943 that suppression of the black market was impossible if shopkeepers could replenish their stock only in committing 'grave irregularities' and if industrialists could obtain raw materials only on the black market.[151]

German purchasing aggravated the supply crises, bid up prices, fostered networks for illicit exchange, and privileged money and influence. For French business, collaboration was often a matter of survival, to obtain essential resources, employ resources and retain workers. In commerce, retailers depended on new intermediaries to obtain supplies. The added transactional layer increased costs and reduced efficiency, relied on dissimulation and deception, but connected buyers to goods they otherwise could not obtain. Honest manufacturers and shopkeepers lost business; honest state officials suffered deprivation and demoralization. Worst off were those without wealth or privilege, especially the urban working and middle classes, struggling to cope with the rising cost of goods essential to their survival from day to day.

---

[151] AN F/7/14895, 'Note au sujet de la position des Services français de Contrôle en ce qui concerne la lutte contre le marché noir', likely April 1943: 'the nearly complete absence of some indispensable products ... obliges almost all industrialists and shopkeepers to turn to the black market'.

Paris police reported in June 1941 'The material impossibility for the families of workers, employees, civil servants, to ensure a minimum of indispensable victuals, causes definite anxiety that is manifested most often in bitter words with regard to state powers and the Occupation authorities.' In queues outside shops, the waiting customers talked of the injustice. 'The middle and working classes state that circumstances tend to divide consumers into two distinct clans: on one side the owning classes that, by the "black market", can provision themselves almost normally, and on the other, the working class that lacks essentials. The words of the head of state announcing the equality of all in facing restrictions are bitterly underlined.'[1]

Differences in access to necessities accentuated social divisions: between rich and poor, between urban workers and rural farmers, between those whose employment or personal connections gave them access to material goods and those without. It fostered animosity against the visibly privileged who could obtain sufficient clothing and food without undue hardship. The Paris police and many prefects cautioned that these inequities could lead to violence, through Communist-inspired urban protest by hungry workers and mothers, or by those deprived of goods seeking revenge against those who profited from their misery. In the Haute-Marne, prefect Robert Cousin commented on the deprivation of workers and *petits rentiers* in 1942: 'Social injustice is increasing; more than ever we see the triumph of money, sometimes even indecently displayed. It should not be concealed that a grave malaise results from this, ably exploited by an active propaganda'; demonstrations can only be violent when the point of explosion is reached.[2]

---

[1] APP 220W 4, 'Situation à Paris', 16 June 1941. The department of the Seine's *Contrôle économique* stated in 1942, of the traffic in bread coupons, that there were those who could afford counterfeit tickets at 200 or 250 francs per sheet and those who could not. The first ate all the bread they wanted; the second starved. APP BA 2258, departmental head of the *Contrôle économique* to the prefect of police, 7 Aug. 1942.

[2] AN AJ/41/377 (Haute-Marne), prefect bi-monthly report for Nov.-Dec. 1942.

Consumers lost power as their choice of goods and providers contracted. Jean Dutourd framed the relationship bluntly in his novel *Au bon beurre*. Before the war, the customer had always been right, and dishonest shopkeepers could anger their clients and end in bankruptcy. Occupation shortages changed that profoundly. The Poissonards, proprietors of the dairy shop Au Bon Beurre, quickly realize the power that possession of goods will give them. Dutourd writes of their shop as a seat of government in which they rule as tyrants over a powerless clientèle. Madame Poissonard at her cash register 'reigned over a little people who each day brought her tribute'.[3] Charles-Hubert builds a black market empire based on consumers' need for the shopkeepers with whom they register to receive their rations: 'Treat him like a dog, he'll always come back: he doesn't want to die of hunger.'[4] For Louis Baudin, an economist who wrote on consumer issues, the shortages reversed the prewar power relationship. 'The consumer loses his former primacy; the king is now a valet.'[5]

Yet wealth and privilege could not monopolize market power. Ordinary consumers could seek alternative ways to access needed goods and resist exploitation by merchants engaging in fraudulent practices. As the state relaxed its enforcement of rationing rules to allow families to supplement their rations, the rules were stretched, and this fostered new illicit traffic. Consumers exploited connections with family and friends. They seized opportunities for public protest to demand that Vichy deliver on its claims to support the lives of families and improve moral behaviour. They demonstrated to obtain more food and to coordinate their opposition to state policies that produced increasingly perverse results.

Women bore an even greater weight as consumers and providers. The loss of prisoners, volunteers and labour conscripts to Germany shifted the gender balance and the roles for daily life in France.[6] Women had traditionally been responsible for purchasing food and clothing for their families. During the Occupation they headed households, took on more paid employment, and often became sole managers of family consumption. As purchasing became more difficult, it demanded more of their time, effort and ingenuity:

Woman reigns in the domain of consumption, a domain that has become one of cards, inscriptions, queues, in other words of patience, devotion, sacrifice .…

---

[3] Jean Dutourd, *Au bon beurre: Scènes de la vie sous l'Occupation* (Paris: Gallimard [1952]; Folio ed.), 107. The subtitle was added in 1972.

[4] Dutourd, *Au bon beurre*, 134–135, 143.

[5] Baudin, *Esquisse de l'économie française*, 153–154.

[6] Sarah Fishman, *We Will Wait; Wives of French Prisoners of War, 1940–1945* (New Haven, CT: Yale University Press, 1991); Miranda Pollard, *The Reign of Virtue*; Hanna Diamond, *Women and the Second World War in France 1939–1948: Choices and Constraints* (Essex: Pearson Education Ltd., 1999).

Each moment brings new worries and the slightest error – missing one's turn in a shop, the ticket lost, a mistake – is punished with the worst of sanctions: hunger.[7]

Vichy rhetoric accorded women high status for their roles as mothers, bearing children, raising families, and providing the organizational structure for the family as 'the very foundation of the social edifice', the state's top priority.[8] Vichy family policy was hierarchical and authoritarian, demanding conformity and sacrifice, and giving women less power over their families and their bodies.[9] But as mothers, often as the head of families, and as chief purchasers, women had increased visibility and used it to challenge the state on its responsibility to maintain and support families. They protested shortages, demanded food for their children, and sought alternatives when state food supply failed to meet family needs. As consumers lost power in the official economy of penury, women redirected their purchasing power to demand more of the state and sought means to provide for their families from alternative sources, including the black market.

The Consumer Deficit Economy

Until the Depression, consumption in France had been increasing through rising disposable income and the spread of mass-produced consumer goods, marketed in new stores, offering easier access, wider variety and lower prices. Consumers were served by markets that integrated national production and international trade; the growth of markets and consumer choice relied on the transport of goods. Under German Occupation, consumption contracted sharply. Output fell, with local isolation from international and national trade, declining disposable income, and a higher share of income needed for necessities. The German demand for consumer goods took output from this shrinking economy. Cautious and calculating producers and wholesalers withheld goods from markets; anxious consumers rushed to buy and hoard supplies. Department stores emptied of goods and shopkeepers searched to replace stock in the buying frenzy in 1940. The modern consumer

---

[7] Louis Baudin, 'Introduction' to Paulette and Louis Baudin, *La consommation dirigée en France en matière d'alimentation* (Paris: Librarie générale de droit et de jurisprudence, 1942), 6, 8–9. Baudin dedicated his *Esquisse de l'économie française* (1945): 'To my dear wife, whose daily devotion has assured my existence during these years of hardship, and without whom this work would not have been written.'

[8] Maréchal Pétain, 'La politique sociale de l'avenir', *Revue des Deux Mondes* (Sept. 1940): 114–115: 'The family is the essential cell; it is the very foundation of the social edifice; it is on this that we must build; if it weakens, all is lost; as long as holds, all can be saved.'

[9] Pollard, *Reign of Virtue*.

economy based on the display of consumption possibilities, increasing purchasing power, and the arrival of new consumer goods, reversed direction. Consumers had to adapt. In Dominique Veillon's words, 'One had to learn to live differently.'[10]

In place of abundant goods and choice, consumers faced the daunting combination of rationed goods and queues, queues even to obtain the ration documents they needed to queue for rationed goods. The opportunities to purchase rationed goods were limited, with empty shelves in many stores and declining product quality. Some goods, especially imports, were replaced with inferior substitutes: *gazogène* engines to power automobiles with wood or charcoal, artificial fabrics for clothing, and *ersatz* ingredients to take the place of real tobacco and coffee.[11] *Café national* had roasted barley as its main ingredient. Proposals for a *tabac national* considered various leaves to mix with tobacco for cigarettes, looking for a blend that would extend tobacco supplies without ruining the flavour, burning too quickly, or poisoning the smoker.[12] These 'national' blends, inferior to prewar products, linked Vichy to the obvious decline in quality. Unrationed goods disappeared, as did any substitutes for which official prices had been set too low. Official markets offered ever less in terms of quantity, quality and choice.

Many state officials, industrialists, shopkeepers and consumers assumed that the initial shocks in 1940 would be followed by a return to normal, with food and material goods coming back to markets as the impact of defeat receded and economic activity recovered. Collaboration would make a place for France in the European new order under Nazi Germany. Vichy's trinity of virtues, *Travail, famille, patrie* (Work, family, fatherland), replaced the Republican trinity of *Liberté, égalité, fraternité*

---

[10] Veillon, *Vivre et survivre*, 105. The impact of the Occupation on consumption has received attention mainly for hardships imposed, rather than changes in consumer practice. The most detailed study remains Veillon, *Vivre et survivre*. Marie-Emmanuelle Chessel devotes two pages to the Occupation in *Histoire de la consommation* (Paris: La Découverte, 2012); Jean-Claude Daumas avoids the Occupation years in *La révolution matérielle: Une histoire de la consommation, France XIXe–XXIe siècle* (Paris: Flammarion, 2018), as do the essays on France in Alain Chatriot, Marie-Emmanuel Chessel and Matthew Hilton, eds., *Au nom du consommateur: Consommation et politique en Europe et aux États-Unis au XXe siècle* (Paris: La Découverte, 2004). In *Les entreprises de biens de consommation sous l'Occupation*, ed. by Sabine Effosse, Marc de Ferrière le Vayer and Hervé Joly (Tours: Presses universitaires François-Rabelais de Tours, 2010), the editors' introduction and Jean-Claude Daumas' conclusions comment on this 'often forgotten' dimension of Occupation experience, 10–14, 334–335.

[11] Dominique Veillon, 'Une politique d'adaptation spécifique: les ersatz', in *Cahiers de l'IHTP* 32-33 (1996): 59–74.

[12] 'Tabac national', *Journal des Débats*, 4 Nov. 1941, René Armand interview with the director of tobacco manufacture in Marseille.

(Liberty, equality, fraternity).[13] Vichy's collaboration failed in the obvious inability to improve food rations and the provision of necessities. As the quality of material life deteriorated, ordinary citizens blamed the Germans for their exactions, but rapidly came to see the Vichy administration as holding equal or greater responsibility. The prefect for the Paris region observed in February 1941 that no government measures involving collaboration with the Germans would be understood if material conditions did not improve.[14] Police reports stated repeatedly that the shortages and the failure to increase food rations destroyed public belief in collaboration. Workers, they reported in June 1941, who suffered 'from malnutrition and the privations imposed by insufficient food supply, distance themselves more and more from a collaboration in which they claim to be the only ones to bear the cost'.[15]

The impact of defeat was obvious in July and August 1940, particularly in areas with many German troops buying goods. The exodus from Paris in June reduced the population of the city and suburbs by more than two-thirds. Stores and markets closed, and the infrastructure for food supply ground almost to a halt. As residents returned, with the city back to half its normal population in early August, the prefect of the department of the Seine faced food supply challenges that ranged from the lack of transport and fuel to the price differentials between Paris and producers' local markets (reducing supply to Paris), and German requisitions. In September he emphasized 'the precariousness of food supply', including the increase in purchasing that escaped state control and a 'crooked commerce' that always found the means to obtain vehicles and fuel by paying higher prices.[16] Consumers faced limited access to food (meat and dairy in particular), rising prices and long queues at the few stores that were open. When he asked Parisians on 2 August to avoid making unnecessary food purchases, to assure access for all to the limited supplies, consumers bought more and hoarded, seeing in his appeal a sign that the situation would worsen.[17] Hoarding continued as the loss of

---

[13] Pétain explained the rejection of the revolutionary logic in 'La politique sociale de l'avenir', *Revue des Deux Mondes* (Sept. 1940): 113–117.

[14] AN AJ/41/390, Charles Magny to Ambassador Noël, 3 Feb. 1941. Magny emphasized that improvement in material conditions would be the best propaganda; no propaganda could explain to Parisians the reasons for the current material deprivation. Prefect monthly report for November, 1 Dec. 1941.

[15] APP 220W 4, 'État d'esprit de la population parisienne 21 et 22 juin 1941'.

[16] AdP Perotin 1012/57/1 3, prefect of the Seine (Achille Villey-Desmeserets) to M. Noël, French ambassador, delegate of the government of occupied territories, 8 Aug. 1940 and 13 Sept. 1940.

[17] APP 220W 1, 'Situation à Paris' reports of 5 and 12 Aug. 1940.

imports and falling domestic production presaged shortages; consumers purchased any and all available goods as reserves.[18]

Local authorities had implemented piecemeal food rationing measures during the summer; these were replaced by a national program on 23 September 1940. The consumer response combined a sense of relief that order would be restored to the unpredictable market for food with alarm at the low level of rations, particularly for bread and meat. The normal adult ration was set at 350 grams of bread per day (reduced to 275 grams in April 1941) and 360 grams of meat per week (reduced to 250 grams in April 1941).[19] The queues for dairy products shortened and 'collaboration' was thought initially to portend negotiations to increase rations, particularly for workers and children.[20] Disillusion followed. Rations did not improve, essential supplies to markets remained barely sufficient, and basic products were scarce: especially butter, eggs and cheese, as well as pork, milk, soap, and imported goods like coffee. As winter set in, shortages of coal, gas and electricity meant consumers had little power for heat and cooking food.

In the centralized food distribution, retailers and wholesalers believed Paris would receive adequate supplies only if prices were fixed and direct purchase by individuals prohibited, to ensure that food supplies moved from farms to markets without diversion to the black market.[21] The Gendarmerie saw public opinion shift decisively as rationing and inequities in purchasing power forced most consumers to make do with rations while others escaped the constraints with black market purchasing. 'Rationing thus underlines the consequences of inequalities of wealth, when the introduction of food rationing was intended to assure everyone a minimum, regardless of their resources.'[22]

Customers in queues voiced declining confidence in state management. Their patience with low rations and long market queues was limited, and vulnerable to growing evidence that 'sacrifice' was principally shared by those without wealth or privilege.[23] German purchasing, official and

[18] ABdF 1069201226 22, DGEE, 'Résumé des rapports économiques', ZO, Aug.–Oct. 1940.

[19] Cépède, *Agriculture et alimentation*, 383.

[20] APP 220W 1, 'Situation à Paris' reports of 23 and 30 Sept. and 21 Oct. 1940.

[21] APP 220W 1 and 2, 'Situation à Paris' reports weekly through the fall of 1940, as well as prefect reports in AN AJ/41/390, particularly Prefect of the Seine to Minister of the Interior, 28 Jan. 1941.

[22] AN AJ/41/397, de Laurencie, 'L'opinion publique en zone occupée et certains aspects de l'attitude allemande – Gravité de la situation', 16 Oct. 1940.

[23] APP 220W 3 and 4, 'Situation à Paris' reports in the first half of 1941. The report 'État d'esprit de la population française 21 et 22 juin 1941' concluded: 'Finally, we can affirm that the working class and all those who suffer from undernourishment and the shortages imposed by insufficient food supply are more and more alienated from a collaboration in which they are the only ones to bear the cost.'

private, took large quantities of meat, cheese and butter as these goods arrived in Paris. Wholesalers and retailers complained of the lack of coordination in food administration, the price policies in producing departments that kept goods from urban markets, and consumer dismay at the difficulties in having ration tickets honoured, especially for meat.[24] The allocation of goods, after German requisitions, gave priority to hospitals, cooperatives, workplace canteens, the *Secours national*, and perhaps most gallingly, to restaurants that served a privileged elite, including German officers. *Au Pilori* compared the restaurants for the privileged to bootleggers in the United States during prohibition. While millions of French citizens tightened their belts, tens of thousands of those privileged by fortune could eat sumptuous meals whenever they wished, at 200 to 300 francs per person.[25] The supply system favoured restaurants frequented by Germans and retailers in wealthy neighbourhoods.[26] For those depending on rations and waiting in queues, the French administration was to blame for these inequities.

The press in Paris, eager to claim that Parisian collaborators would do better in power, blamed Vichy for the shortages. Marcel Déat accused Vichy of deliberately starving Paris to sabotage genuine collaboration.[27] Journalists accused Jean Achard, the minister of food supply, of gross incompetence and personal profit from an administration that fostered systemic fraud. Achard was forced to resign in July 1941. Pétain blamed Achard and a system that benefitted wholesalers at the expense of producers and consumers. Official food supplies and rations did not improve.[28] The rations for staple foods – bread, meat and fats – were reduced in April 1941; supplies of butter, eggs and pork went increasingly to the black market. The prefect of the Gironde observed that public ill will would be less acute if restrictions were in fact equally shared. But, thanks to the black market, the public could 'at any time see that the wealthy have the possibility to evade the common law'.[29]

---

[24] APP BA 1807, note dated 4 Jan. 1941.

[25] Quoted in APP 220W 5, 'Situation à Paris', 11 Aug. 1941.

[26] APP 220W 5, 'Situation à Paris', 20 Oct. 1941, and similar comments in reports for 13 and 27 Oct.; and 220W 6, 'Situation à Paris', 17 and 24 Nov. 1941.

[27] Marcel Déat, 'Le blocus de Paris', *L'Œuvre*, 7 Jan. 1941, as well as his articles on 6, 13 and 23 Jan. 1941.

[28] APP 220W 3 and 220W 4, 'Situation à Paris' reports on press criticism in 1941. Notable critics included Déat in *L'Œuvre*, Jacques Doriot in *Le Cri du Peuple*, Aimé Caesar in *La Gerbe*, Charles Dieudonné in *La France au Travail*, André Algarron in *Le Petit Parisien*, and René Jolivet in *Le Matin*. For the campaign against Achard, see Grenard, *Les scandales du ravitaillement*, 75–91; Pétain commented on Achard's dismissal in his *vent mauvais* speech of 12 Aug. 1941; Pétain, *Discours aux Français*, 167.

[29] AN F/60/502, extract from the prefect monthly report, 17 July 1941.

The declining public faith in state management marked a critical loss of legitimacy for Vichy. Marketplace queues still voiced support for tough measures to track and punish black market activity.[30] Marcel Bucard suggested that the state shoot twenty 'great bandits animating the black market' and a dozen of their richest clients, to set an example.[31] Consumers blamed Vichy for shortages, believing that under the counter and back-door sales and abundant supplies to the 'rich neighbourhoods' and the 'great restaurants' proved that the system worked against them. Restaurants served lavish meals to the wealthy, while honest folk depending on rations found their tickets honoured after long delays, if at all.[32] Wages were frozen while prices rose, making essential food purchases ever more difficult for workers, artisans, middle-class employees and civil servants. As consumers awaited the second winter of shortages in the autumn of 1941, they had ever greater incentive to work outside the rules, and declining tolerance for the controllers trying to enforce a system they experienced as inequitable and corrupt.

Tickets and Queues

Consumers learned new routines in a purchasing regime that now required individual ration cards, coupons and tickets for their entitlement to legal purchase. The queue established a new social space: for creating and maintaining friendships, for exchanging information, for observing new social hierarchies, and for mobilizing frustrated consumers.[33] Ration books and coupons added a new form of currency that could be bought, sold, traded, stolen, or counterfeited. As the consumer deficit economy took more durable form, the queues became an unmistakable display of inefficiency and injustice, so much so that authorities sought to reduce their visibility (easier than reducing the need for them).

---

[30] APP 220W 4 and 220W 5, 'Situation à Paris' reports in summer and fall 1941.

[31] *Le Franciste*, 6 Sept. 1941, quoted in APP 220W 5, 'Situation à Paris', 8 Sept. 1941.

[32] APP 220W 5, 'Situation à Paris', 15 Sept. 1941, and reports for 22 Sept.; 13, 20 and 27 Oct. 1941; 220W 6, 1 Dec. 1941.

[33] The most immediate recognition of these factors was the reporting by Paris police on opinions and behaviour in queues in their 'Situation à Paris' reports and in newspaper attention to queues. Paul Achard's *La queue: Ce qui s'y disait, ce qu'on y pensait* (Paris: Éditions de la Belle Fontaine, 1945), written in 1942, was not published until the end of the Occupation. For a wartime representations, see Jules Véran, *En faisant la queue ou Les spectacles du jour* (Paris: Librairie Aristide Quillet, 1942) and Louis Le François, *J'ai faim . . . ! Journal d'un Français en France depuis l'Armistice* (New York: Brentano's, 1942). For comment on the queue's importance, see Baudin, *Esquisse de l'économie*, 119–122; Veillon, *Paris allemand*, 113–125 and *Vivre et survivre*, 127–132; and Alary et al., *Les Français au quotidien*, 266–271.

The food rationing system in September 1940 imposed quantities as dictated by the Germans for starvation-level rations of dietary staples, bread and meat in particular. It required consumers to register with local authorities, usually the town hall, in order to obtain a ration book, and a combination of coupons for goods allocated on a monthly basis and tickets for goods rationed by weekly and daily allowances. Customers needed to register with shops for most basic needs. Ration categories, as explained in Chapter 2, ranged from infant through three age categories for youth (J1, J2, J3), to adult, with special adult categories for workers in agriculture and heavy labour, and the elderly. Keeping track of the coupons and tickets required close attention.[34] Every ticket lost meant a lost opportunity to purchase. The tickets and coupons could be used only when valid *and* when the rationed goods were available. Newspapers provided daily updates for local and regional coupon use. For products with supply disruption, including meat and dairy, there were periods when tickets could not be used for weeks at a time.

Jean Dutourd's avaricious shopkeepers in *Au bon beurre* regularly cheat their customers on weight and quality of goods and take extra tickets from the inattentive.[35] The Poissonards are extreme in their duplicity and hypocrisy, but shopkeeper dishonesty was widespread and targeted by state controllers, and a common element in consumer critiques of the Occupation. 'The honest shopkeeper no longer exists', lamented Alice Noël in her diary in December 1941. 'All shopkeepers are thieves', Jean Bailleul recalled from his boyhood.[36]

Compared to their contact with adjacent customers in line, consumers' interaction with shopkeepers was brief. Waiting in queues was one of the most common elements in Occupation experience, and the time in lines, waiting for the *possibility* to purchase rationed goods, imposed the heaviest burden on those who could not afford alternatives. Dominique Veillon cites the case of one Parisienne who waited more than four hours in queues in October 1942, beginning at 7:30 a.m., and obtained no food.[37] Wealthy clients could avoid queues by purchasing direct from farmers or on the black market, and having scarce foods delivered to their door. Or they could pay someone to wait in line. Such *queuetières* were

[34] Veillon, *Vivre et survivre*, 130.

[35] Dutourd, *Au bon beurre*, 133–136, 148–149, 251–252.

[36] Noël diary entry for 31 Dec. 1941 quoted in Michel Boivin, *Les Manchois dans la tourmente de la Seconde Guerre mondiale*, vol. 4, *L'Occupation: Résistance, répression et vie quotidienne* (Marigny: Editions Eurocibles, 2004), 146; Bailleul in Jean-Pierre Guéno, ed., *Paroles de l'ombre: Lettres, carnets et récits des Français sous l'Occupation 1939–1945* (Paris: Librio, 2009), 49.

[37] Dominique Veillon, 'La vie quotidienne des femmes', in *Vichy et les Français*, ed. by Jean-Pierre Azéma and François Bédarida (Paris: Fayard, 1992), 631–632.

often mothers, who stood in lines and had their children deliver the purchased goods while they moved to another queue.[38]

Although most shoppers in queues were women, there were single men and children as well. Single workers with day shifts, male and female, shopped later when stocks were often depleted (stores were required to keep evening hours to serve them); children took turns in line; seniors and men living alone queued for goods they needed, an unusual social experience for many.[39] While queues were still a novel experience in the autumn of 1940, *Le Matin* ran a contest for the men and women waiting in line, offering 100 francs if they identified themselves as the circled face in a published photograph.[40]

Queues offered opportunities to gather information, learn of news and rumours, forge new acquaintances, and exchange views on current problems, especially for the acquisition of food and cooking with the limited ingredients. Accounts written at the time are structured by the conversations, as is Marcel Aymé's wartime short story 'En attendant'.[41] Queues offered an opportunity for solidarity, but it was manifest most obviously to respect order in the queue and the customers' order of arrival for service. Cries of 'À la queue!' and objections to any *resquilleur* or *resquilleuse* who tried to butt in or sneak ahead in line were common. There was little solidarity in frustration. Uncertainty as to how long one would have to wait, and whether one would obtain any goods, made the queues a site for tension, frustration and incipient conflict. Berthe Auroy recorded her cold mornings in queues in 1940 as follows:

Despite the rigours of the cold and the torture of chilblains . . . it was sometimes necessary to resist for several hours to obtain . . . oh! not much, and sometimes nothing at all, if the merchandise had run out . . . . To get a small ration of frozen meat, the 'risk-everythings' are outside at 5 a.m. (forbidden to go out earlier, otherwise . . .) One finds out possibilities for the right place to pick up a bit of cheese or butter, especially butter; it seems the lack of butter is the greatest privation. The tickets? Oh yes! We have these precious tickets, secure in envelopes of mica, but alas! Too often they represent only pretty promises, illusory, varieties of *chèques sans provisions* ('provisions' is indeed the word).[42]

---

[38] Baudin, *Esquisse de l'économie*, 121; Veillon, *Paris allemand*, 116; Alary et al., *Les Français au quotidien*, 270. Rates of pay ranged from 5 to 10 francs per hour.

[39] The author of *J'ai faim!* describes his experience in queues for food; the queue in Aymé's 'En attendant' consists of seven women, two of whom are mothers, three men and four children.

[40] The contest ran from late October to mid-November. The caption for the photos read: 'In doing your shopping, don't be impatient if you have to wait. You could win one hundred francs.'

[41] Paul Achard, *La queue*; Véran, *En faisant la queue*; Marcel Aymé, 'En attendant', *Le passe-muraille* (Paris: Gallimard, 1943 [Folio edition 1998]), 205–222.

[42] Auroy, *Jours de guerre*, 136–138.

Needs were so desperate and the goods available so rare that shoppers joined queues without knowing what they were for: 'the moment a queue starts, it's because there something difficult to find', one habituée affirmed, noting that she could trade anything she obtained that she didn't need.[43] Customers formed *queues à surprise* if a car pulled up outside a shop door, without knowing what it might deliver: 'the surprise often consisted of the fact that the car was bringing nothing at all!'[44]

Everyone in line wanted their share from the limited supply of goods. The intensity of needs is evident in the conflict created by cards that gave priority to certain customers. *Cartes de priorité* allowed pregnant mothers and mothers with young children to reduce the time they had to wait in line.[45] (Figure 6.1; there were also *cartes d'invalidité* to give priority to war invalids.) The principle was unobjectionable, but the practice sparked controversy. The police decided that separate lines were needed, with service alternating between the two queues, to serve priority cardholders without completely neglecting the ordinary consumers. Without police intervention, it was up to the shopkeepers and clients to initiate the alternation, which mattered very much to the ordinary consumers threatened by the exhaustion of limited supplies.[46] Some cardholders exploited their privilege in lending their cards or making purchases for friends. The cards prompted complaints about this abuse. One exasperated mother wrote to the prefect of the Seine, 'Many use this priority to feed a whole building.'[47] The police admitted there were problems and confiscated cards when they witnessed misuse (usually buying for a third party). But tight control would have required a policeman to watch every queue. Alternatives to restrict cardholders were considered and rejected as impractical.[48]

---

[43] Achard, *La queue*, 19–20.   [44] Baudin, *Esquisse de l'économie*, 121.

[45] Veillon, *Paris allemand*, 116 and *Vivre et survivre*, 129; Pollard, *Reign of Virtue*, 132–134. A decree on 10 Dec. 1940 gave priority cards to veterans of the First World War with status as invalids. Paris police were warned they would be suspended if they took advantage of their official status to jump queues; APP BA 1808, Marchand to all municipal police, 25 Oct. 1940.

[46] APP BA 1808, decrees for maintaining order in queues; separate queues are required in the decrees of 6 May 1941 and 28 June 1942. A decree in January 1942 established that if the queue for *cartes de priorité* was not long, shops should serve two ordinary consumers for every priority customer. The written version of the decree initially reversed this order, stating that two priority customers would be served for each ordinary customer; this was quickly corrected.

[47] APP BA 1808, Mme. Vve. Dabonneulle to the prefect of the Seine, 6 Nov. 1940.

[48] APP BA 1808, has correspondence between the prefect of police and the prefect of the Seine in December 1940 and January 1941; particularly Fontenoy to Magny, 7 Dec. 1940, and director of the *Police générale* to the prefect of Police, 26 Dec. 1940. There were bitter complaints about abuse: 'holders of these cards succeed in being served several times in the course of a day. They collect more merchandise than they need and resell, sometimes at high prices, sometimes to their friends'; APP 220W 9, 'Situation à Paris', 15 June 1942. Darlan noted this as a serious problem in AN F/7/14900, Darlan to

Figure 6.1 'You who are waiting in queues, don't be angry with those who
have priority.' Secrétariat d'état à la famille et à la santé, illustration by
Alain Saint-Ogan, 1941.
Collection Bernard Le Marec © Pierre Verrier, Centre d'histoire de la
Résistance et de la Déportation, Musée de Lyon.

The priority system remained. One man reported waiting for a shop to
open at 9 a.m. at the end of a queue of 250 customers in Place Clichy. The
first customers arrived at 5:45. It was a 'veritable scandal', he wrote, that

the prefects and sub-prefects of Confolens, St. Amand, Montmorillon, 29 Apr. 1941. AD
Pyrénées-Atlantiques 1031W/199 has cases of card confiscations when used to purchase
for third persons in 1941.

priority cardholders, many of whom had probably borrowed cards, could be served after a short wait and continue to another shop 'to do the same again'.[49] A cartoon in 1943 exaggerated the multi-level fraud in having a shopkeeper, serving customers illegally from the back of his store (*arrière boutique*), ask whether any customers in line had counterfeit *cartes de priorité,* in order to serve them first (Figure 6.2). Although the priority for mothers was recognized, customers did not want to lose access to limited food through the illegitimate use of priority cards.

Figure 6.2 'Any false *cartes de priorité*?' from *Devant le marché noir* (1943), private collection.

---

[49] APP BA 1808, Paul Leroudier to the Prefect of Police, 17 Mar. 1942.

In the opening pages of Achard's *La queue*, customers waiting for potatoes in a market are dismayed when the first three sacks are set aside for Jules, Ernest and Nénette, whoever they may be. They protest after someone suggests these sacks will go to *bistrots*, and the woman tending the stall takes advantage of the tumult to set aside two more sacks before selling to those in the queue. The first customers get one kilo per ticket for three kilos, with seven tickets required for a fourth kilo. The length of the queue soon requires a reduction to one half kilo per person. The last customer in line gets nothing.[50] Such scenes became more desperate as market supplies dwindled. Garden produce was particularly vulnerable to seasonal factors, the prices set by local authorities, and diversion to parallel markets. Raymond Ruffin queued for two hours in February 1942 to get two kilograms of carrots, two kilograms of turnips and one cauliflower, a generous haul, as the stall proprietor had not required cards for all his family (his mother was in another queue with three of their five cards). In January 1943, Ruffin waited nearly four hours for 3 kg of Jerusalem artichokes.[51] Complaints were frequent among customers outside butchers' shops. They worried that packages for favoured clients – delivered to their homes, under-the-counter and back-door sales, premiums paid, and exchanges of goods between shopkeepers – reduced the supply for customers in queues.[52]

The dissatisfaction in queues had potential to generate disorder.[53] The police kept the queues under close observation to forestall unrest. In Paris, they issued a litany of rules for shopkeepers and customers to reduce waiting times, prevent obstruction of traffic, and above all, to reduce the numbers of customers waiting. In September 1940, before the official rationing system was put in place, the police anticipated they would need 6,000 *gardiens* to keep order.[54] The Germans recommended having customers register with stores, and storekeepers post signs as to who would be served at what time (alphabetical by family name). The idea met with scepticism in December 1940, but was adopted later in 1941, including measures to allow registration for non-rationed goods, and forbidding queues until thirty minutes before shops opened.[55] In the

[50] Achard, *La queue*, 14–17.
[51] Raymond Ruffin, *Journal d'un J3* (Paris: Presses de la Cité, 1979), 87–89, 165–166.
[52] APP 220W series 'Situation à Paris' reports note these worries repeatedly in autumn 1940 through 1941.
[53] Paula Schwartz, 'The Politics of Food and Gender in Occupied Paris', *Modern and Contemporary France*, 7(1) (1999): 37–38.
[54] APP BA 1808, Prefect of Police to the Prefect of the Seine, 9 Sept. 1940.
[55] APP BA 1808, police commissariat of Saint-Denis-Ville, 13 Dec. 1940; decrees of 24 Dec. 1940, 6 May and 28 June 1941, and prefect of Police to the Commander of the Gendarmerie, Seine Section, 30 June 1941.

6th arrondissement, police noted large crowds in the Buci market, lining up as early as 5 a.m. in December 1940. By 9 a.m. the butcher shops had closed. One butcher with 150 rabbits for sale in half portions had attracted a queue of 2,000. Violence was certain, the police advised, if nothing was done to alleviate the conditions of hunger and cold.[56]

As they observed rising misery and frustration in the queues, the Paris police foresaw not only possible unrest and violence, but also the potential for propaganda critical of the state. The Gaullist resistance received occasional mention, but the greater concern was the communists. Rising prices, the declining purchasing power of workers' wages and the undernourishment of workers' families created 'a climate conducive to communist activity, and largely exploited by their agitators'.[57] Journalists in the collaborationist press criticized Achard and the *Ravitaillement général* for incompetence. Gaullists distributed a pamphlet asking, 'France is hungry; who is starving France?' The PCF urged peasants to refuse to deliver their produce to the state, supported workers' demands for wage increases to cover food costs, and encouraged mothers to demand more food for their families.[58] Food shortages and prices offered common ground for protest against a system that clearly favoured wealth and privilege at the expense of those on fixed incomes.

But customers in queues were difficult to mobilize against retailers, and the reasons show the limits to solidarity in the queues. Queues were inactive by nature, shuffling forward as each customer was served. They gathered anxious and frequently disappointed consumers with potential to spark social disorder. But their inactivity is striking, in contrast to protests to redress market grievances and the 'moral economy' of distribution in earlier periods of food scarcity.[59] Frustrating as they were, the queues promised an orderly distribution of limited food, respecting the order in which customers arrived. The objective was individual (even if purchasing for families) rather than collective, each person drawing from a limited supply. It was a zero-sum game. Any increase in one buyer's share reduced the availability for others in line and increased the number of those who would get nothing. The efforts by shopkeepers and police to

---

[56] APP BA 1808, Le Commissaire de Police de V.P. du 6ème arrondissement to the Directeur général de la Police municipale, 22 Dec. 1940. The report noted that the goods available outside Paris strengthened the belief that Paris was being starved deliberately.

[57] APP 220W 4, 'Situation à Paris', 26 May 1941.

[58] APP 220W 9, 'Situation à Paris', 8 June 1942, reported PCF propaganda advising peasants, 'Peasant, don't give your wheat to Hitler' and 'Peasant, sell your harvest direct to French consumers.'

[59] E. P. Thompson, 'The Moral Economy of the English Crowd in the Eighteenth Century', *Past and Present*, 50 (1971): 76–136.

maintain order were reinforced by customer discipline to ensure that the queue order was respected. Protests were rare, expressing frustration with sellers when price increases caused outrage.[60]

Crowd action against sellers would serve no purpose if there was nothing to distribute. But the empty shelves and the waiting time in queues provided an opportunity to organize protests in public space and challenge state authorities. As one police chief recognized, during the spread of demonstrations in the Alpes-Maritimes in 1942, 'the long waits by customers before shelves with insufficient provisions favour the exchange of unfavourable comments on the conditions of food supply, and can one day be the origin for tumultuous demonstrations'.[61] Collective action and consumer solidarity targeted not shopkeepers but the state, for its potential to bring more goods to empty markets.

Housewives Protest

The stress in feeding families was borne by women, whose role in shopping, cooking and caring for families was complicated by the scarcity of goods, the extra time needed for shopping, and their greater responsibilities as the heads of households when husbands had been lost to the war, POW camps and conscripted labour. Vichy administrators explicitly considered shopping, queues and food protests as women's roles.[62]

The first food demonstrations in the autumn of 1940 were spontaneous. Vichy's emphasis on 'work family, and fatherland' and the importance of mothers bearing children and building strong families, made the public display of mothers' needs a serious challenge to state policy. Officials referred to the women in queues and demonstrations as *ménagères* – housewives – recognizing their status as providers for their families. Communist organizers saw potential to mobilize women shoppers as mothers; they encouraged them to demonstrate accompanied by their children. Protesting coal shortages in the winter of 1940–1941, mothers took their children on Thursdays (a day out of school) to sit in

---

[60] One striking postwar example was the response of the shoppers in the Marché Victor-Hugo in Toulouse in Sept. 1945. In a Saturday market, with no meat having been available in the preceding week, women reacted to merchants selling poultry at higher prices by helping themselves to poultry as well as to pasta, rice, sugar and condensed milk in neighbouring stores. The police estimated that the crowd of 1,500 women took 7,800 chickens and unknown quantities of other goods. AN F/1a/3250, Secretary-General of Police to the Minister of the Interior, 17 Sept. 1945, and Prefect of the Haute Garonne to Minister of the Interior, 18 Sept. 1945

[61] AD Alpes-Maritimes 616W/251; Commissaire central of the city of Nice to the regional prefect, 30 Jan. 1942.

[62] Schwartz, 'The Politics of Food and Gender', 35, 39–41, and Diamond, *Women in the Second World War*, 49–70.

the heated waiting rooms in municipal offices, bringing sewing and letting their children play hide-and-seek. They refused to leave until the mayor met with a delegation and promised more coal for heating.[63]

The protesters targeted municipal offices and department prefectures. The simplicity of their demands – more bread, potatoes, pasta, and dried legumes, so that their children would not starve – made public statement of the failures of state policy. The women challenged the regime's repressive policies and its subordination of 'la femme au foyer', using their visibility to demand more from authorities who failed to provision markets with adequate supplies. They demanded meetings with mayors and prefects. Many demonstrations gained small concessions in food allocation, particularly in the period 1940–1942. But as their protests spread, encouraged by positive results, prefects asked mayors to resist their demands and to reward quiescence with extra distributions 'to the most peaceful communes'.[64]

The shortages prompted a major wave of demonstrations in the south of France in early 1942.[65] In the largest, in Sète on 20 January, more than 1,000 women exasperated by shortages (in previous days markets had only carrots and turnips) gathered outside the town hall. 'Bread for our kids', they chanted, and when they received no response, threw rocks and chanted 'Down with Pétain, down with Pétain.'[66] A few demonstrators were arrested, but municipal authorities responded by distributing a supply of dried vegetables. The Gendarmerie singled out this protest for its threatening character. The PCF argued that success in Sète should encourage more women's demonstrations: it proved that direct action would bring success for their legitimate claims.[67] The other demonstrations, often spontaneous, were smaller than in Sète, but they gained distribution of supplements – dried vegetables, pasta and potatoes. The Gendarmerie added a new category to its monthly summary,

[63] Lise London, *La mégère de la rue Daguerre: Souvenirs de Résistance* (Paris: Seuil, 1995), 102–103, and Veillon, *Paris allemand*, 68–69.
[64] Danielle Tartakowsky, 'Manifester pour le pain, novembre 1940–octobre 1947', *Cahiers de l'IHTP*, 32–33 (1996): 466–474. Tartakowsky finds housewives most successful in obtaining extra food in 1940–1941, prior to the prefect directives.
[65] Jean-Marie Guillon, 'Le retour des "émotions populaires": manifestations de ménagères en 1942', in *Mélanges Michel Vovelle, volume aixois* (Aix: Publications de l'Université de Provence, 1997), 267–276.
[66] *L'Humanité*, 26 Feb. 1942, which reported that the six women sent to talk to the mayor as representatives of the crowd had been arrested, triggering a larger demonstration in which workers joined their wives in protest, the crowd numbering 2500.
[67] *L'Humanité*, 26 Feb. 1942, reported that the six women sent to talk to the mayor as representatives of the crowd had been arrested, triggering a larger demonstration in which workers joined their wives in protest, the crowd numbering 2500. AN AJ/41/24, Gendarmerie summary for January 1942, and the account of the demonstration given later, 'La révolte des ménagères à Sète', *France*, 19 Aug. 1942, in AN F/60/1697.

'Demonstrations by housewives', observing that these were clearly planned and of Communist inspiration. They followed a pattern: assembly in the morning in front of the city hall, sending a delegation to talk to the mayor, giving him time to contact departmental authorities, and returning in the afternoon for his response.[68] The *Contrôle technique* reported that the demonstrations had 'obtained immediate results and consequently risk setting an example, especially because they seem to be prompted by propaganda that opposes the interests of city dwellers to rural people and the poor to the rich'.[69]

Two demonstrations in Paris in 1942 sparked violent clashes with the police.[70] In late May, the PCF distributed tracts calling on mothers to mobilize on behalf of their children on Mothers' Day, stating 'Honour to mothers. They gave children to France. To reward them, the old Pétain and his friend Laval will give them wooden crosses.' They called on mothers to unite and fight to secure life for their children on Sunday, 31 May 1942.[71] Outside the ECO grocery store on the rue de Buci, which was also a food depot for the Germans, militants distributed tracts to waiting customers, urging them to help themselves to essential foods. Several women led by Madeleine Marzin pushed into the store and passed canned goods and sugar to customers outside. ECO staff tried to apprehend them but plans for the demonstration included providing defence groups to protect the women. One male comrade helped free the women in the store; three militants intervened outside when the police tried to arrest them. The women escaped. Their protectors shot five policemen, two fatally; they were arrested nearby.[72]

The police identified the Communist leadership and linked the violence to the PCF's turn to direct action by its *Organisation spéciale*, attacking French police and providing armed protection to Communist speakers. Marzin was arrested the next day, and she and eight men were condemned to death. Three were shot in July, and five students who had been part of the security squad were executed in February 1943. Marzin's sentence was

---

[68] AN AJ/41/24, 'Synthèse des rapports mensuels des Commandants des Légions de Gendarmerie de la Zone Libre (Mars 1942)'.

[69] AN BB/30/1723; 'Synthèse mensuelle des interceptions des contrôles postaux, télégraphiques et téléphoniques', no. 34 (for the period 7 Feb. to 7 Mar. 1942).

[70] For a thorough account and analysis of the rue de Buci protest, see Paula Schwartz, *Today Sardines are Not for Sale: A Street Protest in Occupied Paris* (Oxford: Oxford University Press, 2020).

[71] APP 220W 9, 'Situation à Paris', 1 June 1942.

[72] APP BA 2128, interrogation reports; Schwartz, *Today Sardines are Not For Sale*, 14–38; Megan Barber, 'Popular Street Protests in France', PhD dissertation, UC Santa Barbara, 2012, Chapter 3; and the accounts in Roger Bourderon, *Le PCF à l'épreuve de la guerre, 1940–1943: De la guerre impérialiste à la lutte armée* (Paris: Éditions Syllepse, 2012), 159–160, and Roger Linet, *1933–1943, La traversée de la tourmente* (Paris: Éditions Messidor, 1990), 270–271.

commuted to hard labour for life; comrades helped her escape in the Gare Montparnasse when she was transferred to Rennes in August 1942.[73] Communist tracts encouraged women to take Buci as an example. One tract addressed to 'Housewives, mothers of families' urged: 'Serve yourself! Demand increased rations! Take the goods where they are!'[74] Another praised them in a tract titled 'The women of Paris give us the example': 'They've given the signal to attack in the battle that the population through-out France must wage, to take back what the Boches have stolen from us.'[75]

Violence erupted again on 1 August, outside the Félix Potin grocery store on the rue Daguerre. Lise Ricol climbed on a table to urge house-wives waiting in line to protest the queues and shortages and resist having their husbands and sons sent to Germany. This protest too had been planned. This time fifteen armed militants protected the women, who threw tracts to the crowd. When the police tried to arrest Ricol, the militants shot two officers and one German soldier. The press reported seven civilians wounded, one fatally, which the PCF denied.[76] As well as the PCF, two women's groups were prominent in organizing further protests: the *Comités des femmes françaises* in 1942, and the *Union des femmes françaises* (UFF) in 1943. Further PCF appeals to housewives to take the goods they needed attracted no recorded support. Direct action in markets remained rare, and the use of violence rarer still.[77] The protests on the rue de Buci and the rue Daguerre stand out for their politicizing marketplace actions with armed militants prepared to defend the demonstrators. The strategy was abandoned after these two incidents.

The logic and outcomes of these food demonstrations are strikingly different from those in the 'moral economy' of food protests in eighteenth-century England, analysed by E. P. Thompson as organized responses to food crises.[78] Thompson's crowds took the allocation of supplies at a fair

[73] Schwartz, *Today Sardines are Not For Sale*, 37, 124–130.

[74] APP 220W 9, 'Situation à Paris', 15 June 1942.

[75] APP BA 2067, note of 27 July 1942; Schwartz, *Today Sardines are Not For Sale*, provides excellent analysis of the conflicting Vichy and PCF representations of the protest in 1942 and the 'kaleidoscope of memory' after the war, 143–180.

[76] London, *La mégère de la rue Daguerre*, 158–162; Linet, *La traversée de la tourmente*, 285–291 (Linet was one organizer of FTP security); Barber, 'Popular Street Protest in Vichy France'; Denis Peschanski, 'Manifestation de la rue Daguerre', in François Marcot with Bruno Leroux and Christine Levisse-Touzé, *Dictionnaire historique de la Résistance* (Paris: Robert Laffont, 2006), 736–737; Roger Bourderon, *Le PCF à l'épreuve de la guerre, 1940–1943: de la guerre impérialiste à la lutte armée* (Paris: Syllepse, 2012), 160–162.

[77] Tartakowsky notes that some demonstrations seized goods from merchants suspected of black-market activities and from a pasta factory in the Var, based on research by Jean-Marie Guillon; Tartakowsky, 'Manifester pour le pain', 470. Guillon argues these usually started in empty marketplaces, a return to *Ancien Régime* protests, spontaneous, atomized and regional.

[78] Thompson, 'The Moral Economy of the English Crowd'.

price into their own hands after appealing without success to the state. They maintained 'just' prices and distributed grain produced in their communities rather than allow its export to earn higher profit elsewhere. In food protests in Occupied France, the problem was not high prices. Low output, fixed prices and German requisitions reduced the quantity of goods in the market: often there were no supplies to seize and distribute. The state was the authority that set rules and kept food reserves. Rather than taking over the regulatory functions of government, the women protesters appealed to state authorities to bring more food to markets.

Women took over the political space outside town halls and prefectures and mobilized a force otherwise excluded from politics to challenge state policy on behalf of families. They demanded 'bread for our children'. Tracts charged Vichy with giving the food needed for French families to the Germans. Demonstrators acted because state food policy was failing its most important stakeholders. That failure justified not just public protest, but private action: to find the food supplies needed to survive beyond the bounds of official, controlled markets where official provisioning fell short. Appeals for supplementary rations marked an attempt to stay within the rules. The demonstrators knew that in restaurants, in deals between shopkeepers, in the relative plenty of the countryside, and in the swelling black-market traffic, food supplies were available.

Beyond the Market: Surviving Shortages

The food rations offered 'slow starvation' and trended downwards. The daily allocations for most adults varied between 1,040 and 1,247 calories.[79] International standards held that an adult not engaged in significant exertion needed 2,400 calories to maintain adequate health, and average prewar consumption had been close to 3,000 calories. The rations were higher for children, adolescents, workers engaged in heavy labour, and women who were pregnant or breastfeeding children (the highest rations at 1,900 calories per day). Food supply officials and the medical profession insisted that the rationing regime posed a grave threat to public health.[80] The impact was clear in increasing mortality, disease, weight loss, and slower growth for children and adolescents.[81]

[79] Cépède, *Agriculture et alimentation*, 386.
[80] AN F/60/1546, 'Plan de rationnement alimentaire', 8 Sept. 1940, and Dominique Veillon, 'Aux origines de la sous-alimentation: pénuries et rationnement alimentaire', in *'Morts d'inanition'*, 36–39. Prewar calorie level from Sauvy, *La vie économique*, 111.
[81] The health impact is summarized in Cépède, *Agriculture et alimentation*, 403–417 and Sauvy, *La vie économique*, 189–200. One prefect reported in 1942 that average weight loss in his department since September 1939 was probably 10 kg, based on the declining weight of factory workers at the Usines Solvay in Dombasle, where average weight fell

Insufficient rations made it essential to find supplements. Those with restricted access to food owing to their location, mobility or income felt the greatest impact. Among the worst off were the patients in hospitals and asylums. An estimated 45,000 asylum patients died from malnutrition and weakened resistance, mainly in 1941 and 1942.[82] Also at risk were prisoners, residents in departments lacking diverse agriculture, and residents in large cities without access to food from the countryside.[83] Those closest to rural food sources or with wealth to purchase more (in richer quarters in cities) fared best. Workers, civil servants, middle-class employees and pensioners on fixed incomes struggled to find sufficient food.

The possibilities to increase family consumption varied from purchasing foods sold without ration restrictions (increasingly hard to find) to producing goods at home, bartering goods for food, and a gradation of adaptive purchasing that ranged from exchanges between friends to explicit black-market activity. In the transition from legal purchase to tolerated exchange, and then to illicit activity, there were gradations not only between types of transaction but, as legality became less clear, opportunities for permitted exchange (such as family parcels) used as a cover for black market trade. This bending of rules and stretching of allowances blurs clear distinction between 'grey' and black markets. In practice, they could overlap.[84] Efforts to locate extra supplies proceeded on terms in which opportunity and urgency took precedence over strict legality.

Unrationed foods offered limited opportunity: they were snapped up to replace rationed goods, and subject in turn to rationing, vanishing from markets when authorities set prices at levels the producers found inadequate. This was particularly true for seasonal fruit and vegetables, and for rabbits and poultry, for which the state fixed prices and limited quantities, but did not set rations because the supplies were too inconsistent for planned distribution. Consumers explored alternatives for supply. Those with opportunities to grow a garden and raise animals could add to their own consumption and sell to friends. Poultry and

---

from 72 kg 700 in September 1939 to 70 kg 800 in August 1940, and 62 kg 600 in April 1942. AN AJ/41/379 (Meurthe-et-Moselle), prefect monthly report, 1 May 1942.

[82] Some authors claimed in the 1980s that this was deliberate extermination; Isabelle von Bueltzingsloewen provides careful analysis of the arguments and evidence to refute this in *L'Hécatombe des fous*. The state allocated higher rations for asylum patients in December 1942, reducing their vulnerability.

[83] Von Bueltzingsloewen, ed., *'Morts d'inanition'*, and IHTP studies of *départements affamés* (the Hérault, Alpes-Maritimes and the town of Saint-Claude in the Jura) in *Cahiers de l'IHTP* 32–33 (1996): 171–222.

[84] Debû-Bridel devoted a chapter to 'Marché noir et marché gris', admitting the two overlapped to allow no clear distinction between them; *Histoire du marché noir*, 43–52.

rabbits could be raised in back yards and on apartment balconies.[85] Jean Orieux, on a farm near Limoges, commented, 'It must be said that we never saw, transported or ate so many rabbits as during the war – it was one of the atrocities of this dreadful period. The rabbit was everywhere.'[86] Family gardens provided benefit, but became targets for theft, especially when on the outskirts of cities and towns. Families abandoned their allotments when too much of their produce was stolen.[87]

The next step was to rely on rural family and friends. The possibilities, depending on location, income, and family relations, could allow significant improvement in food access and re-establish or reinforce family connections. Rural properties could be used to grow vegetables.[88] Family in the countryside could be visited on holidays and weekends. Relatives consuming meat from their farms sent meat ration tickets to family in cities, increasing the urban demand. Jean Achard claimed that the number of meat tickets presented to butchers in Paris in early 1941 was equivalent to 10.5 million ration cards.[89] Families planned to send children to stay at rural homes for better access to food. The Groult sisters organized their summers with this in mind, canoeing with friends, helping with summer harvest, or staying with a friend's rural grandparents while studying for exams.[90] Older children could be sent to summer camps or to *colonies de vacances* where they were fed well.[91] Raymond Ruffin went as a *colo* to a farm at la Puisaye (Yonne). His stay, planned for one month in July 1943, extended to mid-October. On his return to Paris, he observed, 'we resume contact with the realities of life under the Occupation'.[92] Micheline Bood, a schoolgirl during the Occupation, often visited

---

[85] Cépède mentions there are no serious statistics for either poultry or rabbits, but that raising rabbits 'saw an enormous increase' to supplement meat rations; *Agriculture et alimentation*, 323. Sauvy cites the 'benevolent rabbit' as 'a valuable resource' for many families and easy to raise. Sauvy, *La vie économique*, 132.

[86] Orieux, *Souvenirs de campagnes*, 332.

[87] AN AJ/41/395, 'Synthèse relative à l'état moral et matériel de la population dans les territoires de la zone occupée au cours du mois de Juillet 1943'; Henri Drouot noted increasing thefts from gardens in 1941, and German troops stealing from gardens and orchards in 1944; *Notes d'un dijonnais*, 197, 276, 289, 310, 318, 550, 664, 689, 695.

[88] Berthe Auroy supplemented her diet with food from rural neighbours, parcels from friends, and kept a vegetable garden in one room of her apartment; Auroy, *Jours de guerre*. Charles Rist had food sent by friends in the countryside and from his country residence, and he grew potatoes and vegetables in his yard in Versailles; Rist, *Season of Infamy*, 115, 191, 221, 254, 284–285.

[89] AN F/60/590, Comité économique interministériel meeting minutes, 28 Mar. 1941.

[90] Benoîte and Flora Groult, *Journal à quatre mains* (Paris: Éditions Denoel, 1962; reprint 2002), 248, 259–264, 320–324, 400–405. Bernard Pierquin went regularly to stay with family in Brittany and noted the abundance of food; *Journal d'un étudiant parisien sous l'Occupation (1939–1945)* (Paris: Bernard Pierquin, 1983), 51, 81, 102.

[91] Pierquin, *Journal d'un étudiant*, 66; Ruffin, *Journal d'un J3*, 172–195.

[92] Ruffin, *Journal d'un J3*, 195.

relatives in Brittany. Returning to Paris in December 1942, she watched her mother and sister exclaim over the 30 kg of food she brought home and wrote, 'It's strange, but when one eats well, one no longer pays any attention to the food.'[93]

Rural families sent food in 'family parcels' to relatives, friends, and to paying customers in the cities. Officially permitted by decree on 13 October 1941, food parcels had been sent to ameliorate shortages since the summer of 1940, and increased as rations and market supplies declined, serving as a major conduit to cities. By the end of 1940, Paris post offices received hundreds of parcels a day. The Paris police attributed the initiative for this growing parcel traffic to the shortages in city markets.[94] The *Comité économique interministériel* (CEI) considered the problem in 1941, concerned that parcels diverted food from official collection. The Germans opposed the 'so-called family parcels', but French negotiators argued that forbidding them or tightening control of their contents would require more manpower in post offices and train stations. The CEI discussed allowing parcel weights up to 30 or 50 kg and opted for the greater weight in October 1941.[95] The Germans demanded their suppression in May 1942 and December 1943; French officials replied that this would simply move the traffic to the black market.

For Raymond Ruffin, the two or three parcels his family received each month brought 'a vital contribution', enough to keep his family at a subsistence level.[96] Parcels in the first winter of the Occupation provided essential food for families unable to obtain their full rations at local stores. Jean Guéhenno, teaching in Paris, survived the winter thanks to food sent by friends and cousins in Brittany.[97] The Groult family received their first parcel from relatives in Brittany in February 1941 with a dozen eggs and a chicken that had started to go bad. They came to depend on food sent from the countryside.[98] Charles Rist wrote of 'a whole system of private shipments' to make up for market shortages.[99] Many diarists and memoirists recorded parcels as a critical supplement, shared at times with friends. Most of these writers were in an economic position to acquire

---

[93] Micheline Bood, *Les années doubles: Journal d'une lycéenne sous l'Occupation* (Paris: Robert Laffont, 1974), 179.

[94] APP BA 1807, note of 29 Dec. 1940.

[95] Veillon, *Vivre et survivre*, 173–176; and AN F/37/5, CEI discussions of 6 June, 10 and 26 Sept. and 1 and 10 Oct. 1941; AN F/60/1546; 'Note pour Monsieur le Délégué Général aux Relations Économique Franco-Allemandes', 11 July 1941 and 6 Sept. 1941, summarizing the negotiations.

[96] Ruffin, *Journal d'un J3*, 93–94, and his subsequent comment that 'we subsist miserably with our rations and the two or three monthly parcels from the provinces', 104.

[97] Jean Guéhenno, *Journal des années noires (1940–1944)* (Paris: Gallimard, 1947), 89 (3 Jan. 1941).

[98] Groult, *Journal à quatre mains*, 188.   [99] Rist, *Season of Infamy*, 115 (7 Feb. 1941).

such benefits. Alfred Sauvy saw the parcels as 'a great manifestation of bourgeois hypocrisy', a means by which wealthy families in the richest *arrondissements* of Paris (the 7th, 8th, 9th and 16th) undermined the egalitarian impulse behind food rationing.[100] The police and the SNCF reported that most parcels went to the wealthy districts.[101]

The designation 'family' meant the contents were for family consumption, not resale. Relations in the countryside could be family, friends, the family of the maid, or 'paid relations' – connections established through classified ads seeking someone to send food.[102] One report commented, in January 1943, 'Many cultivators have, in effect, considerably extended the notion of family, and have sent parcels to a range of individual clients willing to pay excessive prices.' One farmer in the Creuse sent 400 *colis familiaux* per week.[103] The nutritionist Dr Richer estimated that Parisians obtained about 200 calories per day from *colis familiaux* and the black market.[104] As an average, this hides the bias favouring those with connections and income. But his conflation of the sources is apt, as the parcels became a regular means to convey black market food.

In southern cities like Marseille and Nice, where regional agriculture was less diverse, residents had less food in official markets and less opportunity to buy local produce.[105] Jane Hyrem, president of the *Union française des femmes seules*, wrote from Nice to a friend in Grenoble in April 1941, asking him to send a parcel with potatoes, carrots, leeks, eggs, butter, and if possible, a half rabbit or half chicken. Her department was 'badly placed', with flowers as its main agriculture. There was no fruit, few vegetables, and the meat ration had been reduced to 90 grams every two weeks. Ration tickets without food to buy resulted

[100] Sauvy, *La vie économique*, 133–135.

[101] AN F/90/21609; 'Augmentation du trafic', 21 Jan. 1941; APP BA 1806, note of 19 Nov. 1943; and APP 220W 12, 'Situation à Paris', 26 July 1943.

[102] Veillon notes that rural newspapers carried ads seeking farmers who would send food parcels in exchange for payment; *Vivre et survivre*, 174. Robert Gildea found that food sent within families often involved no payment, and the personal relations between buyers and sellers kept prices reasonable for family parcels from the Loire valley, *Marianne in Chains*, 116–118.

[103] AN 72AJ/563, 'Rapport général sur l'agriculture et le ravitaillement en France (janvier 1943)'.

[104] Richer cited in Cépède, *Agriculture et alimentation*, 392. Sauvy estimated an adult consumer obtained about 155 to 240 calories per day from 'Colis de divers sortes', perhaps thus including black market, in a diet that alternative sources raised from 1,087 calories of rationed foods to 1,755 to 2,010 calories. Sauvy, *La vie économique*, 135, figures taken from his 1943 inquiry in Institut de conjoncture, 'Situation économique au début d'Août 1943 (Rapport no. 14)'. On nutritionists monitoring the impact of food shortages, Veillon, 'Aux origines de la sous-alimentation', 31–43.

[105] The 'starving' departments were mostly in the south of France; see Hélène Chaubin, 'L'Hérault', and Jean-Louis Panicacci, 'Les Alpes-Maritimes', in *Cahiers de l'IHTP* 32–33 (1996): 171–193, 195–212.

in 'queues of 3 or 4 hours to get a lemon or often nothing'. 'Everyone here receives packages from the countryside', she continued, 'otherwise we'd die of hunger, it's very sad, but even with money one can't eat'.[106]

The SNCF set up regional sorting stations in autumn 1940 to deal with the increasing volume of food parcels sent from western departments to Paris, routing them from Le Mans to a sorting depot in the Gare Saint-Lazare. The sorting office for *objets recommandés* at the Gare Montparnasse had its daily traffic increase from an average of 40 *paquets* daily in 1938 to 200 sacks of *paquets* each day in August 1940, 400 sacks in September, 600 sacks in October, 900 sacks in November and 1,500 in December.[107] The *paquets recommandés* (a fraction of total traffic, faster than other services) handled there climbed from 784,299 in 1938 to 1.6 million in 1941, 2.8 million in 1942, 4.3 million in 1943.[108] Sauvy reported there were 13,547,000 *colis* shipped in France in 1942, weighing 279,000 tonnes, without stating parcel size.[109] The smaller, faster *paquets* often used for perishable foods such as butter, indicated a massive traffic: 34 million *paquets* in 1941, 45 million in 1942, 55 million in 1943, and 70 million in 1944. If sent at maximum weight, this could have carried up to 135,000 tonnes in 1942, and 210,000 tonnes in 1945.[110]

The opportunity for black-market sales was present from the start.[111] But neither the PTT nor the SNCF had the manpower or the will to block this traffic. Prefects saw the SNCF as 'a wide-open door' for food shipment.[112] Railroad officials were notoriously lax in verifying the contents of parcels, and poor security allowed a high rate of theft for parcels transported, including theft by SNCF employees.[113] Post office staff rarely checked parcel contents, although they were supposed to mark suspect packages with numbered stickers for verification of content. Those collecting the parcels were seldom asked to verify the

[106] AD Alpes-Maritimes 166W/23; Mme. Katherine Rogers to Mr. de Maixmoran, intercepted 22 April 1941.
[107] AN F/90/21609; PTT, 'Note pour Monsieur le Secrétaire général', 21 Jan. 1941; the depot at the Gare Saint-Lazare opened in Jan. 1941.
[108] AN 72AJ/2225; 'Histoire de la guerre 1939–1945, Département de la Sarthe', 13.
[109] Sauvy, *La vie économique*, 134. According to a CE report, Paris train stations received 5,444,358 *colis familiaux* in the last three months of 1943. SAEF B-0057659; DGCE to Pierre Taittinger as president of the Paris Municipal Council, 20 Mar. 1944.
[110] AN F/90/21627; 'Historique des mesures ayant intéressé l'acheminement des correspondances pendant la période de guerre'.
[111] The director of the post office called for vigilance in December 1941, to prevent parcel use for commercial traffic. M. Pignochet, Directeur de la Poste et des Batiments, quoted in André Paul, 'Histoire des PTT pendant la deuxième guerre mondiale', 291.
[112] SAEF 4A-0000003; 'Note sur les facilités donnés par la S.N.C.F. au "marché noir"', 28 Feb. 1941.
[113] AD Ille-et-Vilaine 118W/75, regional prefect reports in autumn 1941, and many reports on thefts in AN F/90/21627, and AN 72AJ/1927.

contents.[114] Butter was a particular problem. It was shipped in packages labelled 'vegetables' by one farmer in Alpes-Maritimes,[115] and wrapped in cabbage leaves or stored in ceramic pots to keep it cool in summer. Georges Simenon mailed butter in 'cracker cans enclosed in sackcloth sewed together with string' to friends in Paris.[116] Sorting depots handled greasy, dripping parcels not just in summer heat, but in winter when parcels were stacked adjacent to depot heating ducts.[117]

The post office and the SNCF compiled lists of individuals sending or receiving unusual quantities for the *Contrôle économique*. The CE had neither the staff nor sufficient information to investigate all such reports. Individuals sending packages used many post offices and gave false names, particularly for black-market traffic. But investigations often found no evidence; persons named on parcel tags often proved impossible to find. Multiple mailings of parcels often went to family members, particularly during the summer when families on rural vacations sent food to their own home address.[118] Ordinary consumers arranged summer travel to buy food in producing regions, which was carried home as extra luggage and shipped in parcels.

The Bank of France director in Clermont-Ferrand termed this a new 'food tourism' (*tourisme alimentaire*).[119] In the surplus departments in the north and west of France, increasing numbers of tourists bought food to stock up for the winter and made deals with farmers to send parcels. Summer visitors showed complete indifference to ration and price rules, buying direct from farms and arranging 'family' parcels to be shipped later. The prefect in Deux-Sèvres attributed the growth of the black market to these summer visitors, noting that this served the well-off in cities, with the parcels as a form of mutual aid, benefiting 'those who can pay well'.[120] Even departments with few resources attracted tourists in

---

[114] AN F/90/21627, 'Contrôle des paquets contenant du beurre', and 'Contrôle des envois postaux présumés contenir des denrées rationnées', and Groult, *Journal à quatre mains*, 383.

[115] AD Alpes-Maritimes 159W/46, case 1195-R.

[116] Georges Simenon, *Intimate Memoirs: Including Marie-Jo's Book*, trans. by Harold J. Salemson (San Diego, CA: Harcourt, Brace, Jovanovich, 1984), 99.

[117] Paul, 'Histoire des PTT pendant la deuxième guerre mondiale', 285–286; Xavier de Guerpel, *Une certaine vie de château au bocage Normand: Témoignage d'un agriculteur, 1939–1945* (Condé-sur-Noireau: C. Corlet, 1973), 118.

[118] SAEF B-0049511; Marseille and Lyon investigations in 1942.

[119] ABdF, 1069199311 9; 'Rapports des directeurs de succursales', Clermont-Ferrand, 2 Sept. 1942, and Annie Moulin, *Les paysans dans la société française: De la Révolution à nos jours* (Paris: Seuil, 1988), 198–208. The practice started in the summer of 1941.

[120] AN AJ/41/392 (Deux-Sèvres); prefect report for September and October 1942, 3 Nov. 1942. Prefects reported *tourisme alimentaire* in Ille-et-Vilaine, Finistère, Côtes-du-Nord and Morbihan. Sophie Focchanère found the same experience in the Landes; 'Du ravitaillement au marché noir: les enjeux des restrictions dans les campagnes landaises',

search of food. In the Hautes-Alpes, food supply officials complained that they had struggled to feed an extra 50,000 summer visitors in the summer of 1942, in a department with a normal population of 88,000.[121] In the Corrèze, the postal control in Brive reported many visitors from southern departments buying food from farms, arranging parcels, and dining in local restaurants at black-market prices.[122]

City residents carrying suitcases loaded with food became known as *valisards*, and their efforts to meet family needs were difficult to distinguish from black market traffic, which adapted to exploit the opportunities afforded by the relaxation of rules for family provisioning. *Valisards* carrying food to urban customers became a particular target for state officials. The prefect of Calvados complained of two forms of open black-market activity in 1943: the truck traffic working with German cooperation, and the traffic *en valise*, 'a swarm of trafiquants' easy to recognize in markets and on trains, talking openly of where they bought goods, how much they paid, and how to travel without tickets.[123] The writer Violette Leduc supported herself in this way, learning the trade from Maurice Sachs in 1942, bringing meat and dairy goods from the commune of Anceins (Orne) to Paris. After Sachs volunteered for labour in Germany in November 1942, Leduc continued to buy from local farms and send food by post to acquaintances in Paris. As her business increased, she had local boys buy for her, and carried the food herself by suitcase to Paris, returning with goods to trade with local farmers.[124] Raymond Ruffin's family shared a train compartment in July 1942 with a woman who went once a week to buy food from farms, at one-third higher than the official price, and sell it in Paris at twice the price. She proudly explained that the employees knew her well, reserved a place for her, and that she paid the SNCF staff and CE inspectors with a pound of butter each.[125]

Heavily burdened travellers were suspect. Their usual practice, when they encountered controls, was to abandon their luggage, often on the quai where they waited to board the train. Two gendarmes based in Cavignac (Gironde) reported on illicit traffic from the station Gauriaget, situated just outside their normal zone of responsibility.

in *Vichy in Aquitaine*, ed. by Jean-Pierre Kosceilniak and Philippe Souleau; (Clamecy: Ateliers de la nouvelle imprimerie Laballery, 2011), 100–101.

[121] AD Bouches-du-Rhône 76W/22; prefect of the Hautes-Alpes to the Minister of Agriculture and Food Supply, undated, likely June 1943.

[122] AD Corrèze 550W/382; Postal control commission in Brive, 'Synthèse de renseignements' for the months April to August 1943.

[123] AN AJ/41/366 (Calvados); prefect monthly report, 4 May 1943.

[124] Carlo Jansiti, *Violette Leduc* (Paris: Grasset, 2013), 117–118, 127–132.

[125] Ruffin, *Journal d'un J3*, 141.

Arriving at the station just before the passage of the 11:10 train to Bordeaux, they saw travellers hide suitcases and canteens of wine in a fuchsia hedge by the station platform. The suitcases contained beef and rationed goods. As the train pulled in, the *valisards* created a mêlée on the platform, which allowed some to grab their luggage and board the train. The Gendarmerie thought this was the work of organized groups trafficking in meat, wine and other rationed foods. They frequently reported abandoned luggage in train stations when they checked travellers for the illegal transport; the suitcases usually contained meat destined for the black market in Bordeaux.[126]

Smaller-scale traffic was more difficult to detect. Regular passengers, such as workers commuting to and from urban centres, transferred a large volume of food into cities. In the Seine-et-Oise, the prefect reported an illicit traffic in beans from the Rambouillet region in 1942. Black-market buyers paid workers to carry family-appropriate quantities, up to 10 kg, back to Paris daily. The *trafiquants* paid the workers' train fares plus a 25-franc bonus. The prefect believed this to be common practice.[127]

The sales to urban consumers took place through a range of regular venues: restaurants, cafés, food shops of all sorts offering under-the-counter and back-door extras, and public markets. Particular restaurants and streets became known for their black-market traffic, as well as metro stations, streets around train stations and flea markets.[128] Prices could be negotiated, and personal relationships between buyer and seller could make a great difference in the terms of exchange, the risks and even the willingness to do business.[129] Wealth and personal connections determined the extent to which ordinary consumers could buy black-market goods. The rising prices restricted purchases by most consumers, but everyone sought extra food. Henri Drouot, observing black-market activity by industrialists and shopkeepers, commented: 'The people, whether

---

[126] AD Gironde 62W/6; Gendarmerie nationale, Compagnie de la Gironde, Section de Blaye, Brigade de Cavignac, report no. 194, 8 May 1943, case no. 1158. Meat in suitcases or trunks, abandoned on station platforms or roadsides, figures in case nos. 97, 1015, 1017, 1106, 1154, 1257, 1680, 1683 and 1684, all in the first six months of 1943. This happened in other departments; it is mentioned as normal practice for *valisards* in northern France in AD Seine-Maritime 51W/57, prefect report for May–June 1943, 30 June 1943.

[127] AD Yvelines 1W/7; prefect monthly report for February 1942.

[128] Grenard, *La France du marché noir*, 159–162; David Drake, *Paris at War 1939–1944* (Cambridge, MA: The Belknap Press of Harvard University Press, 2015), 335.

[129] Kenneth Mouré and Paula Schwartz, '*On vit mal*: Food Shortages and Popular Culture in Occupied France, 1940–1944', *Food, Culture and Society* 10(2) (2007): 276–277; Janet Teissier du Cros, *Divided Loyalties: A Scotswoman in Occupied France* (London: Hamish Hamilton, 1962; Canongate Classics reprint, 1992), 263–266, on her difficulties trading for food in Longpont, south of Paris.

through lack of opportunity or lack of means, would be more honest (except on matters of small-scale family food supplies, which no one can escape).'[130]

Injustice

For consumers, the rationing system looked ever more inefficient as queues and time spent waiting increased for diminishing returns. Diary entries by German and French writers contrasted the substantial restaurant meals of privileged officials and profiteers with the other population required to wait in queues for meagre rations. German officials demanded the suppression of black-market restaurants, claiming to be shocked by the contrast between the abundance in restaurants and the paltry rations for the working classes.[131] Officers in Paris commented on the disparity between the food available for the rich and the scarcity facing workers. Arnold Nüssle saw food supply as the critical issue that would decide French comity or hostility to the German presence.[132]

Three aspects of this visible injustice illustrate the reasons for declining public confidence in the food supply administration and the controls. The first is the obvious advantages enjoyed by the Germans. Their requisitions, direct purchasing, exemption from rules and conspicuous consumption were deeply resented. Henri Drouot noted the exploitation of food resources by Germans in Dijon and the trainloads of food and consumer goods shipped to Germany in his diary.[133] The Communist party used German consumption of French food as a prime reason for popular protest, blaming the Germans for the inadequate supplies of meat, potatoes and wheat.[134]

A second example is the scarcity of food in cities compared with the countryside. The transfer of food to the city by alternative means proved highly unequal. *Tourisme alimentaire* and *colis familiaux*, the two most common means of transfer, favoured those with the income to travel

---

[130] Drouot, *Notes d'un dijonnais*, 639 (24 Mar. 1943).

[131] SAEF B-0049757, de Sailly, 'Rapport au Ministre', 28 Aug. 1942.

[132] Evident in the diaries of Gerhard Heller and Ernst Jünger, and in letters from Paul Lingemann (autumn 1940) and Arnold Nüssle (28 Aug. 1941), reproduced in Aurélie Luneau, Jeanne Guérout and Stefan Martens, eds., *Comme un Allemand en France: Lettres inédites sous l'Occupation 1940–1944* (Paris: L'Iconoclaste, 2016), 63–65, 107.

[133] Drouot, *Notes d'un dijonnais*, the comments run throughout his diary.

[134] AN 78AJ/20; leaflets handed out by PCF militants in 1941–1942. One tract stated: 'Where does our meat go? According to the *Association générale des producteurs de viande*: Each week, 15,000 cattle, 12,000 hogs and thousands of sheep are sent to Germany. Thanks to this, Germans have 800 grams of meat per week, while the French have "60 grams with bone". Throw out those who are starving us!' (Underlined in original.) Another informed mothers that while they had no milk for their children, General von Stulpnagel received 50 litres each day to bathe in.

and buy in the countryside, and wealthier districts with the connections and income to obtain food parcels. Alfred Sauvy saw the parcel traffic's direct impact in reducing state collection, to benefit the rich.[135] These inequities, and popular perceptions of peasant greed, raised fears that the social divide would have violent consequences, and gave further evidence that food was available, but was out of reach for those who needed it, owing to state incompetence and corruption.

A third example is the contrast between abundant food in the restaurants serving the wealthy and privileged and the scarcity for those queuing outside shops. German authorities claimed in April 1943 that 200 Paris restaurants were serving customers all they could eat, and called for greater French effort to suppress black-market restaurants.[136] The restaurants hierarchy included an exclusive set of luxury restaurants in Paris *hors catégorie* – subject to no controls on prices or the food served.[137] The restaurants with privileged access to food supplies presented a world apart, offering 'prewar' menus at prices reflecting wartime scarcity and the affluence of political elites and profiteers. Ernst Jünger memorably characterized food access as a matter of power, contrasting the elegant dining in La Tour d'Argent with the people starving below: 'In such times, to eat, to eat well and abundantly, gives a feeling of power.'[138]

Few French diners had access to such lavish fare. As the CE report on luxury restaurant consumption put it in 1942, the diners were 'people who seem to belong to the business world born of economic circumstances at the present time.'[139] Jean Galtier-Boissière noted of the diners in restaurants in 1941 that 'With cash, lots of cash, you can stuff yourself to the gills, while housewives stand for hours in line in the snow to get a chunk of turnip.'[140] The Paris police commented on public discontent with the privileged access to restaurants access in September and October 1941. The luxury restaurants patronized by Germans and collaborators were a provocation when ordinary citizens could not get enough to eat.[141]

---

[135] Sauvy, *La vie économique*, 133–136; and Institut de conjoncture, 'Situation économique au début du mois de Juillet 1942 (Rapport no. 11)' and 'Situation économique à la fin de Décembre 1943 (Rapport no. 15)'.

[136] AN F/37/4, 'Entretien du 2 Avril 1943 à l'Hôtel Majestic'.

[137] Mouré, 'La capitale de la faim', 317, 321–323; the category existed from October 1941 to July 1942.

[138] Ernst Jünger, *Premier journal parisien, Journal II 1941–1943* (Paris: Christian Bourgeois, 1980), 148.

[139] SAEF B-0049508, report by *Contrôle économique* inspector Savarit, 30 Oct. 1942.

[140] Jean Galtier-Boissière, *Mon journal pendant l'Occupation* (Paris: La Jeune Parque, 1944), 29 (13 Feb. 1941).

[141] APP 220W 5, 'Situation à Paris', 8 Sept. and 27 Oct. 1941 and APP 220W 6, 'Situation à Paris', 24 Nov. 1941.

The Communist party called on housewives to demonstrate in front of 'les grands restaurants' where the rich ate meals costing 600 francs while they waited for miserable rations in queues.[142] Some PCF tracts urged mothers to bring their children into the restaurants frequented by Germans and collaborators and take back the food stolen from the French people.[143] But restaurants attracted resentment rather than protest. Two children observed by Louis Le François marvelled at the food in a luxury restaurant window. Their mother pulled them away. 'She looks in turn, and her eyes express a mix of dreaming, sadness and hatred – a hatred that is not forgotten, nor pardoned. Come along, she says. That's not for us.'[144]

Je n'ai pas envie de sourire

The economy of penury was inescapable in the press. Newspapers provided essential information for the local distribution of rationed goods, ration-ticket validity, and changes to how much of any product could be purchased and transported legally. They reported abuses: black-market arrests, hoarding and provisioning scandals. Cartoons appeared alongside these articles commented on inequities and illicit behaviour with wry humour. In the grim daily routine of shortages, queues, cold, hunger and visible injustice, consumers responded not only with hostility or sullen silence. There was resilience and a combative spirit. It is evident in comments in queues, in housewives' protests, and it is preserved more durably in published articles and cartoons. Despite hardship, difficulties could inspire amusement.

The portrayal of shortages and adaptations to penury gave the harsh conditions of everyday life greater visibility, transcending individual experience and offering common values and vexations in shared experience. Humour provided a release from stress and an opportunity to document experience by making light of hardship. For the *dessinateurs de presse*, recognized as journalists in the interwar period, consumer experience gave occasion for social observation that combined humour and criticism.[145] The 'apparent innocence' of the drawings, depicting challenges in the economy

---

[142] AN 78AJ/20; also in 78AJ/24, PCF tract from 1941, 'Vers la ruine des petits débitants de vin et restaurateurs', and police comments in APP 220W 9, 'Situation à Paris' reports of 1 June, 15 June and 13 July 1941, and *Le Franciste*, 1 Aug. 1942, threatening attacks on restaurants and calling for the suppression of categories to provide a 'national meal' consistent for all consumers.

[143] APP BA 2067; weekly reports to the prefect on PCF activities, 17 Aug. and 24 Aug. 1942. 'In the fine restaurants where the Nazis indulge themselves, burst in with your children and your neighbours, and help yourselves.'

[144] Le François, *J'ai faim . . . !*, 217–218; her comment to the children is 'Ce n'est pas pour nous autres.'

[145] Christian Delporte, *Les crayons de la propagande* (Paris: CNRS Éditions, 1993), 13–23.

of penury and common hardships, could imply criticism of state economic management, but had to do so with care.[146]

For the consumers in cartoons, their adaptations provided a running commentary on the intractability of the shortages. In one, Calino 'doubles' his rations by eating his dinner in front of a mirror (Figure 6.3). In another, a man stands in front of a *crémerie* window to chew his bread ration while he

CALINO DOUBLE SA RATION...

Figure 6.3 'Calino doubles his ration ...', *Le Rouge et le Bleu*, 11 Apr. 1942; France newspaper collection, box 187, Hoover Institution Library and Archives.

---

[146] Nelly Feuerhahn, *Traits d'impertinence: Histoire et chefs-d'oeuvre du dessin d'humour de 1914 à nos jours* (Paris: Bibliothèque publique d'information – Centre Georges Pompidou et Somogy éditions d'art, 1993), 63. André Halimi, *Ce qui a fait rire les Français sous l'Occupation* (Paris: J. C. Lattès, 1979), 109; Halimi finds that the occupier had created all the problems, but the Germans are absent from the cartoons. Emmanuel Thiébot, *Croquer la France en guerre 1939–1945* (Paris: Armand Colin, 2014) distinguishes between caricature (negative, critical) and humour (funny).

contemplates a camembert (Figure 6.4). Longing for more food emphasized its insufficiency. No one was likely to imitate Calino, but the futility of
his tactic and his smile of satisfaction highlight how little one could do. Two
recurring subjects for cartoonists illustrate the tenor of their commentaries.
The first is the degrees of customer tolerance in queues. The second is
restaurant practices, whether rules were followed, and how easily the
wealthy ignored restrictions.

The queues in cartoons were almost all peaceful, showing enormous
patience with the shortages (except *Ric et Rac* cartoonist Dubout's
queues, which are chaotic), and the culture of joining any queue for
whatever might be available. (In one, a woman joins a queue not realizing
it is for a *pissoire*. In another, a man waiting for his date turns to find that
a line of hopeful customers has queued behind him, in case he is the first

Figure 6.4 'And when you've eaten your bread while looking at
a camembert?'
'I'm going to shave while looking at shaving cream.'
L'Œuvre, 22 Apr. 1942, Bibliothèque nationale de France.

— Mais, Madame !... Pour vous délivrer une carte d'habillement il faut me prouver que
c'est nécessaire...
                                                                    (Dessin de Dubout).

Figure 6.5 'But Madame! ... In order to allot you a clothing card, you
must prove to me that you need it ...'
Ric et Rac, 11 June 1941, 1. © British Library Board, MFM.MF247 N.

in line for something they might want to buy.) Most cartoon queues are
for food, but the lines for clothing coupons were depicted, too. In one
Dubout cartoon, ragged customers in patched clothing wait in line to
prove their need for textile coupons to a sceptical official (Figure 6.5).
The frustration of time spent fruitlessly in line was depicted as well; one
customer asks to buy the shelves when no goods remain (Figure 6.6), and
a shopkeeper puts out a series of signs for the goods he has run out of until
he runs out of cardboard for the signs (Figure 6.7). Whether empty
shelves really meant that shopkeepers had no goods was a matter for
doubt. Customer believed that shopkeepers withheld goods for customers
able to pay more. Cartoons depicted shopkeepers using the excuse of no
goods to dismiss customers (Figure 6.8) and selling from their shop back
door (Figure 6.2). Most cartoons focused on consumers, their patience,
and their good faith in following the rules. Protest, unrest, and the
demonstrations by housewives were not subjects for published cartoons.

The scenes in restaurants exaggerated the meagre portions that rations
allowed, especially for meat (Figures 6.9 and 6.10). They mocked the
strict rules for rations and coupons: waiters demand extra coupons for
gravy spilled on a customer, for soap when a customer complains that his
soup tastes like soap, for shoes when a steak is as tough as leather. They
ridicule the careful accounting for minute quantities inherent in rationing
scarce goods. They also show the privileges enjoyed by wealthy customers,

L'OBSTINÉ
— Voyez ! il ne nous reste absolument
rien, les rayons sont vides...
— Donnez-moi un rayon.

(Dessin de Roger Sam.)

Figure 6.6 The Stubborn: 'You see! We have absolutely nothing left, the shelves are empty.' 'Give me a shelf.'
Ric et Rac, 23 Apr. 1943, 1. © British Library Board, MFM.MF247 N.

and the restaurant practices to cover black-market costs (Figures 6.11 and 6.12). The wealthy, whether long established or *nouveaux riches* from black-market gains, were rarely disturbed by the enforcement of controls (Figure 6.13). Prewar meals became an essential point of reference, whether in restaurants boasting that they ignored rationing to serve prewar meals, or in consumer evaluations of the quantity and quality of food no longer available[147] (Figures 6.14 and 6.15). In one cartoon from 1942, a couple reminisce about their prewar wedding, recalling not their love or the celebration with friends, but the roast veal at dinner (Figure 6.16).

---

[147] Pierre Audiat, *Paris pendant la guerre (juin 1940-août 1944)* (Paris: Hachette, 1946), 244; Groult, *Journal à quatre mains*, 149, 418.

(Dessin de H. Monier.)

Figure 6.7 No more coffee; no more butter; no more sugar; no more oil;
no more eggs; no more signs.
Ric et Rac, 21 Aug. 1940, 1. © British Library Board, MFM.MF247 N.

Cartoon content had to pass censorship. It displayed nationalism, and often conveyed official anti-Semitic, anti-Bolshevik, anti-Gaullist and anti-Allied views.[148] The cartoons likewise avoided political criticism. Although often depicting shortages, they provide no explanation. German consumption in stores and restaurants was sharply resented as a factor increasing the shortages in everyday life, as was their interference in the supply and transport of scarce goods, but the Germans are strikingly absent from the cartoons, as if the shortages in France had nothing to do with the Occupation.

[148] Halimi, *Ce qui a fait rire*, 6.

— **Jules, va à la boutique voir ce que veut le client et dis-lui qu'il n'y en a pas !...**
(Dessin de Ferraz.)

Figure 6.8 'Jules, go to the store and see what the customer wants, and tell him we don't have any.'
Ric et Rac, 16 Jan. 1942, 1. © British Library Board, MFM.MF247 N.

Even more striking is the nearly complete absence of the French state, whose policies determined controls and whose police enforced them. The cartoons depict a mostly stateless world in which shortages have no explanation. Consumers maintain public order, and hierarchies of wealth and power determine access to goods. The people in queues are visibly of different class and income than the restaurant patrons who ignore restrictions and dine on meals untouched by scarcity. As a matter of style and choice by the cartoonists, it indicates that the stratification by wealth and privilege was apparent to all, structuring access to goods, and officially acceptable for publication. In collections published after Liberation, the Germans and the state apparatus could be drawn back in.[149] For readers during the Occupation, if most cartoons show consumers relying on their

---

[149] For example, Chancel, *Livre noir 1939–1945* (Paris: Les Éditions de la nouvelle France, 1945).

RESTRICTIONS

— *Je ne vois pas mon gigot !*
— *Regardez bien, il est au chaud sous une pomme frite !*

(Dessin de Pierre Falké.)

Figure 6.9 Restrictions: 'I don't see my *gigot* (leg of lamb)!' 'Look again, it is keeping warm under a French fry!'
Ric et Rac, 13 Nov. 1940, 1. © British Library Board, MFM.MF247 N.

wits, the role of the Germans and the state needed no visual statement. The queues, frustrations and inequities drew from a repertoire of bitter experience they knew too well.

The state used cartoons to encourage compliance with controls. The Department of Agriculture published a collection titled *Devant le marché noir* in 1943, with thematically organized content conscious of present-day penury, and images by some of the best-known press cartoonists. Subjects range from food acquisition in prehistoric times and waste in times of abundance to contemporary challenges: queues, *trafiquants*, restaurants, rural abundance, and the dreams of a future world in which shopkeepers would queue for customers' favour. The state does appear briefly: to arrest *trafiquants* and to monitor restaurant meals. But the state presence is feeble. Minister of Food Max Bonnefous declared in his introduction to the volume that there was nothing funny about any of this and made explicit the volume's didactic purpose: 'I have no wish to smile or to praise "making do". We must convince the French of the need for a strong collective discipline for the

— C'est pas ça votre viande ?...
— Non, c'est un ticket de tramway !...
(Dessin de Bernard Aldebert.)

Figure 6.10 'Isn't that your meat there?' 'No, that's a tram ticket!'
Ric et Rac, 10 April 1942, 1. © British Library Board, MFM.MF247 N.

common good. We must require compliance by those who rebel against it.
I am working on it.'[150]

The newspaper cartoons, alongside the daily notices of rationing rules,
black-market arrests and confiscations, and restaurants closed for control
violations, demonstrated that sacrifice was not equally shared. With little
to eat, imagining food could be the next best thing, whether talking of
recipes adapted to replace missing ingredients, or marvelling at meals
consumed in the past or in a possible future. One queue conversation
described a fabulous 'recent' meal for four, costing only 200 francs, in 'the
little bistro on the corner across from chez Boby'. 'Two hundred francs,
old man, the price of two kilos of butter on a market not completely

[150] Bernard Aldebert et al., *Devant le marché noir* (Bellegarde: SADAG, 1943).

Figure 6.11 'Brandy 1830.' 'That's the year?' 'No, that's the price.'
L'Œuvre, 20 Apr. 1943, Bibliothèque nationale de France.

black.' The 'recent' meal was in 1936.[151] Another told of a bistro on the
rue du Louvre where 'for ten francs you can get a mug of wine, a thick
vegetable soup, a meat dish with trimmings, cheese, and a dessert and
a piece of bread this big and then coffee and an after-dinner drink (*pousse-
café*)'. 'You must be kidding!' the listener responds. 'I am, but you have to
admit, it's a very good price.'[152] In a 1943 poem by Noël-Noël titled
'Marché noir', a passing acquaintance offers to supply the poet with
black-market ham, cheese, soap, bread and coffee, if he pays an advance
of 500 francs. He never sees the acquaintance again, nor his 500 francs,
nor the promised goods. But he reflects:

[151] Achard, *La queue*, 86–87.   [152] Achard, *La queue*, 120.

DU TAC AU TAC
— Monsieur a sa carte de viande ?...
— Oui, vous avez votre carte des vins ?...

(Dessin d'Hervé Baille.)

Figure 6.12 'Monsieur has his meat ration card?' 'Yes, do you have your wine list?'
Ric et Rac, 22 Jan. 1941, 1. © British Library Board, MFM.MF247 N.

That to pay five hundred francs to believe
For two whole days, that you will
Get a kilo of gruyère . . .
A whole Olida ham . . .
Twenty-five bars of prewar soap . . .
Plus : a kilo of unroasted coffee . . .
To pay five hundred francs for all that,
It's cheap! . . .[153]

[153] Quoted in Halimi, *Ce qui a fait rire*, 11.

Figure 6.13 Sign: Closed for 6 months. 'We only had time to eat eight courses: we'll be back to eat the rest in six months.'
L'Œuvre, 2 Dec. 1943, Bibliothèque nationale de France.

Figure 6.14 'We shouldn't have written the menus on the backs of ones from prewar ...'
Ric et Rac, 5 Mar. 1943, 1. © British Library Board, MFM.MF247 N.

(Dessin de Floris.)
— Quelle est votre lecture préférée ?
— Les menus d'avant-guerre.

Figure 6.15 'What is your favourite reading?' 'Menus from before the war.'
L'Œuvre, 14 Apr. 1942, Bibliothèque nationale de France.

Humour filled no one's stomach. But the cartoons representing the daily struggle with shortages gave opportunity for amusement in a shared culture of hardship, to identify with the plight of fellow consumers whose world, in contrast to that of black-market patrons, was greatly impoverished. There was no state visible or responsible for the lurch from abundance to penury, an implicit indictment of Vichy food management. Consumers were on their own, needing to find their own ways to provide for essential needs.

Conclusions

Access to goods, purchasing power and transport were critical determinants of relative power in economic exchange. Most consumers needed goods and had little power. Despite the state claim it would equalize

Figure 6.16 'Do you remember the evening of our marriage?' 'Ah! Yes ... when we ate that succulent roast veal?'
L'Œuvre, 7 Jan. 1942, Bibliothèque nationale de France.

sacrifice, the rich and the well-connected increased their ability to purchase scarce goods. The proliferation of alternative markets and the diversion of output to supply them demonstrated the state's inability to control markets and their terms of exchange. The market-making power of those with the capability to produce and deliver goods had its most influential display in supplying the Germans and the black market. But ordinary consumers retained some agency.

First, consumers demanded greater state effort to provide essentials. The main public demonstrations in the first years of the Occupation were protests by women demanding more food, and they achieved some minor success. They called public attention to the state's failure to fulfil its responsibility to ensure sufficient food for all. Strikes, too, were used to demand more food, again with limited success.[154] Both actions called on

---

[154] On strikes by coal miners and metal workers in the departments of the Creuse (Sept. 1941) and the Loire (Feb. 1942), correspondence in AN F/12/10815; including Couture to Société des Houillières de Montrambert et Société des mines de la Loire,

the state for greater supply of essentials. Vichy authorities had few resources to distribute: the demonstrations made more visible Vichy's failures to protect and provide for citizens.

Second, the main avenues for access to goods developed through exchanges outside state control. The alternatives offered a gradation of kinds of exchange, with some characterized as 'grey' markets to denote official tolerance. In Britain, the key distinction between grey and black markets focused on the motives of the seller – whether or not the exchange was for profit.[155] In France, alternative exchanges were far more widespread and the distinction less clear. Sellers varied their prices according to their relationship with different consumers. Even in legal exchange, rules were routinely violated on quantities and price. Black-market traffic adapted to exploit and stretch the limits of state tolerance.

For most consumers, access to goods, affordable prices and personal connections were more important than market rules. The shortages and injustice delegitimized state controls. The alternatives to obtain essential goods constituted a sliding scale of adaptation, in which needs took precedence over the strict observance of the proliferating rules that reduced access to goods. This sliding scale and the invisibility of most black-market transactions meant that consumers themselves were not always conscious or concerned when they broke the rules. Pierre Laval's insistence that the public need 'bend itself to an economic discipline nevertheless indispensable' would have been better if rephrased as 'an economic discipline nevertheless impossible'.

Consumer use of parallel markets did constitute a form of resistance in everyday life. It was resistance to Vichy economic controls rather than to German economic exploitation, more often in the interest of survival or to satisfy personal needs than for political objectives. Vichy authorities defied their own rules, showing this was opposition to the control regime. This was more personal than political or ideological in its purpose. For most, it was to obtain enough food to eat; for the affluent, to live well despite the shortages. Some black-market activity did redirect resources or disrupt delivery to the Germans. Most notably, Resistance groups in rural areas set up their own systems to regulate distribution and payment, especially in 1944. Georges Guingouin, Resistance leader in the Limousin, set a schedule of 'patriotic prices' to give adequate return to

15 Feb. 1942, which wanted the improvements to miners' rations be announced as a decision of the prefect, so as not to look like it had been a concession forced on him by the strike. For the miners' strikes in the Nord in 1941, see Taylor, *Between Resistance and Collaboration*, 72–97; and the special issue of *Cahiers d'histoire de l'institut de recherches marxistes*, 47 (1991) on 'Les luttes des mineurs de 1940–1944'.

[155] Emphasized in Roodhouse, *Black Market Britain*, 50–76.

farmers and limit consumer prices. He fined those who violated his price regime and signed his price schedules 'Le Préfet du Maquis'.[156]

For most consumers, the violation of controls was in opposition to Vichy's economic policies that aggravated shortages and injustice. Most believed that Liberation would bring rapid improvement in their access to essential goods. In waiting for Liberation, breaking economic rules became common practice, and recourse to the black market an accepted means for survival in the economy of state-administered penury.

---

[156] On Guingouin and his price policies for farmers and consumers, Georges Guingouin, *Quatre ans de lutte sur le sol Limousin* (Paris: Hachette, 1974), 87–107; Kedward, *In Search of the Maquis*, 95–101; and Grenard, *La France du marché noir*, 211–226 and *Une légende du maquis: Georges Guingouin, du mythe à l'histoire* (Paris: Vendémiaire, 2014), 174–179.

7 Illegality Normalized

Honesty, it's a question of personal fortune. Me, I've never been rich enough to be honest.[1] (1942)

The worst is that one no longer knows where fraud begins.[2] (1945)

For Martin, the unemployed taxi driver in Marcel Aymé's story 'Traversée de Paris' (1946) who transports black-market meat across Paris, the black market is a legitimate site for employment and income. Dodging French police and German patrols as he lugs suitcases of fresh meat to Montmartre for a black-market butcher, Martin sees his work as 'honest': 'For him [Martin], an honest man, and you'd have to look hard to find on more honest, he would have liked nothing better than to get rich in the black market.'[3] His belief this is honest work, when black markets are by definition outside the law, exaggerates how views during the Occupation changed with regard to the opportunities for employment, the purchase of food, and moral behaviour. The painter Grandgil, assisting Martin, goes further still in the later (1956) movie version. Paying for their *vins chauds* with one of the 1,000-franc bills he has extorted from the butcher Poliveau, Grandgil claims it is 'honest money, honestly earned'.[4] Aymé's acerbic comments on morality and honesty are deliberately excessive, but the problems he overstates were real. The shortages and increased economic regulation muddied boundaries between licit and illicit activities and created new opportunities for profit working in and across the boundary zone. Strict legality became less clear and of less concern. Everyone reassessed their economic conduct to adapt and survive in the economy of penury.

As seen with regard to agriculture in Chapter 4 and consumption in Chapter 6, licit and illicit exchange overlapped in the 'grey'-market activities impelled by personal and family needs, and could lead in small steps into the 'black' market without clarity as to where the grey turned

---

[1] Achard, *La queue*, 118. [2] Baudin, *Esquisse de l'économie*, 154.
[3] Marcel Aymé, 'Traversée de Paris', *Le vin de Paris* (Paris: Gallimard, 1947), 48.
[4] See Mouré, 'Black Market Fictions', 59–61.

black. The new controls created new crimes and new opportunities. They moved the boundaries between licit and illicit, and outlawed the negotiations of quantity and price that had been normal practice.

War increases criminal activity. The prevalence of violence and weapons, the movement of armies and refugees, the disruption of supply and transport, the shortages of goods, and the degradation of social order and effective policing all can work to create an environment for increased crime against property and persons. The armistice in June 1940 ended military action by official French armed forces, but the economic needs of the French population and the German occupation forces increased the demand for goods. Pillaging of abandoned property in 1940 by the German armies, by French refugees, and by citizens who remained in evacuated regions, began sometimes from simple needs for food and shelter no longer available through normal distribution. Livestock abandoned on farms offered opportunities for theft, slaughter and immediate consumption.[5] New security measures increased the number of policing agencies in France but subordinated them to German oversight. The new agencies and the hierarchy of policing power increased conflict and reduced the coordination of the policing regime in Occupied France.[6]

Shortages prompted a surge in property crime. Convictions for theft increased more than threefold from 1938 to 1942. In 1942, the theft of rationed goods was re-classified as the violation of economic controls rather than as theft, reducing the case numbers for the rise in convictions for theft.[7] In September 1941 the state created a new court, the *Tribunal d'État*, for crimes 'which can have repercussions on the security and the tranquillity of the public'. The three categories of crime it dealt with indicate Vichy's political, economic and moral fixations: abortions, communist activity, and economic crimes such as counterfeiting and trafficking in ration tickets, theft from food parcels (especially those intended for POWs), and black-market profiteering. The Tribunal was established to provide rapid convictions without appeal.[8]

The new possibilities for crime drew ordinary citizens into suspect activity. Practical concerns for survival (of families, farms and firms) could engage them in actions that led incrementally to illicit activity. This complicated the

[5] Martin S. Alexander, 'War and Its Bestiality: Animals and their Fate during the Fighting in France, 1940', *Rural History*, 25(1) (2014): 101–124.

[6] See Jean-Marc Berlière's comprehensive *Polices des temps noirs: France 1939–1945* (Paris: Perrin, 2018).

[7] Bruno Aubusson de Cavarlay, Marie-Sylvie Huré and Marie-Lys Pottier, 'La justice pénale en France: Résultats statistiques (1934–1954)', *Les Cahiers de l'IHTP*, 23 (1993): 82–83, 111. There were 37,400 persons convicted for theft in 1938, and 134,070 in 1942.

[8] Joseph Barthélemy, *Ministre de la Justice, Vichy 1941–1943: Mémoires* (Paris: Pygmalion, 1989), 249.

moral issues of right and wrong, with popular distinctions between acceptable and reprehensible activities changing, depending on who benefited and
by how much. In Jean-Louis Bory's *Mon village à l'heure allemande*, the
Resistance punishes Auguste Boudet's traffic in stolen fuel and burns the
money he made trafficking with the Germans. His sister Elisa distinguishes
between the criminal black market for profit and aiding the Germans, and an
'honest' black market, helping fellow citizens.[9] This distinction was implicit
in the black-market law of 15 March 1942 and in the instructions to
controllers in 1942, increasing punishment for serious black-market activity
that damaged overall supply, while allowing greater tolerance for minor
violations by individuals simply trying to feed their families. The distinction
is evident earlier, in local reports on black market repression. The
Ravitaillement général (RG), organizing to search baggage for illicit goods
arriving in Rennes in September 1941, specified that they were looking for
rationed foods clearly in excess of family needs. For family needs, 'the
greatest tolerance remains in effect'.[10] The police commissioner for the
Les Brotteaux quarter in Lyon reported in November 1941 on the need to
distinguish between the many ordinary citizens 'who are trying to find
enough food, but cannot do it without breaking the rules' and those engaged
in black market activity 'with speculative purpose', for which 'repression is
required ... by its criminal character in present circumstances'.[11]

The changing boundaries between legal and illicit practices created
confusion and encouraged innovations and transgression. This chapter
follows changes in everyday activities to emphasize the pull towards illicit
traffic as behaviour adapted to shortages, beginning with the efforts to
provide for family needs, and proceeding through the black-market temptation in professions that offered easy access to goods, noting the progression from inconsequential acts based on personal need to opportunities to
assist others and then to profit from exchanges of highly sought goods.
State officials allocating goods often avoided or ignored the regulations
established for equitable distribution and could indulge in extravagant
levels of consumption.[12] The chapter's last sections conclude with the

[9] Jean-Louis Bory, *Mon village à l'heure allemande* (Paris: Flammarion, 1945), 32–34, 227,
239–240.
[10] AD Ille-et-Vilaine 118W/72, Ravitaillement général Intendant Hauducoeur to
Commander of the Gendarmerie, Saint-Brieuc, 10 Sept. 1941.
[11] AD Rhône 182W/2, Police commissioner for the Brotteaux district to the Commissioner
for Lyon, 24 Nov. 1941.
[12] This was true everywhere in Europe: for examples, see Lothar Gruchmann, 'Korruption
im Dritten Reich: Zur "Lebensmittelversorgung" der NS-Führerschaft', *Vierteljahrshefte
für Zeitgeschichte*, 42(4) (1994): 571–593; Roodhouse, *Black Market Britain*; Wendy
Z. Goldman, 'The Hidden World of Soviet Wartime Food Provisioning: Hunger,
Inequality, and Corruption', in *The Consumer on the Home Front: Second World War
Civilian Consumption in Comparative Perspective*, ed. by Hartmut Berghoff,

activities of *faux policiers*; the police imposters claiming to enforce the new rules, but in fact using the rules as an avenue for extortion of goods and money, and the increasing official concern that black-market activity was opening an era of moral decline. The reconsideration of activities covered on a sectoral basis in previous chapters is to emphasize how the control regime, in moving the boundaries between licit and illicit commerce, increased the range and the opportunities for illicit transactions. This fostered a normalization of small-scale violations and facilitated the expansion of the criminal black market.

Family and Friends

When Jean-Paul Sartre returned to Paris in March 1941 from a POW camp in Trier, Germany, he criticized Simone de Beauvoir for her black-market purchases of tea. By her account, Sartre's 'strict moral standards' could not be long maintained in Paris, where 'simply to be alive implied some sort of compromise'. She observes after that point that they adapted to the new conditions, and that her letters were full of comments on food. But she mentions the black market again only for its expense, beyond their means, and the 'black-market feasts' of a friend who stole money from his wealthy father. Yet in the spring of 1944, de Beauvoir and Sartre joined evening 'fiestas' with beef stews and abundant alcohol at a time when meat and alcohol would have been very hard to find. Although rations had been reduced, she and her friends find 'sources' for their celebrations; she mentions cycling to Neuilly-sous-Clermont to buy meat from the gate-keeper at the Saint-Gobain factory.[13] The Sartre 'family' adapted, as did most people, to use the black market when they could without moral qualms. Violette Leduc, a de Beauvoir admirer, brought black-market meat and dairy goods from Normandy. She discovered she could make 30,000 francs a month by supplying friends and buyers in Paris.[14]

Jan Logemann and Felix Römer (Oxford: Oxford University Press, 2017), 71–73. For the boundaries between licit and illicit behaviour as recorded in Bremen police records in postwar Germany, see Stefan Mörchen, '"Echte Kriminelle" und "zeitbedingte Rechtsbrecher"': Schwarzer Markt und Konstruktionen des Kriminellen in der Nachkriegszeit', *WerkstattGeschichte*, 42 (2006): 57–76.

[13] Simone de Beauvoir, *The Prime of Life*, trans. by Peter Green (Middlesex: Penguin Books, 1965), 479–480, 504, 528, 562, 572–576, 581. Literary circles friendly with the Germans held events with abundant food; most notably the salon of Florence Gould. Alan Riding, *And the Show Went On: Cultural Life in Occupied Paris* (New York: Alfred A. Knopf, 2010), 257–262.

[14] Violette Leduc, *La bâtarde* (Paris: Gallimard, 1964), 414–449. Carlo Jansiti, *Violette Leduc: Biographie* (Paris: Grasset, 2013), writes of her experience: 'Thanks to the black market, Violette discovered, that she had qualities of courage, endurance, unsuspected

With inadequate rations, all consumers developed strategies to acquire more food, taking advantage of the state tolerance for food transport flexible to accommodate genuine family needs. Alfred Sauvy calculated that an average Parisian adult in mid-1943 obtained 1,087 calories per day from rationed foods. When supplemented by extra rationed goods (120), food from collectives (75 to 125), other market goods (125 to 145), parcels of various sorts (155 to 240), suburban gardens (150 to 225) and food brought from the countryside (10 to 25) and other sources, the total came to 1,755 to 2,010 calories.[15] Sauvy did not have a separate category for black-market food. But the categories he used – family parcels, trips to the countryside to buy direct from farms, barter among friends, and stocking up on unrationed goods – straddled boundaries between licit and illicit acquisitions depending on the prices and quantities. Gabriel Richet estimated average consumption in Paris in 1942 at 1,500 calories, of which 1,000 from rations and 200 from *le marché D* (for *débrouillard*, improvising).[16] Sauvy, analysing the food supply for children, observed that *colis familiaux* did not particularly benefit the children; he suggested renaming the parcels *colis alimentaires* (food parcels).[17]

The proliferation of rules for food purchase and transport, the increasing prices and the frequent changes to permissible quantities, confused consumers as to where, exactly, the line lay between licit and illicit transactions. Charles Braibant observed, after standing in the corridor of a train crammed with sacks of food and travellers returning to Paris in April 1943, 'No one knows any more what one has the right or not to transport.'[18] Uncertainty as to legal limits meant there was a range of activities that, if not strictly legal, were still allowed. It was a short distance from uncertainty to stepping deliberately outside the law. Much extra-to-ration purchasing to feed families fell in this range. Buying extra from the grocer, the butcher or the baker – under the counter or from the back door – was certainly illegal and involved paying a bit more. The mutual (though unequal) advantage to such purchases meant that neither party would report them to the state. Often, neither party cooperated when caught. Case files for retail offences often reported consumers and

willpower, and especially a greed for gain wholly worthy of a Norman peasant'; 117–118 (quote); 127–132.
[15] Sauvy, *La vie économique*, 135, reproducing his findings from Institut de conjoncture, 'Situation économique au début d'août 1943'.
[16] Cited by Veillon, 'Aux origines de la sous-alimentation', 40; Cépède cites a Professor Richer who estimated the Parisian diet as 1,725 calories, 200 furnished by family parcels and the black market. Cépède *Agriculture et alimentation*, 392, n. 2.
[17] Institut de conjoncture, 'Situation économique vers la fin du mois de Novembre 1941'.
[18] Braibant, *La guerre à Paris*, 185 (29 Apr. 1943).

retailers buying from individuals they claimed they did not know and could not identify. With worsening shortages, an increasing sense of injustice and inequity, most consumers engaged in minor infractions with no sense of guilt. Some did so with pride, gaining advantage in a perverse system. Colette commented frequently in her letters to the *petites fermières* who sent her food parcels that the butter, eggs and poultry they sent were unfindable in Paris. When her partner Maurice Goudeket was arrested in December 1941 and released two months later having lost 12 kg., she wrote them, 'Thanks to you, we live!'[19]

Tickets, coupons and ration cards offered a new medium for exchange and opportunity for illegal activity ranging from petty fraud to theft, traffic in *fausses cartes*, and counterfeiting. The ration documents were issued to individuals by name, allowing specified rations to the bearer, but the tickets and coupons were mass-produced and interchangeable, so easily traded or sold.[20] This created a fertile field for unanticipated problems. Family members in rural regions who could rely on meat from their farms sent their tickets to relatives in cities (Chapter 4). Jean Achard wanted to forbid the practice, 'which completely deforms the rules for food supply'.[21] Declarations of lost cards surged in February 1941, requiring stricter rules for the replacement of lost cards. In Saint-Denis the number of lost bread card declarations leapt to 150 per day. 'It is impossible', the police observed, 'that such a quantity of cards and tickets could have really been lost. This method is used by persons of bad faith to double their ration.'[22] At the *Ravitaillement général* office on rue de Mabillon, 4,697 persons claimed to have lost cards or tickets between 21 and 26 February.[23]

Consumers could find or steal other people's ration cards and tickets, could continue using those of family members departed or deceased, and could claim to belong to a ration category that allowed more food. Coupons and tickets were regularly sold and traded. Marcel Aymé satirized the abuses in his short story 'La carte' (1942), in which Parisians negotiate tickets authorizing the number of days they can live each

[19] Colette, *Lettres aux petites fermières*, quote from 81 (26 Feb. 1942).
[20] Culmann argued that exchanges of ration coupons do not alter demand so are an 'opération blanche' with regard to rationing; Culmann, *À Paris sous Vichy*, 94. While this is true for consumers who sold or traded their state-issued ration coupons, the ration documents stolen from *mairies* had to be replaced; thus the stolen and counterfeit tickets added to legal demand.
[21] AN F/60/590, Comité économique interministériel meeting of 28 March 1941.
[22] APP BA 1808, Commissioner of police in Saint-Denis-Ville to the prefect of police, 19 Feb. 1941.
[23] APP BA 1806, Secretary general of the prefecture, 'Note pour Monsieur le Préfet', 28 Feb. 1941.

month.[24] Men and women traded ration documents, as did young and old, particularly in poorer households with limited recourse to the black market. Jean Bailleul recalled that he became 'a great artist' in 1942 at the age of ten: 'I specialized in painting the number 7. On bread cards, there were tickets for 50 and tickets for 750. The 50 on the two tickets was in the same place. I just needed to put a 7 in front of the 50 to transform it to 750!'[25] Micheline Bood, a student in high school, stole food cards on impulse in a municipal office, and doctored counterfeit bread tickets when a Felix Potin clerk refused to accept them.[26] Workers in many professions sought cards as heavy labourers (T) to benefit from the extra rations.

Tobacco was not rationed until August 1941, when the growing disorder in queues for tobacco as smokers tried to stock up on cigarettes required police intervention, and shops faced long lines of angry customers. The state tobacco monopoly (SEITA) discussed how to implement a coherent rationing system in May and June 1941. They wanted to reduce disorder, protect the interests of smokers, and anticipate the redistribution of business when smokers had to obtain their rations from the shop where they registered. To allow rations only to confirmed smokers would pose intractable verification challenges. Tobacconists did not know all their customers. If confirmed smokers signed attestations for smokers who were not known to their tobacconist, they could easily sign up non-smokers to benefit from their rations.[27] SEITA decided to make all men eighteen years of age and older eligible for the *carte de tabac*, the 'easy solution' for equitable allocation. Prisoners of war had allocations that could be collected and sent to them by their families. Women were not allowed tobacco rations.

Non-smokers registered along with the smokers: cigarettes had great exchange value. The numbers signing up for *cartes de tabac* exceeded expectations, requiring a 25 per cent reduction in rations in September 1941. One journalist estimated that of the 14 million men signed up for tobacco rations, 4 million were non-smokers.[28] Cigarettes became a standard of value for illicit exchange. Charles Rist compared it to gold in primitive economies: 'In the barter economy to which, for all

---

[24] The poor, the elderly, and wives of prisoners of war sell some of their tickets; the wealthy buy them up: one M. Wadé buys tickets to live 1,967 extra days in June. Aymé, 'La carte', *Le passe-muraille*, 59–79, first published in *La Gerbe* in April 1942.

[25] Guéno, ed., *Paroles de l'ombre*, 49.   [26] Bood, *Les années doubles*, 262 (1 Mar. 1944).

[27] SAEF B-0061904, Service d'exploitation industrielle des tabacs et allumettes [SEITA], Comité technique, 27 May 1941 and 24 June 1941.

[28] AN 72AJ/1852, Philippe Armel, 'Un peu de statistique', *Les Nouveaux Temps*, 13 Jan. 1942.

practical purposes, we have returned ... tobacco becomes the way to make merchandise suddenly pop out of its hiding place.'[29]

Finding sufficient food was a family affair with fathers often absent and mothers managing family resources with increased responsibilities and difficulty. The need to feed families, particularly children in the J2 and J3 categories (ages six to twelve and thirteen to twenty-one), compelled them to seek new sources of supply. Public opinion and state reporting on black-market activity reflected growing consideration for these needs. The *Contrôle technique* revised its categories for the opinions gathered from monitoring letters and phone calls. In 1943 it created rubrics for 'Necessity of barter to obtain food' and 'Recriminations against the black market', as these opinions showed up with increasing frequency in private communications. In 1944 they added 'Necessity of the black market to assure food needs', as people not only used the black market more often but talked of it more openly.[30] The prefect of the Aube wrote in mid-1943 of the general public indifference to politics, unless it had repercussions for the satisfaction of material needs. The state failures to organize and distribute food resulted in most people developing a taste for '... minor deceptions. The Frenchman of today accommodates himself to illegality. Wanting goods from the black market, he would like us to make an exception in his favour.'[31]

Representations in fiction and in newspaper cartoons showed children taking part in black-market activity in schools, but evidence for their activity is incidental.[32] In Marcel Aymé's *Le chemin des écoliers*, the lycée students Antoine Michaud and Paul Tiercelin conduct their black-market trade outside school; they skip school to enjoy their profits. They are not interested in school when they can earn 35,000 francs a month in black-market deals linked through Tiercelin's father and his black-market restaurant.[33] In Roger Ferdinand's 1943 play *J3*, parents lament the moral decline of their children, but rely on them for black-market food and cigarettes.[34] Ferdinand's play is more concerned with morality and romance than with the economic challenges facing families. A cartoon from *Ric et Rac* in 1943 captures this

[29] Rist, *Season of Infamy*, 191 (16 Nov. 1941). For cigarettes rapidly becoming the currency for exchange of goods in camps for Allied prisoners of war, see R. A. Radford, 'The Economic Organisation of a P.O.W. Camp', *Economica*, 12(48) (Nov. 1945): 189–201.

[30] AN F/7/14930 for this evolution in Clermont-Ferrand. A similar pattern is evident in reports from Lyon, Toulouse, and Montpellier, with slightly different categories; AN F/7/14928.

[31] AN AJ/41/364 (Aube), prefect bi-monthly report for 3 May to 3 July, 3 July 1943.

[32] Veillon gives examples in *Paris allemand*, 226–227.

[33] Marcel Aymé, *Le chemin des écoliers* (Paris: Gallimard, 1946).

[34] Roger Ferdinand, *J3: Comédie en quatre actes* (Paris: La Belle Fontaine, 1947).

exchange of favours: a student doesn't care whether his math answers are correct, knowing he will receive a passing grade because his parents supply the teacher with butter (Figure 7.1). When the Ministry of Education investigated black-market activity in lycées and collèges in June 1945, it found only a few cases of small-scale activity, usually selling chewing gum and cigarettes.[35] But young children were acutely aware of the shortages and the crises in family consumption. Many suffered from malnutrition, and they knew black-market activity by reputation and as witnesses.

Teachers documented this awareness. An analysis of the impact of Occupation on the psychology of children in *écoles maternelles* (ages four to six), based on a survey of teachers in the Marseille region in 1943, had

— Alors, vous trouvez que 7 et 7 ça fait 13 ?
— Qu'est-ce que ça peut vous faire puisque demain je vous apporte une livre de beurre. (Dessin de R. Ganting.)

Figure 7.1 'So, you think that seven plus seven equals thirteen?' 'What do you care, since tomorrow I'm bringing you a pound of butter?' *Ric et Rac*, 1 Jan. 1943, 1. © British Library Board, MFM.MF247 N.

[35] AN AJ/16/7153, 'Trafic illicite et marché noir dans les établissements secondaires'. My thanks to Megan Barber for this reference.

asked about the influences of the war on their students.[36] Teachers reported an increase in bartering, which had been rare before the war; increased theft of food that was consumed on the spot and greed. But they saw acts of generosity as well, and cases of older children looking out for their younger siblings. Children's conversations and games reflected the adult world they observed. Boys played at war and air bombardments. Girls played at being mothers who complain of shortages and waiting in queues. 'When they play store, they carefully set the boundaries for the shop and the back-of-store, indispensable for illicit sales.' For one student, 'the black market, its when the store is closed and you go in anyway'. (Figure 7.2 shows children's consciousness of queues as essential to shopping.) Children found the black market to be 'perfectly lawful. For them, there's the glory of being *débrouillard*.' They talked of their family's

— **On ne peut pas jouer à la marchande : t'es toute seule pour faire la queue !** (Dessin de M. Thierry.)

Figure 7.2 'We can't play store: you're the only one to stand in line!'
Ric et Rac, 7 May 1941, 1. © British Library Board, MFM.MF247 N.

[36] AN F/17/13364, A. Radureau, 'Conférences pédagogiques des écoles maternelles', 17 Dec. 1943.

successes to teachers they trusted. Cathérine told her teacher, 'You know, Madame, Maman went on her bicycle for killing the pig at Madame X's, she brought back the ham in her backpack; today we are eating the blood sausage, but we mustn't tell.' Robert confided, 'Yesterday, we dined really well, we ate a cock, a pie, and a Savoy cake. Maman said it was black market, and that we shouldn't tell.'

The report summarized the circumstances in which children engaged in such deceptions with the comment that 'Life at present is a school of dissimulation, even for the little ones.' Petty theft to gain food for their families came naturally in a world dominated by adaptations to alleviate shortages. For the children, 'They live in a climate where the distinction between good and bad is no longer made, where hiding and stealing are allowed: the important thing is to not get caught.'[37]

State Employees: Food Supply, SNCF, PTT

In this world of urgent needs, dissimulation, and opportunistic appropriation of goods, many employees took advantage of their access to critical supplies. Most disturbing, when such practices came to light, were the state officials who drew personal benefit from their handling of goods and work procedures intended to serve the public. Local newspapers and the collaborationist press in Paris seized on evidence of state mismanagement. Scandals involving food supplies and misappropriations were significant for their frequency, their implicit logic, and the discredit they brought to state authority.

The food supply administration and its management in municipal offices appear to have had the worst record, with *Ravitaillement général* (RG) staff tempted 'to forget their official duties and take advantage of their situation' as one prefect put it, reporting on two RG staff imprisoned for taking ration tickets.[38] The deputy director of food supply in the Marne, arrested in February 1942 for trafficking in ration tickets, had 132 sheets of tickets on his person and another 2,071 in his house. He was sentenced to five years in prison and a fine of 5,000 francs.[39] The *Tribunal d'État* tried food supply employees who had appropriated ration documents for textiles and food supplies, including an employee in Caen sentenced to life at hard labour for the theft and sale of ration tickets for bread and meat in 1943.[40] When the *Ravitaillement général*'s mobile units

---

[37] Radureau, 'Conférences pédagogiques'.

[38] AN AJ/41/372 (Gironde), prefect monthly report, 4 Dec. 1941; the imprisonment was meant to serve as an example to other food supply employees.

[39] AN AJ/41/377 (Marne); prefect monthly reports, 28 Feb. and 30 Apr. 1942.

[40] Reported in APP 220W 12, 'La situation à Paris', 9 Aug. 1943.

for rural enforcement were incorporated into the *Contrôle économique* in 1942, many staff members were dismissed in an effort to reduce corruption.[41]

The *Ravitaillement général* staff had been assembled hastily in 1940 and 1941, extending the system created for military supply to organize food distribution for civilians, and drawing on food industry personnel to organize supply and distribution within departments.[42] New staff, hired on temporary contracts, often left because of poor working conditions and low pay. A district supervisor in 1942 received an annual salary of only 12,000 francs. This might be supplemented with extra salary, a housing allowance, and child allowance, to reach 2,000 francs per month. The low pay contributed to high turnover and a susceptibility to payoffs from those seeking to avoid regulations or escape fines. A report in October 1942 recommended an immediate salary increase of 30 per cent so they could 'honourably' fulfil their responsibilities.[43] Gifts of food to staff in the RG ranks and to administrators were a routine way to bribe them to look the other way. M. Lemaire, the dairy wholesaler in the Somme who supplied butter to RG officials to avoid prosecution, is one example of a common practice.[44] Given the level of fraud, even honest officials were vulnerable to accusations if those they punished complained in retaliation. An RG controller in the Meurthe and Moselle in 1941 was arrested based on a denunciation by a baker whom he had fined for infractions. Jean Casanoue, the chief food supply negotiator, pointed out that, 'If it suffices for a shopkeeper caught committing an offence to make false accusations against a *Contrôle* agent to stop the proceedings against him, repression of the black market will be impossible, and the action of controllers will be completely paralyzed.'[45]

The staff hired to distribute ration documents could benefit from their easy access. Mayors in small towns could supply extra cards to friends. More typically, office personnel could allow extra allocations and card renewals, and in some cases engage in a local traffic in tickets and cards. Municipal staff caught stealing and reselling ration books and sheets of

---

[41] René Bousquet's instructions for consolidation called for a purge of the *Contrôle mobile*, which was often criticized for the recruitment of agents 'whose competence is often lacking'; AD Yvelines 1W/1337, Secretary General for Police Bousquet to regional prefects, 2 July 1942.

[42] The development of advisory committees is summarized in Heilbronner, 'Le ravitaillement', 1645–1653.

[43] AN F/60/1010, André Brulfert report of 27 Oct. 1942; and Raoul Monmarson to Laval, 30 Oct. 1942.

[44] AN F/23/408, 'Affaire Lemaire', Note (M. Julienne) for Inspector General Jeannin, 21 Feb. 1944, discussed in Chapter 4.

[45] AN F/60/1546, 'Note pour le Délégué général aux relations économiques Franco-Allemandes', 7 Aug. 1941.

coupons appeared with notable frequency in the arrests reported by Paris police. Four men and two women from the mayor's office in the 13th *arrondissement* in April 1941; two men and nine women from the 18th *arrondissement* in March 1943; five women employed in the *mairie* of the 9th *arrondissement* in June 1943, who worked with a group of fifteen reselling ration tickets.[46] The mayor's office in Eaubonne (Seine-et-Oise) had several staff arrested for distributing extra bread cards to staff and friends. The municipality had been getting extra ration cards by claiming the town had 10,700 residents, not the actual 9,700.[47] The frequency and volume of ration document distributions meant that such deceptions could easily go undiscovered. The fraud in Eaubonne was discovered by chance. Police had been called in to investigate the theft of textile and coal ration cards. The prefect of the Seine wished to keep reports of employee misconduct in Paris *mairies* out of the press, but their frequency, especially in the 18th *arrondissement*, made that impossible in 1943.[48]

Thefts of ration documents by outsiders increased as well, night-time break-ins to municipal offices and armed robberies in daylight. Most occurred in the first and last days of the month, to seize the next month's distribution. As thefts increased in 1942, municipal officials asked the Gendarmerie to guard their offices after hours.[49] Stolen tickets had to be replaced, increasing the number of 'legal' entitlements in circulation. Stolen tickets, as genuine titles, had higher black-market value than counterfeits. Typically, the thieves were described as young men, aged twenty to twenty-five, armed and usually on bicycles. Three men robbing the municipal office in Tréguier [Doubs] announced they were from the 'class of 1942', taking ration tickets to feed their *réfractaires* comrades.[50] Resistance groups account for many thefts; the ration documents allowed clandestine members to purchase food at legal outlets. Municipal offices offered an easy target for *résistants*, *réfractaires* evading labour conscription, as well as *faux maquis* and black marketeers. The thefts served as a public reminder of the state's failure to provide secure and sufficient food distribution. One cartoon in August 1943 depicted policemen astonished when the thieves take the entire city hall, removing the town's ration tickets later, 15 km away

[46] APP 220W 4, 11 and 13, 'Situation à Paris' reports of 7 April 1941, 8 March and 15 June 1943.
[47] AD Yvelines 1W/9, report from the sub-prefecture of Pontoise, 30 Mar. 1943.
[48] APP BA 2258, R. Bouffet to the prefect of police, Mar. 1943, and Bouffet to the head of the *Contrôle économique* for the department of the Seine, 18 Mar. 1943.
[49] AN AJ/41/395, 'Renseignements concernant la Gendarmerie, recueillis à la date du 31 août 1942', 31 Aug. 1942.
[50] AN F/60/1525, report by Lieutenant Laporterie, 25 Oct. 1943.

(Figure 7.3). Thieves also took textile coupons, municipal stationery and rubber stamps, and typewriters.[51]

Considering more than 500 ration document thefts from municipal offices and mayors' homes in 1943, the authorities devised 'ruses' including having armed guards accompany the transfer of empty document cases to distract the thieves.[52] New rules to secure ration titles in municipal offices and the provision of armed guards for transport and distribution had limited effect, as policing the rationing system required more personnel, weapons and transport than authorities had available.[53] And municipal staff were not necessarily vigilant, especially when they sympathized with the Resistance. Edith Thomas tells of one Resistance group

— Leur audace ne connaît plus de bornes !... On a retrouvé la mairie à 15 kilomètres d'ici, vidée de ses cartes d'alimentaton !...

Figure 7.3 'Their audacity knows no bounds! We found city hall 15 kilometres from here, emptied of its food ration cards!'
L'Œuvre, 24 Aug. 1943, Bibliothèque nationale de France.

---

[51] AN F/60/1522 to 1527. These records also show increasing theft from tobacconists: armed men took cigarettes, tobacco, and matches. Some claimed to be members of the Resistance and paid for the goods in cash but had no ration tickets; some left a promise of payment after Liberation.

[52] AN AJ/41/430, Darnand to regional prefects, 15 Feb. 1944, repeating ideas from Bousquet to regional prefects, 29 Dec. 1943.

[53] AN AJ/41/430, von Neubronn to Bridoux, 5 Feb. 1944, and Minister of Agriculture to Bridoux, 18 Mar. 1944.

near Avignon who notified the local Gendarmerie in advance where they would rob municipal offices, so that the gendarmes could be sent elsewhere. They avoided one small town with only 100 residents until its mayor complained. When they robbed his *mairie*, he fed them lunch and called the Gendarmerie after they were long gone. 'We would have offended him', she was told, 'if we didn't break in there.'[54]

The *Contrôle économique* claimed that its staff did not abuse their official powers. It gave no numbers for staff arrested, sanctioned or dismissed, but claimed in 1943 that corruption cases in its ranks were very rare.[55] But it was not immune, and its cases of malfeasance drew press attention and strict disciplinary measures. Resister Jean-Pierre Levy shared a cell with five men in 1943, one a CE inspector responsible for restaurant surveillance who had ignored infractions in exchange for bribes.[56] The available evidence suggests that CE malfeasance was comparatively rare, but the agency's bad reputation generated assumptions of guilt, and claims by delinquents that they were CE agents. Robert L. of Batignolles, arrested in August 1945, claimed to be a CE *commissaire général* and demanded 40,000 francs from a shopkeeper to close a non-existent case of black-market activity.[57]

The CE agents did not have the same direct access to rationed foods and documents as did *Ravitiallement général* and municipal officials, but their control measures could prompt bribes from traffickers.[58] In December 1943, in response to the bribery attempts, the CE required that controllers inform their supervisor immediately when offered a bribe, and be non-committal in response, in order to arrange a pay-off at which the offender could be arrested.[59] Failure to act on knowledge of illicit activity did result in suspensions and internments.[60] An article published in the CE's journal boasted that controllers required the honesty to

[54] Édith Thomas, *Le temoin compromis* (Paris: Éditions Viviane Hamy, 1995, reprinted 2018), 142–143.

[55] AN F/7/14895, 'Note au sujet de la position des Services français de contrôle en ce qui concerne la lutte contre le marché noir', probably April 1943.

[56] Jean-Pierre Levy, *Mémoires d'un franc-tireur: Itinéraire d'un résistant (1940–1944)* (Brussels: Éditions Complexe, 1998), 121.

[57] SAEF 5A-0000028, 'Activités de la Direction de la Police économique pour la période du 1er au 15 août 1945'. The report commented that this case showed the extent to which public rumours and press stories about 'economic repression' were often actions by individuals who were not part of any state service.

[58] SAEF 5A-0000029; report on accusations of bribe taking by a M. Jeramec, 10 Apr. 1947; B-0049520, a case in which two textile vendors tried to bribe a CE official investigating their illicit sales, Principal Controller, 'Objet: Affaire Sadi et Dachez, corruption de fonctionnaire', 20 May 1946.

[59] SAEF B-0049888, Note de service no. 394, 3 Dec. 1943.

[60] AD Rhône 182W/55; on three price control agents suspended and interned in August 1944 for their failure to report a baker's traffic in counterfeit cards.

withstand any test, including bribes: 'An agent whose annual salary does not exceed 50 to 60,000 francs can find himself refusing an envelope containing 500,000 or 1 million francs.'[61] The short-term nature of agent contracts and their uncertainty as to future employment would have increased the temptation for some.

The post office (*Postes, Télégraphes et Téléphones* – PTT) and national railroads (SNCF) handled a growing volume of food parcels within France and to Germany. Some staff appropriated food for their own use or resale. Theft from parcels to French prisoners of war was particularly reprehensible; the *Tribunal d'État* tried such cases and sentenced perpetrators to life at hard labour.[62] The number of food parcels shipped within France made theft a considerable temptation and a serious problem for supervisory officials. Thefts of goods transported by the SNCF had been rare before the war; 21 thefts in 1938, 58 in 1940. In 1942 they recorded 134,555; in 1943, 176,681. The value of merchandise stolen in 1942 exceeded 89 million francs.[63] The SNCF adopted tighter security measures and asked to arm the guards protecting cars on rail sidings and in station yards.

In many cases, SNCF staff worked with outsiders to steal and resell merchandise. One case in Lyon singled out four SNCF employees from the other nine people trafficking in goods stolen over a period of three months in 1943 from the rail yard at Portes-les-Valences.[64] The number of staff dismissed for theft demonstrate the scale of the problem, as does the decision to post notices warning staff of the numbers already dismissed for theft, listing the names of those dismissed and setting in bold type those who had stolen from POW parcels.[65] More than 1,000 rail workers were dismissed in 1941; 2,311 in 1942, and 2,524 in 1943.[66] Worker solidarity was such that stolen goods were often shared.[67] The

---

[61] Fourment, 'L'évolution du marché noir', 234–235.

[62] AN 4W/27 has statistics for cases in Paris.

[63] Centre d'archives historiques de la SNCF, Le Mans (CAH SNCF) 25LM0240/1, Tables recording the numbers of 'Vol d'objets confiés au chemin de fer'. Ludivine Broch discusses SNCF efforts to deal with the increase in thefts in *Ordinary Workers, Vichy and the Holocaust: French Railwaymen and the Second World War* (Cambridge: Cambridge University Press, 2016), chapter 4.

[64] AD Rhône, 1035W/28, case no. 66.

[65] AN, 72AJ/1927, 'Vols en cours d'expédition par fer', 11 Mar. 1943, gives a slightly higher number of thefts for 1942 – 134, 790; and Director of Central Service to M. le Baron d'André, Mar. 1943. On German permission to arm railroad security guards because of the increasing thefts, see AN AJ/41/336, Paquin to the Secretary of State for Communications, 28 July 1941; and Broch, *Ordinary Workers*, 113–116.

[66] CAH SNCF 25LM0240/1, has tables recording the numbers of 'Vol d'objets confiés au chemin de fer'. The figures for 1941 are for the months from January through September, with 1225 dismissals.

[67] Broch, *Ordinary Workers*, 105–107, 119.

SNCF warned that in addition to theft, the sharing of stolen goods (notably consuming food and drink) would be punished by dismissal, as would the possession of goods supposedly found at the side of the tracks (the rail equivalent of the British reply that stolen goods had 'fallen off the back of a lorry'). The duty of every employee, they were told, was 'not only not to steal, but to repress thefts; anyone accepting goods from a friend that he knows to have been stolen will certainly be dismissed'.[68] In October 1943 the SNCF created a Protection Service to promote vigilance, and the posters listing the names of workers dismissed were displayed in staff areas not open to the public. The public believed the SNCF to be 'a true den of looters', stealing one in three parcels, and that the principal thieves were station employees.[69] The SNCF declared that ending the thefts was essential to regain public confidence.'[70]

In addition to the thefts, SNCF staff assisted black-market networks by accepting their goods for transport in exchange for some benefit in kind and/or in cash, with *trafiquants* usually paying in goods for their cooperation. Whether in contact with a network or an individual *trafiquant*, staff accepted goods for transport without enforcing restrictions on rationed goods and requiring authorizations for transport. Price control agent X. de Francs complained in early 1941 that the SNCF ignored restrictions on food transport, particularly instructions from prefects in producing regions – the Orne, Sarthe, Mayenne, Seine-Inférieure, Nord and Pas-de-Calais. In his view, 'the "black market" finds a door wide open in sending goods by rail'.[71] The *Contrôle économique* found SNCF staff unhelpful in rural areas; they sometimes refused to allow controllers and gendarmes into stations.[72] *Trafiquants* would arrive shortly before trains departed and pay a premium to register their parcels for immediate departure under a false name.[73] Registered baggage accepted as *colis accompagnés* meant that meat could be shipped without declaring the recipient.

[68] CAH SNCF 25LM0240/3, Directionof the Eastern Region, Ordre régional no. 105, 23 Feb. 1942.
[69] AD Alpes-Maritimes 1031W/8, PTT Commission for the *Contrôle technique* in Pau, 'Rapport statistiques du mois de décembre 1943'.
[70] CAH SNCF 25LM0240/3, Direction of the Eastern Region, Ordre régional no. 105, 23 Feb. 1942.
[71] SAEF 4A-0000003, X. des Francs, 'Note sur facilités donnés par le S.N.C.F. au "marché noir"', 28 Feb. 1941, and subsequent notes on 1 May and 18 Aug. 1941, complaining that SNCF agents frequently obstructed CE efforts to investigate in train stations.
[72] AD Ille-et-Vilaine 118W/72, prefect of Morbihan to the regional prefect, 2 May 1942.
[73] AD Seine-Maritime 40W/114, 'Synthèse des rapports des préfets de la région de Rouen du mois d'août 1943'.

In Neufchatel-en-Bray the Gendarmerie found 100,000 kg of meat being shipped in this way in May 1943.[74]

Rail employees also exploited their right to free transit, traveling on days off to rural areas to buy food. Rail staff figured prominently in prefects' reports on black- market activity in 1941 and 1942. The prefect of the Côtes-du-Nord suggested suppressing their permits for free travel.[75] A control operation over five days in September 1941 to seize illicit food parcels included those of thirty railway staff, transporting food that included more than 129 kg butter, 21 chickens, and more than 141 dozen eggs.[76] The regional prefect in Rennes complained of rail workers from the Paris region; one third of the passengers caught for illicit transport in his region in September 1941 were SNCF employees. Only a few counted as 'black market'; most were individuals with 'abnormal quantities of food for purely family needs'.[77] The prefect in the Mayenne noted that if many of the SNCF offenders were simply feeding their families, 'others, on the contrary, more and more numerous it seems, profit from their ease of circulation to work as official transporters for organized bands supplying clandestine food, at a high price, in the Paris region'.[78] In a week-long surveillance of passengers in the Charolles region (Saône-et-Loire), the Gendarmerie caught 385 persons carrying food, 250 of whom were SNCF employees. One report commented on their use of night freight trains, terming them 'specialists in fraudulent supply'.[79]

Post office employees shared similar appetites and sympathies. When controls increased in train stations to check the luggage of passengers returning from the countryside, sending food by post offered an alternative to avoid controllers.[80] The post office staff accepting parcels rarely checked the contents, although they were supposed to report frequent mailings by individuals and to record the identity of senders. Content verification took place at the receiving end, and it was common knowledge that staff ignored the rules restricting the mailing of rationed foods,

---

[74] AN AJ/41/395, 'Synthèse relative à l'état moral et matériel de la population dans les territoires de la zone occupée au cours du mois de Mai 1943'.

[75] AD Ille-et-Vilaine, 118W/75, J. Feschotte to Minister of Food Supply, 29 Sept. 1941.

[76] AD Ille-et-Vilaine 118W/76, Department office for Food Supply in the Côtes-du-Nord, 'Liste des saisies faites dans les colis transportés par les agents de la S.N.C.F. pendant la période du 15 au 20 Septembre 1941', 7 Oct. 1941.

[77] AD Ille-et-Vilaine, 118W/75, regional prefect to the Minister of Food Supply, undated, likely Sept. 1941.

[78] AN AJ/41/378 (Mayenne), prefect report for December 1941, 2 Jan. 1942.

[79] AN AJ/41/24, 'Synthèse des rapports mensuels des commandants des Légions de Gendarmerie de la Zone Libre (Avril 1942)'.

[80] AD Ille-et-Vilaine, 118W/75, regional prefect to the Minister of Food Supply, undated, likely Sept. 1941.

butter in particular.[81] Some postal staff did steal packages. Police summaries in Paris in 1943 included a case of seven employees who stole parcels from the central post office. One employee changed labels on food parcels, readdressing them to his sister and her husband; a group of nine PTT employees caught in July 1943 had stolen an estimated 2,500 parcels.[82] A clerk in Rouen, arrested in July 1942, had stolen ration cards that he sold locally or sent to an uncle who ran a restaurant in Paris.[83] Postal employees in Saint-Lô and Caen were arrested for the theft of ration cards and parcels and the use of postal sacks to ship black-market meat to Paris.[84] The PTT administration warned repeatedly that postal sacks were intended for the transport of mail, and prohibited their use for any other purpose (shipping black-market food).[85] As with rail service, the access to transport and goods provided opportunities to steal and to abet transport by black-market networks.

Workplace Canteens and Cooperatives

As seen in Chapter 5, many factories established workplace canteens to supplement workers' rations. In 1943 work canteens were feeding hundreds of thousands of workers across France; 400,000 in the department of the Seine alone, and another 50,000 in the Seine-et-Marne.[86] In addition to canteens, companies organized food cooperatives, and the state established canteens in schools and state offices. The state also created *restaurants communitaires* to serve meals to low-income workers and their families; they served 6 million meals in their first six months of operation in 1943.[87]

Companies running canteens were encouraged to develop factory gardens tended by workers, rent garden terrain from farmers, and purchase food direct from farms. This created opportunities to gather more food by paying higher prices, and to resell to employees and other customers. The CE supervision of canteens tended towards leniency, given their

---

[81] Groult, *Journal à quatre mains*, 383.
[82] APP 220W 11, 'Situation à Paris', 11 Jan. 1943, and 220W 12, 'Situation à Paris', 28 June 1943.
[83] AD Seine-Maritime 271W/167, Inspectors Giffard and Amouret to the Chief Commissioner, Police de Sûreté, Rouen, 7 Mar. 1944.
[84] Lecouturier, *Le marché noir en Normandie*, 48–49.
[85] Lecouturier, *Le marché noir en Normandie*, 53–54, citing notes to this effect on 23 Nov. 1942, 16 Oct. 1943 and 31 Jan. 1944.
[86] AN 72AJ/1927, Bichelonne note of 13 Sept. 1943; see Grenard, *La France du marché noir*, 139 and 'La question du ravitaillement'.
[87] APP 220W 12, 'Situation à Paris', 26 July 1943.

importance in supplementing workers' diet.[88] Infractions by canteens were mainly in buying and selling at higher than licit prices. But the use of company vehicles and funds for canteen supply gave the means and opportunity for more substantial endeavours. The example of Pétroles Jupiter in Chapter 5, the canteen that organized a slaughterhouse and sold black-market meat in a neighbouring town, shows the way in which organizing food to supply a canteen could lead to larger-scale enterprise. The Société des Hauts-Fourneaux de la Chiers likewise sold part of its output, at the legal price but off the record, to third parties, and used part of the proceeds to buy food for the firm's canteen.[89]

Such cases show how canteens and cooperatives, in the words of the police, 'serve to often to hide a black market from which owners profit with their immediate entourage'.[90] Bank of France regional directors noted that the canteens provided essential food to workers, and rated their purchase of food on the black market and through barter as less serious than black-market purchasing by housewives, because it alleviated worker undernourishment and improved productivity.[91] As official supplies contracted, canteens extended their efforts to find food. Because of the shortages in 1944, the directors of cooperatives for municipal utilities workers in Marseille, whose morals were reported as 'beyond doubt', no longer hesitated to engage in commerce with any seller, 'to procure merchandise at any price without concern to respect even the most elementary formalities'.[92]

Abuse of privilege took place from the start and at the highest levels.[93] Pétain's post-armistice government, provisionally installed at Vichy in 1940, had ministerial food service managers who often crossed legal boundaries to feed their staff. Frequent infractions were reported to the

---

[88] SAEF B-0049888, Notes de Service nos. 315 (1 July 1943) and 383 (19 Nov. 1943) counseled 'nuance' in monitoring canteen activity, while noting that some abused their powers 'to obtain provisions in the clandestine market, under irregular conditions, and to the detriment of the mass of consumers submitting to the control regime' (Note de Service no. 315).

[89] Anne Thomazeau, 'Un ingénieur français et son entreprise: Les Hauts-Fourneaux de la Chiers pendant la Seconde guerre mondiale (août 1939 – septembre 1945)', Masters thesis in contemporary history, Paris-X Nanterre (2001) 97–100; based on the agendas in Fonds Victor Guillermin, IHTP ARC 091.

[90] AD Yvelines 1W/10, Renseignements généraux, Seine-et-Oise, 'Note: Enquêtes dans les usines métallurgiques', 9 Aug. 1943; also 'Note: Enquête dans les usines métallurgiques', 6 Aug. 1943.

[91] ABdF 1069201226 25, DGEE, 'Résumé des rapports économiques', ZO, July 1942.

[92] SAEF B-0049723, reports on the Coopérative de Consommation de la Régie du Gaz de Marseille and the Coopérative de Consommation de la Société des Eaux de Marseille, 4 May 1944.

[93] See Grenard, 'L'approvisionnement clandestin des popotes de Vichy: une affaire soigneusement étouffée', in Les scandales du ravitaillement, 99–113.

minister of justice in spring 1941, hoping to avoid the scandal of public prosecution of ministerial staff. A new rule allocated 15 per cent of the food arriving in Vichy to ministerial *popotes* [food services] and promised that infractions would cease. They did not. The head of food services for Marshal Pétain's personal guard (140 gendarmes) was cited in September 1941 with a dozen others for black-market purchase of rationed foods, collected by the gendarmes every Wednesday. The director explained that he had to find sufficient food, and his superiors closed their eyes to the use of 'clandestine methods'.[94]

The *Contrôle des prix* claimed, at meetings to coordinate action against the black market in December 1941 and January 1942, that they could no longer work in the department of the Allier (for Vichy): 'because all the illicit traffic was working for the food services for the admiralty and ministerial offices'.[95] The cases continued in 1942, making it clear that illicit purchase was standard practice. The prosecutor in Riom, referring a new case to the Garde des Sceaux in June 1942, stated that he had evidence to prosecute, but it was another of 'these interminable *affaires de popote*'.[96] In August the government amnestied eighty-one of the persons involved in ration and price infractions to supply government offices in Vichy, including ministerial staff.[97]

Illicit traffic to supply the ministries continued. One driver, Delorière, thirty-four years old, had bought black-market food for various ministries since August 1940 and worked with the drivers for ministers Pierre Pucheu and Jean Bichelonne. All *popotes*, he claimed, without exception, bought food in the countryside. Having experience with the resources available through black-market purchasing, Delorière continued trafficking on his own account, working with a driver for another ministry, purchasing from his usual suppliers. A search of his room in the Hôtel Villard confiscated food, textiles and alcohol sufficient to stock a small store.[98]

---

[94] AN F/60/291, Attorney General for the Appeals Court, Riom, to the Keeper of the Seals, 17 Oct. 1941.

[95] AN F/60/291, Keeper of the Seals to the deputy premier, 3 Mar. 1942.

[96] AN BB/18/3355, Attorney General for the Appeals Court, Riom, to the Keeper of the Seals, 24 June 1942.

[97] Grenard, *Les scandales du ravitaillement*, 109.

[98] AN BB/18/3355, Attorney General for the Appeals Court, Riom to the Keeper of the Seals, 2 June 1942, underlining his text that this purchasing was a continuing problem. The goods confiscated in the hotel included: 20 sausages, 60 camemberts, 95 1 kg cans of chicken and beans, one can of tomatoes, 9 cans of 'Maltées' flour, 98 spools of thread, 66 pairs of women's stockings, 4 pairs of men's socks, 16 bottles of sparkling wine, 5 bottles of other wines, 23 litres of aperitifs, 45 tent canvases and one large tarpaulin, tent pegs, 100 kg salt, military clothing (383 châles militaires, 1 chandail militaire, 1 grande

The Bank of France used its trucks to transport food for its canteen (Chapter 5); the PTT and the SNCF too had transport capacity to supply their staff canteens. The PTT trucks distributing mail in rural areas brought food for canteens on their return trips.[99] The SNCF was caught transporting thousands of kilograms of meat from clandestine slaughter and using SNCF vehicles to supply their canteens. In one case they sent a special train from Paris to Limoges with a flatbed wagon to transport a car for prospecting in the region and a truck to carry 3,100 kg of meat from illicit slaughter back to Paris. Another case arranged to bring 10,000 kg of meat to Paris. The CE director reporting on these stated: 'the canteens of the SNCF abuse the transport facilities accorded by their situation to systematically violate the economic legislation with the tacit assent of the high personnel in the company'. Given similar offences by the PTT and continuing abuse by both organizations, the state in effect subsidized the clandestine activity that used state transport to supply state employees.[100]

Even the Ministry of Justice was caught in violations. The CE confiscated 150 kg of butter intended for the Ministry of Justice canteen in early 1945. Controllers cracking down on the resurgence in black-market activity paid particular attention to the canteens and cooperatives benefiting from special privileges for their supply.[101] The CE reported as 'current practice' that the truck drivers they stopped routinely claimed the goods they carried were for a canteen, with the authorization for their cargo not yet received. This replaced the use of German army trucks bringing goods to the Paris black market.[102] It was 'a traffic for profit, difficult to thwart, practiced under cover of the canteens and cooperatives'. But until official distribution worked more effectively, such abuse had to be tolerated, within defined limits.[103]

Retail Trade

Shopkeepers and restaurant owners, as well as profiting from customer needs, found opportunities for mutually beneficial exchange, violating controls to replenish stock. Shopkeepers sought deals with manufacturers,

couverture militaire), three jerrycans, two of which were full, butchers' knives, a 65 litre cask of wine and a 45 to 50 litre cask of alcohol.

[99] SAEF B-0075660, L. Cruse, 'Note pour M. le directeur du cabinet', 23 Jan. 1945, reporting the seizure of 1200 kg meat transported by a PTT truck.

[100] SAEF B-0057660, L. Cruse, 'Note au ministre' concerning 'Transports irréguliers de denrées contingentés effectués pour le compte de la S.N.C.F.', 26 May 1945.

[101] SAEF B-0057660, Mauriol to the Keeper of the Seals, 12 Feb. 1945.

[102] SAEF 5A-0000028, Contrôle économique 'Rapport mensuel', Feb. 1945.

[103] SAEF 5A-0000029, Director of the *Contrôle économique* to Minister of the Economy and Finance, 5 May 1945, noting abuses in canteens run by the army, the Resistance, the *Milice patriotique*, the Czechoslovakian consulate and the Galeries Lafayette.

wholesalers, and a new layer of freelancing intermediaries. Just as low official prices discouraged farmers from bringing goods to official markets, price controls and shortages of raw materials diverted manufactured goods from normal channels to illicit exchange. Shopkeepers bought, when and where they could, paid premiums off-the-book for goods they found and sold at higher prices to recover their costs. Restaurants were regulated but difficult to monitor. Controllers in Paris estimated in early 1941 that nearly half the restaurants were guilty of price, rationing and accounting infractions. But if rationing measures were strictly observed, many restaurants would have to close.[104]

Ordinary customers faced daily ordeals in the queues for food, keeping track of ration coupons and tickets for their purchases, sharing meagre supplies among family members, shortages of fuel for heat and cooking, and empty shelves in retail markets and stores. Shopping consumed more time and energy, with less to show at the end of the day. Urban residents lost weight and suffered higher rates of infant mortality and tuberculosis linked to malnutrition; chilblains on hands and feet were a painful daily reality, a malady that disappeared when food supply improved after the war.[105] Everyone not only wanted, but *needed* to find supplementary sources for food, clothing and material goods. Their ability to do so depended partly on wealth, but critically on location and opportunities for connections to provide transport and means of payment (including barter) for goods.

In June 1942, Paris police reported that housewives harshly criticized the shopkeepers that they believed kept goods to exchange with other shopkeepers or to sell 'in the back of the store ... to wealthy clients who pay at far above the fixed prices'.[106] But the shopkeepers were not the main target for complaint. German requisitions and Vichy food administration received most of the blame, and the French authorities for according purchasing privileges to 'canteens, cooperatives and other collectivities' ahead of retailers and ordinary consumers.[107]

Consumer power lay in finding alternative sources for goods and the necessary means of payment that did not distinguish carefully between the licit and illicit. This turn to improvisation, the capacity to develop alternatives and work around the law, which was termed *le système D*, the ability to 'make do', or resourcefulness (from the verb *se débrouiller*). It

---

[104] SAEF B-0049757, 'Note' dated 1941 on control operations in the Paris region beginning 31 March; and APP BA 1808, note of 29 Nov. 1941.

[105] The health impact is summarized in Cépède, *Agriculture et alimentation*, 403–17, and Veillon, 'Aux origines de la sous-alimentation'.

[106] APP 220W 9, 'La situation à Paris', 15 June 1942.

[107] APP 220W 12, 'La situation à Paris', 12 July 1943.

became a catch-all category for finding access to goods. Whether the alternatives were strictly legal – contents in family parcels from the countryside, or the barter of scarce materials for food, for example – or more often pushed legal boundaries, the emphasis was on results, *débrouillardise*.[108] This improvisation to ameliorate the shortages in official markets often meant finding ways around the laws that restricted market activity: prices, quantities, and permits for transport. Any leeway for transgression could be stretched. As state rules became more restrictive and alternate paths increased in importance, there was increasing creativity and a progressive de-legitimation of the state controls. The multiplication of controls exceeded the state's capacity to police them: *le système D* exemplified and valorised consumer improvisation to circumvent state control.

Faux policiers

This gap between state capacity to police controls and the rising level of illicit traffic was filled in part by new criminal initiative. It fostered a surge in activity by *faux policiers*: police imposters using intimidation, extortion and theft for personal gain.[109] Alarmed at the surge, the Ministry of the Interior asked the Paris police to report on all 'affairs called *faux policiers*'. Their list, kept by the police from April 1942 to March 1944, counted 820 cases in the Paris region alone, and involved thousands of individuals, as the *faux policiers* often worked in groups.[110] As one inspector observed in September 1941, the early *faux policiers* exploited individuals unlikely to report aggressive police behaviour: Jews, black market *trafiquants*, and dealers in gold around the Paris Bourse.[111] Later in the Occupation, families sheltering resistance members and *réfractaires* evading the labour draft became targets as well.

---

[108] Veillon, *Vivre et survivre*, 186–195. The term originated in the French army in North Africa in the 1850s and became widely known for soldiers' survival tactics in the First World War; see Libby Murphy, *The Art of Survival: France and the Great War Picaresque* (New Haven, CT: Yale University Press, 2016), 43–63.

[109] Kenneth Mouré, 'The *faux policier* in Occupied Paris', *Journal of Contemporary History*, 45(1) (2010): 95–112, also Vinen, *The Unfree French*, 239–242, and Auda, *Les belles années du 'milieu'*, 148–150.

[110] APP BA 2115, Secretary General of the police to the prefect of Paris police, 23 Apr. 1942; this official count understates *faux policier* activity in reporting only the cases reported and the offenders caught.

[111] APP BA 2115, Inspector principal adjoint Lucien Schmitt, 29 Sept. 1941. The black market for gold, and German tolerance and use of the market are explored in Georges Gallais-Hamonno, Thi-Hong-Van Hoang and Kim Oosterlinck, 'Price Formation on Clandestine Markets: The Case of the Paris Gold Market during the Second World War', *Economic History Review* 72, no. 3 (2018): 1048–1072.

Most *faux policiers* claimed to be German police, flashed their official badges too quickly for victims to verify, and relied on imitating the arrogance and intimidation exercised by German military and police. Many official roles could be adopted to gain entry to private apartments and commercial premises, there to steal money, jewellery, furs and other clothing, canned goods and hams. *Faux policiers* claimed to be CE agents, food supply administrators, electrical and gas company meter readers, and even shoe inspectors. The most extreme in their violence and extortion were the 'French Gestapo'; the French citizens, many freed from prison, working with the Germans who provided them with official police status (termed 'true *faux policiers*' in Grégory Auda's account of their activity)[112] and engaging in theft, extortion and murder. Members of the *Milice française*, created by Vichy in January 1943 to battle the growing Resistance, engaged in criminal activity for their own benefit. Some *faux policiers* then claimed to be French Gestapo or *Milice* to intimidate victims and leverage their extortion. A news digest in 1944 reported: 'There are an increasing number of bogus policemen, bogus Gestapo agents, and bogus gas company employees who break into private houses, produce forged credentials and search the premises, sweeping off money and jewels from under the noses of the owners.'[113] *Faux policiers* activity had as context the economy of penury. They exploited the proliferation of controls, their widespread violation, public confusion about and fear of the multiple policing authorities, the disorder and violence characteristic of the German police, and the Vichy regime's inability to contain and repress the escalation of criminal activity.

Moral Crisis

The *faux policiers* provide an extreme and perverse example of the ways in which shortages, controls limiting access to needed goods, and the state's incapacity to police economic crimes all encouraged violations. The logic varied, from mild transgressions to feed families, to practices intended to keep businesses running and workers employed, to trafficking in goods for the Germans and squeezing profit from the needs of ordinary consumers. There was slippage between behaviour that was clearly within legal bounds or stretching legal limits, and engaging in clearly illegal activity. The ill-defined boundaries between licit and illicit transactions that could

---

[112] Auda, *Les belles années du 'milieu'*, 86. The most infamous group was the Lafont-Bonny gang of the rue Lauriston, but other 'French Gestapo' groups were located on rue de la Pompe, avenue Foch, and in Neuilly. Concisely surveyed in Berlière, *Polices des temps noirs*, 487–508.

[113] AN F/1a/3966, News Digest no. 1443.

be exploited with little apparent risk provided opportunity for all. New economic rules had outlawed the normal negotiation of terms of exchange. The determination of price between buyer and seller, fundamental to market transactions, was no longer legal if prices or quantities exceeded the legal ceilings. *Trafiquants* exploited the opportunities opened by the greater needs and the blurred boundaries. Goods and transactions moved to extralegal terrain where buyers and sellers could negotiate for desired goods. Once outside the law, all limits could be renegotiated or transgressed. The shortages, restrictions, and urgency of demand for essentials created a logic and dynamic for developing connections and transactions outside legal limits.

This broad intermediary zone for the extralegal activity vital for survival was the terrain in which Charles Rist's 'unscrupulous intermediaries' thrived. Opportunities to satisfy needs and turn a profit could appear as rational, logical, and even patriotic. Ineffective and erratic law enforcement, the structuring of legal activity to serve German needs, and the obvious inequities in access to goods, especially for necessities in a system claiming to 'share sacrifice', undermined the legitimacy of state controls. Louis Baudin described the system as a 'vaudeville économique' in which 'the swindler swaggers, the misfit whines, incapable of finding sufficient food and swamped by formalities, the hero who won't use the black market and does not have relatives in the countryside is distinguished by his thinness and his pallor'.[114]

The spread of illicit commerce raised fears that the increasing criminal behaviour marked the start of a major crisis in morality. In the economy of penury, Vichy's purported 'new moral order' was obviously losing ground to criminal behaviour and moral abandon. Prefects worried about declining moral standards, with black-market activity a key signal for their concern. Marc Chevalier, prefect of Seine-et-Oise, saw a rampant moral crisis in 1943, against which the state was powerless because the crisis was so widespread. Youth, in particular, were threatened: 'The spirit of lucre, the indiscipline, the disobedience, are the main traits of a younger generation that has only bad examples before their eyes.'[115] The Paris police and the Gendarmerie commented regularly on moral decline linked to economic need. Bank of France directors observed 'a weakening of morality and the rapid spread of black market behaviour'.[116] Diary entries by notable private citizens lamented this decline. For Charles Rist, the war experience marked 'a material and moral regression that would have

---

[114] Baudin, *Esquisse de l'économie*, 150, 155–156.
[115] AN AJ/41/391 (Seine-et-Oise), prefect monthly report, 31 July 1943.
[116] ABdF 1069201226 25, DGEE, 'Résumé des rapports économiques', ZO, Mar. 1942.

seemed unbelievable just a few years ago'. Charles Braibant, director of the Navy's archive and library service in Paris, remarked on the theft of 3,000 envelopes from his secretary's desk: 'People steal more and more. If this war were to last, it would mean the end of all probity, all morality.'[117]

The moral crisis, as citizens adapted behaviour to disregard the law in favour of *débrouillardise*, was clearly in response to economic circumstances. As the Paris police observed, reporting on public opinion and the increase in property crimes in 1943, 'The difficulties of existence and the high cost of living bring a permanent malaise and contribute, to a large extent, to the degradation of morality.'[118] The confusion and uncertainty about the boundaries for economic exchange, between licit and illicit, or more accurately, between infractions tolerated or unacceptable, heightened concerns for the dangers of a normalization of illegality. The sense of moral crisis would intensify as black-market activity increased after Liberation, which many had believed would bring immediate improvement to material conditions.

---

[117] Rist, *Season of Infamy*, 364 (6 Dec. 1943), adapted to accord with the original French; Braibant, *La guerre à Paris*, 211–212 (20 May 1943). These fears are explored at greater length in Kenneth Mouré, 'Marcel Aymé and the Moral Economy of Penury in Occupied France', *French Historical Studies* 34 (4) (2011): 713–743.

[118] APP 220W 11, 'Situation à Paris', 8 Mar. 1943.

8   Liberating Markets and Consumers

> For four years radio from London has shown us with statistics that the Germans were pillaging France and that their excessive levies were starving the population. The Germans are gone. The Allies have come to our aid and yet the food situation continues to worsen: we no longer understand.[1] (1945)

'For the first time in my life and probably the last, I have lived for a week in a great city where everybody is happy', American journalist A. J. Liebling wrote from Paris on 1 September 1944. Resistance movements had sped the city's liberation in August, with Parisians taking a proud role in securing their freedom from German oppression. Food shortages and cycling, he reported, gave French women 'the best figures in the world'. Although food was scarce, 'the day of the black-market people is ending, because there are great quantities of butter, meat, and vegetables in Normandy, Brittany, and Anjou at about an eighth of Paris prices and bringing them here is now simply a matter of transportation'. With so much food within easy reach, shortages would soon end. Liebling's advice? French consumers should 'do without for a few weeks, because such a situation can last only under the rule of the Germans'.[2] Bank of France directors noted that across France everyone believed the end to German exactions would bring rapid recovery in food supply.[3]

Pushing out the Germans relaxed only one of the constraints causing the shortages, economic distress and black-market growth. Liberation itself disrupted supplies, markets, and the enforcement of controls. German exploitation came to an end in an economy crippled by war and Occupation. Allied supply management focused on delivering

---

[1] AN F/1a/3250, 'Note pour Monsieur le Directeur général de la Sûreté nationale', 22 Mar. 1945.

[2] A. J. Liebling, 'Letter from Paris', *The New Yorker*, 9 Sept. 1944; written 1 Sept. 1944, reprinted in *A. J. Liebling: World War II Writings* (New York: Library of America, 2008), 522–523. Liebling revised these superficial views in a subsequent column, see chapter conclusion.

[3] ABdF, 1069201226 27, DGEE, 'Résumé des rapports économiques', Sept. 1944.

military support to defeat Germany. French output contracted and transport for civilian goods remained at a fraction of prewar capacity with extensive damage to infrastructure. The problem was more than 'simply a matter of transportation' and would take time to solve. The black market slowed at Liberation, then flourished anew. Bank of France directors wrote in March 1945 that it had reached its highest levels of activity and prosperity since 1940.[4] Reductions in personnel and shortages of vehicles and fuel restricted control efforts and weakened state power to repress illicit activity. Vichy's moral 'new order', through material deprivation, collaboration and corruption, seemed to have fostered a culture of deception, crime and aversion to hard work. Jean Chaintron, the prefect of the Haute-Vienne, observed, 'We have to repair not only the material ruins of our country, but also the moral ruins the enemy has left behind.'[5]

Visitors from Britain found conditions in France alarming. The economist Thomas Balogh, in Paris in January 1945, began his analysis of French economic problems for the British Treasury: 'The French economic and social position presents a picture of disaster, distress, and increasing tension, superimposed on the great relief and enthusiasm brought forth by the liberation.' Balogh estimated French industrial production at 30 per cent of its prewar levels, and agricultural output at 50 per cent. The black market kept ordinary citizens alive.[6] The British embassy's air attaché toured industrial sites near Lyon in March and summed up the black market there as: 'essentially a market for things which are necessities and which cannot be got in sufficient quantities elsewhere'. Authorities were powerless against it. Although 'rackets' had amassed 'huge fortunes' for the few, he concluded: 'the hard fact to remember in making moral judgments, is that without the Black Market France could not exist'.[7]

A Czech diplomat visiting Paris in January 1945 was struck by the visibility and the necessity of the black market. 'Everybody needs the black market inevitably to keep alive; but in fact it is not a black market at all, because it goes on quite openly, I should almost say supervised by state authorities. It is in fact the real source from which the French draw life and most of the goods they need in order to maintain their normal

---

[4] ABdF 1069201226 27, DGEE, 'Résumé des rapports économiques', Mar. 1945.
[5] AN F/1a/4022, Commissaire de la République report for the Limoges region, 1–15 June 1945; 'Allocution prononcée à Radio Limoges par M. Jean Chaintron, Préfet de la Haute-Vienne, le 1er Juin 1945'.
[6] TNA FO 371 49131, T. Balogh, 'The Economic Problem of France', Jan.–Feb. 1945.
[7] TNA FO 371 49096, 'Lyons – 3rd March, 1945'. The attaché noted that low official rates of pay for truck drivers meant most preferred to work transporting black-market goods.

living standards.' Continual adaptations to work outside the rules had reconfigured the delivery of goods. 'For instance, you would not get your meat at the butchers, but at the petrol pump, your petrol not at the pump, but in the pub and a bottle of brandy not in the pub, but in a beauty shop ... In PARIS one can buy anything that even the most fastidious taste could want – and all of the finest pre-war quality and cut, but of course at fantastic prices.'[8] His observation underlines the question of how serious the shortages really were, and whether the diversion of goods to the black market had created a parallel economy that was better supplied and more efficient than the official market under state control.

French officials grappled with the transition from administering a crippled and fragmented economy serving German demands to reconstructing their economy in the interests of French producers and consumers. The challenges proved to be formidable and largely unforeseen. In a situation of acute shortages, limited productive capacity, and popular demands for wage increases, continued controls were deemed essential. Alfred Sauvy had cautioned in 1942 that widespread public opinion blaming the Germans for the shortages led to a dangerous expectation that access to goods, food in particular, could rapidly return to prewar norms when hostilities ended.[9] He returned to the problem in January 1945, noting the widespread belief that 'considerable riches' had been hidden or lost, which led to the conclusion that the state administration was responsible for shortages.[10] The need for controls appeared greater than ever. But the state resources for enforcement were shrinking, as was public tolerance for controls and controllers. This led to violent confrontations and, in mid-1947, a retreat from strict enforcement. This chapter covers the flourishing of black-market activity from Liberation through 1947, including the black market for US Army goods, and the official fears of moral decline as black-market practices continued to spread illicit activity, subverted state controls, and imperilled plans for economic recovery.

---

[8] TNA FO 371 49096, Czech letter in translation to A. Hayek, 30 Jan. 1945; the author is likely Alexander Kunosi (my thanks to Susan Howson for identifying the author), writing to Friedrich A. Hayek. François Brigneau similarly comments that it became normal 'to buy butter at the hairdresser's, cigarettes from the bootlace vendor, and cloth from the accountant on the third floor', in *Mon après-guerre* (Paris: Éditions du Clan, 1966), 117.

[9] Institut de conjoncture, 'Situation économique au début de mars 1942 (Rapport no. 10)', 56–57.

[10] Institut de conjoncture, 'Situation économique vers le 15 janvier 1945 (Rapport no. 2)', 48–49.

The Limits of Consumer Liberation

In the final months of the German Occupation the French economy contracted further, choked by shortages of raw materials, transport and energy. Coal, gas for heat and gasoline were in short supply and electricity output fell dramatically, limiting work in factories and workshops. The Paris police observed in April that restrictions on electricity 'are paralyzing economic and commercial life, and provoke frequent recriminations by industrialists, directors of entertainment venues, and notably by artisans who complain they can no longer complete work for their clients'.[11] The Bank of France reported spreading economic paralysis in March and April as the Allied bombing of railyards, locomotive depots, arms factories and bridges reduced supplies of fuel and raw materials. Factories fell idle, their finished goods undeliverable to customers.[12] As production declined, workers were paid less, accentuating the gap between their earnings and the rising cost of living. In late March, 1,340 bakeries in Paris were closed to ration the wood for bakery ovens, and the police discussed whether to close restaurants three days a week rather than two.[13] Public transit had been slashed in 1941 (eliminating above ground buses and closing about 100 metro stations). Service contracted further in 1943–1944, reducing the number of lines still running, the stations served and the hours of operation.[14]

Food supplies were particularly vulnerable. Officially, weekly meat rations allowed 120 grams per person in Paris, but many consumers received no meat rations for three weeks in March.[15] Parisians joked that the meat ration could be wrapped in a metro ticket. Employers increased the number of meals they provided in cafeterias, served meals for the unemployed, and gave workers increased time off to find food.[16]

[11] APP 220W 15, 'Situation à Paris', 3 Apr. 1944.
[12] ABdF 1069201226 12, DGEE, 'Résumé des rapports économiques', Mar. and Apr. 1944. On the bombing in preparation for Normandy and its cost in civilian lives, see Olivier Wieviorka, *Normandy: The Landings to the Liberation of Paris* trans. by M. B. DeBevoise (Cambridge, MA: The Belknap Press of Harvard University Press, 2008), 122–131. The shift in RAF targets from February to 6 June, to attack 'railway targets' in March and to focus on French targets in May 1945 before the Allied invasion, can be followed in the RAF bombing reports published in Martin Middlebrook and Chris Everitt, eds., *The Bomber Command War Diaries: An Operational Reference Book, 1939–1945* (Harmondsworth: Viking, 1985), 471–520.
[13] APP 220W 15, 'Situation à Paris', 17 Apr. 1944.
[14] Michel Margairaz, 'Les deux compagnies de transports urbains parisiens entre rationalisation, collaboration d'État et collaboration technique (1940–1944)', in *Transports dans la France en guerre 1939–1945*, ed. by Marie-Noëlle Polino (Mont-Saint-Aignan: Publications des Universités de Rouen et du Havre, 2007), 270–271. Drake, *Paris at War*, 382, notes at end of July 1944 there were just 8 lines in operation, on reduced hours.
[15] APP 220W 15, 'Situation à Paris', 3 and 17 Apr. 1944.
[16] APP 220W 15, 'Situation à Paris', 12 June 1944.

Anticipating transport disruption, municipal authorities had discussed a 'Distress Plan' for food supply in 1943, to determine how to feed 4 million Parisians in the event of major disruption. The plan considered four scenarios, the last of which – the stoppage of all road and rail transport – found that reliance on horse and human power (including bicycles with trailers) would not be able to feed the city.[17] An Allied invasion to liberate France was the obvious reason to plan for 'distress' in transport.

The Allied landing in Normandy naturally impacted food supply. Official rations fell. Bread rations in cities were reduced, even in Normandy, to 100 grams per day. In some parts of southern France, needing wheat from the north, bread rations dropped to as little as 50 grams per day.[18] Fuel allocations to state services stopped, and the retreating Germans took cars and bicycles. Employees rendered their service vehicles inoperable. Some trucks were hidden with wheels in one location, engines in another, chassis in a third, awaiting reassembly after Liberation.[19] De Sailly claimed his administration was 'totally paralyzed' in late June, and the pause in control efforts meant the resumption of controls after Liberation needed re-thinking. Some local Liberation committees suspended control functions and regional newspapers criticized rationing and price controls.[20] Writing to price control directors in liberated departments at the end of August, de Sailly urged them to contact local officials and help re-establish state authority and price stability. Resuming price verifications needed to take place in stages, he cautioned, 'with tact and with particular care for the educational role of the Service'.[21]

[17] APP BA 1807, 'Plan de détresse', following meetings between officials from the Paris municipal police, the *Ravitaillement général* and the transport services (Ponts et Chaussées) on 7 July and 8 September 1943, sent to the Minister of the Interior on 21 Nov. 1943.

[18] TNA FO 371 42017, for rations of 100 grams of bread per day in Caen in June, and that three-quarters of the city's food reserves had been destroyed by Allied bombing in early July; Capt. E. G. de Pury, 'Recce Report on CAEN', 12 July 1944. The US Seventh Army's Civil Affairs reports on conditions in southern France in late August noted that feeding the civilian population was the principal civil affairs challenge. In the Var, 300-gram bread rations in May had been cut to 100 grams per day in June; in Cannes bread was available only on the black market, with no bread rations distributed in the previous ten days. TNA WO 204 3732, Seventh Army Civil Affairs Report No. 2, 19 Aug. 1944 (the Var) and Civil Affairs Report No. 9, 26 Aug. 1944 (Cannes).

[19] TNA WO 204 3732, 'Civil Affairs Report No. 2', 19 Aug. 1944, commenting on transport shortages in southern France, and the hiding of vehicles as reported by the Département des Ponts et Chaussées.

[20] SAEF B-0057659, de Sailly notes to the director of price controls in the Charente-Maritime, 3 and 17 Aug. 1944, and 'Note au cabinet du ministre', 7 Oct. 1944; Grenard, *La France du marché noir*, 267.

[21] SAEF B-0057659, Director of price controls (Paris) to department directors, 31 Aug. 1944; the CE annual report termed the Liberation a period of 'anarchy'. DGCE, *Rapport sur l'activité de la DGCE au cours de l'année 1944*, 1–3.

Allied forces provided some food as they liberated French territory, but their focus was defeating the Germans and managing transport to supply their armies in the field. Allied planning had foreseen the need for continuing price control and rationing to manage scarce supplies. In their view, 'the total elimination of Black Markets during the period of military occupation is neither feasible nor desirable'.[22] Whether black-market activity could be reduced would be decided by local conditions. Civil affairs officers in Normandy reported great enthusiasm for Liberation and a sharp decline in black-market activity. They called for propaganda to discourage a return to black-market practices, which had been patriotic when denying supplies to the Germans but would now deprive French consumers.[23]

De Gaulle's provisional government saw no alternative but to continue Vichy controls, policing markets to stabilize prices and maintain an equitable distribution of essential goods. Free French planners realized that although public sentiment wanted a rapid end to controls, without them, the shortages would produce an inflationary surge, the decline of the franc, and deprivation for those unable to pay higher prices. Price stability was essential for reconstruction and required 'tighter control'.[24] The essential role for controllers would be to track down 'the black market itself', de Sailly advised, while allowing greater flexibility for all infractions motivated by 'the legitimate desire to maintain business activity and satisfy the urgent needs of French consumers'.[25] In other words, strict control would be counterproductive; illicit traffic was essential to meet legitimate and urgent needs.

The Black Market Thrives

A return to prewar consumption would require prewar levels of output, trade and transport to move raw materials to producers and finished goods to market. A concatenation of factors crippled official markets

---

[22] NARA RG 331, Box 61, quote from SHAEF Civil Affairs Division, London, to Chief of Staff, CAD, SHAEF (Attn. Planning Section), 8 Feb. 1944.

[23] NARA RG 331 Box 26, 'Basic Content for Broadcasts to Combat Hoarding and Black Market Activities in Liberated Territories', 29 June 1944; and SAEF 5A-0000183, J. Ricquebourg, 'Note sur la propagande à faire en matière de prix et de ravitaillement', 11 Aug. 1944.

[24] SAEF 5A-0000181, 'Note sur la réglementation économique', undated, and 5A-0000182, 'Esquisse de la politique financière de la France', undated (quoted). On public opinion rejecting controls, see AN AG/3(2)/418, Section N.M., 'Enquête sur le sentiment public en France à l'égard des problèmes politiques et économiques de l'après-guerre', Nov. 1943.

[25] SAEF B-0049889, Note de service no. 507, 21 Sept. 1944; he advised giving warnings rather than fines.

and promoted alternative networks. Black-market prices climbed as buyers sought goods. Some local liberation committees suspended price controls and raised wages. Free French planners believed wage increases were essential to recover part of the purchasing power lost by the middle and working classes, particularly the lowest paid workers.[26] Wage increases were decided on a regional basis, ranging from 33 per cent to 50 per cent in the first months after Liberation.[27] The Bank of France characterized industrial production in July and August as almost completely inactive as a result of shortages. In regions of military action, production stopped.[28] Bank directors anticipated that the end to German purchasing would allow an increase in official rations, but only if transport could bring food to markets.[29]

Transport posed the critical challenge, and the black market had greater capacity to solve transport difficulties with its higher profits and its organization to work outside the rules. It provided food from farms, wine from the south of France, and an array of US Army goods, especially food, clothing, cigarettes, gasoline and vehicle tyres and parts. Public opinion, expecting rapid improvement in material circumstances, turned sharply critical of state management. The public demanded the punishment of *trafiquants* as traitors and condemned the state officials who, having worked for Vichy, remained in office to demoralize the population and sabotage the efforts of the provisional government.[30] One critic characterized the government services as operated by 'imbecile administrators' following the obstructionist doctrines of the *Vichyboches* who had ruled Occupied France.[31]

The disruption of transport meant that local output determined food availability in many regions. Normandy and Brittany could no longer send food by rail or truck to cities and deficit regions. Damage from the battles in agricultural regions reduced output, but local consumption increased for perishable dairy goods and meat.[32] The black market for

[26] SAEF 5A-0000182, 'Note sur la question des salaires à la Libération de la France', undated, spring 1944, advised against an across-the-board wage increase because of regional and class differences in cost of living and wages. Better to increase wages for those in greatest need without feeding inflation and the black market.

[27] Grenard et al., *Histoire économique de Vichy*, 137; Chélini, *Inflation, État et opinion*, 311–322.

[28] ABdF 1069201226 27, DGEE, 'Résumé des rapports économiques', July-Aug. 1944.

[29] ABdF 1069201226 27, DGEE, 'Résumé des rapports économiques', Sept. 1944.

[30] AN F/1a/4023, the Commissaire de la République report from Marseille for 15 to 30 Nov. 1944 stated that food was scarce in all departments, especially in the Alpes-Maritimes: 'the population is not satisfied with the organization of food supply, and some talk of this as organized sabotage'.

[31] AD Manche 1004W/2312, intercepted letter from Dr. Blandamour, 2 Oct. 1944.

[32] Jean Quellien, 'Le Calvados à l'ombre du Mur de l'Atlantique', in *Cahiers de l'IHTP* 32–33 (1996): 463–464.

local goods disappeared for a few weeks in Normandy. The end to German exactions and the impossibility of shipping food to other regions provided local abundance. Rationing was suspended temporarily, then resumed in late July, along with the black market.[33] The need for transport put perishable foods at risk. Some 70,000 eggs delivered to the railway station in Laval could not be sent to Paris or distributed locally for lack of transport; they were sold to US troops.[34] In Rennes, the Commissaire de la République reported that his most urgent need was fifty 5- to 10-ton trucks for use in the department and one hundred 15-ton vehicles to ship food to other regions.[35]

Allied planning gave some attention to supplies for liberated civilians and refugees but prioritized military needs. Famine conditions were possible in Occupied regions; hundreds of thousands had starved in Greece in 1941–1942 and civilian food supply was a persistent challenge for Allied forces in Italy. The troops landing in France were instructed to rely on their own supplies. Civil Affairs officers organized relief supplies to prevent disease and unrest in regions of military occupation and in 'hiatus areas' from which enemy troops had withdrawn. The volume of supplies needed for liberated civilians posed logistical challenges, to provide food, medicine and transport, and to keep civilian relief separate from the military supplies, and organize the manpower needed to unload and distribute supplies. Plan A called for 700,000 tonnes of food to be delivered in France in the first six months after Liberation, but it relied on civilian labour for distribution. In the Saint-Tropez region alone, US authorities estimated they needed 5,000 French workers in August 1944.[36] On the landing beaches in Normandy, disorganization limited the arrival and transport of relief supplies; in the first sixty days, barely one third of the arriving civilian goods could be distributed. Organization improved rapidly thereafter.[37]

Commissaires de la République and department prefects stressed their need for transport and the critical shortages of trucks and gasoline. The premiums paid for black-market goods encouraged the use of available transport for illicit traffic. Some French army officers used their trucks

[33] AN F/1a/4007, 'Renseignements sur la situation économique en Normandie libérée', 31 July 1944.
[34] AN F/1a/4006, Coulet (Commissaire de la République for the Normandy region) to Commissar for the Interior, 'Mission en Bretagne et à Laval', 9 Aug. 1944.
[35] AN F/1a/4006, Pierre Laroque to the General Military Delegate for the Zone Nord, 13 Aug. 1944.
[36] F. S. V. Donnison, Civil Affairs and Military Government North-West Europe 1944–1946 (London: HMSO, 1961), 303–318; on labour at Saint-Tropez, TNA WO 204 3732, Civil Affairs Report No. 2, 19 Aug. 1944.
[37] Donnison, Civil Affairs, 313.

(US-built) for black-market traffic.[38] The Ministry of Justice and Ministry of War both had truckloads of food seized as black-market supplies for their canteens.[39] The CE paid particular attention to factory canteens, whose purchasing privileges and vehicles supplied black-market operations. One example was a truck carrying three tons of meat for Renault factory canteens at Billancourt (Renault had twelve canteens serving 14,500 workers[40]), caught in March 1945 using falsified transport documents. Controllers tried to confiscate the cargo; workers seized the truck and delivered the meat to their factory. The canteen director warned controllers that 200 workers had come out this time; next time it would be the entire factory.[41] Similar incidents occurred with supply for the canteens of the Galeries Lafayette and several military units, leading the *Contrôle économique* to comment that 'there is no doubt that a lucrative traffic, difficult to suppress, is practiced under cover of the canteens and cooperatives.[42]

Drivers caught at roadblocks with illicit cargo of rationed foods often claimed they were transporting food for industrial canteens. If stopped by controllers, they said that they worked for factory or state canteens; they had requested authorization but not received it in time, for food urgently needed in the canteen. The canteen director would then request authorization and release of the food, stressing the social importance of the canteens. In many cases, controllers believed, truck owners and canteen directors worked in concert. The directors covered up the illicit transport if the trucks were stopped and shared in the profits from food sold on the black market.[43] 'It must be recognized that the "black market" in Paris, formerly supplied in large part by German trucks, is now supplied in this way ... without the knowledge of directors of the social services we have targeted, whose work is normally in unselfish pursuit of humanitarian ends.'[44]

Factories traded manufactured goods for food. Some required that buyers provide food for their canteens as part of payment for factory

---

[38] SAEF 5A-0000028, 'Rapport mensuel', for Feb. 1945 cites several cases, as does SAEF B-0057660, Cruse, 'Note pour le Ministre: Transports irréguliers sous couvert d'ordres de mission', 5 May 1945.

[39] SAEF B-0057660, Director of the Contrôle économique to the Minister of Justice, 12 Feb. 1945, for Department of Justice butter supplies; and SAEF 5A-0000029, Dubarry, 'Note pour le Ministre', 5 June 1945, for a Ministry of War truck transporting the classic B.O.F. combination of butter, eggs and cheese.

[40] SAEF B-0049510, Controller Astich to the brigade chief, 28 Apr. 1945.

[41] SAEF B-0057660, Mauriol (Director of the Contrôle économique), 'Note pour le ministre', 15 Mar. 1945.

[42] SAEF B-0057660, Cruse, 'Note pour le ministre', 5 May 1945.

[43] SAEF 5A-0000028, 'Rapport mensuel, Février 1945'.

[44] SAEF 5A-0000028, 'Rapport mensuel, Février 1945'.

products.[45] When CE agents checked on a shoe factory in Orange for the 'irregular' delivery of shoes in exchange for food for its workers, the manager summoned his workers to threaten the controllers. He said that he had fed them since the imposition of restrictions, and that the CE was now trying to punish him for having looked after them. At a cement factory outside Paris, management sounded the factory siren to summon workers who pushed out controllers checking on the illicit exchange of cement for food. Workers were easily mobilized to oppose control interventions when directors told them that the controllers wanted to end their provisioning of factory cooperatives.[46]

The renewed effort to enforce price controls frustrated producers and consumers, particularly in regions of agricultural surplus. There, farmers considered black-market prices to be normal in covering their costs. As a result, the *Ravitaillement général* had difficulty getting deliveries of meat, butter and milk. In the Ardennes, despite abundant food for local needs, producers and middlemen kept their prices high to sustain wartime levels of profit.[47]

Victor Le Gorgeu, *Commissaire de la République* in Britanny, reported rising public anger in September 1944 as price controls and rationing restored Occupation conditions of consumer deprivation in a region of agricultural surplus. City residents wanted lower prices and increased rations, while farmers accustomed to black-market profits wanted higher official prices. Le Gorgeu recommended increasing wages, bread rations, and an effort to reduce the extraordinary number of intermediaries who raised consumer prices.[48] The region had surplus food to send to Paris, but lacked vehicles and fuel, and needed food from Northern France in exchange. The director of food supply in the Côtes-du-Nord termed it 'a veritable economic heresy' that in a transport crisis with critical food shortages, trucks that carried 66 tonnes of butter, eggs and potatoes to Paris returned empty. Black-market trucks, too, came empty from Paris to buy farm goods, especially butter, reviving 'the infernal cycle of the black market'.[49] The police chief in Tours lamented that transport made the food situation worse than during the Occupation. Black-market

---

[45] AN F/1a/3360, 'A.S. du ravitaillement des cantines d'usines', 3 July 1946, states there were many such cases.

[46] SAEF B-0057661, Burnod, 'Note pour le sous-sécretaire d'État à l'économie', 27 Feb. 1946.

[47] SAEF 5A-0000183, M. G. Denis, 'Situation générale', Department of the Somme, 17 Oct. 1944; M. G. Denis, 'Situation des prix', Department of the Ardennes, 14 Oct. 1944.

[48] AD Ille-et-Vilaine 43W/128, Commissaire de la République to Pleven, 10 Sept. 1944, and his reports of 2 and 12 Sept. 1944.

[49] AD Ille-et-Vilaine 43W/128, Director of Food Supply to the prefect of the Côtes-du-Nord, 4 Sept. 1944.

trucks carried food to Paris, and black-market restaurants relied on army trucks for supplies, in a one-way flow of food away from his region.[50]

In contrast to Normandy and Brittany, deficit departments like the Gard and Alpes-Maritimes in south-eastern France desperately needed food from surplus departments. Rapid liberation in August 1944 had sparked hopes for dramatic improvement. But the US Army reported in September that conditions in Nice were worse than in any other part of France. Bread distribution had fallen to 175 grams. One month later, they termed the food situation 'catastrophic' with starvation rations. 'It is a well-established fact that the people ate better under the Nazi occupation, though the black market was running rampant, but we are now employing all facilities to halt the black market and they no longer can rely on this source of food.'[51] Many consumers believed that the food supply administration deliberately sabotaged the system and supported black-market sales.[52] Consumers criticized the farmers for supplying black markets, wholesalers for diverting goods, retailers for saving goods for preferred customers (at black-market prices), collectives for abusing their purchasing privileges, and the state for its incompetence.[53]

A poor harvest, scarce transport, and the failure of surplus departments to send promised quantities of grain, vegetables and meat resulted in sustained shortages after Liberation. In February 1945 the police in Nice reported that the food situation was still alarming, with insufficient rationed goods: 'Recourse to the black market is still obligatory.'[54] Prefect Paul Escande, frustrated by the lack of attention to his regional needs in Paris, tried to draw local produce back to market by raising prices to an intermediate level between official and black-market prices. Local newspapers referred to the minister of food supply, Paul Ramadier, as 'Ramadiète' and 'M. Zéro-Ramadier-Promesse'.[55]

Shortages, prices too low to cover costs, the renewed effort at control enforcement, and limited transport capacity challenged producers and consumers alike. The rapid resurgence of black-market activity was not just greed for profit, but also a means to solve problems, and a frustrated

[50] Gildea, *Marianne in Chains*, 371.
[51] Civil Affairs reports from Nice on 6 Sept. and 5 Oct. 1944 in Harry L. Coles and Albert K. Weinberg, *Civil Affairs: Soldiers Become Governors* (Washington, DC: Office of the Chief of Military History, 1964), 782.
[52] AN F/1a/4023, Commissaire de la République report for the Marseille region, 15 to 30 Nov. 1944.
[53] AD Alpes-Maritimes 616W/253, letters of complaint from the *Union locale des syndicats ouvriers de Nice*, the CGT, and especially from the *Mouvement populaire des familles*.
[54] AD Alpes-Maritimes 30W/39, 'Bulletin bi-mensuel', Nice, 5 Feb. 1945.
[55] Jean-Louis Panicacci, 'Les Alpes-Maritimes', in *Cahiers de l'IHTP* 32–33 (1996): 204–212.

response to the unintended and perverse consequences of state controls. Bank of France regional reports for November 1944 explained the delayed recovery of industry and commerce as a result of shortages and war damage, but most critically that the 'bottleneck' choking all parts of production, distribution and consumption was the lack of transport. Until the critical shortages of rail traffic and coal supplies were resolved, no recovery would be possible. Truck traffic was even more precarious, owing to the limited number of vehicles, their poor state of repair, and the scarcity of tyres and fuel. The growing consumer needs without new supply left retailers worse off than under the Occupation. The months since Liberation had seen no improvement in material conditions, which continued to deteriorate for most of the population.[56] Even the black market suffered. In the Ardennes, the industrial black market, 'very active until August, has completely disappeared because of lack of transport'.[57] Operators with clandestine stocks developed their own distribution networks. Uncoordinated local decisions produced a range of prices and levels of consumption. The Bank of France described this as a state of anarchy in food supply.[58] In deficit regions, high demand attracted *trafiquants*; the greater the distance from producing regions, the greater the reliance on the black market and higher prices.[59]

But by March 1945 promising signs of economic recovery appeared. They were fragile, the start of a *convalescence difficile*. All realms of transport – rail, road and rivers – showed improvement, and industry needed more skilled workers. Food supply remained the primary concern. The key problem was still the prices paid to producers, and state administration tended to complicate problems rather than solve them. The black market had reached a record level of activity surpassing that during the Occupation. The hopes at Liberation for a return to abundance and an end to the black market had been disappointed. 'After a very brief pause, it has recovered and even increased its hold on the French economy: neither controls nor fixed prices have been able to contain it. To break it, a better distribution of goods seems to be the necessary condition.'[60]

In Lyon, Yves Farge called for a 'serious struggle' to punish black-market commerce in January, and lamented in February that low agricultural prices encouraged the black market.[61] Residents in the Ille-et-Vilaine

[56] ABdF 1069201226 27, DGEE, 'Résumé des rapports économiques', Nov. 1944, underlined in original.
[57] SAEF 5A-0000183, M. G. Denis, report from Ardennes, 14 Oct. 1944.
[58] ABdF 1069201226 27, DGEE, 'Résumé des rapports économiques', Nov. 1944.
[59] ABdF 1069201226 27, DGEE, 'Résumé des rapports économiques', Dec. 1944.
[60] ABdF 1069201226 27, DGEE, 'Résumé des rapports économiques', Mar. 1945.
[61] AN F/1a/4023, Commissaire de la République reports for 16–31 Jan. and 1–15 Feb. 1945.

were angered by food shortages in a department of surplus production, blaming state incompetence and corruption that forced them to rely on the black market for meat, dairy, and especially for butter.[62] The Gendarmerie echoed the recurring theme of deep division between those who ate well and everyone else: 'The French are divided in two blocs, those who eat all they want, and those who use all their ingenuity to obtain the strict minimum they need.' Everyone used the black market for food: 'The black market takes on the character of an institution to which everyone has recourse.'[63]

The end of the war in Europe in May 1945 brought little improvement. According to the Gendarmerie reports in July, 'The black market is still practiced on a vast scale, because the low rations force all who can to use it.'[64] Prisoners of war and deportees arriving home from German camps were shocked at the state of their country. 'The prisoners had known a France prosperous and happy; they have returned to a poor country where everyone is burdened with worry for tomorrow. The disillusion is profound', they reported in June; and in July, 'Most of them see with amazement and sadness the state in which France finds itself.'[65]

Pierre Mendès France, the Minister of National Economy from the Liberation to April 1945, argued for tight control of prices and the confiscation of illicit profits, integrated with economic planning for reconstruction. His planning included a currency exchange. All currency would be deposited in banks, in exchange for a fixed, limited amount of the new currency notes (for current needs). Obtaining new currency for the remainder of large cash holdings would depend on how the money had been earned, allowing the state to identify wealth gained from economic collaboration and the black market. Hoarded currency (to avoid penalties) would be rendered worthless.

Belgium implemented a currency exchange in October 1944: the 'Gutt Plan' reduced franc notes in circulation by two-thirds.[66] Free French forces had imposed a currency exchange in Corsica in 1943. Minister of

---

[62] AD Ille-et-Vilaine 43W/133, Contrôle techniques, 'Synthèse régionale d'information no. 1, Mois de janvier 1945', 31 Jan. 1945.

[63] AN 72AJ/384, Col. Meunier, 'Synthèse pour la période du 15 février au 15 mars 1945', 12 Apr. 1945.

[64] AN 72AJ/384, Col. Meunier, 'Synthèse pour la période du 15 mai au 15 juin 1945', 16 July 1945.

[65] AN 72AJ/384, Col. Meunier, 'Synthèse pour la période du 15 avril au 15 mai 1945', 13 June 1945 and 'Synthèse pour la période du 15 mai au 15 juin 1945', 16 July 1945.

[66] Herman Van der Wee and Monique Verbreyt, *A Small Nation in the Turmoil of the Second World War: Money, Finance and Occupation (Belgium, Its Enemies, Its Friends, 1939–1945)*, trans. by Frank Parker (Leuven: Leuven University Press, 2009), 391–393, 417–423. The Gutt Plan allowed only 2,000 new francs per household member. The reform was delayed to early October, waiting on the arrival of new currency notes printed in Britain;

Finance René Pleven opposed the plan in France, as did French bankers. The *Comité français de libération nationale* (CFLN) had favoured austerity and a currency exchange when planning financial policy for liberated France. But once in France, Pleven and financial opinion opposed both. De Gaulle opted for a policy of 'facility' rather than 'rigour'.[67] Instead of the currency exchange, his government issued a national Liberation loan in November 1944 to reduce the note circulation, promising that if the loan was successful, 'you'll be spared the Belgian experience'.[68]

Mendès France resigned in April 1945 after repeated frustration of his plans to curb inflation and punish illicit trade. He warned de Gaulle, in his first letter of resignation on 18 January, that the government had chosen the path of inflation, increasing purchasing power before increasing the quantity of goods.[69] Rationing was essential, he explained in March; he wanted a stronger, centralized, 'rational' system in place of the current disorder. Consumers and producers had to rely on the black market. Producers needing raw materials bought on the black market and hoarded goods. The state then had fewer goods to distribute and determined rations on the basis of declarations by industrialists that were 'less and less controlled and more and more inaccurate'. The rationing system, he said, was 'devouring itself': it controlled ever fewer goods, while the black market thrived.[70] Everyone looked to the black market for food and blamed the state for a situation that had never been this bad.[71]

The scale of black-market activity, difficult to establish during the Occupation, is even less quantifiable in the postwar surge of illicit trade (Table 3.1 shows black market infractions). The decline in state enforcement and the disappointment of consumers when material conditions improved little after Liberation increased recourse to the black market and discredited state economic policies and enforcement. The black

---

this allowed some profiteers to convert hoarded Belgian notes into material goods or other currencies.

[67] For the conflict between Mendès France and Pleven, see François Bloch-Lainé and Jean Bouvier, *La France restaurée 1944–1954: Dialogue sur les choix d'une modernisation* (Paris: Fayard, 1986), 66–71; Margairaz, *L'État, les finances et l'économie*, 781–793; Christian Bougeard, *René Pleven: Un Français libre en politique* (Rennes: Presses universitaires de Rennes, 1994), 137–159; and Alain Chatriot, *Pierre Mendès France: Pour une République moderne* (Paris: Armand Colin, 2015), 55–62.

[68] Paul Delouvrier and Roger Nathan, *Politique économique de la France* (Paris: Institut d'études politiques, 1958), 143–144, 162–164, quote at 164.

[69] Mendès France to de Gaulle, 18 Jan. 1945, reprinted in Mendès France, *Œuvres complètes* vol. 2, 115–125.

[70] SAEF 5A-0000029, Mendès France to the Minister of Industrial Production, 23 Mar. 1945.

[71] AN 72AJ/384, Col. Meunier, 'Synthèse pour la période du 15 février au 15 mars 1945', 12 Apr. 1945.

market was essential to survival for businesses and consumers alike in liberated France.

The American Bazaar

Allied policy changed the direction for black-market traffic.[72] German occupation personnel had engaged in multiple schemes to seize French resources, using the black market to tap hoarded goods and illicit production for massive official and private purchasing. The Allied forces landed with an awesome array of weapons, transport capacity and military equipment, food and clothing. Civilians in Normandy delighted in the treats that US troops handed out freely: chocolate, candy, 'chouine-gomme', a wondrous range of canned rations, and cigarettes made from American tobacco.[73] Edmond Dubois marvelled at their entry into Paris: 'this democratic army, rich with its endless convoys, its inexhaustible reserve of fuel, tyres, food … Paris holds out its arms and they give condensed milk, cigarettes, chocolate, coffee, tea, canned goods.'[74] With the wealth of goods came opportunity: to alleviate shortages, to slake the demand for food and clothing, and to profit from trading this vast Allied material wealth.

Allied planners anticipated shortages of food and medicine in liberated regions. The Allied *Field Handbook for Civil Affairs* described the food control system in France as 'complex and confused', and estimated that 40 per cent of the food subject to controls reached consumers through the black market. Continued controls would be essential to prevent a complete collapse of food supply and increased recourse to the black market.[75] General Eisenhower instructed Allied troops that civilians in Nazi-occupied Europe had suffered 'great privations' and lacked 'even the barest necessities'. Allied troops would be fully supplied. His message on 6 June declared: 'You must not deplete the already meagre local stocks of food and other supplies by indiscriminate buying, thereby fostering the "Black Market", which can only increase the hardship of the inhabitants.'[76]

---

[72] Noëmie Fossé uses 'The American Bazaar' in her study of the black market for US Army goods in Seine-et-Oise. Noëmie Fossé, 'Libération, délinquance et trafics en Seine-et-Oise: Restrictions, consommation et marché noir des produits de l'U.S. Army (1944–1950)' (PhD dissertation, Paris I Panthéon-Sorbonne, 2015).

[73] See the civilian testimonies used by Mary Louise Roberts in *D-Day through French Eyes: Normandy 1944* (Chicago: University of Chicago Press, 2014), 161–171.

[74] Edmond Dubois, *Paris sans lumière 1939–1945: Témoignages* (Lausanne: Librairie Payot, 1946), 213.

[75] SAEF 5A-0000183, Supreme Headquarters of the Allied Expeditionary Force *Field Handbook of Civil Affairs, France, Provisional first edition* (no date), 186.

[76] Eisenhower message to troops of the A.E.F., 6 June 1944, in *The Papers of Dwight David Eisenhower. The War Years: III*, ed. by Alfred D. Chandler et al. (Baltimore, MD: The Johns Hopkins Press, 1970), 1914.

Civil Affairs officers planned to coordinate closely with local officials in liberated regions, to secure supply lines for the advancing armies and minimize the military resources needed for civil administration. Conflict at the highest levels over recognition of de Gaulle as leader and the CFLN as a provisional government for liberated regions complicated the Allied arrival in France. The decision to issue Allied Military Government (AMG) francs to the troops, as they had done in Italy (AMG lire), was particularly controversial. De Gaulle cancelled the appointment of French liaison officers assigned to work with Civil Affairs, then relented on 7 June, to allow twenty of the originally planned 120 officers. But Allied military personnel and French administrators developed practical solutions at the operational level.[77]

According to US Army policy in May 1944, soldiers could not purchase goods needed by French civilians, especially food, and these rules were adopted for all Allied troops.[78] In their first exchanges with civilians in Normandy, troops handed out candy and cigarettes, while the French offered flowers, wine, fresh produce and calvados.[79] The abundant food produced in the Normandy region increased the supply for civilians, and Allied troops had opportunities to purchase the surplus of perishable foods. As troops advanced and the liberated regions became transit zones for supplies to the battlefront, gifts frequently gave way to calculated exchange. Soldiers were eager to obtain fresh food, alcohol and sex. Paid in AMG francs, they had ready money to buy from the French, although soldiers spent only a fraction of their pay, returning most (over 90 per cent in July 1944) to their paymasters for saving.[80] They also had

---

[77] For the difficulties managing civil affairs in France without official recognition of de Gaulle's provisional government, see Forrest C. Pogue, *United States Army in World War II: The Supreme Command* (Washington, DC: Office of the Chief of Military History, 1954), 231–236, and Eisenhower, 'Memorandum', 3 June 1944 in *The Papers of Dwight David Eisenhower. The War Years: III*, 1904. The controversy over the use of AMG francs without de Gaulle's authorization is explained in Mouré, 'Spearhead Currency', 286–288.

[78] SAEF B-0033002, SHAEF G-5 Division, 'Report on Investigation of Some Financial Aspects of the Liberation of Normandy', 12 Aug. 1944 provides an overview of the regulations, with Memorandum No. 6 on 20 May 1944 prohibiting soldiers from making individual purchases. British troops were instructed to follow the same rules; SAEF B-0033003, 'Note by the War Office on Measures Taken to Prevent Excessive Spending by Troops in Normandy', 19 Aug. 1944, reproducing a War Office memo issued on 21 June 1944.

[79] The sequence of initial contacts is captured well in the French testimonies in Roberts, *D-Day Through French Eyes*, 97–120, especially the account by Bernard Gourbin, 106.

[80] SAEF B-0033002, G-5 Division, 'Some Financial Aspects'. More generally for currency to pay Allied troops, see Walter Rundell Jr., *Military Money: A Fiscal History of the U.S. Army Overseas in World War II* (College Station: Texas A&M Press, 1980) and Vladimir Petrov, *Money and Conquest: Allied Occupation Currencies in World War II* (Baltimore, MD: Johns Hopkins Press, 1967).

material goods to sell. Local residents were eager to obtain any and all goods that Allied troops could offer: food and cigarettes, clothing, blankets, gasoline, tyres, and medicine. The supplies were US government property, but their abundance and the goods soldiers could purchase at low price in post exchange (PX) stores offered opportunities to soldiers and civilians. Unlike the German black-market purchasing, the Allied soldiers engaging in black-market activity work supplied French civilians rather than depriving them. In mid-September the US Army newspaper *The Stars and Stripes* reported soldiers auctioning K-rations and cigarettes at the foot of the Eiffel Tower: 'For our money, any soldier who can march into Paris as a liberator and within two weeks become a speculator deserves to be shot.' Shot not as a profiteer, a 'selfish, soulless, brainless punk', or a thief and a cheat, but 'because he's a disgrace to the millions of GIs in this theater who came here to fight a war against indecency'.[81]

The opportunity for profit was immense. Some soldiers deserted soon after they landed in France and set up black-market operations run as criminal gangs. The gangs developed in haphazard fashion. The AWOL soldiers often met in bars in Paris and, having no income, used their weapons and uniforms to appropriate Army supplies, by fraud or by force, and sold the goods to a needy consuming public.[82] The Vincennes Gang led by Pfc. James Clyde Blackburn and the Voltaire Gang under Pfc. Walter Medley began stealing gasoline for black-market sale in September 1944, using stolen Army trucks and forged transport orders to obtain the gasoline from supply depots, and selling it in Paris.[83] Corporal James R. Mills, a driver in a Quarter Master Truck Company, deserted in early September and participated in gasoline theft and black-market sales by three groups of AWOL soldiers before his arrest in mid-November.[84] In January 1945, the arrest of seven men from two Quarter Master Truck Companies prompted a summary report stating: 'Investigation revealed huge black market leakage from Berre and Miramas dumps. U.S. soldiers with fraudulent and forged requisitions and misappropriated trucks obtained and sold at least 22 truckloads of gasoline.'[85]

[81] 'Step Right Up – Going, Going, Gone', *The Stars and Stripes* (Paris), 21 Sept. 1944.

[82] Charles Glass, *The Deserters: A Hidden History of World War II* (New York: Penguin Books, 2014).

[83] Kenneth D. Alford, *American Crimes and the Liberation of Paris: Robbery, Rape and Murder by Renegade GIs, 1944–1947* (Jefferson, NC: McFarland and Company, 2016), 88–102, 106–115.

[84] Judge Advocate General's Department, *Holdings and Opinions Board of Review, Branch Office of the Judge Advocate General, European Theater of Operations*, vol. 20, CM ETO 9288.

[85] NARA RG 498 Box 4255, Criminal Investigation Reports and Procedures, title page missing, 24 Feb. 1945, case #233.

American press coverage of the military black-market activity depicted a problem of alarming proportions. *Life* magazine ran a story in March 1945 titled 'Paris Black Market Robs U.S. Army' with a photo series on the tracking down of the Voltaire gang. It claimed that some 2,500 GIs had deserted and turned to crime in France.[86] *Yank* gave details on rampant black-market activity by 'GI Racketeers in Paris' with their highest profits made from trafficking in US Army gasoline, and gangs 'organized with the same sweet, ruthless efficiency that marked the Capone mob of Chicago in the 1920s'. The gangs were successful because the Army gasoline was so easily available. According to one 'convicted racketeer': 'Any damn fool could make a fortune without even trying.'[87]

The most publicized case was the theft and sale of supplies by the 716th Railway Battalion. Responsible for the transport of supplies from Dreux to Paris, the 716th had pilfered goods from railcars and sold them, cigarettes especially, in Paris (at 500 to 600 francs per carton).[88] The press covered the 'cigarette trials' for 190 enlisted men and eight officers, including the battalion commander, charged with theft from Army supplies. The prosecution demanded harsh punishments to set an example: up to fifty years at hard labour and dishonourable discharge. Most of the battalion had taken goods from railway cargoes from September through November 1944. *The New York Times* reported that soldiers trading cigarettes and gasoline immediately after troops landed had created 'a giant black market in which Paris gangs interspersed with American Army deserters hijack trucks on the open highway and fight gun battles with the American military police'.[89]

In southern France, greater scarcity increased the demand for Allied supplies. Allied supply planning, expecting strong German resistance, was 'combat-heavy' with the first civilian supplies scheduled to arrive forty days after the initial landing on 15 August.[90] The 'innocent' practice

---

[86] 'Paris Black Market Robs US Army', *Life* 18 (13), 26 Mar. 1945.

[87] Sgt. Allan B. Ecker, 'GI Racketeers in the Paris Black Market', *Yank*, 4 May 1945.

[88] Judge Advocate General's Department, *Holdings and Opinions Board of Review, Branch Office of the Judge Advocate General, European Theater of Operations*, vol. 19, CM ETO 8234 and 8236.

[89] Dana Adams Schmidt, 'Deserters, Gangs Run Paris Racket', *The New York Times*, 23 Jan. 1945. Schmidt mentions the cigarette trial of 182 soldiers; the battalion is also mentioned as a worst-case example of group approval of black-market sales of government property in Malcolm R. McCallum, 'The Study of the Delinquent in the Army', *American Journal of Sociology* 51, no. 5 (1946): 482.

[90] This was accelerated so that the first civilian supplies were landed after just 25 days. Jeffrey J. Clarke and Robert Ross Smith, *The European Theater of Operations: Riviera to the Rhine* (Washington, DC: Center of Military History, United States Army, 1993), 217–220.

of troops trading cigarettes for wine when they landed 'grew to enormous proportions thereafter as the Base Section and Port soldiers discovered that they could get astronomical prices for the PX rations and Army supplies'. The Civil Affairs history for Southern France records that the many arrests there were 'a drop in the bucket', and that roadblocks to interdict stolen army property caught only a fraction of the traffic.[91] Officials estimated that thefts took as much as 20 per cent of the supplies unloaded in Marseille.[92] French police were not authorized to stop Allied military vehicles, and most of the traffic was carried in US Army trucks. One soldier in Marseille boasted that everyone in his outfit had made at least $5,000 selling to the black market.[93] Raymond Aubrac, Commissaire de la République for the Marseille region, noted with gratitude in his memoir the aid provided by US soldiers who sold rations to starving civilians.[94]

In Paris, Provost Marshal Col. Ernest G. Buhrmaster attributed the spectacular growth of the black market and its violence to the 'fabulous price in francs' for US Army goods and the great civilian needs: 'there is a market for anything that a soldier can sell'.[95] Demand and price played a part, as did the profusion of Allied supplies and the confusion possible with millions of troops in Europe drawing from massive supply dumps.[96] *The Stars and Stripes* reported in January 1945 that the number of AWOL soldiers had climbed to between 18,000 and 19,000 in the European Theatre of Operations (ETO) and quoted Brigadier General Pleas B. Rogers, commander of the Seine Section, that more than half the AWOL soldiers were involved in the black market.[97] The Gendarmerie identified American troops as the principal suppliers for black-market

---

[91] History of Civil Affairs Operations for Southern France, quoted in Coles and Weinberg, *Civil Affairs*, 772.

[92] Clarke and Smith, *Riviera to the Rhine*, 219; they give no numbers or value for stolen supplies.

[93] NARA RG 226, reference card 117049 C for report on France and black market, 19 Feb. 1945.

[94] Raymond Aubrac, *Où la mémoire s'attarde* (Paris: Odile Jacob, 1996), 154.

[95] Schmidt, 'Deserters, Gangs Run Paris Racket'. The official exchange rate overvalued the franc, at 50 to the US dollar; black market rates were 200 francs to the dollar.

[96] One explanation of the railway battalion trial noted, regarding officers who overlooked minor pilfering, 'Such irregularities ... were naturally incident to the confusion that necessarily attended hurried and overextended military operations where the maximum results were required in a minimum of time, with decidedly secondary consideration to the cost and the manner in which such results were obtained.' NARA RG 498 Box 6200, 'Supplemental Opinion of the Staff Judge Advocate in the Cases of Captain Olson, Lieutenant Loop and Lieutenant Springer', 29 June 1945.

[97] '18,000 U.S. Soldiers AWOL in ETO, Upped Rate Linked to Theft Rise', *The Stars and Stripes* (Paris), 27 Jan. 1945. The article stated that the Provost Marshal's records showed 5,192 soldiers arrested in Paris so far in January, and that of 850 men awaiting trial, more than 400 were charged with selling Army property, theft, and other crimes.

cigarettes and gasoline in Paris.[98] The gasoline was shipped from Britain for use in the Allied war effort: there was in fact no legal market for gasoline in the ETO. Black-market gasoline was stolen from the US Army.[99]

The cases brought to trial demonstrated the powerful attraction of black-market opportunities for US troops and highlighted poor discipline. The court martial cases, particularly for the 190 men from the 716th Railway Battalion, were used to set an example, to impress the public and to discourage any troops tempted by opportunities for profit. The men found guilty in the 'cigarette trials' were given harsh sentences, but they were offered the opportunity to serve under suspended sentences in a special combat battalion.[100] The chief charge against them, larceny of government supplies, warranted terms of imprisonment ranging from 6 months to a maximum of 5 years, depending on the value of goods taken. Some of those charged had benefited from significant black-market sales, but others had sold no goods. The 'pillage' of supplies began when the unit had not received its rations and took them from supplies in transit. For many, the value of goods taken was under $20, normally subject to a maximum imprisonment of 6 months. The sentences handed down ranged up to forty and fifty years at hard labour. The trials garnered major press attention in Europe and the United States, and the harsh sentences showed Army determination to punish disciplinary infractions. The process for clemency that followed was not publicized. The JAG review in June 1945 clarifies the purpose of the trials:

It is observed with satisfaction that the exemplary purpose of the highly publicized trials was fully served by the severe sentences; that the public shock necessarily resulting therefrom was mitigated, and the bulk of the convicted soldiers restored and salvaged as soldiers and citizens, through the measures of mass clemency successfully executed; and finally that the novel form of the charges, necessarily devised to warrant the exemplary punishment required, have been held legally sound, and the trials thereunder fully sustained.[101]

On the French side, if the desire for Allied supplies is obvious, the extent, importance and methods of black-market commerce merit closer

---

[98] AN 72AJ/384, Col. Meunier, 'Synthèse pour la période du 15 Décembre 1944 au 15 Janvier 1945', 12 Feb. 1945.

[99] Judge Advocate General's Department, *Holdings and Opinions Board of Review, Branch Office of the Judge Advocate General, European Theater of Operations* vol. 15, CM ETO 5539, Private Albert L. Hufendick, tried on 16 Nov. 1944 in Paris; gasoline price discussion, 138–141.

[100] In all, 159 served suspended sentences; 115 of them joined a special combat unit in February and were shipped to fight in the Pacific.

[101] NARA RG 498 Box 6200, Col. C. E. Brand (JAGD), 'Final Report, Railway Pillaging Cases', 21 June 1945.

attention. The tales of armed gangs led by US deserters, driving US Army vehicles and wielding weapons, are dramatic. Less visible are the lower-level exchanges that would have had a wider impact. Noëmie Fossé's research in French records for black-market traffic in US Army goods in the Seine-et-Oise provides instructive evidence and analysis. The department of the Seine-et-Oise surrounded Paris; any black-market traffic to Paris had to pass through it. Three major Allied supply routes traversed the department, including the Red Ball Express. Initiated in late August to carry supplies from the English Channel to Chartres, the Red Ball Express was extended as the vital transport connection from Normandy beaches to the First and Third Armies until rail service could take over in mid-November. The Seine-et-Oise became a crucial transit zone, and thus, a site for black market traffic in US Army goods. Red Ball Express trucks were loaded and travelled with little supervision, and they used two transfer points in the department. On average 5,400 trucks were dispatched daily, carrying an average payload of 5.3 tons.[102] Small losses from this volume of traffic were difficult to notice and trace, but entire trucks and cargoes disappeared and were sold on the black market. Drivers were told to remove the rotor arm from their vehicle's distributor when leaving their vehicle unattended; this rapidly fostered a black market for rotor arms.[103]

Fossé found that the main goods in the black-market trade for US Army supplies were gasoline and cigarettes, followed by food and clothing. More revealing for the extent and nature of the traffic, the cases caught and prosecuted by French authorities most often involved small-scale 'local traffic', usually initiated by US soldiers, in exchanges with citizens who worked in US camps or lived close to them. The prices were lower than on the Franco-French black market, and most of the French *trafiquants* tried and punished had no previous criminal record.[104] Unlike the black-market gangs operating as 'big business' and organized crime, this was predominantly local traffic, trading in goods the troops had in abundant supply. Prosecutions included people who took discarded food and clothing from Allied dumps, material that had been damaged or deemed unsuitable for use. When US troops were leaving, it was often

---

[102] In eighty-one days the Red Ball Express moved 412,193 tons of supplies. Roland J. Ruppenthal, *Logistical Support of the Armies*, vol. 2: *September 1944–May 1945* (Washington, DC: Office of the Chief of Military History, 1959), 134–139.

[103] David Colley, *The Road to Victory: The Untold Story of World War II's Red Ball Express* (Washington, DC: Brassey's, 2000), 125–131.

[104] Fossé, 'Libération, déliquence et trafics', 364–367. Fossé found that the majority of those caught were male, operated in small groups, and were between twenty and thirty-nine years of age, many in their thirties, so flexible in their adaptation to wartime and postwar changes.

easier to destroy stocks of goods than ship them home. These surplus US goods were transferred on a small scale to needy French consumers.

Criminal gangs were most likely to operate where opportunities for crime and for invisibility were greatest, in the cities: Paris, Marseille, Lyon, and Bordeaux. In the Seine-et-Oise, Fossé found a 'gangsterization', imitating American style holdups and gang organization, with the gangs run in part by US Army deserters. The 'gang de Gagny', included American deserters, several French men, and French women who rented the gang's lodgings and sold their black-market goods. The gang stole cars and threatened French police with an all-out military assault when six members were arrested in February 1945. The 'gang du Vésinet' included three American deserters and likewise engaged in armed robbery.[105] Gang activity was greater in cities, which offered greater opportunities for crime, as well as for entertainment and recruitment, including other AWOL soldiers.[106]

French public opinion turned against the US troops in many regions as cases of thefts and pillage increased, and the soldiers' incessant demand for alcohol from bars, commercial establishments and private homes tried local patience. Allied deserters powered a rising tide of armed robberies, summary executions and use of firearms and explosives: 'These crimes generally go unpunished. The Gendarmerie and the police lack the means to attack armed bands that dispose of automobiles and benefit from the silence of the population, sometimes complicit, often terrorized.'[107]

The trade in US Army goods changed when the war in Europe ended in May 1945, as did the Judge Advocate General's (JAG) efforts to suppress supply losses and the black market for US Army goods. There were fewer supplies in transit; authorities paid closer attention to inventory; soldiers had more time in base camps and on leave, and more contact with French civilians. In June 1945, the JAG office estimated there were at least 30,000 US soldiers in Paris at any given time. The base camps in north-western France became known as 'cigarette camps' and attracted civilians interested in trading anything they could for US Army goods – cash, food, liquor, sex.[108] The number of soldiers passing through base camps and the frequency of

---

[105] Fossé, 'Libération, déliquence et trafics', 242–245; details on the gangs are sketchy. Marc Hillel comments on an 'the heyday for *grands trafiquants* and pimps' and the climate of violence and debauchery linked to Americans in criminal gangs in France; Marc Hillel, *Vie et moeurs des G.I.'s en Europe, 1942–1947* (Paris: Balland, 1981), 145–148.

[106] Glass, *The Deserters*.

[107] AN 72AJ/384, Col. Meunier, 'Synthèse pour la période du 15 janvier au 15 février 1945', 14 Mar. 1945.

[108] See Mary Louise Roberts, 'The Price of Discretion: Prostitution, Venereal Disease, and the American Military in France, 1944–1946', *American Historical Review*, 115(4) (2010): 1019, and Jean-Claude Marquis, *Les camps cigarette: Les Américains en Haute Normandie à la libération* (Rouen: Médianes, 1994).

conflict with local citizens soured French opinion of the Americans, who they saw as unruly and undisciplined in comparison with British troops. Aggression by soldiers seeking alcohol and sex generated a stream of complaints to Paris. The Minister of the Interior responded to the many reports he received on 'the frequency and gravity' of conflicts between French citizens and American troops. He suggested tighter restrictions on the sale of alcohol and an increase in police patrols. These could remedy the problem, but only *if* French police worked in conjunction with American military police.[109]

The Provost Marshal's quarterly reports for the postwar period reached similar conclusions to Fossé's on the black-market traffic linking GIs seeking easy profit with French civilians in need of scarce consumer goods. These reports on activities across the European Theatre of Operations concluded in early 1946 that the increased black-market activity in winter months was the result of greater civilian need for food and clothing, with most activity being barter between individuals rather than the work of organized gangs. 'The market flourishes because it provides items that are greatly needed and desired by civilians while comparatively plentiful, and hence of small value, to military personnel.'[110]

The black market for US Army goods is most striking for the contrast between US Army abundance and French scarcity. The harsh punishments for soldiers in the 716th Railway Battalion show the Judge Advocate General's use of exemplary punishment to discipline troops and impress public opinion. Neither American military nor French legal proceedings provide quantitative evidence to establish the full extent of black-market traffic or its importance to French provisioning. Much went unrecorded in the gap between US Army and French civilian policing. But the disparity between Allied supplies and civilian deprivation made the generosity of Allied troops a striking and memorable gesture of good will on their arrival, which promised future recovery from the desperate shortages of the Occupation years.

Greed for Gain

Luc Martin's father fought in the Resistance in southern France and was killed two days before the liberation of his region. The state sent the fourteen-year-old Luc to Paris to be raised as a 'pupil of the nation'. On arrival, he was hustled to a state reception for Resistance orphans. Told

---

[109] AN F/1a/3305, Ministry of the Interior, 'Note au sujet des attentats et aggressions commis par des soldats américains', 5 Sept. 1945; the note appends a long list of incidents involving US troops in August 1945.
[110] NARA RG 498 Box 4255, Office of the Theater Provost Marshal, 'Report of Operations 1 January – 31 March 1946'.

that the officials would take his dog, Luc left the reception in the company of a black marketeer named Vanderputte and his two supposed children. From them, Luc learned to cadge cigarettes from US soldiers and sell Vanderputte's black-market goods to French buyers. Most of the goods came from American military supplies and a nearby UNRRA (United Nations Relief and Rehabilitation Administration) warehouse. Luc progressed from the black market to petty theft, then auto theft, and ultimately to armed robbery. His career in crime seemed to illustrate the corruption of youth and the moral decline of France.

Authorities feared for French youth in the turbulent world of shortages and supply improvisation, *le système D*, where the black market offered better opportunities for income and adventure. Vichy had fostered a black-market culture that encouraged illicit activity, easy profits, the avoidance of hard work, and the destruction of family. 'The principal spiritual heritage of Vichy,' resister Jean Cassou wrote in 1953, 'is the mystique of the Black Market. It triumphs in all hearts, and the système D and scheming have replaced all methods of thought and production.'[111]

Luc Martin is the main character in Romain Gary's novel *Le grand vestiaire* (1948). His story reflected popular anxieties for France and its future in the post-Liberation swerve into increasing illegality.[112] These anxieties are evident, too, in Marcel Aymé's 'Le faux policier', his story of an accountant, another Martin, who supplements his low salary by impersonating state officials, punishing black marketeers and illicit trade for his own profit. Martin stopped this activity at Liberation, then resumed on a larger scale to maintain his income. In Jean Dutourd's black-market novel *Au bon beurre*, the Poissonards multiply their wartime black-market fortune with increased traffic after Liberation.[113] The fictional accounts exaggerate elements in lived experience, but nonetheless distil common fears of the ways in which war experience had corrupted law-abiding citizens.

Fears for France's youth increased in contemporary reports on crime and economic difficulties after Liberation. The Third Republic had created agencies to manage children whom officials feared were victims of 'moral abandon' (inadequate or inappropriate parental supervision).[114]

---

[111] Jean Cassou, *La mémoire courte* (Paris: Éditions de minuit, 1953), 94–95.
[112] Romain Gary, *Le grand vestiaire* (Paris: Gallimard, 1948). After serving as a pilot with Free French forces in London, Gary wrote *Le grand vestiaire* while working for the French legation in Sofia. David Bellos provides an illuminating comparison of the novel with Dickens' *Oliver Twist*, with Luc as Oliver and Vanderputte as an anti-Semitic Fagan. David Bellos, 'Oliver Twist à Paris, Romain Gary à New York: *Le grand vestiaire* et les tabous de l'après-guerre', *littératures*, 56 (2007): 173–181.
[113] Marcel Aymé, 'Le faux policier', *Vin de Paris*, 153–169; Dutourd, *Au bon beurre*.
[114] Sylvia Schafer, *Children in Moral Danger and the Problem of Government in Third Republic France* (Princeton, NJ: Princeton University Press, 1997).

The state showed exaggerated concern for the absence of paternal authority during the war and Occupation (fathers killed or prisoners of war), which they blamed for the increase in juvenile crime. The Occupation crime wave was notable for theft and property crimes, more credibly explained by economic hardship.[115] But fears for the adverse consequences of absent fathers, coupled with concern for population decline, increased crime, and the resurgence of black markets after Liberation, produced great anxiety for their country's future.

Reports on opinion in Brittany by the *Service des contrôles techniques* at the end of January 1945 articulated the problem in terms that echoed those of Vichy condemning the Third Republic for France's defeat in 1940. A crisis in morality affected many in France in whom four years of occupation had inculcated the taste for lucre, laziness, and an opportunism in seeking pleasure: 'Demagogy and black market, that's become the slogan for success.' Youth were of particular concern, because of their 'excessive love of money and pleasure, of dancing and laziness'.[116] But this was 1945, and the legacy of Vichy's economic contraction and moral disorder posed a threat to national recovery. The military commander in Brittany observed that food shortages and disorder in political life promoted a mentality characterized by 'selfishness, greed for gain by any means'. The state of mind of youth was 'disturbing': 'Most of the new generation has not understood the lesson of the liberation and shows no sign of manliness. The taste for pleasure and laziness has taken the place of that for work and dignity.'[117] A *trafiquant* buying Armagnac in the Gers and reselling it in Paris could earn 25,000 francs per truckload; one young man earned 3 million francs in this way in 1944. 'Honest work is completely devalued and yields place, more and more, to machinations harmful to the general interest.'[118]

The Gendarmerie expressed repeated concern for the moral crisis and its effects on young adults in the last months of the war. They saw French youth as divided into 'two perfectly distinct classes': those who had supported Resistance and answered the call of the nation, and those who tried to continue their 'easy life' without making any serious effort to aid their country. 'The young people in this category are ready for all the work, for the shadiest trafficking, the most unhealthy

[115] Sarah Fishman, *The Battle for Children: World War II, Youth Crime, and Juvenile Justice in Twentieth-Century France* (Cambridge, MA: Harvard University Press, 2002).

[116] AD Ille-et-Vilaine 43W/133, 'Synthèse régionale d'information', 31 Jan. 1945.

[117] AD Ille-et-Vilaine 43W/133, General Allard, 'Rapport bi-mensuel pour la période du 1er au 15 janvier 1945', Rennes, 25 Jan. 1945.

[118] AN 72AJ/384, Col. Meunier, 'Synthèse pour la période du 16 juillet au 15 août 1945', 15 Sept. 1945.

machinations.'[119] In December and January they reported widely held opinion that youth needed protection from the temptations of the easy life possible in black-market trafficking.[120] In February, they posited that four years of Occupation had changed attitudes towards work, with youth in a state of moral abandon and unwilling to make any effort.[121] And in May 1945: 'Too many "idle" young people draw their resources from unsavoury acts, a consequence of bad habits they developed during the Occupation.' In the national interest, French youth, particularly in Paris, needed 'moral re-education'.[122] The Gendarmerie solution, as a police force under military direction, was to enlist youth in military service.

By April 1945 the black market was a national institution to which everyone had recourse, and economic injustice and food shortages were becoming political questions that provoked disturbances and threatened public order.[123] Many state officials and private individuals had expressed concern for the decline in morality under the harsh economic conditions of the Occupation. Even the Catholic Church had accepted minor consumer infractions as permissible to alleviate desperate needs for food and clothing.[124]

Such anxieties about moral behaviour increased after Liberation. Alfred Brauner, who had worked with children and young adults in Spain, and then with refugees and concentration camp survivors in France, included a section on 'The French child since the war' in his 1946 study of the impact of war on children. He saw wartime shortages as the seedbed for economic crime. Like the Gendarmerie, Brauner found that youth who had finished school and were too young for the army were too often at loose ends, neglected by the state and 'in moral danger'. 'The current difficulties in production and in food supply offer thousands of opportunities to savvy *trafiquants*. Easy money tempts the young, who are drawn to risk and adventure.'[125] The Communist party shared these

---

[119] AN 72AJ/384, Col. Girard, 'Synthèse pour la période du 15 septembre au 15 octobre 1944', 13 Nov. 1944.

[120] AN 72AJ/384, Col. Girard, 'Synthèse pour la période du 15 octobre au 15 novembre 1944', 11 Dec. 1944, and 'Synthèse pour la période du 15 novembre au 15 décembre 1944', 12 Jan. 1945.

[121] AN 72AJ/384, Col. Meunier, 'Synthèse pour la période du 15 décembre 1944 au 15 janvier 1945', 12 Feb. 1945.

[122] AN 72AJ/384, Col. Meunier, 'Synthèse pour la période du 15 mars au 15 avril 1945', 22 May 1945.

[123] AN 72AJ/384, Col. Meunier, 'Synthèse pour la période du 15 février au 15 mars 1945', 12 Apr. 1945.

[124] Renée Bédarida, *Les catholiques dans la guerre, 1939–1945: Entre Vichy et la Résistance* (Paris: Hachette, 1998), 46–49, 57, 89–90.

[125] Alfred Brauner, *Ces enfants ont vécu la guerre* ... (Paris: Les Éditions sociales françaises, 1946), 259–261.

concerns. The principal duty of the *Union des femmes françaises* (UFF), its organization to mobilize women on issues of family and household issues stated, was to provide children with a secure home life and raise them with high moral standards, 'inculcating in them the taste for work, filial respect, love of country and civic sense'.[126]

Foreign observers remarked on this moral dimension. Robert Parr of the British Foreign Office saw 'a very serious moral cancer ... spreading through every level of society' in April 1945, particularly dangerous for the attraction it held for young adults. Only improved food supply and transport would reverse the growing influence of the black market. His colleague W. L. Fraser, from talks with friends in Paris, observed a national decline in moral values: 'They appear to be steeped in black market practices, tax dodging, corruption, selfish and materialistic influences, and exhibit no obvious desire to serve the community ... . Black market stories are legion.'[127]

Raymond Aubrac and Paul Haag, successive Commissaires de la République for the Marseille region from Liberation through the summer of 1945, commented on the inevitability of illicit activity when official rations were insufficient. Haag warned repeatedly of the 'profound moral crisis' resulting from ration levels.[128] The prefect of the Haut-Vienne had spoken of the need to repair 'the moral ruins the enemy has left behind'.[129] And the moral decline extended to state administrations. Reductions in civil service staff and low salaries in a period of declining standard of living and high black-market profits posed a challenge that administrators decried as a moral danger. The SCRCE (*Service de coordination des recherches sur la collaboration économique*), investigating cases of economic collaboration, warned of physical danger to its staff. They were investigating people 'often, from a moral point of view, disreputable' who could resort to violence in defence of 'ill-gotten gains'. Their staff were in moral danger as well, given the power of money and their own desperate needs. The SCRCE proposed paying a 'risk indemnity': 'Our investigators, in the nature of their work, are every day in contact with people having ready money and

---

[126] Claudine Michaut at the First National Congress of the Union des femmes françaises, quoted in Sandra Fayolle, 'L'Union des femmes françaises et les sentiments supposes féminins', in *Émotions ... Mobilisation!* ed. by Christophe Traïni (Paris: Presses de la FNSP, 2009), 170.

[127] TNA FO 371 49097, Mr. Parr to Mr. Eden [Z 5241/102/17], 27 Apr. 1945, and W. L. Fraser, 'Notes on the French Situation', 23 Apr. 1945.

[128] AN F/1a/4023, Commissaire de la République reports for January through July 1945, quote from report covering 15–31 July 1945.

[129] AN F/1a/4022, Chaintron radio address of 1 June 1945.

for whom corruption is common practice. As a result, we must give them the means to resist temptation.'[130]

The 'crisis of morality' was a product of circumstances: the lack of improvement in living conditions, the necessity and vitality of the black market, and anxiety about whether, when and how a French economic recovery would be possible. Two contemporaries less alarmed by the atmosphere of crisis gave more measured judgment of the linkage between scarcity and economic offences. Joseph Dubois, writing in *L'Esprit*, argued that black-market activity was not immoral, but amoral, an inevitable consequence of state regulation. It gave access to essential goods and stimulated production, which would speed recovery and a return to abundance.[131] Retired teacher Berthe Auroy observed in August 1945 that most people thought they were living in the most corrupt era ever: 'Everything is rotten.' France suffered morally as well as materially, and the future looked grim. 'Despite all that', she continued, 'hope is permitted: hope for better days, hope for greater liberty that is better understood, hope for improved morality as life returns to normal'.[132]

Popular Protest and the Retreat of the State

As material conditions failed to improve and public frustrations increased, demonstrations and violence against state officials increased. Black-market activity, consumer and shopkeeper protests, and assaults on state officials manifested widespread opposition to state controls. Consumers and producers had greater freedom to protest and higher expectations for the state, the speed of recovery, and the return to prewar consumption levels. Essential to the protests and the state's ability to maintain controls were the public perceptions of the legitimacy, equity and purposes served by the control system.

The winter of 1944–1945 was bitterly cold, with less coal and in some regions less food than during the Occupation. The Gendarmerie composed a note for US authorities comparing the food supply and public opinion in Paris in January 1945 with January 1944. With the Germans gone, food rations were still 'far from being sufficient'. The railways no longer brought family parcels to Paris, a critical element in Occupation food supply. In 1944 there had been some coal for heat; now there was no coal, no wood, and little electricity. Grateful for Liberation, Parisians were disappointed in the

---

[130] SAEF B-0049475, SCRCE note for Ministry of National Economy, 13 Mar. 1945.
[131] Joseph Dubois, 'Amoralité et utilité du marché noir', *L'Esprit*, 1 June 1945, 79–91.
[132] Auroy, *Jours de guerre*, 411 (15 Aug. 1945).

American failure to alleviate shortages. The note concluded: 'Please send trucks and tires to equip the few trucks we have left.'[133]

Public demonstrations were now possible without the risk of harsh repression. Workers demanded higher wages, lower prices, suppression of the black market, and improved rations. Hundreds of demonstrations called for more food, and unions relied on public protests rather than strikes to press for improvement for working-class consumers.[134] The *Union des femmes françaises* (UFF) organized food demonstrations in the early months of 1945, as did the Catholic *Mouvement populaire des familles*, encouraging housewives to protest insufficient food, black-market profits, and poor state administration. The UFF called for the arrest of 'the kings of the black market' and the elimination of laws and state organizations created by Vichy: 'if France remains under-nourished, it's mainly because representatives of VICHY still figure as part of the Administration'.[135] The Gendarmerie noted, of housewives' protests from January to April, that 'the public mood grows more bitter each day, the criticisms are more violent, demonstrations multiply and the public services held responsible are accused of maintaining, and even of deliberately aggravating a situation that has never been this bad'.[136] Police measures against the black market became increasingly unpopular, particularly those of the *Controle économique*, which focused (still) on small quantities carried by consumers rather than on producers.

The Gendarmerie recorded fifty-two demonstrations from mid-February to mid-March, and ninety-three from mid-March to mid-April; thirty-one protests had more than 1,000 participants. The largest, organized by the *Union des syndicats ouvriers du Rhône* in Lyon on 11 March, was reported as gathering 100,000 demonstrators. The most frequent discontent was the food supply.[137] Yves Farge, as Commissaire de la République in Lyon, sympathized with their complaints. In the three

---

[133] Service historique de la Défense, Vincennes (SHD), GR/8P/31, 'Comments on the food situation in Paris in January 1945 compared to January 1944', undated.

[134] Danielle Tartakowsky, 'Manifester pour le pain', 471–475; ; Danielle Tartakowsky, *Les manifestations de rue en France 1918–1968* (Paris: Publications de la Sorbonne, 1997), 498–519 (Tartakowsky counted 499 street demonstrations from August 1944 to December 1945, 304 concerned food supply); and Herrick Chapman, *France's Long Reconstruction: In Search of the Modern Republic* (Cambridge, MA: Harvard University Press, 2018), 33–37.

[135] AD Pas-de-Calais M5416, contains UFF letters from communes throughout the department, a concerted campaign, most of them dated 5 April 1945.

[136] AN 72AJ/384, Col. Meunier, 'Synthèse pour la période du 15 février au 15 mars 1945', 12 Apr. 1945.

[137] AN 72AJ/384, Col. Meunier, 'Synthèse pour la période du 15 février au 15 mars 1945', 12 April 1945, and 'Synthèse pour la période du 15 mars au 15 avril 1945', 22 May 1945.

industrial cities in his domain, Lyon, Grenoble and Saint-Étienne, Farge reported: 'It is incontestable that everyone is dying of hunger in the industrial centres of the region.' Shortages of transport, low prices paid to farmers, and workers needing to buy food outside official markets encouraged black-market activity and demand for higher wages.[138] Farge believed that poor state administration lay at the root of public disaffection. 'As much as it is the hunger they feel, it is the administrative incoherence that pushes people to the limit.' Lyon had been repeatedly promised increased food, but few supplies were delivered. Resistance hopes for political renewal were frustrated by the return of Third Republic politicians and civil servants, while need for the black market meant that 'our economy is now based entirely on the butter standard'.[139] The police agreed. Six months after Liberation, material conditions had deteriorated and the fault lay in the incompetence of the food supply administration.[140] After the massive 11 March demonstration, reported on radio in Paris as against the black market, *Lyon Libre* protested: 'The black market is only a result of the policy adopted, which has been content to allow men appointed by Vichy to apply methods which Vichy has devised.'[141] The UFF mobilized women to demand more food and protest against 'the Vichyites still in place, against those causing hunger with the black market, against the trusts'.[142]

Popular opposition to controllers turned more often to violence, with the *Contrôle économique* as the most frequent target. Attacks on controllers had begun soon after the establishment of the control regime in October 1940 and the development of an enforcement apparatus in 1941.[143] Growing opposition after Liberation showed the declining legitimacy of the economic controls. Consumers, merchants, the police, and most levels of state administration knew that low prices for local produce had immediate consequences: farmers withheld goods to sell at higher prices. Needy consumers followed the goods, not the rules. The CE recommended harsher penalties: average fines, which had more than doubled from 1943 to 1944, needed to be higher still to develop 'a healthy fear among the fraudsters'.[144]

Policing the black market was 'more and more unpopular', the Sûreté reported in March 1945. '[E]very day operations by CE agents are

---

[138] AN F/1a/4023, Commissaire de la République reports for 16–31 Jan. and 1–15 Feb. 1945.
[139] AN F/1a/4023, Commissaire de la République report for 15 Feb. to 15 Mar. 1945.
[140] AD Rhône 283W/101, police commissioner in Villeurbaine to the commissioner in Lyon, 27 Feb. 1945.
[141] TNA FO 371 49096, Robert Parr despatch no. 25, 12 Mar. 1945.
[142] AN F/1a/4023, Commissaire de la République report for 15 Mar. to 15 Apr. 1945.
[143] Grenard, *La France du marché noir*, 127–132.
[144] DGCE, *Rapport sur l'activité de la DGCE au cours de l'année 1944* (1945), 34.

thwarted. The reason is these operations generally involve small quantities of food carried by consumers.'[145] Where local committees had increased rations and raised prices to draw goods to market, the controllers encountered resistance and sometimes violence in re-imposing the price and ration rules, after the war ended in May 1945. 'We demand the suppression of the *Contrôle économique*', one committee told the prefect of the Gironde: 'the petty, bureaucratic spirit is exercised magnificently for the accounts of shopkeepers, rule-followers, but ignores with a blindness that borders on complicity the outlaws of the black market.[146] In Aumale, near Rennes, residents confronted four food supply inspectors who tried to close local butchers' shops that sold meat from illicit slaughter. Gendarmes rescued the inspectors.[147] In Saint-Sever, a hostile crowd roughed up a state meat purchaser named Félix Meslin, who was requisitioning cattle. Meslin had worked in the same capacity for Vichy. He was pulled from his car, along with the food he had collected (several dozen eggs, butter, sausages, hams and 10 kilograms of lard). The crowd overturned his car, smashed the windscreen, slashed the tyres, set the car on fire, then took off his trousers and 'crowned him with butter'. The newspaper *Franc-Tireur* warned the Minister of Food Supply that there were many Félix Meslins in France. Referring to the farmers as 'the best sons in the world', it asked, 'how can they be blamed for wanting to return to a free economy after their experiences with a "controlled economy"?'[148]

Confrontations followed a similar pattern in 1946 and 1947. The return of bread rationing in January 1946 sparked street protests across France. Most were peaceful, but protesters in Tours, Saint Quentin, Auneuil and Valençay invaded municipal offices and burned bread ration cards. The police reported these as spontaneous, mainly workers, but including many women and children.[149] Meat shortages provoked local protests, blaming CE controllers for the problems. Any instance in which controllers mistreated consumers and shopkeepers or an obstreperous restaurant customer refused to pay was attributed to the *Contrôle économique*. An agent of the *Police économique* in Bonny-sur-Loire was chased by a crowd armed with sticks and shovels, choked with his scarf, and threatened, 'Next time, it's death!' when he took refuge in his hotel. The crowd believed he was a CE

---

[145] AN F/1a/3250, Direction générale de la Sûreté nationale, 'Note pour Monsieur le Directeur général de la Sureté nationale', 22 Mar. 1945.

[146] AD Gironde 57W/25, ordre du jour voted by the Comité cantonal de Libération de Blaye, sent to the prefect of the Gironde, 26 May 1945.

[147] AN F/1a/3250, Seine-Inférieure, 21 Aug. 1945.

[148] 'L'affaire de Saint-Sever', *Franc-Tireur*, 3 Sept. 1945; copy in SAEF 5A-0000029.

[149] AN F/1a/3250, note by M. Pelabon, 6 Jan. 1946, and analysis by the Direction des Renseignements généraux, 6 Jan. 1946.

controller. The CE administration lamented the hostility of the press, which presented them as an institutional holdover from Vichy 'whose sole purpose is to attack consumers and small retailers, to deprive them of the goods they might acquire'.[150] Its agents encountered frequent opposition, but the director believed that easing controls would simply encourage illicit traffic without benefit for the honest shopkeepers and consumers.[151] Prefects claimed that the locals who attacked controllers were 'badly informed', in taking the side of shopkeepers against the state, which tried to protect them from the black market.[152] But in many confrontations, the controllers seemed to be protecting consumers from the opportunity to purchase more of the food produced in their region.

Relations with consumers and sellers deteriorated further in 1947. Léon Blum's interim government tried to deliver a psychological shock to reduce inflationary pressures, announcing in a radio address on New Year's Eve that all prices would be reduced by 5 per cent on 1 January and 1 March 1947.[153] *The New Yorker*'s Paris correspondent, Janet Flanner, thought the government hoped 'to scare the trousers off the black market, which is certainly in part the farmers'.[154] To ensure compliance, the CE increased surveillance and the severity of its fines.[155] Inflation slowed and consumers were momentarily optimistic, but opinion turned against the measures as retail sales declined in January. Some consumers delayed purchases, waiting for the second 5 per cent cut planned for 1 March; shopkeepers delayed restocking; some businesses raised prices before implementing the 5 per cent cut. Working-class consumers turned to 'parallel markets' for the essentials now 'unfindable' in official markets.[156]

---

[150] SAEF B-0057661, 'Note pour le ministre: Incident de Bonny s /Loire (Loiret)', 10 Jan. 1946. Both the agent and a colleague, attacked in a separate incident, were attacked. The crowd believed both worked for the *Contrôle économique*.

[151] SAEF 5A-0000028, note on a conference of CE regional directors, 27–28 Nov. 1945, and Burnod, 'Note pour le Ministre', 30 Jan. 1945.

[152] AN F/23/527, *Ravitaillement général* reports from the department of Seine-et-Oise in October and November1945; and Megan Koreman, *The Expectation of Justice: France 1944–1946* (Durham, NC: Duke University Press, 1999), 186–187.

[153] Chélini, *Inflation, État et opinion en France*, 393–400; Margairaz, *L'État, les finances et l'économie*, 867–876.

[154] 'Letter from Paris', 2 Jan. 1947, in *The New Yorker*, 11 Jan. 1947, 60.

[155] SAEF B-0049896, Note de service no. 510; 4 Jan. 1947; SAEF B-0049890, Note de service no. 916, 30 Apr. 1947.

[156] AN F/1a/4735; reports to the Minister of the Interior; 8, 9, 10, 11 and 25 Jan. 1947; the 'unfindable' observation in 'Situation commerciale et industrielle de la capitale', 25 Jan. 1947; SAEF 5A-0000015, 'Résumé des rapports périodiques des inspecteurs généraux et des inspecteurs de l'Économie nationale, Première quinzaine de février 1947'.

President Vincent Auriol noted the pessimism of the prefect reports in his diary: although the situation appeared calm, below the surface lay potentially violent discontent.[157] Farmers withheld food from markets, and meat shortages increased public hostility, especially in cities in live-stock-producing regions.[158] Jacques Le Roy Ladurie, as a former minister of agriculture, blamed shortages on excess regulation and claimed that a large majority of French people would, given the chance, vote against 'the official economic tyranny'.[159] On 6 February, the system for priority meat purchasing to supply cities was ended, sparking an immediate jump in prices and a contagion effect that pushed all food prices higher.[160] The second price reduction on 1 March increased vexation. Protesters called for the suppression of the state organizations and rules that were stifling the economy. Producers, sellers, and consumers of all political stripes were nearly unanimous in criticizing 'outrageous government interference'.[161]

Shopkeepers organized on a local basis to promote resistance and threaten controllers. One speaker advocating resistance claimed that local consumers had hanged five gendarmes in Verdun in 1916 when they tried to arrest a butcher. '*Contrôleurs économiques*', he warned, 'atten-tion, attention ... remember the gendarmes of Verdun ... This is not a threat, but a warning.'[162] The CE encountered local 'committees of self-defence' who alerted their members when controllers arrived, to resist control enforcement. They recorded fifty-nine hostile demonstra-tions in April, May and June 1947, with physical assaults that resulted in eight serious injuries and fourteen cases in which protesters seized and destroyed CE files.[163]

On 19 May in La Roche-sur-Yon, a crowd of 7,000 organized by the *Union départementale d'action des classes moyennes de la Vendée* demon-strated in front of the prefecture. The crowd broke into the offices of the CE, taking and burning all the files. Others broke into tax offices, setting fire to files and stealing office property. They tried to break into the

---

[157] Vincent Auriol, *Journal du septennat* vol. 1, *1947* (Paris: Armand Colin, 1970), 37 (26 Jan. 1947).

[158] AN F/1a/4735, Headquarters of the Sûreté nationale, 'Le problème de la viande', 13 Jan. 1947, and daily reports in January titled 'Le ravitaillement et le mécontentement populaire'.

[159] AN F/1a/4735, police report on the article he published in *Reconstruire* on 25 January, 27 Jan. 1947.

[160] AN F/60/674, prefect of the Finistère to the premier, 17 Feb. 1947; prefect of the Haute-Garonne to the premier, 18 Feb. 1947.

[161] ABdF 1069201226 29, DGEE, 'Résumé des rapports économiques', Apr. 1947.

[162] AN BB/18/3737, case 33A47/F-95.

[163] DGCEE, *Rapport sur l'activité de la DGCEE au cours de l'année 1947*, 12–13.

offices of the department's Committee for Confiscation of Illicit Profits (CCPI), without success.[164]

The next day, 8 to 10,000 demonstrators answered the call for a *journée décisive* in Dijon, protesting the continuation of Vichy regime economic controls. Posters called for protest against, not just the shortages caused by state regulations, but also against state interference in the economy: 'We can no longer produce, manufacture, sell, transport, circulate, without going through countless requirements imposed by BUREAUCRATS WHO INCREASE IN NUMBER DAILY.' Government bureaucracy and regulations cost 40 billion francs, they claimed, with pathetic results. 'We must allow the French to WORK, to PRODUCE, to RECONSTRUCT. The tradesmen know more about how to do this than the **bureaucrat**.'[165] The demonstration began by singing 'La Marseillaise', the standard opening for Vichy-era protests, and heard speeches at the Bourse de Commerce. Demonstrators delivered their complaints to the prefect's office. Then several hundred attacked the offices of the *Contrôle économique*, the *Ravitaillement général*, and the CCPI. Forcing their way past police, they taunted officials with cries of 'Long live liberty!' They ripped bars from the windows to gain entry to offices, threw files and furniture outside, set fires, and destroyed the documents they could lay their hands on.[166]

The protest in Dijon was followed by smaller demonstrations and the threat from Léon Gingembre's *Confédération générale des petites et moyennes enterprises* (CGPME) to close shops across France in a national strike protesting state controls. The CGPME, created in October 1944 to represent small business owners who had little voice in the national employers' association, had expanded in 1946 to include shopkeepers.[167] In early June, the ministries of finance, national economy and industrial production met with Gingembre and the CGPME, and representatives from the *Confédération générale de l'artisanat français* and the *Comité de l'alimentation parisienne* to avoid the strike. They agreed to a series of measures to increase liberty

---

[164] SAEF 30D-0000002, Attorney General, Appeals Court in Poitiers to the Minister of Justice, 22 May 1947.

[165] AD Côte d'Or 40M/278, copy of poster, emphasis as in original (capitals, underlining and bold letters).

[166] SAEF 30D-0000002, 'Des manifestants mettent à sac des services du Contrôle économique du Ravitaillement et du Contrôle laitier', *Le Bien Public*, 21 May 1947; AD Côte d'Or, 40M/278, prefect report of 21 May 1947.

[167] Sylvie Guillaume, *Confédération générale petites moyennes entreprises: Son histoire, son combat, un autre syndicalisme patronal 1944–1978* (Talence: Presses universitaires de Bordeaux, 1987), and Henry W. Ehrmann, *Organized Business in France* (Princeton, NJ: Princeton University Press, 1957), 172–184.

for commerce.[168] Meetings continued in mid-June, and the CE issued directives to cut back on the most disliked methods of control enforcement. Henceforth, owners had to be present for controllers to enter locked premises and were entitled to legal representation; and the methods for imposing fines were revised to reduce fines in accord with evidence provided.[169] Controllers could no longer pose as buyers to provoke illicit sales, except in cases of suspected large-scale traffic; the method was explicitly forbidden in cases of individuals seeking food for their families.[170] The aggressive enforcement of controls in retail markets was relaxed.

Controllers still encountered organized opposition, with at least thirty confrontations in the remainder of 1947, forty-eight in the first half of 1948, and twenty-four in the second half, lessening in frequency as supplies improved and controls relaxed. In September 1947, two CE inspectors who had written citations for offences by a butcher and a baker in St-Aignan-sur-Cher stopped for lunch nearby. The butcher sought them out in the restaurant, demanding to see their identification and trying to take their briefcase and files. A crowd outside threatened to hang them (cries of '20 metres of rope') and set fire to their car.[171] In other incidents, the food supply administration, the *Police économique,* and even the national office for grain supply had staff threatened when crowds suspected they were from the *Contrôle économique.* In Margerit-à-Rosières, two tax inspectors from the *Contributions indirectes,* checking grain and flour stocks, were swarmed by a crowd of 300 and forced to hand over their files and promise they would not return. The crowd believed they were CE controllers and would have done worse, the Gendarmerie explained, had the inspectors not been able to show they worked for the tax office.[172]

The retreat from strict control is striking in the decline of CE *procès-verbaux* filed. In the first half of 1947 they filed reports on 129,324 cases; in the second half, 62,567 (down 51.6 per cent).[173] Although the CE was not the only administration under attack, it was by its own account 'the target of a particular hatred, and the work of our

---

[168] 'La grève du 4 juin aura-t-elle lieu?' and 'Tous ouverts le 4 juin', *Le Monde,* 2 and 4 June 1947.

[169] SAEF B-0049890; Note de service no. 931, 21 June 1947.

[170] SAEF B-0049890; Note de service no. 980 and its annex, 17 Sept. 1947.

[171] AN BB/18/3737, case 33A47/F-91.

[172] AN BB/18/3737, case 33A47/F-88. Dez reported a similar case in 1947, a *Contribution indirectes* inspector attacked at a flour mill in Saint Amand-sur-Sèvres because the crowd believed he was a CE controller. Dez, 'Économie de pénurie', 175, n. 25.

[173] SAEF B-0009860, DGCEE, *Rapport sur l'activité de la DGCEE au cours de l'année 1947,* 11–14.

service has been rendered practically impossible in numerous departments'.[174] But economic conditions were improving slowly. Policies attributed to Vichy's controlled economy continued to obstruct the economic initiatives needed to produce new growth. French producers and businesses accepted moderate price increases as necessary incentives. As controls relaxed in 1948, the CE noted that changes in the economic situation and behaviour rendered black-market prices less useful as an indicator. Administratively, the black market was losing its economic character and becoming a matter of fiscal fraud.[175] After reduced harvest in 1947, in part owing to poor weather, the harvests improved in 1948 and 1949. Inflation brought a convergence of official and black-market prices. Rationing was suspended for many foods in 1948 and ended for the remainder in 1949.[176]

Conclusions

A. J. Liebling, optimistic in September 1944 that the black market would soon end, quickly realized that the shortages would continue. Increased mortality, disease, and broken bones resulting from dietary deficiencies meant that his initial amazement at 'the thousands of pretty girls on bicycles who greeted us Americans in Paris on the day of its liberation' had missed the essential story. A few weeks later he wrote, 'Young women dying from tuberculosis do not ride bicycles.'[177] Until official supplies and distribution improved, consumers and industry needed the black market.

The resurgence of black-market activity after Liberation was a product of continuing shortages, diminished state enforcement, and renewed effort by producers and intermediaries at all levels to organize better distribution. Transport was essential to distribute scarce goods and rebuild productive capacity. The importance of army trucks and factory vehicles used to carry black-market goods offers a prime example of how official resources were repurposed to serve market demand. Public protests, initially to demand more food, spread to obstruct the enforcement

---

[174] SAEF B-0009860, DGCEE, *Rapport sur l'activité de la DGCEE au cours de l'année 1947*, 13.

[175] SAEF B-0049890, Note de service no. 1084, 4 June 1948; the CE index for black market prices was reduced from 32 items to just 9.

[176] INSEE, *Mouvement économique en France de 1944 à 1947* (Paris: Imprimerie Nationale, 1958), 66–69.

[177] Liebling, 'Letter from Paris', 26 Oct. 1944, in *The New Yorker*, 4 Nov. 1944, reprinted in Liebling, *World War II Writings*, 696. 'Now that the Germans have stopped draining France of anything edible, the food situation must improve, but it cannot improve greatly until the French railroads and trucking systems have been sufficiently restored to ensure distribution of what is available, which will not happen for some time.'

of ration and price controls, and then to challenge the control regime seen as one of 'economic tyranny'. The escape from Occupation penury needed price incentives and reward more readily found in the black market. Producers and consumers wanted liberation from the control regime that had been designed by Vichy and was visibly failing after Liberation in its essential purpose to provide sufficient and equitable distribution.

9   Justice for *les profiteurs de la misère publique*

The suffering and injustice inflicted by Germans and by French collaborators during the Occupation fostered expectations and a deep emotional conviction that those who worked with the Germans or benefited from their presence must be held accountable. Those who paid a high price during the Occupation – in damage to their lives and loved ones, as well as their exploitation in the economy of penury – wanted justice. The *Conseil National de la Résistance*'s 'Action Programme' of 15 March 1944 set an agenda to restore France's moral and social equilibrium and to build 'a more just social order'. Measures included the confiscation of goods belonging to traitors and *trafiquants* and a tax on profits 'realized at the expense of the people and the nation during the occupation'.[1] Jean Mairey, Commissaire de la République for the Dijon region, insisted after Liberation that it would not be enough to punish only those who traded with the enemy: '[I]t is necessary to strike quickly and mercilessly at those who profited from public misery, who without having collaborated in the literal sense of the term, have nonetheless made scandalous fortunes.'[2]

Justice and retribution would correct the abuse and violence effected under Vichy rule. The public demand for justice included sentiments of injury, anger, and desire for vengeance. It had a moral foundation: the inequities, injustice and abuse under Vichy needed to be recognized and punished. Those who betrayed their families, their friends, their colleagues, their communities, their country, those who had 'forgotten they were French', must be held accountable. But how?

The *épuration sauvage* of the Liberation period, when partisans and local communities exercised popular justice, gave immediate satisfaction in punishing some of the most obvious and detested collaborators; those

---

[1] 'Program of the Conseil National de la Résistance' as translated in Peter Novick, *The Resistance versus Vichy: The Purge of Collaborators in Liberated France* (London: Chatto and Windus, 1968), 198.

[2] SAEF B-0049475, Commissaire de la République in Dijon to the Minister of National Economy and the Minister of the Interior, 26 Sept. 1944.

who had not slipped away. De Gaulle's provisional government needed to demonstrate its ability to restore order and legal process, to end the 'wild purge' and establish clear procedures to try those accused of betrayal of the nation's principles and trust. The most urgent trials focused on ideological and political collaborators and the perpetrators of Vichy's violence against the Resistance. Economic collaboration and black-market activity had less visibility and posed problems for definition and evidence, but this form of collaboration had been widespread.[3] Most industrial firms worked for the Germans, and black-market activity coloured almost every aspect of domestic consumption. The purge yielded uneven results. In Henry Rousso's summation, 'It was unequal in time and in space, it was sometimes incoherent, notably in leaving out of reach the most important collaboration, that is, economic collaboration.'[4]

This chapter reconstructs foundational elements in the economic purge: the planning as part of the preparations for national economic reconstruction; the retributive violence against profiteers and *trafiquants* at Liberation; and the establishment of legal procedures to punish collaboration and black-market activity by confiscating 'illicit profits'. Disillusion and disappointment in the economic purge were profound. Pierre Mendès France warned in November 1944 that many *trafiquants* and profiteers would escape punishment. He cautioned in January 1945 that the country's disappointment would be great 'when it sees that the immense majority of the nouveaux riches – guilty or not – have escaped any punishment'.[5] The main structures for the economic purge – the national and regional purges of professionals and the department committees to confiscate illicit profits – would evaluate hundreds of thousands of cases and impose sanctions affecting tens of thousands of collaborators and profiteers. Many escaped or were punished lightly, and public opinion considered the economic purge to have failed.

How and to what degree the purge failed will be assessed. Justice required investigation and due process. In Michel Debré's words, 'The

---

[3] I use the term 'economic collaboration' to retain the emotional force of the term in the period of the purge. Its use is contested, as immediately pejorative and covering too wide a range of adaptations to circumstances, including working with the Germans unwillingly and as unhelpfully as possible. For major steps in distinguishing degrees of collaboration and coercion, see Stanley Hoffmann, 'Collaborationism in France during World War II', *Journal of Modern History* 40, no. 3 (1968): 375–395; and Burrin, *France under the Germans*. For a well-argued critique of the term, see Sébastien Durand, 'Les entreprises françaises face aux occupants (1940–1944): Entre collaboration, opportunisme et "nécessité de vivre"', *French Politics, Culture and Society* 37, no. 2 (2019): 1–26.

[4] Henry Rousso, 'L'épuration en France: une histoire inachevée', *Vingtième Siècle*, 33 (1992): 101.

[5] Address to cabinet on 17 Nov. 1944 and letter to Charles de Gaulle on 18 Jan. 1945 in Mendès France, *Œuvres complètes*, vol. II, 62, 117.

justice of the Republic is not that of Vichy.'[6] In specifying how and why the purge was limited, this analysis shows the conflicts in the need to reconcile due process with public demand for rapid action, and the impracticality of punishing *all* black-market activity given its extent. The purge posed challenges for legal procedure, state policy, and the employment of scarce resources. Was economic justice possible in the effort to build a more just social order? Explaining the expectations, compromises and frustration with the economic purge is important in order to understand the linkages between legal process, justice, public opinion, economic recovery, and the difficulty of holding all collaborators and profiteers to account.

Planning to Punish *Collaboration économique*

The economic purge after Liberation would punish 'the profiteers of the defeat': those who gained financially from collaboration with the Germans and exploitation of their fellow citizens.[7] The categories intertwined. Serving German interests deprived French consumers, and exploiting French consumer needs derived profit from the German occupation. The connection was obvious in cases of traders selling to both the Germans and the French black market. Less visibly, those producing goods for the Germans often relied on black markets for raw materials and on German protection from French control. Any undeclared enrichment drawing benefit from the German Occupation would be subject to confiscation. Punishing economic collaboration would strike those who aided the Germans, the black marketeers, and state officials who supported and profited from both.

A Resistance note in 1943 posed the question: where was the money printed by the French state to pay German occupation costs? It was in the hands of all those who collaborated: in politics, in industry, in commerce, state officers who protected the black market, and those who organized the pillage of Jewish property. It was in the hands of the many 'who saw the Occupation only as a source of profit, and who made great efforts to supply our enemies with what they needed to prolong their war'. Requiring declarations of wealth acquired during the Occupation and stamping bank notes to identify wartime gains would avoid financial catastrophe after Liberation.[8] Mendès France advocated a mandatory

---

[6] Michel Debré, *Trois républiques pour une France: Mémoires* (Paris: Albin Michel, 1984), 328.

[7] Phrase used in AN AG/3(2)/419, Ollier-Delest, 'Une étude sur les mesures à prendre concernant les fortunes édifiées par la collaboration', received in London 29 Aug. 1943.

[8] AN AG/3(2)/419, Ollier-Delest, 'Une étude sur les mesures à prendre'.

currency exchange to reduce inflationary pressure, but also to identify war profiteers and enable the confiscation of illicit profits.[9]

Crimes against French civilians in occupied regions during the First World War had gone unpunished, the planners believed. Suffering in the present war was greater, and failure to punish those responsible could lead to popular violence. War tribunals would mete out justice at liberation to prevent a wave of popular violence: 'On the day of victory, the French people will appreciate, in learning of the condemnations pronounced against wartime traitors, that they have been defended effectively by the government of FIGHTING France.'[10] Satisfying the grassroots demand for justice would punish collaborators and restore democratic practice. Locals would participate in 'liberation committees', mobilizing their knowledge of local behaviours to support the post-liberation purge.[11]

France had taxed excess profits in the First World War as 'war benefits'. That legislation laid the foundation for the confiscation of 'illicit profits'.[12] The liberation of Corsica in September 1943 gave the French National Liberation Committee (CFLN) an opportunity to test how to identify and punish economic collaboration and black-market profits. The CFLN issued decrees to confiscate 'illicit profits' and require an exchange of bank notes. All currency had to be turned in for exchange; each depositor would receive 500 francs of new currency, with the release of further new currency in stages, as sources of wealth were verified. Mendès France, the CFLN commissar for finances, believed policy in Corsica to be especially important in setting the precedent for France.[13] The confiscation decrees for Corsica, prepared in late 1943, were finally issued in May 1944, communicated to Corsican authorities in June, and Mendès France flew to Ajaccio to meet with administrators in early July.[14] The purge in Corsica had limited success. Its late start allowed collaborators to hide evidence, witnesses to change their testimony, and friends of the accused to attest to

---

[9] Chélini, *Inflation, État et opinion*, 265–274.

[10] AN AG/3(2)/419, 'Création d'un tribunal de guerre en France dans la zone ex-non-occupée', 11 May 1943.

[11] On the role of *Comités départementaux de la Libération* as part of the democratic renewal at Liberation see Chapman, *France's Long Reconstruction*, 29–37.

[12] Béatrice Touchelay, 'D'une sortie de guerre à l'autre: de la contribution sur les bénéfices de guerre (1916) à la confiscation des profits illicites (1944–1945), l'État a-t-il appris à compter?' in *L'épuration économique en France à la Libération*, ed. by Marc Bergère (Rennes: Presses universitaires de Rennes, 2008), 33–50; and Philippe Verheyde, 'Guerres et profits en longue durée, une approche politique et morale de l'économie', in ibid., 27.

[13] AN AG/3(2)/419, Mendès France to M. Mederic, 16 Feb. 1944.

[14] Drafts of the legislation, stressing the importance of taxing black-market profits, are in SAEF B-0058865, especially Mendès France to the prefect of Corsica, 23 June 1944; and in AN AG/3(2)/419.

their good conduct.[15] The president of the *Commission des enrichissements illicites* in Ajaccio reported a series of difficulties caused by the delay. Many who profited during the Occupation evaded the exchange of currency, and illicit profit investigations tended to identify the small-scale operators, letting the *gros trafiquants* escape. People knew who the latter were and saw the currency exchange as punishing those who followed the law, while the truly guilty escaped justice.[16]

In France, Gaullists considered rapid action to punish collaborators and profiteers so as to establish the authority and the legitimacy of the provisional government. Resistance newspapers and Free French radio broadcasts had warned that traitors would be brought to justice at Liberation, including those who profited from the German presence.[17] To divert wartime hatred from the murderous path of popular violence, the government needed to establish the path for official justice, 'A justice rapid, because the anger will not wait, a justice simple, because procedural artifices permit the shrewd to deceive, a justice extensive because there are many to hold accountable, a justice that does not sully, but cleanses.'[18] In deliberate contrast to the arbitrary justice under Vichy, 'impersonal and brutal', liberated France would follow the rule of law and protect citizens against arbitrary decisions and state violence.[19]

Speed was essential to ensure that the guilty did not disappear or hide their gains (as in Corsica). Local and regional authorities were authorized to freeze assets, block accounts and sequester businesses to prevent collaborators escaping with their assets as liberation took place. But authorities used these measures inconsistently, with increasing concern for the disruption they caused. Profiteers liquidated assets and escaped. Inconsistent state measures disrupted employment and output, particularly the work of construction firms. One writer declared that all such measures affecting production and recovery should follow a simple rule: 'Repress to clean up, with a constructive goal.'[20]

---

[15] AN AG/3(2)/419, 'Trois problèmes de la libération. Leur solution dans le cadre de la Corse', 26 May 1944.

[16] SAEF B-0049475, President of the Commission for Illicit Enrichment [Ajaccio] to the Commissar of Finances in Algiers (Mendès France), 11 Oct. 1944.

[17] Herbert R. Lottman samples these warnings in *The Purge: The Purification of French Collaborators after World War II* (New York: William Morrow and Company, 1986), 28–31.

[18] AN AG/3(2)/419, 'Les responsabilités et les sanctions', undated.

[19] Michel Debré's policies as Commissaire de la République for the Poitiers region provide a good example; see Marc Bergère, *Une société en épuration: Épuration vecue et perçue en Maine-et-Loire. De la Libération au début des années 50* (Rennes: Presses universitaires de Rennes, 2004), 69.

[20] SAEF B-0049475, 'Note sur les services de province' (quoted) and 'Note sur le blocage des comptes et sur l'exécution des séquestres', undated. Department prefects,

The purge experience in Corsica showed that changes were needed to improve on the results achieved.[21] Liberation in France sparked popular violence against collaborators, the Milice (the French special police force to combat the Resistance) and profiteers. Liberation authorities used arrests, internments, and the imposition of fines and confiscations to punish 'profiteurs de la misère' and obtain funds to feed their local population. Local and departmental committees of liberation (CLL and CDL) punished economic collaborators in anticipation of state action by the provisional government. They imposed fines, payable immediately, on economic collaborators and black-market dealers, including farmers who benefited from food sales.[22] The Occupation policies and restrictions that had confined individuals in small communities now produced intense demands for retributive violence to punish local abuses and exploitation.[23]

Officials feared that uncoordinated and irregular actions by local committees would compromise the re-establishment of republican order. Local sanctions could potentially function more like ransom by gangs than as state confiscations.[24] The director of *Contributions directes* in the Côtes-du-Nord warned of this. Better organization was needed to punish illicit commerce and produce 'immediate and tangible' results; to maintain social peace and be certain that funds seized as fines would be paid into state coffers.[25] In the Gers, the CDL imposed heavy fines on Armagnac producers, demanding immediate payment and threatening arrest. In a letter on behalf of Armagnac producers, Pierre du Vignau protested that these 'war fines' lacked due process and legal authority, and left the victims vulnerable to additional fines and taxation. Local

Commissaires de la République and Bank of France directors were empowered to freeze assets, block accounts, and take control of collaborationist firms.

[21] SAEF B-0033849, 'Rapport sur l'évolution de la situation monétaire en Corse et sur l'application de l'Ordonnance du 2 Octobre 1943', undated. The delay in the illicit profit measures was one problem. The first phase of the currency exchange in October 1943 required the deposit of all currency notes of 500, 1,000 and 5,000 francs; depositors received up to 5,000 francs in new notes immediately. Most notes deposited were 1,000-franc notes; 60 per cent of the deposits were for exactly 5,000 francs, likely by people paid a commission to exchange someone else's illicit gains. On measures in Corsica, SAEF B-0049475, President of the Commission for Illicit Enrichment (Ajaccio) to the Commissar of Finances in Algiers, 11 Oct. 1944.

[22] Grenard, *La France du marché noir*, 241–243; Rochebrune and Hazera, *Les patrons sous l'Occupation*, 331–340. AD Pyrénées-Atlantiques 34W/8 has a receipt book with fines issued in autumn 1944; fourteen of twenty-four receipts are for the payment of fines by farmers.

[23] A logic stressed by Conway, 'Justice in Postwar Belgium', 142–143.

[24] SAEF 30D-0000004, Pignerol, 'Enquête sur l'application de l'ordonnance du 18 octobre 1944', 30 Nov. 1944.

[25] SAEF B-0058865, *Contributions directes* to the director in Paris, notes of 2 and 30 Aug. 1944.

authorities demanded fine payments just as Armagnac producers needed funds to purchase wine for their production season; the fines would ruin some producers.[26]

The new republican regional *commissaires* acted promptly against economic collaborators. In Lyon on 3–4 September, Yves Farge announced he would punish profiteers 'who grew scandalously rich in collaborating with the enemy', and arrested Lyon's most prominent industrialist, Marius Berliet. He placed major industries under state administration, appointing temporary administrators while directors' degrees of collaboration and illicit profit were determined.[27] In Bordeaux, Gaston Cusin called for 'a justice impartial and enlightened, as well as prompt', using all possible means to punish black-market *trafiquants* and collaborators, many of whom had escaped justice. In the following months he interned many business leaders.[28] In Marseille, Raymond Aubrac requisitioned fifteen firms, mainly in the transport and metallurgy sectors, putting them under workers' control.[29] Jean Mairey, the Commissaire in Dijon, blocked corporate bank accounts, a measure he declared necessary to accommodate 'the public's exasperation in the face of the impunity of collaborators and *trafiquants*'.[30]

De Gaulle's provisional government issued a decree to confiscate illicit profits on 18 October 1944. It stressed the need to satisfy public demand. Confiscations were a matter of elementary fiscal justice, turning over to the Treasury all gains made possible by the German occupation: 'When the nation was being impoverished, it is inadmissible that some grow rich at its expense.' Departmental committees would identify firms and individuals who had earned 'illicit profits' and confiscate those earned between 1 September 1939 and 31 December 1944. The decree defined illicit profits as profits earned from all commerce with the enemy that had not been imposed, and from the violation of economic laws – price controls,

---

[26] SAEF B-0058865, Treasury in the Gers, 'Relève détaillé des amendes infligées par le Comité départemental de libération aux profiteurs de guerre', 2 Oct. 1944; 'Procès-verbal de la Commission réunie à la Préfecture du Gers le 22 Septembre 1944', 26 Sept. 1944; and Pierre du Vignau to the prefect of the Gers and the president of the CDL, 5 Sept. 1944.

[27] Hervé Joly, 'L'épuration économique a bien (provisoirement) existé: l'exemple de la région Rhône-Alpes', in *Une poignée de miserables*, ed. by Marc Olivier Baruch (Paris: Fayard, 2003), 301–335. Quoted in Lottman, *The Purge*, 194. The first firms sequestered are listed in a note from Commissaire de la République Farge to the prefect of the Loire, 8 Sept. 1944, in AD Rhône 283W/91. The Berliets' arrest (Marius and his four sons) and trials are recounted in Rochebrune and Hazera, *Les patrons sous l'Occupation*, 82–103.

[28] Cited in Durand, 'Les entreprises de la Gironde occupée', 1196; Cusin quote from 28 Aug. 1944.

[29] Aubrac, *Où la mémoire s'attarde*, 138–144; Robert Mencherini, *La Libération et les entreprises sous gestion ouvrière: Marseille 1944–1948* (Paris: L'Harmattan, 1994).

[30] SAEF B-0049475, SCRCE, 'Note pour le Ministre', Oct. 1944.

currency exchange, gold, and food supply regulations. For simplicity and efficiency, the committees would estimate total illicit profits rather than needing to document precise gains.[31] The confiscation of profits served as a blunt fiscal measure, simpler than determining unpaid taxes on unrecorded illicit commerce. In addition, the committees could punish willing collaboration and deliberate fraud to conceal illicit activity with fines up to three and even four times the profits confiscated.[32] These measures aimed explicitly 'to make pay up those who got rich thanks to the misfortunes of the country and tried to conceal their profits'.[33] René Pleven stated the government was determined to punish 'the profiteers of distress'.[34] The decree made the departmental committees the sole authority to decide penalties and taxes owed for collaboration and black-market activity, taking this power back from local authorities.[35]

Department committees were composed of the directors from the *Contributions directes*, *Contributions indirectes*, *Contrôle économique*, *Douanes*, the department treasurer, and three members appointed by the *Comité departmental de la Libération*. Most departments established a single committee, but eight with populations greater than 800,000 had two (Pas-de-Calais, Nord, Gironde, Rhône, Bouche-du-Rhône, Seine, Seine-et-Oise, Seine-Inférieure). The Department of the Seine (Paris) began with two committees, increased to six, and then to twelve. The extent of commerce with the Germans and black-market trade meant the task ahead was vast. The need to follow due process and decide confiscations and fines based on evidence required trained personnel, material resources for gathering and evaluating the evidence, the development of consistent procedure, and time to accomplish this work with exactitude. In May 1946 Paris, with six CCPI, estimated they would have 30,000 cases that could take five to ten years. Finance inspectors reporting on the progress across France in April 1945 found that committees were well established, but in many departments the numbers of cases far exceeded their capacity.[36] Most of the committee work took place in 1945 and

---

[31] SAEF B-0058865 for draft versions of the decree and its exposé des motifs, and discussion of the legislation by staff in the *Contributions directes*, the Ministry of Finance (20 Sept. 1944), and the *Direction des affaires criminelles* (21 Sept. 1944).

[32] The process in Corsica allowed fines up to the amount of the confiscation. The draft legislation increased this to double, and in exceptional cases to triple the confiscation; in June 1945 this was increased again to four times the confiscation.

[33] SAEF B-0058865, 'Projet de loi tendant à confisquer au bénéfice de la Nation les profits réalisés du fait des circonstances de guerre ou de l'occupation ennemie', 29 Aug. 1944.

[34] AN 560AP/33, Pleven (Minister of Finance) press conference of 12 Dec. 1944.

[35] SAEF 30D-0000001, Minister of Finance to regional Commissaires de la République, 20 Oct. 1944.

[36] SAEF 30D-0000004, Guyot to the Minister of Finance, 13 April 1945, and Pignerol, 'Mission de contrôle des comités de confiscation', 7 April 1945.

1946. The slow and careful process frustrated observers. Many businesses feared they would be subject to confiscations, while the public saw little progress in punishing the firms and individuals they knew to be guilty.

The National Assembly called a halt to the process in 1947. A law of 21 March 1947 set deadlines, with no new cases to be started after 30 June, and committees to decide their cases by the end of the year in all departments with fewer than 800,000 residents. The official reasons were that CCPI staff were needed in the tax departments and the continued threats of confiscation were reducing investment needed for reconstruction.[37] The major cases had been dealt with, smaller cases could be handled as tax evasion, and resentments against controllers, including those from the CCPI, were mounting. Contemporaries were unimpressed. The currency exchange, implemented finally in June 1945, did not touch illicit profits: 'most of those who got really rich would doubtless have had time to transform into hidden real values ... the greater part of their illicit gains'.[38] Former tax officials concluded that most illicit profits had escaped confiscation. The effort had been necessary to punish *trafiquants*, but it conformed to a general rule: taxes weigh most heavily on honest business, while the crooks and *trafiquants* escape.[39]

Confiscating Illicit Profits

But the process had not failed. The archival sources now available yield insights into the challenges the committees faced, the workings of economic collaboration and black-market traffic, and the illegibility of much of the activity the state had struggled to repress. The new committees faced material and procedural hurdles in establishing a consistent and effective process for confiscations and fines. They needed to determine how much illicit profit had been earned, and how and whether the money could be found for confiscation. To start the process, they needed to decide the departmental committee members, set meeting schedules (often once a week), find office space and secretarial staff, and assign agents for the investigative work needed to gather evidence. With committees of eight to ten members, the CCPI members would have

---

[37] SAEF 30D-0000002, Certeux to the president of the CCPI for the Department of the Seine, 16 Apr. 1948.
[38] Gaetan Pirou, 'Le problème monétaire en France depuis la Libération', *Revue d'économie politique*, 55 (1945): 27.
[39] Jules Chauveneau, Pierre Mahuzier and Edmond-Jean Carton, *La confiscation des profits illicites* (Paris: Rousseau et Cie, 1947), 41–44.

numbered close to 1,000, and they needed investigators, who numbered about 1,800 in 1946.[40]

Investigators required mobility, particularly to work in agricultural departments. Most had to rely on public transport or their own vehicles. A suggestion that each committee be allocated one vehicle was declined. Appeals for funds to reimburse investigators for mileage expenses and to allocate fuel and tyres documented how poorly equipped they were.[41] The president for the Rhône lamented the time lost by investigators who, if they had a car, had no gasoline.[42] One request in February 1945 began: 'The current lack of transport risks paralyzing completely the action of the service charged with on-site investigations and seriously damaging the enforcement of the decree of 18 October 1944.'[43]

Once established, the committees needed to identify their targets. Committee members were drawn from state agencies for taxation and controls. Article 6 of the decree establishing the CCPI required state agencies to notify the committees of persons who had contravened economic regulations. The CE, having written the largest share of more than 1 million *procès-verbaux* during the Occupation, focused on sending cases involving penalties of more than 20,000 francs or prison terms. They sent more than 111,000 cases to departmental CCPI, including cases that escaped prosecution thanks to German protection. Louis Rosenstock-Franck, director of the CE in 1949, estimated that his agency's efforts accounted for 35 per cent of the Treasury's revenue from CCPI confiscations and fines.[44] The *Contributions directes* staff provided the most effective agents conducting inquiries.[45] The legislation included public notoriety as grounds for investigation. This encouraged denunciations, which suffered the same grave defect as those for black-market activity during the Occupation: their instrumentalization for personal rivalries and revenge. They consumed investigative time with paltry results. In Bretagne, more than 50 per cent of the denunciations were for economic offences, either collaboration or black-market traffic. Luc Capdevila

---

[40] Marc Bergère gives 1,800 in 1946 and 1,300 in 1947, slightly less than half of them each year worked full time on their investigations, the rest were 'intermittent'. Bergère, 'Contribution à un premier bilan national de la confiscation des profits illicites, 1944–années 1960', in *L'épuration économique*, 76.

[41] SAEF 30D-0000004, Pignerol, 'Mission des comités de confiscation', 22 Jan. 1945.

[42] AD Rhône 283W/170, President of the CCPI to the regional Commissaire de la République, 19 Dec. 1944.

[43] SAEF 30D-0000004, note from the director, 24 Feb. 1945.

[44] SAEF 5A-0000028, Louis Rosenstock-Franck, 'Rapport sur le concours fourni par le Contrôle économique à l'application de la législation relative à la confiscation des profites illicites', 30 Apr. 1949; the amount was roughly 11.5 billion francs.

[45] Their importance is stressed in finance inspector reports on process; for example, in SAEF 30D-0000004, Guyot to Minister of Finance, 13 Apr. 1945.

reproduces a letter from a retired gendarme who denounced his son, brother, and son-in-law for black-market activity in December 1944. The prefect noted in the letter's margin, 'Sad mentality'.[46]

Department committees gave first attention to their most important cases. These entailed gathering and evaluating financial records to determine confiscations and fines that could be in millions of francs. The public wanted rapid, punitive decisions. As authority passed from committees of liberation to the CCPI, the pace of prosecution and punishment slowed abruptly. The number of cases and the need for due process conflicted with the speed and visibility desired by the public. The CCPI investigations needed to remain secret while underway, to prevent the destruction of evidence and minimize the disruption to business activities, especially for firms needed for reconstruction.[47] The public thus received little news of investigation targets or progress, and learned of punishments only when the confiscations and fines had been decided.

Many individuals and firms feared they would be targets for investigation. Inspectors reported on the negative impact of this uncertainty. From Brittany, where black-market activity had been extensive, 'It is highly regrettable that the committees have not been able to inform the public of at least some of the profiteers they decided immediately to investigate.' The range of potential targets was 'immense;' the public wanted assurance that committees would target notorious collaborators and *trafiquants* and leave in peace the large category of clearly honest people as well as those whose profits had been modest.[48]

The committees needed to determine standards for their decisions, with no knowledge of how appeals would be dealt with by the *Conseil supérieur de confiscation des profits illicites* (CSCPI). They had no precedents to help determine appropriate confiscations and fines. Determining black-market profits from deficient or fraudulent accounting was 'necessarily very approximate'. Especially in black-market cases, increased wealth could be obvious, with no record of how the profits had been earned. Uncertainty delayed progress in many committees, and public opinion turned against them.[49] Some stalled on making decisions; others imposed harsh confiscations to set an example. Many profiteers sentenced in the initial phase appealed, and the CSCPI reduced the

---

[46] Luc Capdevila, *Les Bretons au lendemain de l'Occupation: Imaginaires et comportements d'une sortie de guerre (1944/1945)* (Rennes: Presses universitaires de Rennes, 1999), 250, 256–257.

[47] SAEF 30D-0000003, Guyot to Minister of Finance, 8 Mar. 1945.

[48] SAEF 30D-0000004, 'Note sure les comités de confiscation des profits illicites dans la région de Bretagne', 7 Jan. 1945.

[49] SAEF 30D-0000004, Guyot to the Minister of Finance, 13 Apr. 1945 (on CCPI work in Division VII, Toulouse and southwestern France).

confiscations and fines in cases where the departmental committees had been overzealous or careless. Over time, public expectations were disappointed and committees recalibrated their penalties to accord with the emerging CSCPI standards for evidence and punishment. High fines often proved unpayable, reducing the recovery of funds and the department's per cent of recovery. (Both were metrics to judge the success of their work.) Under the influence of *Conseil supérieur* decisions, the CCPI moved from an 'essentially repressive' logic at the outset to a 'fiscal' logic, focused on careful investigations of business accounts when these were not rejected as fraudulent.[50]

Commerce with the Germans left more financial records than black-market activity. Committees were often able to determine income from sales to the Germans in setting the confiscations and fines. For firms that actively sought business with the Germans, engaged in deliberate deception in their accounting, or had significant black-market activity, the committees imposed fines of two or three times the confiscation. In some cases, collaborationist firms were requisitioned or nationalized (notably Renault, Berliet, and the firms requisitioned in Marseille). In cases where the CCPI confiscations took all the profit, the fines were essentially unpayable, but they demonstrated the intent to punish.

Some heavy confiscations and fines were intended to bankrupt the firm or individual. If this was not the case, committees had to set reasonable penalties and a timeline for payments by instalment. There was a conflict between establishing public credibility by imposing tough sanctions and losing credibility when the penalties were not paid.[51] One inspector commented in July 1945, 'It is necessary to recognize that the very high fines were generally imposed under the pressure of public opinion, vigorously supported by the representatives from the Liberation Committees, concerned to punish anti-national actions rather than to render executable decisions.'[52] Of the first ninety-eight decisions in 1945, fifty-five were appealed to the CSCPI.[53] The appeal process required departmental committees to review their cases, and appeals were frequent in cases of high penalties. The reconsiderations with new evidence reduced the fines

---

[50] SAEF 30D-0000003, Guyot to the Minister of Finance, 3 Apr. 1947. The committees had higher recovery rates when their penalties were moderate; A. Poisson, 'Note sur la situation des travaux du Comité de confiscation des profits illicites dans les Hautes Pyrénées', 17 Feb. 1946; P. Arnoult, 'Note sur une demande d'information concernant le recouvrement des profits illicites dans la bonneterie troyenne', 28 June 1946; Guyot to Minister of Finance, 3 Apr. 1947.

[51] SAEF 30D-0000002, Hoppenot, 'Rapport de la mission de Contrôle des Comités de confiscation de profits illicites', 9 Mar. 1945.

[52] SAEF 30D-0000004, Guyot to the Minister of Finance, 8 July 1945.

[53] SAEF 30D-0000002, Hoppenot, 'Rapport de la mission de contrôle', 9 Mar. 1945.

and sometimes the confiscations, correcting 'exaggerations committed under the pressure of public opinion'.[54]

For legitimacy of the process, the decisions had to be based on evidence, not hearsay, and allow appeals to introduce further evidence when decisions were contested. The Service Coordinating Research into Economic Collaboration, created in September 1944 to coordinate research to punish collaboration, estimated there were 30 tonnes of German documents to be sorted, including 7 tonnes left by the Germans in the Chamber of Deputies (that they did not have time to burn), the records of the Organisation Todt, and French government and business records.[55] Some commerce had been legal, imposed by German and/or Vichy authorities, and had earned little profit. Many cases concerned French businesses who contracted to supply German troops billeted in French towns, to provide support services, and to build military installations: the Atlantic Wall, airfields, coastal defences, barracks. German troops needed French supplies of food and equipment, labour, and the work of French construction firms (BTP – *Bâtiment-travaux publics*).

The construction industry was critical for the French war effort, for German wartime needs, and for reconstruction.[56] In areas of German troop concentration, preparing to invade Britain and later to defend Fortress Europe (particularly the Atlantic coast), not only were almost all French BTP firms drawn into construction, but foreign firms as well,[57] and foreign workers. Of 290,000 Organisation Todt workers for defence construction in France in June 1944, 85,000 were French, 15,000 German, 25,000 came from French colonies and 165,000 were 'foreign' workers.[58] Many BTP firms had little choice: they could work for the Germans, or they could lose their raw materials, equipment and workers. The work by itself was not sufficient reason to condemn firms. Some had

---

[54] SAEF 30D-0000003, Guyot to the director of the coordination service, on decisions in Division VII to 30 April; 18 May 1947.

[55] SAEF B-0049475, SCRCE, 'Note au Ministre', undated, and Ministère de l'Économie nationale, 'Note sur le Service de Coordination des Recherches sur la Collaboration Économique', Jan. 1945.

[56] Danièle Voldman, 'Le bâtiment, une branche solicitée', in *La vie des entreprises sous l'Occupation*, 91–116; and Dominique Barjot, 'L'industrie française des travaux publics (1940–1945)', *Histoire, Économie et Société*, 11(3) (1992): 415–436.

[57] The Danish firm Christiani and Nielsen provides an interesting example; see Steen Andersen, 'The French Opportunity: A Danish Construction Company Working for the Germans in France, 1940-1944', in *Economies under Occupation: The Hegemony of Nazi Germany and Imperial Japan in World War II*, ed. by Marcel Boldorf and Tetsuji Okazaki (London: Routledge, 2015), 262–279.

[58] Rémy Desquesnes, 'L'Organisation Todt en France (1940–1944)', *Histoire, Économie et Société*, 11(3) (1992): 546–547.

put up resistance, slowing their pace of work and aiding Resistance groups. Others had sought rapid profit, including the *entreprises champignons* – 'mushroom firms' that sprang up overnight – a common occurrence in the construction sector. One firm in Chaumont (Haute Marne), having had little business in the 1930s (and bankruptcy in 1932), obtained profitable contract work for painting in German military installations. An initial CCPI decision in March 1945 imposed a confiscation of 1,736,800 francs and a fine of 850,000. The owners appealed. Further investigation and a separate condemnation for 'intelligence with the enemy' revealed they not only actively sought German business, but billed for work they had not completed, trafficked in materials obtained from the Germans, and tried to double-bill the Germans. The CSCPI increased their fine to 3,300,000 francs.[59]

Patrick Veyret's evaluation of BTP activity in Lyon found the largest firms all worked for the Germans, almost exclusively by 1944, but they also often supported the Resistance and sheltered workers from being sent to Germany.[60] Claude Malon's examination of the purge in Le Havre documents the complexity of BTP cases.[61] All the BTP firms in the coastal region worked for the Germans. The most notorious, in public opinion, was the construction firm Thireau-Morel. The liberation committee in Le Havre declared it 'collaborationist', claiming it worked for the Germans throughout the Occupation on friendly terms. Thireau-Morel accounts had been destroyed in the Allied bombing of Le Havre on 5 September. According to bank records, work for the Germans totalled 43 per cent of their Occupation earnings. The departmental CCPI imposed a confiscation of 8 million francs in March 1946. The firm appealed, with new evidence to show their subjection to German demands and their significant support to the Resistance. Thireau-Morel was now helping reconstruct Le Havre. The confiscation was annulled in 1949.[62]

Less visible to the public, the *Société française des travaux routiers* (SFTR) was a classic *entreprise champignon*, three firms in fact, controlled by one family, growing from small-scale operations prewar to employ 1,200 workers in 1943 and earn 90 per cent of its receipts from the Germans, building defence works for the Organisation Todt. Yet

[59] SAEF 30D-0000056, case 141R, 25 Sept. 1945.
[60] Patrick Veyret, *Lyon 1939–1949: De la collaboration industrielle à l'épuration économique* (Chatillon-sur-Chalaronne: Éditions La Taillanderie, 2008), 181–192.
[61] Claude Malon, *Occupation, épuration, reconstruction: Le monde de l'entreprise au Havre (1940–1950)* (Mont-Saint-Aignan: Presses universitaires de Rouen et du Havre, 2013), 251–268.
[62] Malon, *Occupation, épuration, reconstruction*, 252–255.

SFTR, too, provided information to the Resistance. Although liberation authorities arrested its directors and sequestered the firm, it escaped confiscations and fines.[63] The coastal regions where collaboration had been extensive to build the *Atlantikwall* were often the heaviest hit by Allied bombing and land battles, with great need for construction firms to help rebuild, even if they had worked for the Germans.[64]

Compared to commerce with the Germans, black-market traffic was typically undocumented or concealed by accounting deceptions. Local communities wanted the black marketeers who exploited their desperate material needs to be punished.[65] Farmers and small firms, widely dispersed and small-scale in dealing with the Germans or with French *trafiquants*, rarely kept transaction records. Targets for committee investigation were determined by prior offences and public notoriety. In the absence of accurate records, investigators calculated changes in their subjects' wealth and *train de vie* from prewar to the end of the Occupation, assessing whether increased wealth and income had been reported and taxes paid. This involved estimations, potentially subjective in character (depending in part on the target's degree of cooperation with the investigation). It determined the likely illicit profits earned. When notified of the CCPI confiscation and fine, the person or firm could provide documents to prove the assessment wrong and specify their actual profits. Most *trafiquants* kept no such records.

The CCPI had discretionary power in imposing fines. In early cases they set fines of 200 or 300 per cent to punish wilful collaboration, fraudulent accounting, and obstruction of their investigations. Departments without significant German forces and military construction had more black-market activity than collaboration, and less accounting evidence. In such departments, the public was eager to see major *trafiquants* punished. Heavy fines against farmers and butchers who had engaged in illicit slaughter and black-market sales were unpayable 'by definition', as the confiscation took their profits.[66] In the Haute-Garonne, under pressure from public opinion, the CCPI imposed fines of 200 and 300 per cent on top of high confiscations. In the Hérault, public disinterest allowed committee decisions that were moderate and more likely to be paid.[67] In areas where the traffic in food supplies had engaged almost

[63] Malon, *Occupation, épuration, reconstruction*, 116–121, 255–258.
[64] As well as Malon's work, see Julie Chassin, 'Épurer ou reconstruire? Le secteur du bâtiment et des travaux publics du Calvados', in *L'Épuration économique*, 257–269, and Sébastien Durand, 'Les entreprises de la Gironde occupée' on BTP in the Bordeaux region, 1234–1237.
[65] Capdevila, *Les Bretons au lendemain de l'Occupation*, 237–260.
[66] SAEF 30D-0000002, Hoppenot, 'Rapport de la mission de contrôle', 9 Mar. 1945.
[67] SAEF 30D-0000003, Guyot to the Minister of Finance, 3 Apr. 1947.

everyone, farmers, shopkeepers and consumers, public opinion turned
against investigations of black-market commerce that kept families fed.[68]

Investigations were complicated by the fact that commerce with the
enemy and black-market profits often intertwined. The supplies to
German troops routinely required black-market purchasing, and
German demands far exceeded their military needs, evolving into
a systematic pillaging of French resources. The complicity of the
French state and the violence of the German authorities required that
investigators distinguish carefully to target for confiscation the cases
where black-market use had been 'active' and 'direct', and recognizing
that German demands often could not be opposed.[69]

Businesses that worked for the Germans pleaded that they had no real
choice, they had to serve the Germans or face requisitions, seizure of raw
materials, workers sent to Germany, and business collapse. The paper
trail from this commerce sometimes allowed the CCPI to assess the
degree of constraint. Ernest D., a wine wholesaler in Trèbes (near
Carcassonne), claimed that he had delivered wine to the Germans
under constraint. The Vichy administration had appointed him president
of the regional *Syndicat des marchands de vin en gros* to oversee wine sales to
the Germans. Refusal, he claimed, would have meant 'the most serious
consequences' for him personally and for the wine industry. French wine
producers and the French Treasury benefited from organized sales to the
Germans and tax payments to the state. In their initial assessment, the
CCPI imposed a confiscation of 1,852,990 francs in illicit profit, and
a fine of 5,558,970 francs, three times the confiscation. His appeal
resulted in a careful CCPI analysis that detailed how, rather than having
been forced by the Germans and made minimal efforts on their behalf as
he claimed, D. had in fact sought German business and maintained
cordial relations with them. He encouraged French producers to sell to
the Germans 'in an interest better understood of our commercial future'
and had stated his willingness to make a 'maximum effort' to serve his
German clients. In its final decision, the CSCPI maintained the confiscation and reduced his fine slightly, from 300 per cent to 250 per cent of the
confiscation.[70]

The committee in the Gironde made a similar case against Marcel
Borderie, a wine merchant with political connections to Vichy politicians,
who had escaped disciplinary measures and profited from selling wine
and apéritifs to the Germans. His profits had enabled him to buy up

[68] SAEF 30D-0000004, Guyot note, 13 Apr. 1945.
[69] SAEF 30D-0000004, Le Prado, 'Essai' on the confiscation of illicit profits, 23 Dec. 1944.
[70] SAEF 30D-0000112, case no. 1976.

vineyards in the Saint-Émilion region. The initial CCPI decision on 3 May 1945 was a confiscation of 316,360,000 francs and a fine of 700 million.[71] Borderie appealed. The CSCPI annulled the original decision for procedural error but imposed the same confiscation and fine for deliberate avoidance of taxes and for commerce that had been voluntary.[72]

Poultry wholesaler Émile G, in Varennes-sur-Allier (Allier), had been appointed by the department's *Ravitaillement général* to organize the collection of butter, eggs and poultry. He used his position to traffic in these foods, selling to government offices. His traffic had been subject to a series of infraction reports and his professional cards for wholesaling had been withdrawn for three months, but Vichy ministers intervened to prevent his being punished. The CCPI found his account books 'very incomplete', with no explanation for his increased wealth during the Occupation. In April 1945 the CCPI decided the confiscation of 1.5 million francs in illicit profit. For abuse of power as an RG official and failure to declare his wealth and income, they imposed the maximum fine of 6 million francs. On appeal, the CCPI review reduced the fine to 1 million francs, in order to make it recoverable. The CSCPI upheld the department decision.[73]

The Ministry of Finance supervised the confiscation process. Their *Inspection générale* reports give valuable insight into two key dimensions of the illicit activity under investigation: the business practices to conceal evidence of illicit commerce, and the development of broader resistance to CCPI investigations by a public that had initially demanded punishment of those who profited from the German presence.

They found accounting fraud to be pervasive. The increased regulation through price controls and rationing encouraged all manner of deceptions, from neglecting to record sales, to the use of *soultes* alongside bills of sale showing legal prices, to keeping more than one set of books, one set recording licit prices to show controllers. Inspector Robert Guyot described this culture of fraudulent bookkeeping: 'Five years of price control have shown merchants and industrialists the art of hiding the premiums they are paid (soultes), and the account books, when they are kept, are almost always in order.'[74] The textile merchant Joseph P., for example, falsified his purchase prices (recording higher prices) and the

---

[71] SAEF 30D-0000132, case no. 1388R; Durand, 'Les entreprises de la Gironde occupée (1940–1944)', 1233–1234.

[72] SAEF 30D-0000132, case no. 1388R, Report of the director of *Contributions directes*, doc. no. 91274, undated (1947).

[73] SAEF 30D-0000112, case no. 780; report of CSCPI committee president, 29 July 1946.

[74] SAEF 30D-0000004, Guyot to the Minister of Finance, 8 July 1945.

names of manufacturers (to obstruct price verification). He concealed merchandise stock even while he was under investigation, had not kept complete accounts of purchases and prices, overcharged his customers, and failed to ticket his merchandise with legal prices.[75]

Commerce with the Germans involved not only state-approved contracts, but methods of direct purchasing that included the most notorious black-market operations like the Bureau Otto, which operated on a first-name basis in cash.[76] French suppliers transacted sales with no signatures and cash payments, issued receipts with untraceable last names, and kept accounts that were incomplete and inexact. Accountants were easily found to falsify the books. *Trafiquants* hid profits 'thanks to account books that looked correct'. The fines for accounting fraud were 1,000 francs for the first offence and rising by 1,000 francs for each offence thereafter; paltry sums in relation to black-market profits.[77]

Large firms could afford more complex accounting deceptions and defence strategies. The case of the cosmetics firm covered in Chapter 5 is illustrative. It declared losses in three of five years from 1940 to 1945. The CCPI took testimony from the firm's former manager, who stated they had extensive black-market business, sales to the Germans, and an extensive system of fraudulent accounting.[78] The firm had extensive production for the black market in France and accounting fraud to conceal its profits.[79] Its off-book sales began in 1937 to avoid taxation. The CCPI imposed a confiscation of 250 million francs and a fine of 375 million in July 1948.

In agriculture, the number and geographic distribution of producers and the lighter expectations regarding accounts meant that there was little documentation for widespread black-market activity. In most agricultural departments, black-market cases were more frequent than commerce with the enemy; the activity was smaller in scale, widely scattered, and left less evidence. Committees tried to distinguish between notorious collaborators and profiteers, who deserved harsh penalties, and the smaller-scale black market traffic in food that had been essential to survival. Accounting fraud did not weigh heavily in the latter, in the absence of any records.

---

[75] SAEF 30D-0000155, case no. 1626, Maine-et-Loire.

[76] Rochebrune and Hazera, *Les patrons sous l'Occupation*, 248; Chauveneau et al., *Confiscation des profits illicites*, 24. See Chapter 5 for more detail on accounting fraud.

[77] SAEF 30D-0000004, Polaillon, XIe division, 'Note sur les comités de confiscation', 20 Jan. 1945.

[78] AdP, Perotin, 3314–71–1–8 44.

[79] On the basis of worker productivity, the CCPI estimated that the firm's account books recorded 20 per cent of output.

The second dimension evident in reports is the turn in public opinion against the CCPI. The continuation of Vichy regulations with no improvement in the food supply turned consumers and producers against the state regulators. Public sympathy increased for the illicit traders under investigation for control infractions, whose services were still needed. Finance inspector Robert Guyot cited examples: a cattle merchant in the Tarn-et-Garonne, whom the CDL had energetically sought to punish for his activities during the Occupation, and who was now seen as helping with food supply; and a potato wholesaler who supplied Perpignan at prices well above the legal limit when none were available in markets. Guyot summarized this turn in opinion in April 1945: if strictly followed, the decree of 18 October would require the investigation of so many shopkeepers and farmers that everyone would have a parent, a friend or a provider facing investigation for illicit profits. 'We can be sure that public opinion will side with those we are investigating, given that the decree was made to reach the traitors and profiteers. In addition, the public will soon see the persons cited as victims for the services they have rendered, even under stressful circumstances, to assure indispensable supplements for insufficient official food supply.' Everyone charged higher prices.[80]

Bank of France directors observed repeatedly that the threat of confiscations curbed business investment, limiting the capacity to borrow the funds needed for reconstruction and recovery.[81] In the Basses-Pyrénées, the department CDL protested the confiscation methods that disrupted commerce and called on the confiscation committee to pay attention to the cases of the 'big beneficiaries of the black market' before proceeding against those with minor illicit gains.[82] Everywhere, inadequate rations had generated extensive and complex supplementary systems of supply that violated state controls. Because these involved nearly everyone, reasonable limits were needed to restrict those who would be prosecuted. Urban residents often assumed that all farmers had made significant black-market gains. Cattle merchants were believed to have profited from all transactions, their sales to state purchasers and to the Germans, as well as the black-market sales to French citizens.[83] In the Maine-et-Loire, the CCPI believed that all butchers participated in illicit slaughter and sales.[84] The CCPI in Seine-Inférieure estimated that Roger

[80] SAEF 30D-0000004, Guyot to Minister of Finance, 13 Apr. 1945.
[81] ABdF 1069201226 27, DGEE monthly reports from February to June 1945.
[82] SAEF 30D-0000004, 'Voeu présenté par le Comité départemental de Libération des Basses-Pyrénées', 22 Feb. 1945.
[83] SAEF 30D-0000004, Guyot to the Minister of Finance, 2 Apr. 1945.
[84] SAEF 30D-0000005, CCPI report for the Maine-et-Loire, 13 Jan. 1947.

G., a butcher in Rouelles, had earned more than 2 million francs in illicit profit. He admitted to illicit slaughter during the Occupation, as a means to counter the German war effort. He had served a large working-class clientèle: clients and local *résistants* spoke in his favour. They elected him mayor at Liberation and vice-president of the CDL.[85]

The finance inspectors' assessments of the progress in handling confiscations show the development of resistance to state controls in a progression from violating regulations to protecting illicit trade that served community needs. In the Pau region, CCPI committee members sympathized with those they investigated and criticized the work of their own investigators (who had a particularly difficult task in a department with a long history of smuggling).[86] Local culture, resentment of state interference, and community benefit from illicit trade all encouraged resistance to CCPI inquiries. Administrators needed to distinguish between large-scale commerce with Germans and black-market profits, for which popular opinion demanded punishment, and the everyday accommodations to circumvent rules and connect buyers with goods they needed.

Inspector Robert Guyot's analyses for his region in southern France give valuable insight into the difficulties encountered. Unlike commerce with the Germans, black market activities opened a vast field of enquiry. Interested parties knew this and resisted. Public opinion approved tough sentences for notorious *trafiquants*, but otherwise supported black-market activity.[87] Cooperation with investigations varied according to the scale of the black-market trade under scrutiny.

Although resistance varied by region and product, the language in inspection reports depicts growing sympathy for the smaller-scale black market activities that improved local access to essential goods. Guyot wrote in July 1945: 'The conspiracy of silence is taking hold, in favour of the "black market": it is good form to vituperate in indignant terms, but no one would dare give precise details on the subject, and interventions are becoming ever more frequent in favour of those under investigation.'[88] The violation of rules to gain access to scarce goods had been normalized, and local sellers could now be seen as victims. *Trafiquants* whom local opinion had wanted punished in 1944 were now seen in a different light. Guyot cited the example of a cattle trader in Toulouse, whose black-market trade had been seen as a reason for meat shortages, but in April 1945 he was

---

[85] Malon, *Occupation, épuration, reconstruction*, 275–276.
[86] SAEF 30D-0000004, André Poisson, 'Seconde note sur le fonctionnement du Comité de confiscation des Basses Pyrénées', 18 April 1945.
[87] SAEF 30D-0000003, Guyot, 'Clôture des citations (Opportunité et délais)', 24 June 1946.
[88] SAEF 30D-0000004, Guyot to the Minister of Finance, 8 July 1945.

newly appreciated by consumers facing worsening shortages. 'If the shortages continue and grow worse, the *trafiquant*, formerly condemned, will pass before long as a victim of the committee and a benefactor long unrecognized by the population.'[89]

Some major collaborators and profiteers were caught; others fled France or concealed financial evidence. Critical opinion of black marketeers became more tolerant for the practices that served consumers in the postwar era of penury. The cynical popular view of the failure of the economic purge traces this path of disillusionment. Anyone in a community served by black-market trade, anyone working in a factory that produced goods for the Germans, anyone who suffered from shortages and had seen others around them benefit from illicit commerce, had seen cases where they believed that profiteers had escaped punishment. The extensive reach of economic collaboration and illicit trade, whether by *trafiquants* drawing huge profit or by ordinary consumers surviving thanks to le *système D*, made inevitable a punishment process that would be 'partial' in both senses: incomplete and biased by local circumstances.[90]

Deceptions

Contemporaries believed the confiscation of illicit profits had failed miserably. Dorothy Pickles judged confiscations in 1946 to be 'ridiculously small', allowing most *trafiquants* to escape unpunished. Ronald Matthews termed the revenue from confiscations 'a joke, and not a very good one'.[91] Civil servants who worked on the committees stated that the principal targets had escaped punishment: 'the profiteers of the French black market and the trafiquants of black market commerce with the enemy can slip through the net, from not being known, or are the object, if caught, of confiscations and fines that the greater part will not be recovered'.[92] Raymond Aron commented on the clash between expectations and realities, to explain why the purge was so widely viewed as a failure. He saw conflict between the legal determination of what constituted 'collaboration' and the state need for 'competent men' to restore the state and economy.[93]

[89] SAEF 30D-0000004, Guyot to the Minister of Finance, 13 Apr. 1945.
[90] As Philippe Verheyde has pointed out, judgements on the success of the purge and confiscations were bound to differ according to what they assessed and how they calibrated their final judgement; 'Guerres et profits', 30.
[91] Dorothy Pickles, *France between the Republics* (London: Love and Malcomson Ltd., 1946), 188–189; Ronald Matthews, *The Death of the Fourth Republic* (London: Eyre and Spottiswoode, 1954), 192.
[92] Chauveneau et al., *La confiscation des profits illicites*, 41–42.
[93] Raymond Aron, 'Les désilusions de la liberté', *Les Temps Modernes*, 1 (1 Oct. 1945): 76–105, quote 77–78.

Characters in novels like Marcel Aymé's *Uranus* (1948) and Jean Dutourd's *Au bon beurre* (1952) made fortunes from the black market and escaped punishment. But public opinion was neither constant nor consistent over time. While believing that *gros trafiquants* escaped punishment, public sympathy increased for the local *trafiquants* who continued to serve local communities in conditions of continued scarcity.

The public demand for justice had pressured officials to punish those who profited from the German presence. *Commissaires de la République* and liberation committees imprisoned collaborators not just for prosecution, but also to protect them from public violence. Vichy sympathizers exaggerated the scale of the popular violence, claiming tens, and even hundreds of thousands of summary executions in the 'wild purge'.[94] The numbers as tallied by prefects in 1948 and 1952 came to about 10,000.[95] Historians' best estimates now place it lower, slightly more than 9,000.[96] Public outrage in local communities needed to be contained and channelled into fair legal process. The economic purge was less violent and less visible than the political retribution exacted during and after Liberation. Was it less successful?

The local anger unleashed in the 'wild purge' influenced the official purge. After the initial violence in summer 1944, renewed waves of popular retribution occurred in the winter of 1944–1945 and in the spring of 1945, in response to the return of deportees from German concentration camps and the early release of suspected collaborators.[97] Public demand influenced the harsh early decisions by confiscation committees.[98] By May 1945, the public was widely critical of an official process that seemed to be 'fuelled by resentment',[99] and failed to punish

---

[94] Foulon discusses these exaggerations in Charles-Louis Foulon, *Le pouvoir en province à la libération: Les commissaires de la République, 1943–1946* (Paris: Armand Colin, 1975), 156–157, the greatest being T. de Vosjoli, *Lamia*, who claimed 500,000 summary executions.

[95] Cited by Novick, with figures of 9,673 in the first survey and 10,822 in the second, both approximations on incomplete evidence. Novick, *The Resistance versus Vichy*, 204.

[96] The numbers and controversy are explained well in François Rouquet, 'L'épuration: histoire d'un chiffre, mémoire du nombre', in *Une poignée de misérables*, 515–529.

[97] Megan Koreman, 'The Collaborator's Penance: The Local Purge, 1944-5', *Contemporary European History*, 6(2) (1997): 177–192, and Patricia Boyer, 'L'épuration et ses représentations en Languedoc et Roussillon (1944–1945)', *Vingtième Siècle*, 68 (2000): 17–28. The waves of violence are evident in Gendarmerie summaries in AN 72AJ/ 384.

[98] As well as finance inspectors' reports in SAEF 30D-0000003, cited above, see Patricia Boyer and Nicolas Marty, 'L'épuration des entreprises en Languedoc-Roussillon: enjeux, organisation et demande sociale', in *L'épuration économique*, 103–123; Bergère, 'Les pouvoirs publics et la conduit des processus d'épuration', 127; and Joly, 'Épuration et propriété privée', 417–418.

[99] Marie-Claude Albert and David Hamelin, 'L'épuration économique dans le département de la Vienne au prisme de deux procès d'industriels', in *L'épuration économique*, 163.

profiteers. Many people believed that the purge only 'accidentally' struck the serious black-market dealers;[100] it punished *lampistes* – the small fry without protection by complicit state officials.

Gendarmerie reports provide a valuable chronicle of the evolution in public opinion. In November 1944 they reported dissatisfaction with the speed of the purge process; in December, those who had suffered during the Occupation and been promised 'a justice rapid, merciless and dispassionate' now found that 'if it is dispassionate, it is not often merciless and even less rapid'.[101] In February they characterized the purge as 'too tepid, too slow'; in March and April as flawed and too slow: 'The purge, with its errors, its omissions, its slow pace, and its excessive clemency or excessive severity, creates a climate ill-favoured for union and for work.' And it failed to punish the worst offenders: 'While the "little guys" pay, they say, "the true leaders are still at large".'[102] The public wanted 'a justice well-ordered, implacable, and especially rapid bringing to an end a situation painful and which, if prolonged, can only harm the cohesion of efforts'.[103] Justice proved to be neither rapid nor merciless.

The reasons for this disappointment are easier to see in retrospect. The purge began with optimism about the potential to purge traitorous activity and build a morally and politically revitalized, democratic France. The clash with reality began with the need to channel popular demands for justice from local reprisals into state courts and legal process. The number of cases, the need to gather evidence and give the accused an opportunity to defend themselves, the need to act quickly, and the need to consider the impact of investigations on national reconstruction all tempered the speed, scale and outcomes of the confiscation effort. The slow pace and lack of information about investigations underway discouraged public confidence. Notorious *trafiquants* were not all punished; the CCPI recalibrated penalties on the grounds of justice and payability.

Robert Guyot summarized the problems in 1948 based on his observation of nine departments in southern France. Strong public opinion in early 1945 believed penalties on notorious cases, 'even spectacular' ones, to be insufficient. Public interest weakened as the CCPI processed lesser cases for violations of price and ration legislation. The continuing

[100] Capdevila, *Les Bretons au lendemain de l'Occupation*, 238, from a public opinion survey in December 1944.
[101] AN 72AJ/384, Col. Girard, 'Synthèse pour la période du 15 septembre au 15 octobre 1944', 13 Nov. 1944, and Col. Meunier, 'Synthèse pour la période du 15 octobre au 15 novembre 1944', 11 Dec. 1944.
[102] AN 72AJ/384, Col. Meunier, 'Synthèse pour la période du 15 février au 15 mars 1945', 12 Apr. 1945.
[103] AN 72AJ/384, Col. Meunier, 'Synthèse pour la période du 15 mars au 15 avril 1945', 22 May 1945.

shortages brought new recognition of the role of illicit producers and commerce in alleviating shortages. Small-time *trafiquants* came to be seen as victims of the confiscation process. 'From the point of view of public opinion, it would have been better to end a year earlier, as the potential for citations weighed heavily on small and medium commerce, especially in mainly rural departments.'[104]

Ending the Illicit Profits Purge

Although appeals continued through the 1950s into the 1960s, investigations wound down in 1947. As with price controls and rationing, public discontent curbed state action. In the case of the CCPI, the confiscations to tax undeclared profits were supposed to be transferred to a reformed tax administration, creating new *Commissions de taxation d'office* (CTO). The National Assembly set deadlines in 1947 to allow no new illicit profit cases after 30 June and to decide cases by 31 December. Any remaining cases would be dealt with by 'fiscalization', transferring them to CTO, which would have technical expertise similar to the CCPI.[105] The CTO would continue 'the battle against fraud and notably against certain categories of fraud (*trafiquants*, intermediaries) who, on the margins of fiscal laws, earn significant profits to the detriment of the Treasury and honest taxpayers'.[106] A memorandum in December 1946 asked CCPI presidents for suggestions on how to organize the new CTO. Their responses reveal their frustrations with CCPI process, and their views on what worked well and why the confiscation of illicit gains should continue.

The presidents supported the creation of the CTO to continue their efforts to tax the wealth gained by means concealed from the state. The efforts were important in 'an era where, it must be recognized, tax evasion has been raised to the rank of an institution'.[107] Tax fraud was not unique to wartime; the CTO would pursue tax evasion that escaped illicit profit confiscations.[108] The practices they recommended as having worked in their investigations included: requiring a declaration of wealth and income to identify unexplained (and untaxed) increases in wealth; giving

---

[104] SAEF 30D-0000003, Guyot to the Minister of Finance, 15 Feb. 1948.

[105] SAEF 30D-0000005, Head of the Service de la coordination des administrations financières to the presidents of CCPI, 30 Dec. 1946, relaying the content of legislation creating the CTO passed on 23 Dec. 1946.

[106] SAEF 30D-0000005, 'Commissions de taxation d'office, exposé des motifs'.

[107] SAEF 30D-0000005, CCPI for the Seine-et-Oise, 'Note sur les Commissions de taxation', 21 Jan. 1947.

[108] SAEF 30D-0000005, CCPI for the Maine-et-Loire, 'Note sur les dispositions des articles 51 et 52 de la loi n. 46–2914 du 23 décembre 1946', 13 Jan. 1947.

the CTO the same financial expertise as the CCPI, without its political component (CDL members); and making sure they had adequate staff including trained financial investigators to verify bookkeeping and accounts. Shortages of staff and investigators had hampered CCPI investigations, and some presidents warned against starting the CTO while the CCPI were still at work, as this would exacerbate their staff shortages. The CTO should not be paralyzed by the need for accounting evidence they could not obtain.[109] They saw no need for a board for appeals: it would suffice to give firms and individuals the opportunity to contest the CTO estimates of untaxed gains and to correct errors.

French taxation was in disarray, with rising budget deficits and inflation in the face of reconstruction needs. Finance inspectors devised a major reform in 1947, to combine the offices of the *Contributions directes* and *Contributions indirectes* and centralize tax administration in the *Direction générale des impôts*, created in April 1948.[110] They saw little purpose in continuing the intensive labour of the CCPI, terminating the CTO initiative. A 'global' assessment of enrichment by a unified tax administration would provide more efficient and reliable detection of fraud and illicit profit.[111]

Conclusions

The CCPI examined 123,717 cases.[112] By 31 July 1950 they had imposed confiscations and fines totalling 146,913,337,000 francs, and the state had recovered 38,053,231,000 francs (26 per cent).[113] Departments with more than 800,000 residents continued to review cases in 1948 and 1949. Appeals lasted into the 1960s, and the CSCPI closed shop in 1968. The effort was considerable. The results, disappointing to contemporaries, and extended over more than a decade, were erratic in who they punished.[114]

---

[109] SAEF 30D-0000005, president of the CCPI for the Aisne to the head of the *Service de la coordination des administrations financières*, 16 Jan. 1947.

[110] Frédéric Tristram, *Une fiscalité pour la croissance: La direction générale des Impôts et la politique fiscale en France de 1948 à la fin des années 1960* (Paris: CHEFF, 2005), 23–60.

[111] SAEF B-0028333, Laure, Valls and de Lattre, 'Contrôle unique', Aug. 1947.

[112] Bergère, 'Contribution à un premier bilan', 71; this number as of 30 April 1948.

[113] SAEF 30D-0000001, 'Note pour le ministre', C.P.I. 14.851, 9 Oct. 1950. The fines imposed totaled slightly more than the confiscations: 68,318,042,000 francs in confiscations and 78,595,095,000 in fines. The recovery rate on confiscations was much higher than that on fines: in early 1948 the recovery rates were 42.5 per cent on confiscations, only 7.5 per cent on fines. SAEF 30D-0000002, 'Note pour le ministre', C.P.I. 8407, Mar. 1948.

[114] For concise summaries, see François Rouquet and Fabrice Virgili, *Les Françaises, les Français et l'épuration (1940 à nos jours)* (Paris: Gallimard, 2018), 303–309, 321–323, and Grenard et al., *Histoire économique de Vichy*, 324–331.

The imperative to hold all collaborators and 'profiteers from distress' accountable could not consider every case when virtually everyone broke economic rules to survive the shortages. The black market was indeed 'an institution to which everyone has recourse'.[115] Most firms engaged in some degree of commerce with the enemy, whether under constraint or seeking profit. In the sectors of greatest interest to the Germans – armaments, metals, vehicle manufacture and BTP – almost all firms had to work for them. Some willingly. Illicit activity was ubiquitous. The purge had to limit its range, and no clear line could be drawn to separate cases requiring punishment from those to be dropped.

Resource constraints limited CCPI investigations. The first was the limits on personnel and material resources. All financial administrations suffered staff shortages; the CCPI needed members and investigating agents from other administrations with the expertise needed for difficult cases. Agents struggled to keep pace with the workload.[116] The second was the quantity of evidence: extensive, widely dispersed, yet deficient for most cases where financial records were incomplete or falsified. The coordination of research was essential. The SCRCE, created in September 1944, received little help from rival ministries (it was under the Ministry of National Economy), and it was amalgamated against its will with a rival administration, the *Direction du blocus* (Management of the Blockade). The SCRCE claimed there were twenty-six different government agencies involved in prosecuting economic collaboration. In their view in December 1945, punishment had been 'notoriously insufficient'. Apart from the notable exception of the nationalized Renault factories, many big suppliers escaped punishment: 'the repression concentrated on the small and medium culprits, while the large companies that set the example for economic collaboration are neither sought nor prosecuted'. The CCPI penalties, impressive in magnitude, were 'feeble in proportion to the profits realized'.[117] The process, intended to be 'rapid, merciless and dispassionate', proved to be neither.

The penalties collected in confiscations and fines provide a misleading measure of CCPI success. The total imposed, nearly 147 billion francs, included estimated profits that were not necessarily recoverable, and fines

---

[115] AN 72AJ/384, Col. Meunier, 'Synthèse pour la période du 15 février au 15 mars 1945',12 Apr. 1945.

[116] SAEF 30D-0000003; finance inspector reports give details. For example, Robert Guyot, 'Service des comités de confiscation: Clôture des citations (opportunité et délais), Etat d'avancement des travaux – Insuffisances locales en personnel et mesures à prendre pour y faire face', 24 June 1946.

[117] SAEF B-0049475, SCRCE, 'Note sur la répression de la collaboration économique', 4 Dec. 1945. The critique of lack of coordination among multiple agencies was shared by three former inspectors; Chauveneau et al., *Confiscation des profits illicites*, 21–22.

were imposed to demonstrate the scale of wrongdoing, not realistic payment. Except when high fines were intended to bankrupt firms, reducing
the confiscations and fines recognized the difficulty in estimating illicit
profits and obtaining payment. For firms to remain in business, committees needed to establish viable schedules for payments. In the Troyes
region, as of June 1946 the *bonneterie* industry had thirteen cases decided,
with confiscations of roughly 150 million francs and fines of 100 million.
The funds recovered were less than 10 per cent of the total: 24,600,009
francs. But this was because the CCPI for the Aube had scaled payments
to accommodate levels of business activity. Although only 10 per cent of
the total had been paid, that was actually 94 per cent of the payments
required by June 1946. The scaling of payments reconciled penalty
payment with economic survival.[118] Despite the accommodations, the
CCPI came under bitter attack from the industrialists, and the collection
of penalties in the department was given to the *Contributions indirectes*.[119]
Demands for harsh punishments had to yield, in sectors where output was
needed, to the practical limits of what was possible.

Contemporaries termed the profits purge a fiasco. The slow pace of
justice and the declining levels of confiscations and fines disappointed
many. The SCRCE commented in December 1945: 'The result is
a subversion of opinion, and the people, who no longer believe in the
justice exercised by the state, find themselves needing to administer
private justice ... What is more serious, is that all confidence in the
economic policy of the government disappears.'[120]

Anger and resentment had few avenues for expression and punishment
when the state took control of the purge to assure due legal process. Jean
Meckert's novel *Nous avons les mains rouges* (1947) renders a chilling
portrayal of disillusioned *résistants* in southern France. They employ
'direct action' (murder) against collaborators and black-market profiteers
to correct the 'rotten justice' of the postwar years. One member of the
group comments: 'No ... the war is not over! ... We fought for an ideal of
peace and justice. And we've found neither peace, nor justice!'[121]

---

[118] SAEF 30D-0000003, P. Arnoult, 'Note sur une demande d'information concernant le
recouvrement des profits illicites dans la bonneterie troyenne', 28 June 1946.
[119] SAEF 30D-0000004, 'Note sur le comité de confiscation de l'Aube', 12 July 1946.
[120] SAEF B-0049475, 'Note sur la répression de la collaboration économique'.
[121] Jean Meckert, *Nous avons les mains rouges* (Paris: Gallimard, 2020 [1947]), 250.

10   Black Markets in Wartime

In Paula Schwartz's apt phrase, 'the black market was not a secret *place*; it was a vast underground system of exchange, at once everywhere and nowhere'.[1] Everywhere, and used at some point by nearly everyone, and essential to French strategies for survival in an economy of penury. Nowhere because it had no fixed address and no official records. The archival records used in this study report on control efforts and violations, French negotiations with the Germans, and public opinion as observed by those seeking to control and suppress the black market, but they leave much of market experience obscured. The more serious the illicit traffic, the greater the efforts to hide it. Individuals recounting their experience in letters and diaries talked frequently of shortages, but few mentioned or elaborated on their own illicit activities to ameliorate them. In the adaptations and the deceptions it fostered, the black market was not only everywhere and nowhere; in its machinations, anything was possible. As Jacques Delarue, the police commissaire who wrote *Trafics et crimes sous l'Occupation,* put it many years later, 'all imaginable situations actually occurred'.[2]

The statistics for French output, distribution and prices in the official economy are misleading (Chapter 2), understating output and prices. The clandestine economy was less visible and left fewer records. Black-market prices defied indexation; they ranged from below official prices to ten and twenty times higher, and they varied by region, season and the relationship between buyer and seller. Averages indicate trends and hide lived experience that seldom corresponds to the average. The actual volume of black-market traffic is unknown. The government defined black-market activity as all practices in contravention of economic controls, but in practice it allowed transgressions of the food regulations by those 'trying to get enough to eat, but who can't do it without breaking the rules'.[3] The line between legal and illicit was not clear.

---

[1] Mouré and Schwartz, 'On vit mal', 276.
[2] Quoted in Sanders, 'Economic Draining', 137.
[3] AD Rhône 182W/2, Police commissioner for the Brotteaux district to the Commissioner for Lyon, 24 Nov. 1941.

We also have no record for the additional time and effort invested in the circuitous paths for production, transport and distribution of illicit goods. We have no accurate metrics for system legitimacy and the extent to which people lost faith in state controls and official markets. But even without the precision to determine exact contours and limits, the logic and the patterns of behaviour in black market activity are clear. In practice, black market use became so widespread because it became a necessary part of the strategies for survival in a policy regime that failed to provide essential goods.

Two characterizations of the black market common during the Occupation can be readily dismissed. The first are the statements by Vichy authorities, especially in the first two years of the Occupation, which blamed the growing black market on foreigners and Jews. As Fabrice Grenard notes, these claims were the product of Vichy anti-Semitism and xenophobia, claiming the black market 'an anti-French work orchestrated by the enemies of the nation'.[4] The black market was used to justify persecution: the first mass arrest of Jews in Paris in May 1941 was explained as an action against foreign Jews for their significant part in black-market traffic.[5] Jews excluded from legitimate business by anti-Semitic decrees, and foreigners marginalized by Vichy employment policies, did engage in black-market activity, in part by default, as they had fewer legitimate options than other citizens. The state propaganda justified Vichy anti-Semitic measures and deflected attention from state mismanagement and German purchasing.[6] The mass of evidence in CE files and the sectoral analyses in Chapters 4 through 6 make clear that there was little 'orchestration' and a great deal of innovation to deal with immediate problems. German Occupation policies and practice fostered and promoted illicit activity, but the breadth and influence of the black market came from its utility for French producers, commerce and consumers.

The second characterization is that of the black market being more efficient than the official markets. The fact that the black market could deliver goods unavailable in official markets did not demonstrate its efficiency. Given the need to conceal traffic and evade regulatory safeguards, more goods were lost in the complexities of illicit production and distribution. The spoiling of perishable food, the breaking of fragile

---

[4] Grenard, *La France du marché noir*, 53–58, quote at 54.
[5] 'Cinq mille juifs', *L'Œuvre*, 15 May 1941; the article claimed that the courts in Paris were burdened by black-market cases in which those charged were 'almost always Jews of foreign nationality'.
[6] Michael R. Marrus and Robert O. Paxton, *Vichy France and the Jews*, 2nd ed. (Stanford, CA: Stanford University Press, 2019), 91–92, 131–133.

goods, the higher cost of illicit transport and storage, and the payment of more numerous and greedy intermediaries meant that it worked with higher costs and greater product losses than legal commerce. In the classic 'B.O.F.' products of butter, eggs and cheese, Colette's letters to her *anges nourrisseurs* in Brittany mention broken eggs (thirty broken in one parcel received on 4 March 1942; fifteen broken the following week) and melted butter.[7] Postal workers in package depots had grease-blackened sleeves from the butter shipped by mail that melted in summer heat, and in winter too.[8] Customers buying black-market meat learned to eat it immediately, knowing how quickly it could spoil.[9] Perishable goods seized by the state sometimes went bad before they could be redistributed. In Normandy in May 1943, a truckload of 3700 kg of meat could not be refrigerated quickly enough to avoid this.[10] The purported 'efficiency' of the black market lay in its ability to procure goods that were otherwise unavailable. Apart from exploitation for profit, the black market won growing social acceptance because of local appreciations of its ability to provide goods in the economy of penury. At a price.

This final chapter draws conclusions regarding the importance of the black market in France, and the conditions that made French experience exceptional in light of European and Allied experience with shortages, economic controls and black markets. By contextualizing French experience, it underscores the vital importance of market responses to solve supply challenges. It re-emphasizes how the controls on market transactions created new problems and new opportunities when the bounds of licit activity narrowed, outlawing normal market responses. Problem-solving energy shifted to illicit trade, including the black market, where a range of incentives (not just profit) promoted innovations and work-arounds to serve not just individual, but business, family and community interests. It tapped 'individual ingenuity', as the Bank of France termed it, with that ingenuity being 'such that the authorities prove powerless to stop this trend'.[11]

Black Markets in Wartime

Black markets developed in all belligerent countries. Mobilization for total war increased the competition for goods and necessitated state intervention to allocate resources for the war effort and to manage the impact on civilian

---

[7] Colette, *Lettres aux petites fermières*, 82, 92.
[8] Paul, 'Histoire des PTT pendant la deuxième guerre mondiale', 286.
[9] Cécile Rol-Tanguy interview, Paris, 13 Mar. 2015.
[10] SAEF B-0049509, correspondence in May, June and July 1943 concerning meat seized by the *Contrôle économique* on 15 May.
[11] ABdF, 1069201226 24, DGEE, 'Résumés des rapports économiques', ZO, Aug. 1941.

consumption and prices.[12] The singularity of French experience is clearer in reviewing the context of more desperate and more favourable circumstances in other countries during the Second World War.

In Eastern Europe, black-market activity became vital to distribute food and essential goods; German exploitation was brutal and undisguised. In Ukraine, the German postal censor's office reported extensive corruption, especially in widespread black-market activity: 'Illegal trading and black marketeering are in full bloom. ... Ukraine is a black market paradise.'[13] Heinrich Böll, an unhappy Wehrmacht conscript, marvelled in his letters from Eastern Europe at the variety of goods available on the black market: one could buy anything, if one had a thick enough wallet.[14] In Poland, literary critic Kazimierz Wyka wrote of German rationing policy as a 'social fiction' because under its rules, no one could survive. For the Polish population in the General Government, 'the only important question was: *how to survive despite the regulations*'.[15] Even the General Government relied on the black market for survival.[16] In the Soviet Union, the state legalized some market trade and encouraged growing private gardens to increase the food supply to the cities. The Red Army relied on the black market to obtain needed goods ranging from boots to alcohol, and soldiers profited from selling the goods they had stolen or confiscated.[17] In Greece, the black market became pervasive, the lifeline for survival, after famine in 1941–1942 had killed an estimated half a million.[18]

---

[12] Alan S. Milward provides a clear explanation in *War, Economy and Society 1939–1945* (Berkeley: University of California Press, 1977), 99–131.

[13] Aly, *Hitler's Beneficiaries*, 110–117; Aly quotes at length from the post censors' report, 113–116, quote from 116. On Kiev, see Karel C. Berkhoff, *Harvest of Despair: Life and Death in Ukraine Under Nazi Rule* (Cambridge, MA: Harvard University Press, 2004), 174–186; on barter and black markets in Eastern Europe, Klemann and Kudryashov, *Occupied Economies*, 281–288.

[14] Heinrich Böll, *Briefe aus dem Krieg 1939–1945* Band 2 (Cologne: Verlag Kipnheuer und Witsch, 2001), 975 (7 Jan. 1944), 987–988 (30 Jan. 1944).

[15] Kazimierz Wyka, 'The Excluded Economy', in *The Unplanned Society: Poland During and After Communism*, ed. by Janine R. Wedel (New York: Columbia University Pres, 1992 (first published in Aug. 1945)), 25.

[16] Ramona Bräu, 'The Economic Consequences of German Occupation Policy in Poland', in *Paying for Hitler's War*, 438, ed. by Scherner and White; and Jerzy Kochanowski, 'Black Market in the General Government 1939–1945: Survival Strategy or (Un)Official Economy?', in *Coping with Hunger and Shortage*, 27–47.

[17] On adaptations in the USSR, see Wendy Z. Goldman, 'Not By Bread Alone: Food, Workers, and the State', in *Hunger and War: Food Provisioning in the Soviet Union during World War II*, ed. by Wendy Z. Goldman and Donald Filtzer (Bloomington: Indiana University Press, 2015), 44–97. For the Red Army, see Catherine Merridale, *Ivan's War: Life and Death in the Red Army, 1939–1945* (New York: Henry Holt and Co., 2006), 136–140, 237–238, 348–349.

[18] Mark Mazower, *Inside Hitler's Greece: How the Nazis Ruled Europe* (New Haven, CT: Yale University Press, 1993), 23–52; and Violetta Hionidou, *Famine and Death in Occupied Greece, 1941–1944* (Cambridge: Cambridge University Press, 2006).

German policies in Western Europe were less brutal, but black markets still provided critical supplements for low rations. Belgium, more dependent on food imports than France, experienced near-famine conditions in the first winter of Occupation. The black market, termed the 'free market', was vital to consumers and industry, and fraud became 'the very condition not just for economic activity, but even for existence' in a system where rations did not provide the minimum needed for survival.[19] In the departments in northern France administered by the German military command in Brussels, Belgians with freedom to travel gained notoriety for their black-market acumen and were a repeated target for complaints by French prefects.[20]

The use of controls in the United Kingdom, Canada and the United States offered a striking contrast. These states did not suffer occupation or interference by an exploitive foreign administration. They used price controls and rationing to allocate resources in circumstances that rallied most citizens to accept restrictions and limited sacrifice as a contribution to their national war effort. Mark Roodhouse found that 'Black markets were everywhere and nowhere in austerity Britain.' Even with widespread violations, he terms the British controls a success, and distinguishes between the grey market, 'a mixture of self-help and mutual aid' that fostered community cohesion, and the black market that worked for profit, serving 'illegitimate greed' rather than 'legitimate need'.[21] In North America, further from the war damage and benefiting from increased agricultural and industrial output to meet war demand, civilian rations were generous. Black markets developed for the regulated goods most needed in the war effort: gasoline, tyres, sugar, liquor and meat. They diverted a smaller proportion of output to illicit trade, did less damage to the supply to official markets, and were condemned by popular opinion.[22]

Black markets in these countries worked on the margins, rather than at the centre, of national economic life. The generous rations in North

---

[19] Fernand   Baudhuin,   *L'économie   belge   sous   l'Occupation   1940–1944*   (Brussels: Établissements Émile Bruylant, 1945), 318, 202, 209.

[20] AN AJ/41/342, the file titled 'Fraude à la frontière belge: surveillance douanière 1940–1943' has extracts from prefect reports complaining of the lack of border controls and control effort by German authorities. Also, Ralf Futselaar, 'Incomes, Class, and Coupons: Black Markets for Food in the Netherlands during the Second World War', *Food and History* 8, no. 1 (2010): 171–198.

[21] Roodhouse, *Black Market Britain*, 253–257.

[22] Geoffrey Mills and Hugh Rockoff, 'Compliance with Price Controls in the United States and the United Kingdom during World War II', *Journal of Economic History*, 47(1) (1987): 197–213; Harold Vatter, 'The Material Status of the U.S. Civilian Consumer in World War II: The Question of Guns or Butter', in *The Sinews of War: Essays on the Economic History of World War II*, ed. by Geoffrey T. Mills and Hugh Rockoff (Ames: Iowa State University Press, 1993), 219–242; and Jeff Keshen, 'One For All or All For One: Government Controls, Black Marketing and the Limits of Patriotism, 1939–47', *Journal of Canadian Studies*, 29(4) (1994): 111–143.

America and their sufficient provision in Britain *guaranteed* adequate nourishment. The US War Ration Book No. 2 stated explicitly: 'This is your Government's guarantee of your fair share of goods made scarce by war.'[23] Rationing policy in Britain promised 'Fair shares for all', a slogan central to their campaign for public acceptance of rationing.[24] The British reliance on imports and vulnerability to blockade made planning for food supply more urgent than elsewhere.[25] It also facilitated state monitoring of supplies; imported food arrived in a few ports in large quantities, rather than originating on millions of widely dispersed farms. W. B. Reddaway, one of the experts working in the British system, defined state policy as to provide 'orderly distribution and a certain degree of equity' in rationing scarce goods; the 'real test' was that rationing 'should produce a more acceptable pattern of distribution than would emerge from the alternative "system" of queues, favoured customers, shop-crawling, and the like'.[26]

In the United States and Canada, administrators appealed for strong public support to make controls effective. The price controls in Canada, beginning in October 1941, depended on voluntary compliance to minimize administrative costs; better to have shoppers monitor prices than to hire an army of price controllers.[27] The Wartime Prices and Trade Board recruited women to its Consumer Branch and women's groups mobilized volunteers to assist in ration document distribution and price controls. In a poster from May 1944, men from the armed forces and the civilian economy saluted a shopper with the commendation: 'THANK YOU MRS CONSUMER – for WATCHING PRICES! BUYING ONLY WHAT YOU NEED! INVESTING IN WAR SAVINGS! KEEP IT UP!'[28] The rationing system

---

[23] Quoted in Amy Bentley, *Eating for Victory: Food Rationing and the Politics of Domesticity* (Urbana and Chicago: University of Illinois Press, 1998), 1. The importance of providing rations as an essential minimum was fundamental: see John Kenneth Galbraith, *A Life in Our Times: Memoirs* (Boston: Houghton Mifflin, 1981), 156; Frederick James Marquis Woolton, *The Memoirs of the Rt. Hon. The Earl of Woolton* (London: Cassell, 1959), 191–192. British planners resisted the extension of rationing in 1941 on the basis of this implied guarantee; R. J. Hammond, *Food and Agriculture in Britain 1939–45: Aspects of Wartime Control* (Stanford, CA: Stanford University Press, 1954), 114.

[24] Zweiniger-Bargielowska, *Austerity in Britain*, 12–45; on the program's shortcomings, and 'Fair Shares? The Limits of Food Policy in Britain during the Second World War', in *Food and War in Twentieth Century Europe*, ed. by Ina Zweiniger-Bargielowska, Rachel Duffett and Alain Drouard (Farnham: Ashgate, 2011), 125–138.

[25] Alan F. Wilt, *Food for War: Agriculture and Rearmament in Britain before the Second World War* (Oxford: Oxford University Press, 2001).

[26] Reddaway, 'Rationing', 182–183.

[27] K. W. Taylor, 'Canadian Wartime Price Controls, 1941-6', *The Canadian Journal of Economics and Political Science*, 13(1) (1947): 87.

[28] Joseph Tohill, '"The Consumer Goes to War": Consumer Politics in the United States and Canada during the Second World War', in *Shopping for Change: Consumer Activism and the Possibilities of Purchasing Power*, ed. by Louis Hyman and Joseph Tohill (Ithaca, NY: Cornell University Press, 2017), 137–150, poster reproduced at 147; and his

had remarkable popular support; one survey in 1945 found that 'rationing has consistently given evidence of being the most popular among Canada's wartime controls, a fact that is especially significant when one remembers that it has been more a part and parcel of everyday living than any of other controls'.[29] The American price control program learned and borrowed from British and Canadian experience. The Office of Price Administration encountered greater resistance from the business community but recruited hundreds of thousands of volunteers to distribute ration books and monitor retail prices.[30] Most consumers in both countries appreciated the national controls and willingly sacrificed some of their purchasing to support their fighting troops.

In contrast, French consumers were expected to make ever greater sacrifice in a flagging economy, by a 'national' government that worked, increasingly obviously, as a puppet regime whose regulations served German interests. Barren official markets and ration tickets unused for lack of goods proved that the system benefitted the Germans and the privileged, including collaborators, and it failed most French consumers. The legitimacy of the control regime for producers and consumers alike lay in its perceived equity and efficiency. It needed to meet basic needs, operate with visible equity, and deliver clear benefit to those who complied with controls. When it failed in these regards, those who tried to abide by the rules realized they were 'dupes'. The system served German interests, rewarded *trafiquants* and corrupt state officials, deprived producers of fair return for their effort, and discouraged the delivery of essential goods to market. It was a system to be resisted and rejected in favour of clandestine markets.

The Black Market in France

German policies aggravated the problems of economic management throughout Occupied Europe. Their demands varied according to regional resources, the racialized character of Nazi policy, and the local government structures on which they could lean for administrative

---

detailed examination of Canadian price controls in Joseph J. Tohill, "'A Consumers' War": Price Control and Political Consumerism in the United States and Canada during World War II' (PhD dissertation, York University, 2012), chapter 3.

[29] Ian Mosby, *Food Will Win the War: The Politics, Culture, and Science of Food on Canada's Home Front* (Vancouver: University of British Columbia Press, 2014), 83–84; for his coverage of the WPTB and its successes, 74–89.

[30] In peak periods as many as 300,000 women volunteered for temporary tasks; Harvey C. Mansfield and Associates, *A Short History of OPA* (Washington, DC: US Government Printing Office, 1951), 244. On US management of price controls and rationing, see Meg Jacobs, *Pocketbook Politics: Economic Citizenship in Twentieth-Century America* (Princeton, NJ: Princeton University Press, 2005), 179–220, and the works cited above by Joseph Tohill.

support.[31] In France, the Germans seized goods, requisitioned supplies, demanded French labour, and intensified their economic exploitation to supply their war effort on the Eastern Front. France paid more in tribute to Germany than any other occupied country, owing in part to the size and productivity of her economy, and in part to collaboration.[32] Vichy collaboration aimed to gain administrative autonomy, a better deal from the Germans to avoid 'Polonization', and an influential place in Hitler's Europe. But it did not do much to shield France; it facilitated German ends. Vichy administrators sought to preserve some French control in a system of intensifying German exploitation. The Wehrmacht victories in 1940 did not, as first seemed possible, produce a Europe at peace under German domination. The invasion of the Soviet Union and war against the United States intensified the total war effort and increased German demands on occupied economies.

France adopted price controls in September 1939 and preliminary rationing measures in early 1940, and it developed these into a comprehensive system after the defeat in June 1940. The Vichy regime faced the triple threat of a sharp contraction of supply and productive capacity, intensifying German demands, and the need for new controls and enforcement. Improvisation by producers and consumers to meet critical needs and work around controls outstripped the state's organizational capacity and fostered rapid innovation to acquire goods and develop paths for alternative supply. Some innovations deliberately violated rules from the outset, but others became illegal as the control regime tightened. Three factors fostered the extensive black-market growth in France.

First and most obvious (and true for regulation and evasion everywhere): the shortages, when combined with controls on prices and quantities, encouraged the diversion of goods by anyone with goods to sell or with purchasing needs frustrated by market controls. Previously legal bargaining practices were forbidden. Buyers and sellers now had to choose whether to abide by new restrictions or improvise ways around them to obtain the goods they wanted. At the outset, many consumers

---

[31] The German and Japanese economic demands are explored in new research in Boldorf and Okazaki, eds., *Economies under Occupation*, and Jonas Scherner and Eugene N. White, eds., *Paying for Hitler's War: The Consequences of Nazi Hegemony for Europe* (Cambridge: Cambridge University Press, 2016).

[32] Calculated per capita, including the credits to Germany for defence construction, France did not pay as heavily as the Netherlands and Norway; Klemann and Kudryashov, *Occupied Economies*, 201–207. But monetary calculations at the national level and per capita averages obscure the immediate, real impact of German exploitation where the damage was felt: at the local and individual level.

wanted state regulations to organize access and equity for goods they needed. But the restrictions created new opportunities for profit.

Second, German interference encouraged and often structured black-market growth. The German authorities insisted on regulations, especially rigid price controls and rationing, to facilitate their exploitation of French resources (for both military and private purchasing), to punish French consumers, and to encourage collaboration, minimizing their need for administrative personnel and maximizing their yield in material goods and French labour. The rules were for the French. French police were not authorized to stop, search or confiscate goods from German forces. *Trafiquants* who worked for the Germans (or who believed they could escape French control by claiming to), if caught by French police, sought German intervention to free them. The Germans took the confiscated goods, and often demanded the case files as well.

French black markets and their networks of intermediaries developed in part to serve German purchasers who exploited black-market opportunities, in part to deliver goods to French buyers outside the constraints of the control system, and in part to seize opportunities for exceptional gain – to 'profit from misery'. Alternative markets provided consumers with critical supplements needed for survival. Businesses used them for access to raw materials and to sell their product at prices that recouped costs. For producers and consumers alike, the inequities created by the ration and price system, and the increasing diversion of productive effort and goods to black markets, demonstrated inept state management of markets and encouraged the recourse to alternative markets. The fact that controls served the Germans added patriotic incentive as a justification (or an excuse) for black-market use. Consumers and businesses adapted their purchasing, production, and sales methods to work around the state controls that interfered with their access to goods.

Legitimacy was the third, and key element in black-market growth. Even those who wanted controls and those who worked in the state administration lost faith in the utility and fairness of the control regime, and alternative markets offered more dependable access to needed goods: commerce turned increasingly to illicit trade. The controls and controllers then became obstacles to production and consumption. There was a cumulative logic to the development of controls, their rigid enforcement, their evident inequities, and the shift in activity to illicit markets. Prefect reports, *Contrôle technique* eavesdropping, Bank of France economic assessments, and police and enforcement agency reports all show the spread and growing acceptance of the black market as necessary to economic survival, and legitimized by that necessity. It is reflected in the *Contrôle technique* adding new rubrics to its categories of opinion in 1944 to include 'Necessity to barter for food' and 'Necessity of the black market to ensure food needs'.[33] As shortages became acute in 1944, alternative markets did much more to help consumers survive than they had in 1941. This help was both needed and possible in part because of the diversion of goods from official markets.

No metrics measure system legitimacy directly. The number of control infractions tell us more about the enforcement effort than the actual number of violations. The rising number of enforcement personnel over time signals increasing problems; and the staff numbers were conditioned by the funds and personnel available, and the will to enforce controls. The CE complained repeatedly of insufficient staff, expressing their concern for the increasing violations and their conviction that rapid punishment could suppress black-market activity. But ration levels required consumers to find more food, and the public had declining interest in helping to enforce controls. The state retreat from enforcing the rules for petty infractions in 1942 and the leniency of the courts in judging economic crimes conceded this general need to evade controls. The black market became one of the practical means to meet essential needs. It also came to be seen as a way to strike back, not just indirectly at Germany, but directly at the Vichy regime, for its failure in its fundamental responsibility to protect the welfare of its citizens.

The CFLN in 1943–1944 and the provisional government after Liberation saw no alternative but to continue Vichy controls. A return to normal consumption was not possible in 1944–1945. But shortages for some goods became more serious after Liberation and the continuation of controls and legislation providing harsher punishments for black-market activity clashed with public expectations of improvement. The continuity in Vichy controls increased frustration. Resistance to controls increased. Consumers complained that they had been better off under the Germans, and that civil servants from the Vichy era deliberately sabotaged supplies. For Charles Rist in December 1945, 'This winter, after a year and a half of liberation, is as painful as all those that preceded it.' Food and clothing remained scarce, coal shortages and power cuts made keeping warm the greatest challenge. 'We are the slaves of an administration that has not changed any of its habits, including bad humor and inertia.'[34]

Escape from black-market dependency required increased output and the recovery of transport capacity; yet the rebuilding of the productive power necessary to both would take time. Resources and entrepreneurial

---

[33] AN F/7/14930, reports from Clermont-Ferrand. The black market for food needs rubric was added in May 1944; the reports had long had a rubric for 'Récriminations contre le marché noir'.

[34] Rist, *Season of Infamy*, 433 (9 Dec. 1945).

energy had to be persuaded back from illicit commerce to legal endeavours. The breadth of the parallel economy and the continued need for it after Liberation indicate its practical importance. And the scale of illicit activity posed a formidable challenge for postwar prosecution: after years of suffering and privation, liberated French citizens wanted justice, an economic purge to punish those who had worked for the Germans and 'the bad citizens who grew scandalously rich while the entire nation was impoverished'.[35]

But many of the biggest *trafiquants* escaped punishment, with confiscation committees unable to find sufficient evidence against them. Lower-level dealers, the *lampistes*, were sometimes punished, and sometimes protected as they continued their trade to satisfy demands that official markets could not. Local communities eager for retribution in 1944 resisted investigations and penalties when these threatened to close down the illicit traffic on which they had come to depend. The mild economic purge was a necessary compromise, accepting suspect wartime activity in order to restore productive power and return productive effort to legal paths. Inflation from 1944 to 1949 likewise compromised between monetary rigour and incentivization: it weakened the franc, it damaged government authority, but it provided necessary stimulus by raising prices. As output recovered, black market and official prices converged. Rationing could be lifted and black-market use declined. Inflation provided an easier path to recovery than the strict enforcement and system-based injustices of strict price control.

Vichy's Control Regime

The resistance to Vichy's economic controls can be placed in a longer-run perspective on the interdependence of states and markets and the politics of everyday consumption. In modern capitalism, the law defines legal markets and thus sets the 'black' markets outside the law. Markets do not exist without rules, some formal and some tacit, to establish property rights and regulate conduct, to make contracts enforceable, to provide security and guidelines for fairness and appropriate conduct in market exchange. The development of the state and its police in the seventeenth and eighteenth centuries took place with increasing attention to the circulation, quality, and accessibility of the goods necessary for survival of the state's population: 'To the early public economists – including the young Adam Smith – "police" was precisely what ensured the abundant

---

[35] SAEF B-0049475, regional Commissaire de la République to the prefects of the Nord and the Pas-de-Calais, 13 Dec. 1944.

provision of necessary foodstuffs and commodities.'[36] Market activity without regulation has potential to destroy security, wealth, social relations and government. States exert control through a system of laws and the policing capacity needed for law enforcement to protect 'every member of society' from injustice and oppression. As well as the law, there are socially defined boundaries for acceptable behaviour; markets are socially embedded.[37] State regulations are most effective when they align with societal standards and obtain broad compliance through the acceptance of the rules and self-regulation. State regulation and social standards then work together to restrain the impulses for rapacious action, theft and violence, and to identify and discipline violations.

In wartime, the increase in violence and the scarcity of goods can have catastrophic consequences. States increase economic regulation, especially to protect access to essential resources. The regulations need societal acceptance and willingness to respect the new restrictions. This in turn requires belief that the changes are necessary and temporary to deal with war's impact, that they will benefit society and the economy at large and work to benefit most individuals (in restricting some to protect all).

The power of market capitalism lies in its capacity for dynamic response to challenges and opportunities, including the opportunities for profit. State regulation and market freedoms exist with ever-present tensions between the regulation necessary to protect property, players and the market, and the will of the players to work within or to escape regulation.[38] Liberal market economies function with shared belief that players will respect the rules of exchange that protect property and social welfare, and will therefore regulate their own and each other's behaviour.

The Vichy regulatory regime was a product of improvisation, based on traditional concerns for the stability and strength of the franc and the dangers of inflation. To the pressures of war and occupation present elsewhere in Europe, French experience added the complication of a French government administering controls that served German interests. This added a conflict over the legitimacy of the Vichy state and its

---

[36] Bernard E. Harcourt, *The Illusion of Free Markets: Punishment and the Myth of Natural Order* (Cambridge, MA: Harvard University Press, 2011), 20.

[37] The classic account of markets as socially embedded and their destructive power without regulation is Karl Polanyi, *The Great Transformation: The Political and Economic Origins of Our Time* (Boston: Beacon Press, 2001 [1944]). Adam Smith, writing to promote the development of 'commercial society' in the 1770s, recognized that the liberty of individuals in society depends upon an impartial administration of justice to protect property and rights; *The Wealth of Nations* (1776), Book V, chapter 1.

[38] Again, Allan H. Meltzer's second law of regulation: 'Regulations are static. Markets are dynamic.' Meltzer, *Why Capitalism?*, 9, quoted in Chapter 3, with the reminder that market behaviour, not just regulation, is the product of human volition.

control system to the stress of increased regulation in a period of economic and political crisis. Vichy tried to police increased controls in a population and marketplace that was accustomed to political and economic liberty. The control regime rapidly lost legitimacy in 1941, despite the strong initial public support for equity in sharing necessary sacrifice.

After Liberation, trapped by the circumstances of deprivation and public defiance of the controls inherited from Vichy, the provisional government saw no alternative but to continue Vichy policies, unable to establish a new legitimacy for the unpopular control regime. The scale and persistence of black-market activity in the years of democratic government following authoritarian control show the continuity in the tensions between state regulation and market dynamism. From these tensions, four aspects of French experience merit emphasis.

First, the powerful factor driving black-market growth was the demand for scarce goods, especially food, needed by everyone. The state effort to manage this demand with increased emphasis on price control to prevent inflation proved inept, targeting the symptoms. In official markets, the state rationed and fixed prices for essential consumer goods. The quantities of goods delivered fell, and producers and distributors increasingly redirected their efforts to meet consumer demand in 'alternative' markets. Vichy could not control the demand by German purchasers or the speculative actions by producers and intermediaries. Black-market activity by most consumers was for essential goods, with the bargaining and allocation by price making access to scarce goods possible.

Second, the state focus on fixing prices deadened the signals essential to market regulation of supply and demand by price. Productive effort in agriculture, industry and commerce sought paths where it would obtain at least an adequate (and for some, an extraordinary) return. The market's ability to foster innovation and encourage supply of scarce goods relies on incentives. Motivations other than profit play a part, but they rely on financial feasibility.

State pricing policy damaged that capacity to encourage production and bring the output to market. The problem-solving power migrated to black markets for greater financial reward, as well as to satisfy family and community needs and political and patriotic objectives. Profit played its strongest role in the traffic to satisfy German demand and to exploit misery. But the black market gained its breadth, earned toleration, and was valued for its capacity to supply families and communities and to deliver needed goods to various French purchasers. Farmers and manufacturers made their production choices in considering whether they would draw some profit or at least avoid losses. This was particularly evident in agriculture (Chapter 4), where low prices discouraged the production and marketing of some essential foods, caused output to be withheld from legal markets, and fostered alternative practices ranging from family parcels and direct sales to intentional production for the black market. State measures needed to provide some incentive other than price to direct productive effort to desired ends when fixed prices reduced or eliminated profit. But the easiest means to do so, price flexibility and subsidies to sustain output and reduce consumer cost, were impossible in the face of German insistence on low prices and extraction of excessive occupation costs.

Third, once beyond the bounds of market rules, irresponsible behaviour had few constraints. The black market served two broad categories of demand outside official markets: that for essentials, which was widespread and encountered some community controls; and that of the privileged for any goods they wanted (especially the Germans and those in positions of power). Both categories offered opportunities for profit, but with far greater profit in serving the latter. Those exploiting the shortages included the Germans using black markets and their French imitators who collaborated in the worst abuses – like the Bonny-Lafont gang of the rue Lauriston. This black market thrived on power and privilege. For the Germans and their collaborators, their economic power was constrained neither by formal rules nor by community standards. They worked outside of, and were not responsible to, the communities they exploited. The secondary French players allowed to share in this power then joined in the abuse; black market activities by the French Gestapo and suppliers to the Bureau Otto are good examples, as are sensational black-market profiteers like Joseph Joinovici and Michel Szkolnikoff. There was a clear compatibility in the lawlessness of Nazi behaviour and the French use of the black market, including by collaborators, with contempt for Vichy and its state controls.

Fourth, the black market functioned in hiding violations from controllers. The transactions to obtain critical supplies for producers and consumers and to exploit sales opportunities relied on concealment from official supervision, and this opened the way to greater opportunities for exploitation and abuse. Market efficiency and public trust need knowledge and transparency: knowledge of the quantities of goods available, their quality and their prices, allows the rational calculation of costs and appropriate prices. This transparency makes competition more effective, rewarding efficient production and distribution. Purchasers can judge and respond to the prices and the quality of goods they seek, and their purchasing decisions can serve to discipline conduct. Policing is essential to monitor this self-regulating action in markets, and to punish offenders on the margins, reinforcing respect for honesty and fairness in the market.

Shortages not only reduce buyers' choice and disciplinary power; they also encourage concealment of goods and terms of exchange, increasing the traffic in the shadows as official markets lose goods to illicit commerce. Inept controls exaggerate the retreat from transparency and increase both the need for policing and the difficulties of doing so. As we have seen (especially in Chapter 3), Vichy controllers spent much of their time trying to enforce the new requirements for 'legibility'. The violations of pricing, ticketing and receipt rules were easier to find and punish than the transactions those violations concealed.

The restoration of democratic government allowed greater freedom for evasion of regulations and for public protest, and the state faced higher demands for transparency.[39] Coercive power could increase compliance; its retreat facilitated evasion. So, too, did the declining legitimacy of the control regime. Expectations for greater honesty and openness set higher standards for state conduct and for the use of controls. In adopting Vichy's controls and grappling with the Vichy legacy of postwar financial and monetary crises, republican officialdom needed an honesty in state conduct and an acceptance of public sacrifice that it could not obtain.

The public expected rapid improvement after Liberation: in real wages, lower prices, and a greater supply of goods. When black-market activity declined, it did so thanks in part to the unwanted inflation that raised official prices, which drew both goods and purchasers back to legal markets (Chapter 8). Inflation proved to be the line of less resistance. Postwar policies allowed wage and price increases that in turn brought the convergence of official and black-market prices. This was the less-coercive path for drawing production back into official markets.

The sectoral analysis of black-market use in *Marché noir* highlights the dynamics, the logic, the pervasiveness, and the vital importance of black markets in France. The French control regime lost legitimacy because the economic controls implemented by Vichy quickly demonstrated that they worked in German interests, demanded extra effort from producers, and delivered no significant return. Consumers, unable to depend on official markets for sufficient food, clothing and heat, sought expedients by means that bent, broke or circumvented rules that otherwise would confine them to inadequate supplies of essential goods. Consumer behaviours changed to locate essential goods and resist the restrictions that served particular interests, especially those of the Germans and their collaborators. Their alternative strategies developed to survive shortages had a political content in resisting Vichy regulations at the individual

---

[39] Stefanos Geroulanos, *Transparency in Postwar France: A Critical History of the Present* (Stanford, CA: Stanford University Press, 2017).

level. An analyst of food supply and the black market in 1943 commented on the way black market use spread from the wealthy and extended its reach to ordinary consumers, as a 'democratization of the black market'. The *petits consommateurs* realized that if they did not buy on the black market, the scarce goods would all go to the rich. The honest producers and consumers who tried to stay within the rules 'ended up looking like dupes and resigned themselves in turn to participating in the *débrouillage général* (finding their own solutions, *le système D*)'.[40]

The black market in wartime France demonstrated the failure of the Vichy regime in its fundamental governing role to protect the welfare of its citizens. The rejection of Vichy's political and economic programs became increasingly persuasive as support for popular and democratic reforms. Vichy's economic failures were evident in the queues outside shops and market stalls, in the demonstrations of housewives demanding food for their children, and in the use of the adjective 'national' for the *ersatz* goods that replaced valued commodities with inferior products.[41] They were evident in the black market's exceptional growth and breadth, and its increasing acceptance by ordinary citizens, producers and consumers alike, as a necessary avenue of access to essential goods. Vichy's failures were obvious, too, in the black market's having been developed in part by the Germans and their collaborators, who generated the worst abuses and the most vicious exploitation in Vichy's economy of penury.

---

[40] AN 72AJ/563, 'Rapport général sur l'agriculture et le ravitaillement en France', Jan. 1943.

[41] The use of 'national' persisted after Liberation, 'to qualify anything that was of poor quality, was not what it claimed to be'. Richard Cobb, *French and Germans, Germans and French: A Personal Interpretation of France under Two Occupations 1914–1918/1940–1944* (Hanover, NH: University Press of New England, 1983), 132.

Select Bibliography

Contemporary Works

Achard, Paul. *La queue: Ce qui s'y disait, ce qu'on y pensait.* Paris: Éditions de la Belle Fontaine, 1945.

Aldebert, Bernard et al. *Devant le marché noir.* Bellegarde: SADAG, 1943.

Arnoult, Pierre. *Les finances de la France sous l'Occupation allemande (1940–1944).* Paris: Presses universitaires de la France, 1951.

Audiat, Pierre. *Paris pendant la guerre (juin 1940-août 1944).* Paris: Hachette, 1946.

Baudin, Louis and Paulette. *La consommation dirigée en France en matière de l'alimentation.* Paris: Librairie générale de droit et de jurisprudence, 1942.

Baudin, Louis. *Esquisse de l'économie française sous l'Occupation allemande.* Paris: Librairie de Médicis, 1945.

Brauner, Alfred. *Ces enfants ont vécu la guerre …* Paris: Les Éditions sociales françaises, 1946.

Cassou, Jean. *La mémoire courte.* Paris: Éditions de minuit, 1953.

Chauveneau, Jules, Mahuzier, Pierre and Carton, Edmond-Jean, *La confiscation des profits illicites.* Paris: Rousseau et Cie, 1947.

Chelmicki, Teodozjusz. *Le marché noir.* Louvain: Institut de recherches économiques et sociales, 1950.

Cluseau, Max. *Taxation, rationnement et science économique: Étude théorique et pratique des prix réglementés et d'une économie distributive.* Paris: Librairie Médicis, 1943.

Contrôle économique (4 issues published by the Ministry of Finance for staff of the Contrôle économique, 1943–1946).

David, Michel. *Le marché noir.* Paris: SPID, 1945.

Debû-Bridel, Jacques. *Histoire du marché noir, 1939–1947.* Paris: La Jeune Parque, 1947.

De Felice, Pierre. *La confiscation des profits illicites.* Paris: CHAIX, 1945.

Dubergé, Jean. *Le contrôle des prix en France au regard de la théorie économique.* Paris: Librairie générale de droit et de jurisprudence, 1947.

Farge, Yves. *Le pain de la corruption.* Paris: Éditions du chêne, 1947.

Floriot, R. and Champigny, D. *La hausse illicite et le marché noir: toute la jurisprudence.* Paris: Presses universitaires de France, 1943.

Franck, Louis. *French Price Control from Blum to Pétain.* Washington, DC: The Brookings Institution, 1942.

Galbraith, John Kenneth. *A Theory of Price Control: The Classic Account.* Cambridge, MA: Harvard University Press, 1952.

INSEE. *Enquêtes diverses sur les prix et les consommations de 1941 à 1944.* Paris: Imprimerie nationale, 1947.

Jeantet, Fernand-Charles. *Le code des prix et les principes fondamentaux du droit classique.* Paris: Montchrestien, 1943.

Lebrun, Rémi. *La police des prix: ses pouvoirs de recherche et de constatation du délit de hausse illicite.* Paris: Librairie Dalloz, 1944.

Magnaval, Pierre. *Code des prix et du ravitaillement. Le marché noir. Toute la jurisprudence.* Paris: Presses universitaires de France,1944.

Matthews, Ronald. *The Death of the Fourth Republic.* London: Eyre and Spottiswoode, 1954.

Mazard, Jean. *Les infractions au rationnement.* Paris: Sirey, 1943.

Mendès France, Pierre. *Œuvres complètes, vol. II Une politique de l'économie 1943–1954.* Paris: Gallimard, 1985.

Mérigot, Jean-Guy. *Essai sur les comités d'organisation professionnelle.* Paris: Librairie générale de droit et de jurisprudence, 1943.

Moreau-Néret, Olivier. *Le contrôle des prix en France.* Paris: Sirey, 1941.

Pickles, Dorothy. *France between the Republics.* London: Love and Malcomson Ltd., 1946.

Pétain, Philippe. *Discours aux Français, 17 juin 1940 – 20 août 1944,* ed. Jean-Claude Barbas. Paris: Albin Michel, 1989.

Rueff, Jacques. 'The Case for the Free Market', *Foreign Affairs* (Spring 1948).

Véran, Jules. *En faisant la queue: ou les spectacles du jour.* Paris: Librairie Aristide Quillet, 1942.

Diaries, Letters and Memoirs

Aubrac, Raymond. *Où la mémoire s'attarde.* Paris: Odile Jacob, 1996.

Auroy, Berthe. *Jours de guerre: Ma vie sous l'Occupation.* Paris: Bayard, 2008.

Barthélemy, Joseph. *Ministre de la Justice, Vichy 1941–1943: Mémoires.* Paris: Pygmalion, 1989.

Beauvoir, Simone de. *The Prime of Life,* trans. by Peter Green. Middlesex: Penguin Books, 1965.

Böll, Heinrich. *Briefe aus dem Krieg 1939–1945,* 2 vols. Cologne: Verlag Kipnheuer und Witsch, 2001.

Bood, Micheline. *Les années doubles: Journal d'une lycéenne sous l'Occupation.* Paris: Robert Laffont, 1974.

Braibant, Charles. *La guerre à Paris (8 Nov. – 27 Août 1944).* Paris: Corrêa, 1945.

Colette. *Lettres aux petites fermières,* ed. by Marie-Thérèse Colléaux-Chaurang. Paris: Le Castor Astral, 1992.

Culmann, Henri. *A Paris sous Vichy: Témoignage et souvenirs.* Paris: Les Éditions la Bruyère, 1985.

Debré, Michel. *Trois républiques pour une France: Mémoires.* Paris: Albin Michel, 1984.

Drouot, Henri. *Notes d'un Dijonnais pendant l'Occupation allemande, 1940–1944.* Dijon: Éditions universitaires de Dijon, 1998.

Dubois, Edmond. *Paris sans lumière, 1939–1945. Témoignages*. Lausanne: Librairie Payot, 1946.

Galbraith, John Kenneth. *A Life in Our Times: Memoirs*. New York: Houghton Mifflin, 1981.

Galtier-Boissière, Jean. *Mon journal pendant l'Occupation*. Paris: La Jeune Parque, 1944.

Gancel, Hippolyte. *Crime et résistance en Normandie*. Rennes: Éditions Ouest-France, 2008.

Grenadou, Ephraïm. *Grenadou, paysan français*. Paris: Éditions du Seuil, 1966.

Groult, Benoîte and Flora. *Journal à quatre mains*. Paris: Éditions Denoël, 1962; reprint 2002.

Guéhenno, Jean. *Journal des années noires, 1940–1944*. Paris: Gallimard, 1947, 2002.

Guéno, Jean-Pierre, ed. *Paroles de l'ombre: Lettres, carnets et récits des Français sous l'Occupation 1939–1945*. Paris: Librio, 2009.

Guerpel, Xavier de. *1939–1945. Une certaine vie de château au bocage Normand: Témoignage d'un agriculteur*. Condé-sur-Noireau: C. Corlet, 1973.

Guingouin, Georges. *Quatre ans de lutte sur le sol Limousin*. Paris: Hachette, 1974.

Jamet, Fabienne. *One Two Two*. Paris: O. Orban, 1975.

Jünger, Ernst. *Premier journal parisien, Journal II 1941–1943*. Paris: Christian Bourgeois, 1980.

Levy, Jean-Pierre. *Mémoires d'un franc-tireur: Itinéraire d'un résistant (1940–1944)*. Brussels: Éditions complexe, 1998.

Liebling, A. J. *A. J. Liebling: World War II Writings*. New York: Library of America, 2008.

Limouzin, René. *Le temps des J3: Une adolescence paysanne pendant la guerre de 1939–1945*. Paris: Éditions les monédières, 1983.

Linet, Roger. *1933–1943: La traversée de la tourmente*. Paris: Éditions Messidor, 1990.

London, Lise. *La mégère de la rue Daguerre: Souvenirs de Résistance*. Paris: Seuil, 1995.

Luneau, Aurélie, ed. *Je vous écris de France*. Paris: L'Iconoclaste, 2014.

Luneau, Aurélie, Guérout, Jeanne and Martens, Stefan, eds. *Comme un Allemand en France. Lettres inédites sous l'Occupation*. Paris: L'Iconoclaste, 2016.

Maspero, François. *Le sourire du chat*. Paris: Editions du Seuil, 1984.

Orieux, Jean. *Souvenirs de campagnes*. Paris: Flammarion, 1978.

Pierquin, Bernard. *Journal d'un étudiant parisien sous l'Occupation (1939–1945)*. Paris: Bernard Pierquin, 1983.

Rist, Charles. *Season of Infamy: A Diary of War and Occupation, 1939–1945*, trans. by Michele McKay Aynesworth. Bloomington: Indiana University Press, 2016.

Ruffin, Raymond. *Journal d'un J3*. Paris: Presses de la Cité, 1979.

Sadoul, Georges. *Journal de guerre*. Paris: Les Editeurs Français Réunis, 1977.

Sauvy, Alfred. *De Paul Reynaud à Charles de Gaulle*. Tournai, Casterman, 1972.

Schroeder, Liliane. *Journal d'Occupation. Paris, 1940–1944. Chronique au jour le jour d'une époque oubliée*. Paris: François-Xavier de Guibert, 2000.

Simenon, Georges. *Intimate Memoirs: Including Marie-Jo's Book*, trans. by Harold
    J. Salemson. San Diego, CA: Harcourt, Brace, Jovanovich, 1984.
Teissier du Cros, Janet. *Divided Loyalties: A Scotswoman in Occupied France.*
    London: Hamish Hamilton, 1962; reprint Canongate Classics, 1992.
Thomas, Édith. *Pages de journal 1939–1944, suivies de journal intime de Monsieur
    Célestin Costedet.* Paris: Éditions Viviane Hamy, 1995.
    Le temoin compromis. Paris: Éditions Viviane Hamy, 1995, 2018.
Toesca, Maurice. *Cinq ans de patience (1939–1945).* Paris: Éditions Émile-Paul,
    1975.
Toklas, Alice B. *The Alice B. Toklas Cookbook.* New York: Harper and Brothers,
    1954.
Trouillé, Pierre. *Journal d'un préfet pendant l'Occupation.* Paris: Gallimard, 1964.
Vallotton, Gritou and Annie. *C'était au jour le jour. Carnets (1939–1944).* Paris:
    Payot et Rivages, 1995.
Werth, Léon. *33 jours.* Paris: Éditions Viviane Hamy, 1992.
    Déposition, Journal 1940–1944. Paris: Éditions Viviane Hamy, 1992.
Woolton, Frederick James Marquis. *The Memoirs of the Rt. Hon. Earl of Woolton.*
    London: Cassell, 1949.

Fiction and Theatre

Aymé, Marcel. *Le passé-muraille.* Paris: Gallimard, 1943.
    Le chemin des écoliers. Paris: Gallimard, 1946.
    Le vin de Paris. Paris: Gallimard, 1947.
    Uranus. Paris: Gallimard, 1948.
Bory, Jean-Louis. *Mon village à l'heure allemande.* Paris: Flammarion, 1945.
Calaferte, Louis. *C'est la guerre*, trans. by Austryn Wainhouse. Evanston, IL: The
    Marlboro Press/Northwestern University Press, 1999.
Dutourd, Jean. *Au bon beurre: Scènes de la vie sous l'Occupation.* Paris: Gallimard,
    1952; Folio, 1972.
Ferdinand, Roger. *J3: Comédie en quatre actes.* Paris: La Belle Fontaine, 1947.
Gary, Romain. *Le grand vestiaire.* Paris: Gallimard, 1948.
Leduc, Violette. *La bâtarde.* Paris: Gallimard, 1964.
Meckert, Jean. *Nous avons les mains rouges.* Paris: Gallimard, 2020 [1947].
Triolet, Elsa. *A Fine of Two Hundred Francs.* New York: Penguin Books, 1986
    [Éditions Denoël, 1945].

Secondary Literature

France

Abramovici, Pierre. *Szkolnikoff: Le plus grand trafiquant de l'Occupation.* Paris:
    Nouveau monde, 2014.
Alary, Eric. *L'histoire des paysans français.* Paris: Perrin, 2016.
Alexander, Martin S. 'War and Its Bestiality: Animals and Their Fate during the
    Fighting in France, 1940', *Rural History*, 25(1) (2014): 101–124.

Amouroux, Henri. *La vie des français sous l'Occupation*. Paris: Fayard, 1961.

La grande histoire des français sous l'Occupation, 10 vols. Paris: Fayard, 1976–1993.

Arnaud, Patrice. *Les STO: Histoire des Français requis en Allemagne nazie 1942–1945*. Paris: CNRS Éditions, 2010.

Arnoult, Pierre. 'Comment, pour acheter notre économie, les allemands prirent nos finances (1940–1944)', *Cahiers d'Histoire de la Guerre*, 4 (1950): 1–28.

Aubusson de Cavarlay, Bruno, Huré, Marie-Sylvie and Pottier, Marie-Lys, 'La justice pénale en France: Résultats statistiques (1934–1954)', *Les cahiers de l'IHTP*, 23 (1993): 7–148.

Auda, Grégory. *Les belles années du 'milieu' 1940–1944: Le grand banditisme dans la machine répressive allemande en France*. Paris: Éditions Michalon, 2002.

Avakoumovitch, Ivan. 'Les manifestations des femmes', *Cahiers d'Histoire de l'Institut de Recherches Marxistes*, 45 (1991): 5–54.

Azéma, Jean-Pierre and Bédarida, François, eds. *Vichy et les Français*. Paris: Fayard, 1992.

La France des années noires, 2 vols. Paris: Seuil, 1993.

Barjot, Dominique. 'L'industrie française des travaux publics (1940–1945)', *Histoire, Économie et Société*, 11(3) (1992): 415–436.

Barral, Pierre. *Les agrariens de Méline à Pisani*. Paris: A. Colin, 1968.

'Agriculture and Food Supply in France', in *Agriculture and Food Supply in the Second World War*, ed. by Bernd Martin and Alan S. Milward. Ostfildern: Scripta Mercaturae Verlag, 1985, 89–102.

Baruch, Marc O. *Servir l'État français: L'administration en France de 1940 à 1944*. Paris: Fayard, 1997.

Baruch, Marc Olivier and Duclert, Vincent, eds. *Serviteurs de l'État: Une histoire politique de l'administration française, 1875–1945*. Paris: Éditions de la Découverte, 2000.

Baruch, Marc Olivier, ed. *Une poignée de misérables*. Paris: Fayard, 2003.

Bédarida, Renée. *Les catholiques dans la guerre, 1939–1945: Entre Vichy et la Résistance*. Paris: Hachette, 1998.

Belser, Christophe. *La collaboration en Loire-Inférieure 1940–1944*, vol. 1, *Les années noires*, vol. 2, *Intelligence avec l'ennemi*. La Crèche: Geste éditions, 2005.

Beltran, A., Frank, R., and Rousso, H., eds. *La vie des entreprises sous l'Occupation*. Paris: Belin, 1994.

Berger, Suzanne. *Peasants against Politics: Rural Organization in Brittany 1911–1967*. Cambridge, MA: Harvard University Press, 1972.

Bergère, Marc. *Une société en épuration: Épuration vécue et perçue en Maine-et-Loire. De la Libération au début des années 50*. Rennes: Presses universitaires de Rennes, 2004.

ed. *L'épuration économique en France à la Libération*. Rennes: Presses universitaires de Rennes, 2008.

Berlière, Jean-Marc. *Polices des temps noirs: France 1939–1945*. Paris: Perrin, 2018.

Bertin, Célia. *Femmes sous l'Occupation*. Paris: Stock, 1993.

Bloch-Lainé, François and Bouvier, Jean. *La France restaurée 1944–1954: Dialogue sur les choix d'une modernisation*. Paris: Fayard, 1986.

Bloch-Lainé, François and Gruson, Claude. *Hauts fonctionnaires sous l'Occupation*. Paris: Éditions Odile Jacob, 1996.

Boivin, Michel. *Les Manchois dans la tourmente de la Seconde Guerre mondiale, 1939–1945*, 6 vols. Marigny: Éditions Eurocibles, 2004.

La vie quotidienne des Manchois sous l'Occupation 1940–1944. Marigny: Éditions Eurocibles, 2014.

Boldorf Marcel and Schermer, Jonas. 'France's Occupation Costs and the War in the East: The Contribution to the German War Economy, 1940–4', *Journal of Contemporary History*, 47(2) (2012): 291–316.

Boudard, Alphonse. *L'étrange Monsieur Joseph*. Paris: Robert Laffont, 1998.

Boudot, François. 'Aspects économiques de l'Occupation allemande en France', *Revue d'Histoire de la Deuxième Guerre Mondiale*, 54 (1964): 41–62.

Bourderon, Roger. *Le PCF à l'épreuve de la guerre, 1940–1943: De la guerre impérialiste à la lutte armée* Paris: Syllepse, 2012.

Boussard, Isabel. *Vichy et la Corporation paysanne*. Paris: Presses de la foundation nationale des sciences politique, 1980.

Boutet, Gérard. *Ils étaient de leur village . . .* vol. 3, *Ils ont vécu l'Occupation*. Paris: Jean-Cyrille Godefroy, 1990.

Boyer, Patricia. 'L'épuration et ses représentations en Languedoc et Roussillon (1944–1945)', *Vingtième Siècle*, 68 (2000): 17–28.

Broch, Ludivine. *Ordinary Workers, Vichy and the Holocaust: French Railwaymen and the Second World War*. Cambridge: Cambridge University Press, 2016.

Bueltzingsloewen, Isabelle von, ed. *'Morts d'inanition': Famine et exclusions en France sous l'Occupation*. Rennes: Presses universitaires de Rennes, 2005.

L'hécatombe des fous: La famine dans les hôpitaux psychiatriques français sous l'Occupation. Paris: Flammarion, 2007.

Burrin, Philippe. *France under the Germans: Collaboration and Compromise*, trans. by J. Lloyd. New York: New Press, 1995.

Capdevila, Luc. *Les Bretons au lendemain de l'Occupation: Imaginaires et comportements d'une sortie de guerre (1944/1945)*. Rennes: Presses universitaires de Rennes, 1999.

Cazals, Claude. *La gendarmerie sous l'Occupation*. Paris: Éditions de la Musse, 1994.

Cépède, Michel. *Agriculture et alimentation en France durant la IIe Guerre mondiale*. Paris: Éditions M.-Th. Génin, 1961.

Chapman, Herrick. *France's Long Reconstruction: In Search of the Modern Republic*. Cambridge, MA: Harvard University Press, 2018.

Chatriot, Alain. 'Syndicalismes et corporatisme agricole en France', in *Le corporatisme dans l'aire francophone au XXe siècle*, ed. by Olivier Dard. Berne: Peter Lang, 2011, 29–48.

Pierre Mendès France: Pour une République moderne. Paris: Armand Colin, 2015.

'L'ONIC ou la régulation étatique et professionnelle d'un marché politique sensible (1940–1953)', in *Histoire des modernisations agricoles au XXe siècle*, ed. by Margot Lyautey, Léna Humbert and Christophe Bonneuil. Rennes: Presses universitaires de Rennes, 2021, 137–151.

Chatriot, Alain, Chessel, Marie-Emmanuel and Hilton, Matthew, eds. *Au nom du consommateur: Consommation et politique en Europe et aux États-Unis au XXe siècle*. Paris: La Découverte, 2004.

Chélini, Michel-Pierre. *Inflation, État et opinion en France de 1944 à 1952*. Paris: CHEFF, 1998.

Chessel, Marie-Emmanuelle. *Histoire de la consommation*. Paris: La Découverte, 2012.

Chevandier, Christian and Daumas, Jean-Claude, eds. *Travailler dans les entreprises sous l'Occupation*. Besançon: Presses universitaires de Franche-Comté, 2007.

Cobb, Richard. *French and Germans, Germans and French: A Personal Interpretation of France under Two Occupations, 1914–1918/1940–1944*. Hanover, NH: University Press of New England, 1983.

Dard, Olivier, Daumas, Jean-Claude and Marcot, François, eds. *L'Occupation, l'État français et les entreprises*. Paris: ADHE, 2000.

Daumas, Jean-Claude. *La révolution matérielle: Une histoire de la consommation, France XIXe–XXIe siècle*. Paris: Flammarion, 2018.

Delouvrier, Paul and Nathan, Roger. *Politique économique de la France*. Paris: Institute d'études politiques, 1958.

Delporte, Christian. *Les crayons de la propaganda*. Paris: CNRS Éditions, 1993.

Desquesnes, Rémy. 'L'Organisation Todt en France (1940–1944)', *Histoire, Économie et Société*, 11(3) (1992): 535–550.

Diamond, Hanna. *Women and the Second World War in France, 1939–1948: Choices and Constraints*. Harlow: Pearson Education, 1999.

Delarue, Jacques. *Trafics et crimes sous L'Occupation*. Paris: Fayard, 1968.

Douzou, Laurent. 'A Perilous History: A Historiographical Essay on the French Resistance', *Contemporary European History*, 28(1) (2019): 96–106.

Drake, David. *Paris at War 1939–1944*. Cambridge, MA: The Belknap Press of Harvard University Press, 2015.

Dreyfus, Jean-Marc. *Pillages sur ordonnances: Aryanisation et restitution des banques en France 1940–1953*. Paris: Fayard, 2003.

Dumez, Hervé and Jeunemaitre, Alain. *Diriger l'économie: L'État et les prix en France (1936–1986)*. Paris: L'Harmattan, 1989.

Durand, Sébastien. 'Les entreprises françaises face aux occupants (1940–1944): Entre collaboration, opportunisme et "nécessité de vivre"', *French Politics, Culture and Society*, 37(2) (2019): 1–26.

Dutton, Paul V. *Origins of the Welfare State: The Struggle for Social Reform in France 1914–1947*. Cambridge: Cambridge University Press, 2002.

Faure, Christian. *Le projet culturel de Vichy: Folklore et révolution nationale, 1940–1944*. Lyon: Presses universitaires de Lyon, 1989.

Fayolle, Sandra. 'L'Union des femmes françaises et les sentiments supposés féminins', in *Émotions ... Mobilisation!* ed. by Christophe Traïni. Paris: Presses de la FNSP, 2009.

Feuerhahn, Nelly. *Traits d'impertinence: Histoire et chefs-d'œuvre du dessin d'humour de 1914 à nos jours*. Paris: Bibliothèque publique d'information – Centre Georges Pompidou et Somogy éditions d'art, 1993.

Fishman, Sarah. *We Will Wait; Wives of French Prisoners of War, 1940–1945*. New Haven, CT: Yale University Press, 1991.

The Battle for Children: World War II, Youth Crime, and Juvenile Justice in Twentieth-Century France. Cambridge, MA: Harvard University Press, 2002.

Fogg, Shannon L. 'Denunciations, Community Outsiders, and Material Shortages in Vichy France', *Proceedings of the Western Society for French History*, 31 (2003): 271–289.

The Politics of Everyday Life in Vichy France: Foreigners, Undesirables, and Strangers. New York: Cambridge University Press, 2009.

Geroulanos, Stefanos. *Transparency in Postwar France: A Critical History of the Present*. Stanford, CA: Stanford University Press, 2017.

Gildea, Robert. *Marianne in Chains: In Search of the German Occupation of France 1940–1945*. London: Macmillan, 2002.

Goldschmidt, André. *L'Affaire Joinovici: collaborateur, resistant . . . et bouc émissaire*. Paris: Éditions Privat, 2002.

Gordon, Bertram M. *War Tourism: Second World War France from Defeat and Occupation to the Creation of Heritage*. Ithaca, NY: Cornell University Press, 2018.

Grenard, Fabrice. 'Les implications politiques du ravitaillement en France sous l'Occupation', *Vingtième Siècle*, 94 (2007): 199–215.

La France du marché noir (1940–1949). Paris: Payot, 2008.

'L'administration du contrôle économique en France, 1940–1950', *Revue d'Histoire Moderne et Contemporaine*, 57(2) (2010): 132–158.

'La soulte, une pratique généralisée pour contourner le blocage des prix', in *Les entreprises de biens de consommation sous l'Occupation*, ed. by Sabine Effosse, Marc de Ferrière le Vayer and Hervé Joly. Tours: Presses universitaires François-Rabelais de Tours, 2010, 29–43.

Maquis noir et faux maquis 1943–1947. Paris: Vendémiaire, 2011.

'La dénonciation dans la répression du marché noir', in *La Délation dans la France des années noires*, ed. by Laurent Joly. Paris: Perrin, 2012, 139–161.

Les scandales du ravitaillement: Détournements, corruption, affaires étouffées en France, de l'Occupation à la guerre froide. Paris: Payot, 2012.

Grenard, Fabrice, Le Bot, Florent and Perrin, Cédric. *Histoire économique de Vichy: L'État, les hommes, les entreprises*. Paris: Perrin, 2017.

Gueslin, André, ed. *Les hommes du pneu: Les ouvriers Michelin à Clermont-Ferrand de 1940 à 1980*. Paris: Éditions de l'atelier/Les éditions ouvrières, 1999.

Guillon, Jean-Marie. 'Le retour des "émotions populaires": manifestations des ménagères en 1942', in *Mélanges Michel Vovelle, volume aixois: Sociétés, mentalités, cultures. France (XVe–XXe siècles)*. Aix-en-Provence: Publications de l'université de Provence, 1999.

'Les manifestations des ménagères: Protestation populaire et résistance féminine spécifique', in *Les femmes dans la Résistance en France*, ed. by Mechtild Gilzmer, Christine Levisse-Touzé and Stefan Martens. Paris: Tallandier, 2003.

Halimi, André. *Ce qui a fait rire les Français sous l'Occupation*. Paris: J. C. Lattès, 1979.

La délation sous l'Occupation. Paris: Alain Moreau, 1983.

Hesse, Philippe-Jean and Ménard, Olivier. 'Contrôle des prix et rationnement: l'action du gouvernement de Vichy en matière de régulation de l'offre et de la demande', in *Le droit sous Vichy*, ed. by Bernard Durand, Jean-Pierre Le Crom and Alessandro Somma. Frankfurt am Main: Vittorio Klostermann, 2006, 165–208.

Hoffmann, Stanley. 'Collaborationism in France during World War II', *Journal of Modern History*, 40(3) (1968): 375–395.

Husson, Jean-Pierre. *La Marne et les Marnais à l'épreuve de la Seconde Guerre Mondiale* 2 vols. Reims: Presses universitaires de Reims, 1995.

Jäckel, Eberhard. *La France dans l'Europe de Hitler*. Paris: Fayard, 1968.

Jansiti, Carlo. *Violette Leduc*. Paris: Grasset, 2013.

Joly, Hervé, ed., *Les comités d'organisation et l'économie dirigée du régime de Vichy*. Caen: Centre de recherche d'histoire quantitative, 2004.

    ed., *Faire l'histoire des entreprises sous l'Occupation: Les acteurs économiques et leurs archives*. Paris, 2004.

    ed., *L'économie de la zone non occupée 1940–1942*. Paris: Comité des travaux historiques et scientifiques, 2007.

Joly, Laurent, ed. *La délation dans la France des années noires*. Paris: Perrin, 2012

Kaplan, Steven L. *The Bakers of Paris and the Bread Question, 1700–1775*. Durham, NC: Duke University Press, 1996.

    Le pain maudit: Retour sur la France des années oubliées 1945–1958. Paris: Fayard, 2008.

Kedward, H. R. *In Search of the Maquis: Rural Resistance in Southern France 1942–1944*. Oxford: The Clarendon Press, 1993.

Koreman, Megan. 'The Collaborator's Penance: The Local Purge, 1944-5', *Contemporary European History*, 6(2) (1997): 177–192.

    The Expectation of Justice: France, 1944–1946. Durham, NC: Duke University Press, 1999.

Kramer, S. P. 'La crise économique de la Libération', *Revue d'Histoire de la Seconde Guerre Mondiale*, 111 (1978): 25–44.

Kuisel, Richard F. *Capitalism and the State in Modern France: Renovation and Economic Management in the Twentieth Century*. Cambridge: Cambridge University Press, 1981.

Laborie, Pierre. *Le chagrin et le venin: La France sous l'Occupation, mémoire et idées reçues*. Paris: Bayard, 2011.

Lacroix-Riz, Annie. *Industriels et banquiers sous l'Occupation: La collaboration économique avec le Reich et Vichy*. Paris: Armand Colin, 1999.

Le Bot, Florent. *La fabrique réactionnaire: Antisémitisme, spoliations et corporatisme dans le cuir (1930–1950)*. Paris: Presses de la FNSP, 2007.

Lebovics, Eugene. *True France: The Wars over Cultural Identity, 1900–1945*. Ithaca, NY: Cornell University Press, 1992.

Lecouturier, Yves. *Le marché noir en Normandie 1939–1945*. Rennes: Éditions Ouest-France, 2010.

Lefébure, Antoine. *Les conversations secrètes des Français sous l'Occupation*. Paris: Plon, 1993.

Leleu, J. L., Passera, F, Wuellien, J. and Daeffler, M., eds. *La France pendant la Seconde Guerre mondiale: Atlas historique.* Paris: Fayard, 2010.

Leteux, Sylvain. 'Le commerce de viande à Paris: qui tire profite de la situation?' in *Les entreprises de biens de consommation sous l'Occupation,* ed. by Sabine Efosse, Marc de Ferrière le Vayer and Hervé Joly. Tours: Presses universitaires François-Rabelais, 2010, 81–98.

'Débats et tâtonnements dans l'organisation du marché de la viande en France (1931–1953)', in *Organiser les marchés agricoles: Le temps des fondateurs. Des années 1930 aux années 1950,* ed. by Alain Chatriot, Edgar Leblanc and Édouard Lynch. Paris: Armand Colin, 2012, 127–146.

Lottman, Herbert R. *The Purge: The Purification of French Collaborators after World War II.* New York: William Morrow and Company, 1986.

Lucand, Christophe. *Le pinard des Poilus: Une histoire du vin durant la Grande Guerre (1914–1918).* Dijon: Éditions universitaires de Dijon, 2015.

Le vin et la guerre: Comment les nazis ont fait main basse sur le vignoble français. Paris: Armand Colin, 2017.

Malon, Claude. *Occupation, épuration, reconstruction: Le monde de l'entreprise au Havre (1940–1950).* Mont-Saint-Aignan: Presses universitaires de Rouen et du Havre, 2013.

Margairaz, Michel. *L'État, les finances et l'économie (1932–1952): l'Histoire d'une conversion.* Paris: CHEFF, 1991.

ed. *Banques, banque de France et Seconde Guerre mondiale.* Paris: Albin Michel, 2002.

Margairaz, Michel and Rousso, Henry. 'Vichy, la guerre et les entreprises', *Histoire, Économie et Société,* 11(3) (1992): 337–367.

Marquis, Jean-Claude. *Les camps cigarette: Les Américains en Haute Normandie à la Libération.* Rouen: Médianes, 1994.

Marrus, Michael R. and Paxton, Robert O. *Vichy France and the Jews,* 2nd ed. Stanford, CA: Stanford University Press, 2019.

Mehlman, Jeffrey. 'The Joinovici Affair: The Stavisky of the Fourth Republic', *French Politics, Culture and Society,* 32(1) (2014): 101–110.

Mencherini, Robert. *La Libération et les entreprises sous gestion ouvrière: Marseille 1944–1948.* Paris: L'Harmattan, 1994.

Michel, Henri. *Paris allemand.* Paris: Albin Michel, 1981.

Milward, Alan S. *The New Order and the French Economy.* Oxford: Clarendon Press, 1970.

Moulin, Annie. *Les paysans dans la société française: de la Révolution à nos jours.* Paris: Seuil, 1998.

Mouré, Kenneth. 'The *faux policier* in Occupied Paris', *Journal of Contemporary History,* 45(1) (2010): 95–112.

'Marcel Aymé and the Moral Economy of Penury in Occupied France', *French Historical Studies,* 34(4) (2011): 713–743.

'*La Capitale de la Faim*: Black Market Restaurants in Paris, 1940–1944', *French Historical Studies,* 38(2) (2015): 311–341.

'Spearhead Currency: Monetary Sovereignty and the Liberation of France', *International History Review,* 42(2) (2020): 278–297.

Mouré, Kenneth and Grenard, Fabrice. 'Traitors, *Trafiquants*, and the Confiscation of "Illicit Profits" in France, 1944–1950', *Historical Journal*, 51(4) (2008): 969–990.

Mouré, Kenneth and Schwartz, Paula. '*On vit mal*: Food Shortages and Popular Culture in Occupied France, 1940–1944', *Food, Culture and Society*, 10(2) (2007): 261–295.

Murphy, Libby. *The Art of Survival: France and the Great War Picaresque*. New Haven, CT: Yale University Press, 2016.

Noiriel, Gérard. *Les origines républicaines de Vichy*. Paris: Hachette, 1999.

Nord, Philip. *France's New Deal: From the Thirties to the Postwar Era*. Princeton, NJ: Princeton University Press, 2010.

Novick, Peter. *The Resistance versus Vichy: The Purge of Collaborators in Liberated France*. New York: Columbia University Press, 1968.

Occhino, Filippo, Oosterlinck, Kim and White, Eugene N. 'How Much Can a Victor Force the Vanquished to Pay? France under the Nazi Boot', *Journal of Economic History*, 68(1) (2008): 1–45.

Panicacci, Jean-Louis. *L'Occupation italienne: Sud-Est de la France, juin 1940–septembre 1943*. Rennes: Presses universitaires de Rennes, 2010.

Paxton, Robert O. *Vichy France: Old Guard and New Order 1940–1944*. New York: Alfred Knopf, 1972.

Pollard, Miranda. *The Reign of Virtue: Mobilizing Virtue in Vichy France*. Chicago: University of Chicago Press, 1998.

Ratdke-Delacor, Arne. 'Produire pour le Reich: Les commandes allemandes à l'industrie française (1940–1944)', *Vingtième Siècle*, 70 (2001): 99–115.

'Die "Gelenkte Wirtschaft" in Frankreich: Versuch einer vergleichenden Untersuchung der technokratischen Strukturen der NS-Besatzungsmacht und des Vichy-Regimes (1940–1944)', in *Figurationen des Staates in Deutschland und Frankreich 1870–1945*, ed. Alain Chatriot and Dieter Gosewinkel. Munich: R. Oldenbourg Verlag, 2006, 235–254.

Richard, Thibault. *Vivre en région parisienne sous l'Occupation: La Seine-et-Oise dans la guerre (1940–1944)*. Paris: Éditions Charles Corlet, 2004.

Roberts, Mary Louise. 'The Price of Discretion: Prostitution, Venereal Disease, and the American Military in France, 1944–1946', *American Historical Review*, 115(4) (2010): 1002–1030.

D-Day through French Eyes: Normandy 1944. Chicago: University of Chicago Press, 2014.

Rochebrune, Renaud de, and Hazera, Jean-Claude. *Les patrons sous l'Occupation*, revised edition. Paris: Odile Jacob, 2013.

Rouquet, François and Fabrice Virgili. *Les Françaises, les Français et l'épuration (1940 à nos jours)*. Paris: Gallimard, 2018.

Rousselier-Fraboulet, Danièle. *Les entreprises sous l'Occupation: Le monde de la métallurgie à Saint-Denis*. Paris: CNRS Éditions, 1998.

Rousso, Henry. 'L'organisation industrielle de Vichy', *Revue d'Histoire de la Deuxième Guerre Mondiale*, 116 (1979): 27–44.

The Vichy Syndrome: History and Memory in France since 1944, trans. by Arthur Goldhammer. Cambridge, MA: Harvard University Press, 1991.

'L'épuration en France: une histoire inachevée', *Vingtième Siècle*, 33 (1992): 78–105.

'L'économie: pénurie et modernisation', in *La France des années noires* vol. 1, *De la défaite à Vichy*, ed. by Jean-Pierre Azéma and François Bédarida. Paris: Éditions du Seuil, 1993.

Sanders, Paul. 'Prélèvement économique: les activités allemandes de marché noir en France 1940-1943', in *L'Occupation, l'État français et les entreprises*, ed. by Olivier Dard, Jean-Claude Daumas and François Marcot. Paris: ADHE, 2000, 37–52.

Histoire du marché noir, 1940–1946. Paris: Perrin, 2001.

'Economic Draining: German Black Market Operations in France, 1940–1944', *Global Crime*, 9(1) (2009): 136–168.

Sauvy, Alfred. *La vie économique des Français de 1939 à 1945*. Paris: Flammarion, 1978.

Schafer, Sylvia. *Children in Moral Danger and the Problem of Government in Third Republic France*. Princeton, NJ: Princeton University Press, 1997.

Schwartz, Paula. 'The Politics of Food and Gender in Occupied Paris', *Modern and Contemporary France*, 7(1) (1999): 35–45.

Today Sardines Are Not for Sale: A Street Protest in Occupied Paris. Oxford: Oxford University Press, 2020.

Sergg, Henri. *Joinovici: L'empire souterrain du chiffonnier milliardaire*. Paris: Le Carrousel-FN, 1986.

Shennan, Andrew. *Rethinking France: Plans for Renewal 1940–1946*. Oxford: Oxford University Press, 1999.

Sweets, John F. *Choices in Vichy France: The French under the Nazi Occupation*. Oxford: Oxford University Press, 1986.

Taylor, Lynne. 'The Black Market in Occupied Northern France, 1940-1944', *Contemporary European History*, 6(2) (1997): 153–176.

Between Resistance and Collaboration: Popular Protest in Northern France, 1940–45. London: Macmillan, 2000.

Thiébot, Emmanuel. *Croquer la France en guerre 1939–1945*. Paris: Armand Colin, 2014.

Touchelay, Béatrice. *L'État et l'entreprise: Une histoire de la normalisation comptable et fiscale à la française*. Rennes: Presses universitaires de Rennes, 2011.

Tristram, Frédéric. *Une fiscalité pour la croissance: La direction générale des impôts et la politique fiscale en France de 1948 à la fin des années 1960*. Paris: CHEFF, 2005.

Umbreit, Hans. *Der Militärbefehlshaber in Frankreich 1940–1944*. Boppard am Rhein: Harald Boldt Verlag, 1968.

Veillon, Dominique. *Vivre et survivre en France, 1939–1947*. Paris: Payot, 1995.

La mode sous l'Occupation. Paris: Payot and Rivages, 2014.

Paris allemand: Entre refus et soumission. Paris: Tallandier, 2021.

Veillon, Dominique and Flonneau, Jean-Marie, eds. 'Le temps des restrictions en France (1939–1949)', *Cahiers de l'IHTP* (1995):32–33.

Verheyde, Philippe. *Les mauvais comptes de Vichy: L'aryanisation des entreprises juives*. Paris: Perrin, 1999.

Veyret, Patrick. *Lyon 1939–1949: De la collaboration industrielle à l'épuration économique*. Chatillon-sur-Chalaronne: Éditions La Taillanderie, 2008.

Vinen, Richard. *The Unfree French: Life under the Occupation.* New Haven, CT: Yale University Press, 2006.

Zaretsky, Robert. *Nîmes at War: Religion, Politics and Public Opinion in the Gard, 1938–1944.* University Park: The Pennsylvania State University Press, 1995.

Beyond French Borders

Alford, Kenneth D. *American Crimes and the Liberation of Paris: Robbery, Rape and Murder by Renegade GIs, 1944–1947.* Jefferson, NC: McFarland and Company, 2016.

Aly, Götz. *Hitler's Beneficiaries: Plunder, Racial War, and the Nazi Welfare State,* trans. by Jefferson Chase. New York: Metropolitan Books, 2008.

Baudhuin, Fernand. *L'économie belge sous l'Occupation 1940–1944.* Brussels: Émile Bruylant, 1945.

Bellos, David. 'Oliver Twist à Paris, Romain Gary à New York: *Le grand vestiaire* et les tabous de l'après-guerre', *littératures,* 56 (2007): 173–181.

Bentley, Amy. *Eating for Victory: Food Rationing and the Politics of Domesticity.* Urbana and Chicago: University of Illinois Press, 1998.

Berkhoff, Karel C. *Harvest of Despair: Life and Death in Ukraine Under Nazi Rule.* Cambridge, MA: Harvard University Press, 2004.

Boldorf, Marcel and Okazaki, Tetsuji eds. *Economies under Occupation: The Hegemony of Nazi Germany and Imperial Japan in World War II.* London: Routledge, 2015.

Brandt, Karl. *Management of Agriculture and Food in the German-Occupied and Other Areas of Fortress Europe: A Study in Military Government.* Stanford, CA: Stanford University Press, 1953.

Buchheim, Christof. 'Die Besetzten Länder im Dienste der Deutschen Kriegswirtschaft während des Zweiten Weltkriegs: Ein Bericht der Forschungsstelle für Wehrwirtschaft', *Vierteljahrshefte für Zeitgeschichte,* 34 (1) (1986): 117–145.

Certeau, Michel de. *The Practice of Everyday Life,* trans. by Steven Randall. Berkeley: University of California Press, 1984.

Chester, D. N., ed. *Lessons of the British War Economy.* Cambridge: Cambridge University Press, 1951, reprinted Greenwood Press, 1972.

Clarke, Jeffrey J. and Smith, Robert Ross. *The European Theater of Operations: Riviera to the Rhine.* Washington, DC: Center of Military History, United States Army, 1993.

Colard, Jean. *L'alimentation de la Belgique sous l'Occupation allemande 1940–1944.* Louvain: Nouvelles publications universitaires, 1945.

Coles, Harry L. and Weinberg, Albert K. *Civil Affairs: Soldiers Become Governors.* Washington, DC: Office of the Chief of Military History, 1964.

Colley, David. *The Road to Victory: The Untold Story of World War II's Red Ball Express.* Washington, DC: Brassey's, 2000.

Conway, Martin. 'Justice in Postwar Belgium: Popular Passions and Political Realities', in *The Politics of Retribution in Europe: World War II and Its*

Aftermath, ed. by István Deák, Jan T. Gross and Tony Judt. Princeton, NJ: Princeton University Press, 2000, 133–156.

Corni, Gustavo and Gies, Horst. *Brot-Butter-Kanonen: Die Ernährungswirtschaft in Deutschland unter der Diktatur Hitlers*. Berlin: Akademie Verlag, 1997.

Davis, Belinda J. *Home Fires Burning: Food, Politics, and Everyday Life in World War I Berlin*. Chapel Hill: University of North Carolina Press, 2000.

Donnison, F. S. V. *Civil Affairs and Military Government: North-West Europe 1944–1946*. London: Her Majesty's Stationary Office, 1961.

Foucault, Michel. 'Truth and Power', ed., *Michel Foucault: Beyond Structuralism and Hermeneutics*, ed. by Paul Rabinow. New York: Pantheon Books, 1982.

'Governmentality', in *The Foucault Effect*, ed. by G. Burchell, C. Gordon and P. Miller. Chicago: University of Chicago Press, 1991.

Gillingham, John. *Belgian Business in the Nazi New Order*. Ghent: Jan Dhondt Foundation, 1977.

Glass, Charles. *The Deserters: A Hidden History of World War II*. New York: Penguin Books, 2014.

Goldman, Wendy Z. 'The Hidden World of Soviet Wartime Food Provisioning: Hunger, Inequality, and Corruption', in *The Consumer on the Home Front: Second World War Civilian Consumption in Comparative Perspective*, ed. by Hartmut Berghoff, Jan Logemann and Felix Römer. Oxford: Oxford University Press, 2017, 55–74.

Goldman, Wendy Z. and Filtzer, Donald, eds. *Hunger and War: Food Provisioning in the Soviet Union during World War II*. Bloomington: Indiana University Press, 2015.

Gruchmann, Lothar. 'Korruption im Dritten Reich: Zur "Lebensmittelversorgung" der NS-Führerschaft', *Vierteljahrshefte für Zeitgeschichte*, 42(4) (1994): 571–593.

Hammond, R. J. *Food and Agriculture in Britain, 1939–1945: Aspects of Wartime Control*. Stanford, CA: Stanford University Press, 1954.

Harcourt, Bernard E. *The Illusion of Free Markets: Punishment and the Myth of Natural Order*. Cambridge, MA: Harvard University Press, 2011.

Healy, Maureen. *Vienna and the Fall of the Habsburg Empire: Total War and Everyday Life in World War I*. Cambridge: Cambridge University Press, 2004.

Herbert, Ulrich. *Hitler's Foreign Workers: Enforced Labor in Germany under the Third Reich*, trans. by William Templer. Cambridge: Cambridge University Press, 1997.

Hillel, Marc. *Vie et mœurs des G.I.'s en Europe, 1942–1947*. Paris: Balland, 1981.

Hionidou, Violetta. *Famine and Death in Occupied Greece, 1941–1944*. Cambridge: Cambridge University Press, 2006.

Jacobs, Meg. *Pocketbook Politics: Economic Citizenship in Twentieth-Century America*. Princeton, NJ: Princeton University Press, 2005.

Kershaw, Ian. '"Working towards the Führer": Reflections on the Nature of the Hitler Dictatorship', *Contemporary European History*, 2(2) (1993): 103–118.

Keshen, Jeffrey. 'One For All or All For One: Government Controls, Black Marketing and the Limits of Patriotism, 1939-47', *Journal of Canadian Studies*, 29(4) (1994): 111–143.

Saints, Sinners, and Soldiers: Canada's Second World War. Vancouver: University of British Columbia Press, 2004.

Klemann, Hein and Kudryashov, Sergei. *Occupied Economies: An Economic History of Nazi-Occupied Europe, 1939–1945*. London: Berg, 2012.

Lebow, Richard Ned, Kansteiner, Wulf and Fogu, Claudio, eds. *The Politics of Memory in Postwar Europe*. Durham, NC: Duke University Press, 2006.

Liberman, Peter. *Does Conquest Pay? The Exploitation of Occupied Industrial Societies*. Princeton, NJ: Princeton University Press, 1996.

Lüdtke, Alf, ed. *The History of Everyday Life: Reconstructing Historical Experiences and Ways of Life*, trans. by W. Templer. Princeton, NJ: Princeton University Press, 1995.

Lund, Joachim, ed. *Working for the New Order: European Business under German Domination, 1939–1945*. Copenhagen: University Press of Southern Denmark, 2006.

Maddison, Angus. *The World Economy: Historical Statistics*. Paris: OECD, 2003.

Martin, Bernd and Milward, Alan S., eds., *Agriculture and Food Supply in the Second World War*. Ostfildern: Scripta Mercaturae Verlag, 1985.

Mazower, Mark. *Inside Hitler's Greece: How the Nazis Ruled Europe*. New Haven, CT: Yale University Press, 1993.

Hitler's Empire: How the Nazis Ruled Europe. New York: Penguin, 2008.

McAulay, Mary. *Bread and Justice: State and Society in Petrograd, 1917–1922*. Oxford: Clarendon Press, 1991.

Merridale, Catherine. *Ivan's War: Life and Death in the Red Army, 1939–1945*. New York: Henry Holt and Co., 2006.

Middlebrook, Martin and Everitt, Chris, eds. *The Bomber Command War Diaries: An Operational Reference Book, 1939–1945*. Harmondsworth: Viking, 1985.

Mills, Geoffrey and Rockoff, Hugh. 'Compliance with Price Controls in the United States and United Kingdom during World War II', *Journal of Economic History*, 47(1) (1987): 197–213.

Milward, Alan S. *War, Economy and Society 1939–1945*. Berkeley: University of California Press, 1977.

Moeller, Robert G. *War Stories: The Search for a Usable Past in the Federal Republic of Germany*. Berkeley: University of California Press, 2001.

Mörchen, Stefan. '"Echte Kriminelle" und "zeitbedingte Rechtsbrecher": Schwarzer Markt und Konstruktionen des Kriminellen in der Nachkriegszeit', *WerkstattGeschichte*, 42 (2006): 57–76.

Petrov, Vladimir. *Money and Conquest: Allied Occupation Currencies in World War II*. Baltimore, MD: Johns Hopkins Press, 1967.

Pogue, Forrest C. *The Supreme Command*. Washington, DC: Office of the Chief of Military History, 1954.

Rockoff, Hugh. *Drastic Measures: A History of Wage and Price Controls in the United States*. New York: Cambridge University Press, 1984.

Roesler, Jörg. 'The Black Market in Post-War Berlin and the Methods Used to Counteract It', *German History*, 7(1) (1989): 92–107.

Roodhouse, Mark. 'Popular Morality in the Black Market in Britain, 1939-1955', in *Food and Conflict in Europe in the Age of the Two World Wars*, ed. by Frank Trentmann and Flemming Just. London: Palgrave Macmillan, 2006, 243–65.

Black Market Britain 1939–1955. Oxford: Oxford University Press, 2013.

Rundell, Walter Jr. *Military Money: A Fiscal History of the U.S. Army Overseas in World War II*. College Station: Texas A&M Press, 1980.

Ruppenthal, Roland J. *Logistical Support of the Armies*, vol. 2: *September 1944–May 1945*. Washington, DC: Office of the Chief of Military History, 1959.

Scherner, Jonas and White, Eugene N. eds. *Paying for Hitler's War: The Consequences of Nazi Hegemony for Europe*. Cambridge: Cambridge University Press, 2016.

Steege, Paul, Bergerson, Andrew Stuart, Healy, Maureen, and Swett, Pamela E. 'The History of Everyday Life: A Second Chapter', *Journal of Modern History*, 80(2) (2008): 358–378.

Tooze, Adam. *The Wages of Destruction: The Making and Breaking of the Nazi Economy*. London: Allen Lane, 2006.

Thompson, E. P. 'The Moral Economy of the English Crowd in the Eighteenth Century', *Past and Present*, 50 (1971): 76–136.

Tohill, Joseph. '"The Consumer Goes to War": Consumer Politics in the United States and Canada during the Second World War', in *Shopping for Change: Consumer Activism and the Possibilities of Purchasing Power*, ed. by Louis Hyman and Joseph Tohill. Ithaca, NY: Cornell University Press, 2017, 137–150.

Tönsmeyer, Tatjana, Haslinger, Peter and Laba, Agnes eds. *Coping with Hunger and Shortage under German Occupation in World War II*. Cham, Switzerland: Palgrave Macmillan, 2018.

Trentmann, Frank and Just, Flemming eds. *Food and Conflict in Europe in the Age of the Two World Wars*. Houndsmill: Palgrave Macmillan, 2006.

Vatter, Harold. 'The Material Status of the U.S. Civilian Consumer in World War II: The Question of Guns or Butter', in *The Sinews of War: Essays on the Economic History of World War II*, ed. by Geoffrey T. Mills and Hugh Rockoff. Ames: Iowa State University Press, 1993, 219–242.

Wilt, Alan F. *Food for War: Agriculture and Rearmament in Britain before the Second World War*. Oxford: Oxford University Press, 2001.

Winter, Jay and Robert, Jean-Louis, eds. *Capital Cities at War: Paris, London, Berlin 1914–1919*. Cambridge: Cambridge University Press, 1997.

Zierenberg, Malte. 'The Trading City: Black Markets in Berlin during World War II', in *Endangered Cities: Military Power and Urban Societies in the Era of the World Wars*, ed. by Marcus Funck and Roger Chickering. Boston: Brill Academic Publishers, 2004, 152–157.

Berlin's Black Market, 1939–1950. Houndsmill: Palgrave Macmillan, 2015.

Zweiniger-Bargielowska, Ina. *Austerity in Britain: Rationing, Controls, and Consumption, 1939–1955*. Oxford: Oxford University Press, 2000.

Zweiniger-Bargielowska, Ina, Duffett, Rachel, and Drouard, Alain, eds. *Food and War in Twentieth-Century Europe*. Burlington, VT: Ashgate, 2011.

Unpublished theses

Barber, Megan. 'Popular Street Protest in Vichy France.' PhD dissertation, UC Santa Barbara, 2012.

Dez, Jacques. 'Économie de pénurie et contrôle des prix: le contrôle des prix dans l'économie française de 1935 à 1949.' Doctoral thesis, Université de Poitiers, 1950.

Durand, Sébastien. 'Les entreprises de la Gironde occupée (1940–1944): Restrictions, intégrations, adaptations.' Doctoral thesis, Université de Bordeaux Montaigne, 2014.

Fossé, Noëmie. 'Libération, délinquance et trafics en Seine-et-Oise: Restrictions, consommation et marché noir des produits de l'U.S. Army (1944–1950).' Doctoral thesis, Paris I Panthéon-Sorbonne, 2015.

Grenard, Fabrice. 'Le cadre législatif et institutionnel de la lutte contre le marché noir dans la France des années 1940–1946.' Thesis for the DEA, Institut des Études Politiques, 2000.

Kargère, Stephen H. 'L'affaire Joinovici: Truth, Politics, and Justice, 1940–1949.' PhD dissertation, Brandeis University, 1999.

Thomazeau, Anne. 'Un ingénieur français et son entreprise: les hauts fourneaux de la Chiers pendant la Seconde Guerre mondiale.' Masters thesis, Paris-X Nanterre, 2001.

Tohill, Joseph J. '"A Consumers' War": Price Control and Political Consumerism in the United States and Canada during World War II.' PhD dissertation, York University, 2012.

Index